The Souls of Cyberfolk

ELECTRONIC MEDIATIONS

Katherine Hayles, Mark Poster, and Samuel Weber, series editors

Volume 13, Electronic Mediations

The Souls of Cyberfolk

POSTHUMANISM AS VERNACULAR THEORY

Thomas Foster

University of Minnesota Press
Minneapolis • London

Chapter 2 was originally published as "Meat Puppets or Robopaths? Cyberpunk and the Question of Embodiment," *Genders,* no. 18: 11–31; copyright 1993 by the University of Texas Press; all rights reserved. Chapter 3 was originally published as "The Sex Appeal of the Inorganic: Post-human Narratives and the Construction of Desire," in *Centuries' Ends, Narrative Means,* ed. Robert Newman; copyright 1996 by the Board of Trustees of the Leland Stanford Jr. University. Chapter 4 was originally published as "'Trapped by the Body'? Telepresence Technologies and Transgendered Performance in Feminist and Lesbian Rewritings of Cyberpunk Fiction," *Modern Fiction Studies* 43, no. 3 (fall 1997): 688–722. Chapter 5 was originally published as "'The Souls of Cyber-Folk': Performativity, Virtual Embodiment, and Racial Histories," in *Cyberspace Textuality: Computer Technology and Literary Theory,* ed. Marie-Laure Ryan (Bloomington: Indiana University Press, 1999); reprinted by permission of Indiana University Press.

Every effort was made to obtain permission to reproduce the illustrations in this book. If any proper acknowledgment has not been made, we encourage the copyright holders to notify us.

Published by the University of Minnesota Press
111 Third Avenue South, Suite 290
Minneapolis, MN 55401-2520
http://www.upress.umn.edu

Library of Congress Cataloging-in-Publication Data

Foster, Thomas, 1959-
    The souls of cyberfolk : posthumanism as vernacular theory / Thomas Foster.
    p. cm. — (Electronic mediations ; v. 13)
    Includes bibliographical references and index.
    ISBN 0-8166-3405-X (hc : alk. paper) — ISBN 0-8166-3406-8 (pb : alk. paper)
    1. Science fiction, American—History and criticism. 2. Cybernetics in literature.
    3. Literature and technology—United States. 4. Technology in literature.
    5. Cyborgs in literature. I. Title. II. Series.

PS374.C9F67 2005
813'.0876209356—dc22
                                            2004022375

Printed in the United States of America on acid-free paper

The University of Minnesota is an equal-opportunity educator and employer.

12 11 10 09 08 07 06 05   10 9 8 7 6 5 4 3 2 1

FOR EVA AND IVAN

CONTENTS

ACKNOWLEDGMENTS

I N PURSUING THIS TOPIC, I benefited from the intellectual support of N. Katherine Hayles, Don Pease, Robyn Wiegman, Diana Fuss, Andy Clark, Robert Newman, Marie-Laure Ryan, Ann Kibbey, Lisa Nakamura, Nicola Pitchford, Helen Deutsch, and Rachel Lee, many of whom encouraged me to present or publish portions of this work. Their responses and comments were invaluable. The opportunities I had to talk with Bill Martin at the School of Criticism and Theory in 1988 had a lot to do with bringing cyberpunk fiction to my attention as a topic of academic inquiry. I also owe a great debt to the graduate students in my posthuman narrative seminars at Indiana University and to my dissertation students working on technoculture topics, especially Laura Shackelford, Cristina Iuli, and Kevin Marzahl. Two former students, Brian Carr and Kyle Stephan, deserve special mention for engaging me in an extended discussion of Allucquère Rosanne Stone's work as part of an independent readings course they helped organize.

When he was still at the University of Minnesota Press, William Murphy encouraged me to proceed with this project at a crucial point, and I want to thank Diana Fuss for introducing us. Richard Morrison's roles as both editor and interlocutor were indispensable in allowing me to complete the project. In her role as series editor, Katherine Hayles was an ideal reader.

This book would not exist without Eva Cherniavsky's inspiration and her generosity in discussing it with me and allowing me to read her own work in progress.

Cyberpunk = representations of body politics of late capital

INTRODUCTION:
CYBERPUNK'S POSTHUMAN AFTERLIFE

> In a future world where all of life seems stuck on Fast Forward,
> even *boring* people move quickly. . . . Live fast, die young, and
> leave a highly-augmented corpse . . . that's cyberpunk.
> —*Advice for constructing suitably future-shocked cyberpunk*
> *characters in a role-playing game handbook*

> I think that if, in the future, the technology of human enhancement
> is forbidden by bio-Luddites through government legislation, or if
> they terrorize people into having no access to those technologies,
> that becomes a fundamental civil rights struggle.
> —*James Hughes, secretary of the World*
> *Transhumanist Association*

THIS BOOK TAKES AS ITS OBJECT an augmented and enlarged concept of cyberpunk science fiction, beginning (in chapter 2) with cyberpunk's paradigm text, William Gibson's 1984 novel *Neuromancer*. These augmentations include examples of multimedia responses to the original cyberpunk movement within early 1980s print science fiction, but also the incorporation of issues of gender, queer sexualities, ethnic and racial differences, transformations in a nationalist model of citizenship, and global economic flows within the conventions established by fiction like Gibson's. Academic interest in cyberpunk derives largely from this fiction's representation of the body politics of late capital. Cyberpunk's much-vaunted break with earlier traditions of science fiction can be traced to the argument that physical alterations in "the" human body, such as cyborg prostheses or direct brain–computer interfaces, also transform the supposed "essence" of humanity, "our" minds or souls.[1] It is this latter transformation that defines cyberpunk's posthumanism.

In the introduction to *Mirrorshades* (first published in 1986), the first cyberpunk anthology, SF writer and polemicist Bruce Sterling emphasizes the "central themes" of both "body invasion" (including cyborg prostheses as well as genetic engineering and cosmetic surgery) and "mind invasion" (including new, direct human–computer interfaces, artificial intelligence, and the manipulation of brain chemistry and neural structures [xiii]). But in cyberpunk, the emphasis is also on the cultural implications of these "techniques," specifically the ways they redefine "the nature of humanity, the nature of the self" (ibid.). This comment suggests how cyberpunk tries to complicate the utopian/dystopian dialectic structuring much science fiction and most commentaries on new technologies, by defining technology as neither an external threat nor a set of tools under our control, but instead as "pervasive, utterly intimate. Not outside us, but next to us. Under our skin; often, inside our minds" (ibid.).

This intimacy with technology is most famously exemplified by William Gibson's cyberspace metaphor of an immersive computer interface that allows the extension of human consciousness into the topologies of global information networks, which cannot be bounded or internalized by any individual psyche. In later chapters (especially 2, 3, and 4), I will argue that Gibson's cyberspace should also be understood as a form of "mind invasion," as an intervention in the definition of the human and the grounding of that definition in the supposed stability of the human body, not as an escape from either the human or embodiment entirely into a fancied realm of pure mind. But it is also important to note that one of the main goals of the cyberpunk movement was to work through the negative implications of a term like "invasion," as Sterling begins to do in his introduction. "Invasion" implies the separation of human nature from technology and the ontological priority of a pure, individual interiority over our technological supplements or extensions. The result is to conceptualize our relation to technology in exclusively instrumental terms: in this view, technologies are tools whose use does not reciprocally transform the user in any fundamental way, and this view of technology is implicit in the utopian/dystopian polarity structuring so much of science fiction. Whether we control our tools or they control us, "they" remain outside "us." Cyberpunk defines itself by the interrogation of these dualistic habits of thought.

Instead of accepting cyberpunk's own promotional mythology of its difference from earlier science fictions, however, it might better be historicized as an intervention in a set of other posthuman discourses and speculative cultures (either preexisting or emerging around the same time as cyberpunk). All of these discourses and cultures are attempts to "suggest a way out of the maze of dualisms in which we have explained our bodies and our tools to ourselves," as Donna Haraway famously argues about cyborg imagery (*Simians*, 181). But not all of these critiques and imagined lines of flight are politically commensurate; posthumanism is as likely to serve conservative agendas as progressive ones.[2] I will define the posthuman context out of which cyberpunk emerges, and to which it returns, at greater length in chapter 1. The cultural work of cyberpunk fiction can only be fully grasped and evaluated in relation to a longer history of speculations about, for instance, evolutionary theory's challenge to the idea of "the body" as a stable and unchanging ground for human identity, or the origins of the figure of the cyborg in speculations about how humanity might survive an ecological collapse by adapting ourselves to extraterrestrial environments (rather than changing those environments to suit ourselves). This longer history has produced both cyberpunk posthumanism and movements like Extropian transhumanism, which exemplifies how conservative political agendas can survive, even thrive, in technocultural contexts, to the extent that this latter movement conceptualizes technological "self-realization" and transcendence of embodied limits through a libertarian, pro-market model. In addition to these counterexamples of alternate posthumanisms, the next chapter will also discuss the dialogue between these speculations and work in cognitive science, especially evolutionary psychology.

The possibility of rereading cyberpunk not as the vanguard of a posthumanism assumed to be revolutionary in itself, but instead as an attempt to intervene in and diversify what posthumanism can mean is my answer to the question of why cyberpunk still matters at this relatively late date.[3] In fact, in an age when the World Transhumanist Association holds meetings to debate the ethics of technologically mediated forms of embodiment and subjectivity;[4] when Edward O. Wilson laments that we are on the verge of decommissioning natural selection and therefore in danger of losing our "physical soul," the evolutionary legacy of our species unity (303); and Francis Fukuyama warns that biotechnology threatens us with a posthuman future that can only be warded off if we establish state control over our human essence, cyberpunk, as an attempt to intervene in and contest this historical debate, to find alternatives to its limitations and imaginative failures, matters more than ever.[5]

It is a mistake, then, to invoke cyberpunk as the only source for the vocabulary of the "posthuman," despite the fact that one of the most influential contemporary uses of this term can be traced back to Sterling's novel *Schismatrix* (first published in 1985) and its narrative of a far-future conflict between two technological cultures: the Shapers, who practice genetic modifications of the basic human type, and the Mechanists, who prefer cyborg forms of prosthetic enhancement. Sterling's novel is better understood as an intervention in and inflection of a preexisting discourse, which cyberpunk significantly transformed and broadened, providing a new basis for the acceptance of posthuman ideas in contemporary American popular culture. This recontextualization of cyberpunk as an intervention in a preexisting posthuman discourse also helps to explain what has happened to cyberpunk since its heyday in the 1980s and early 1990s. The death of cyberpunk has been announced many times, but one of the

overall arguments of this book is that cyberpunk didn't so much die as experience a sea change into a more generalized cultural formation, just as many of
cyberpunk's characteristic themes and tropes were appropriated and recontextualized from other sources. In the chapters that follow, I will trace some of the
most significant component parts making up the cyberpunk constellation and
their subsequent fates.

There is often a slippery border, however, between the elaboration of such
a cultural formation and its commodification. Almost as soon as cyberpunk
emerged as a named entity (around 1985 or so), it was already being denounced
as just another marketing category for the culture industry, beginning at least
as early as the 1988 special issue of the *Mississippi Review* on the cyberpunk
movement[6] and continuing through such documents as "Confessions of an Ex-
Cyberpunk" by Lewis Shiner (a contributor to the *Mirrorshades* anthology), which
in 1991 announced the death of the movement on the editorial page of the *New
York Times*.[7] Even its most prominent practitioners, Gibson and Sterling, have
distanced themselves from the label of cyberpunk, expressing a barely disguised
anxiety about having their writing categorized and therefore commodified under
that sign, as if the transformation of cyberpunk into a full-fledged concept
rather than a loose association of writers must necessarily reduce the writing
to a formula. In Gibson's words, "I would be very upset if people thought that
I had invented the concept of cyberpunk, because I didn't. Labels are death for
a thing like this. I think that the fact that these labels exist heralds the end of
whatever it was. As soon as the label is there, it's gone" (Tatsumi, "Eye to Eye,"
14).[8] Gibson's comment suggests that many of the cyberpunk writers see the
movement as having fully lived up to the motto the *GURPS Cyberpunk* role-
playing game proposes, as a definition for the cyberpunk sensibility: "live fast,
die young, and leave a highly augmented corpse"—that is, a body enhanced
through mechanical prostheses and cybernetic interfaces.[9] From this point of
view, cyberpunk would now be the province of cultural critics rather than creative writers, and our task is to determine exactly how cyberpunk's death has
augmented the textual corpus of postmodernism, in the literary equivalent of
organ donation. This question might well be understood to contain its own
answer, in the cyborg thematics of the literally augmented body, echoed and
displaced by Gibson's cyberspace metaphor and its representations of virtual
forms of social presence that exist in a very different relation to the physical
bodies that normally ground social personae.

However, I also want to point out how ironic it is that Gibson would declare
cyberpunk dead once it becomes labeled and commodified, a condition that can
apparently be resisted only by affirming that cyberpunk has died young, at the
height of its appeal, and then moving on to something different (a typical
avant-garde strategy). Gibson's resistance to the commodification of his writing

contradicts one of the main insights of Gibson's own cyberpunk fiction—that is, the disappearance of any pure space outside the processes of cultural commodification from the type of postmodern culture and late-capitalist society that Gibson's own novels represent and on which their narrative technique depends. One of the primary forms that this insight takes in cyberpunk fiction is the treatment of the body as a commodity, as literalized in the thematics of the cyborg.[10]

Also implicit in the rhetoric of the death of cyberpunk is an argument for its historical obsolescence, given that cyberspace and Internet cultures have become realities in ways that could not have been predicted at the beginning of the 1980s.[11] But the result of these changes has been a dialectic, not consignment to the dustbin of history. Writers such as Charles Stross see themselves as attempting "to distill . . . cyberpunk into something that works again, from the point of view of someone who has actually gone through a dotcom start-up, worked on the 'Net, worked as a programmer." Stross in fact sees himself as part of a third generation in the cyberpunk "dialogue," a generation for whom it is no longer necessary to "romanticize cyberspace" ("Exploring Distortions," 86).

The organization of this book tracks this sedimented history, starting with the first generation of Gibson's *Neuromancer* (chapter 2) and continuing on through second-generation or "post-cyberpunk" texts such as Neal Stephenson's *Snow Crash* (chapter 7), as well as feminist and queer appropriations of cyberpunk conventions (chapter 4); Richard Calder's rewriting of Gibson to emphasize fetishistic sexual and racial investments in technology, especially "gynoids" or "sexy robots" (chapter 3); the use of black cyborg characters to articulate both cyberspace and body prostheses with African diasporic histories (chapter 5); and the use of cyborg transformations to conceptualize the embattled status of whiteness (chapter 6). I also end chapter 1 with readings of two other third-generation cyberpunk writers, Greg Egan and Ken MacLeod, in order to begin this book by defining what has survived from the original cyberpunk texts: a complex attitude toward embodiment as both a mutable or "plastic" construct and as possessing a materiality that makes textuality or software inappropriate metaphors for this plasticity, because bodies can neither be reduced purely to problems of coding nor easily rewritten and edited (this attitude toward embodiment is usually associated with the trope of "hardwiring" in cyberpunk fiction).[12] On a methodological level, treating cyberpunk as a cultural formation, in Lawrence Grossberg's sense, makes it possible to understand both how cyberpunk lent itself to this kind of dialogic recontextualization and how the specific form taken by the original cyberpunk constellation of ideas, tropes, and practices has influenced the form that these reinventions of it can take.

Grossberg uses the term "cultural formation" to define how "a set of cultural practices comes to congeal and, for a certain period of time, take on an identity of its own which is capable of existing in different social and cultural contexts" (69). In contrast to a genre, which is organized around "the existence of necessary formal elements," a cultural formation is a historical articulation of textual practices with "a variety of other cultural, social, economic, historical and political practices," and the question raised by moving from the idea of genre to the idea of this kind of formation is "how particular cultural practices, which may have no intrinsic or even apparent connection, are articulated together to construct an apparently new identity" (69–70).[13] Grossberg also notes that such a formation cannot be reduced to "a body of texts" but "has to be read as the articulation of a number of discrete series of events, only some of which are discursive" (70). This passage helps to explain the way that cyberpunk's "apparently new identity" came to extend well beyond the boundaries of science-fiction texts to visual media and cultural performance practices.

Grossberg's methodology offers a framework for understanding why the term "cyberpunk" underwent such an inflation and dispersal of reference in the late 1980s and 1990s, why there not only seemed to suddenly be cyberpunk films (starting with *Blade Runner*), TV shows *(Max Headroom)*, comic books *(Cyberpunk)*, role-playing games, and music (a range of techno and rave bands, especially Billy Idol's *Cyberpunk* album), but even people who identified themselves or were identified as cyberpunks (computer hackers). This immediate expropriation and the resulting elaboration of cyberpunk beyond its literary origins suggest how cyberpunk provided a popular framework for conceptualizing new relationships to technology. If Western technological developments are typically informed by the values and assumptions of Enlightenment rationality, such as a belief in progress and the domination of nature, then cyberpunk seemed to offer an alternative value structure for popular needs and interests that remained marginal from the point of view of that Enlightenment model.[14]

Cyberpunk combined or rearticulated a set of already-existing science-fictional tropes, both technological and social, including James Blish's "pantropy" or surgical and genetic forms of body modification; direct neural interfaces; simulated realities (with Gibson coining the new term "cyberspace" to define the combination of such artificial realities with virtual reality and direct neural computer interfaces); artificial intelligence (now understood as "natives" of cyberspace, as Hans Moravec argues in his "Pigs in Cyberspace" essay, reprinted in *Robot*); conflicts between the form of the democratic nation-state and multi- or transnational corporations (a mainstay of the 1950s social satire tradition in SF);[15] and the shift toward some form of postindustrial or post-Fordist information economy, a typical theme in utopian attempts to imagine postscarcity economies. More dystopian versions of this theme, such as John Brunner's *The Shockwave Rider* (1975), emphasize the accelerated pace of change theorized by David Harvey as "time-space compression" or, on a more popular level, by Alvin Toffler as "future shock." These new information economies are one of the main sources for the processes of "decentralization" and "fluidity" that Sterling cites as central to cyberpunk's social settings (*Mirrorshades,* xiv, xii; Sterling specifically refers to Toffler's *The Third Wave* [1981] as "a bible to many cyberpunks" [xii]). One of the key questions in determining cyberpunk's value as a resource for cultural criticism is how self-conscious these writings are about the paradox Harvey defines, in which late capitalism "is becoming ever more tightly organized *through* dispersal, geographical mobility, and flexible responses" (159; I will address this question in the next chapter).

These recognizable textual elements were not just recycled, however, but rearticulated and redefined. Gibson's cyberspace metaphor reinterpreted the unstable simulated realities familiar to readers of Philip K. Dick's science fiction or Thomas Pynchon's postmodern paranoia narratives by reimagining them through the framework of new computer interfaces,[16] as well as the new technological infrastructure that Sterling refers to as "the satellite media net" (understood as part of a new process of "global integration" [*Mirrorshades,* xiv]), and practices of computer hacking (which introduced possibilities of agency and liberatory possibilities into a tradition that associated artificial realities almost exclusively with media manipulation of passive audiences). The cyberspace metaphor also allows a rethinking of the trope of artificial intelligences or simulated persons, who can make cyberspace or other conditions of technologically mediated existence seem "natural." A focus on new processes of subcultural identification, such as punk rock, allowed cyberpunk to reimagine the fragmentation of the national public sphere in relation to practices of resistance rather than as a tragic loss; cyberpunk also took from the punk subculture the same lesson Dick Hebdige finds in it, when Hebdige defines punk as a process of resisting commodity culture through practices of bricolage or the active expropriation and redefinition of commodities and their meanings (as Gibson famously puts it, "the street finds its own uses for things" [*Burning Chrome,* 186]). Sterling's posthuman "technologies made into politics" (*Schismatrix,* 185) situate body-modification technologies culturally, in relation to subcultural body politics; here, again, punk rock's deliberate denaturalization of bodies as style (including hair and makeup that flaunted its own artificiality) provides a model. But Sterling's posthumanism also implicitly situates these technologies in relation to decolonization and multicultural social movements and their more explicitly political challenges to the false universality of Enlightenment humanism. In this sense, the term "posthuman" functions in the same way that Sterling argues the term "cyberpunk" does, to produce "a new kind of integration," specifically between technological and cultural developments (*Mirrorshades,* xi).[17] Sterling's vocabulary of "integration" in fact functions as a popular version of Grossberg's "articulation" theory. To the extent that this process is central to the project of cyberpunk, it represents a self-conscious popular practice of Grossberg's theory.

The forging of these new connections between more or less familiar elements and practices made it possible for cyberpunk to "take on an identity of its own," but more important, for that identity to be "capable of existing in different social and cultural contexts" (Grossberg, 69). In the case of cyberpunk, this process of moving across contexts has also undermined the seeming identity provided by the name, resulting in the conceptual and terminological shift to the "posthuman," understood as a broader term that incorporates and expands on cyberpunk ideas and preoccupations. For example, Dozois's anthology of the posthuman tradition in science fiction cites "cyberpunk attitudes" on "the weakness of the ties between human identity and the human body itself" as merely a transitional moment in or contributing influence to the development of posthumanism (xi).[18]

As this example suggests, while the idea of the posthuman as it circulates today perpetuates cyberpunk in a more or less displaced form, cyberpunk's generalization into posthumanism can also function as a dilution of the original project of cyberpunk and obscure important distinctions among different posthuman projects. The chapters that follow will focus on what was specific about cyberpunk and the cultural formation it became, but in the next chapter I will situate cyberpunk in relation to its competitors, to other variants on the posthuman theme, in part because I believe there are important reasons to retain the cyberpunk impulse against more politically problematic articulations of posthuman ideas and to reread examples of cyberpunk in the emergent context of posthumanism. Cyberpunk offers a distinct set of critical resources, an archive, that postmodern technoculture still needs. This would be my reply to Samuel Delany's assertion that "the continuing interest in the cyberpunks by academics, as something they persist in seeing as alive and still functioning, strikes me . . . as a largely nostalgic pursuit of a more innocent worldview, which . . . to me has no more active historical validity once we pass the Los Angeles King riots" (Dery, "Black to the Future," 756; see chapter 6 for my reading of attempts to use the framework of cyberpunk explicitly to respond to the riots, almost as if in response to Delany's challenge).

One of the pressures driving cyberpunk's transformation from a movement within print fiction to a more mobile cultural formation was the reading of cyberpunk as a literalization of postmodern theory, a working out of the consequences of those theoretical shifts in a recognizable social setting only "20 minutes into the future" (to cite the slogan of the *Max Headroom* television show).[19] Rather than treat cyberpunk as a postmodernizing of science fiction, as Fred Pfeil does, I am interested in the ways in which cyberpunk might be read as a form of vernacular theory. The practice of recontextualization that Grossberg argues characterizes the creation of a new cultural formation can be understood as the particular form that theoretical reflection takes in these popular narratives. As

cyberpunk generalized as posthuman but 2 are not the same

Grossberg puts it, "the practice of articulation reworks the context into which practices are inserted" (54), so that this cultural work of rearticulation makes something new by breaking down distinctions between text and context, foreground and background (55). It is through this practice of questioning contexts that cyberpunk is able to combine proximity or immersion and critical distance and commentary, as Henry Jenkins argues popular forms of knowledge must do (60–61, 66). The result, I argue, is that cyberpunk fiction can be read as a rescripting of key concepts within postmodern theory.

In this book, I am especially interested in the relevance of cyberpunk and posthuman narratives for contemporary political theory, or what Bruce Sterling calls the shift to "fluidarity" rather than solidarity, as the basis for political affiliations. Sterling's use of the term "posthuman" in *Schismatrix* to designate the body politics of technologies (including both genetic engineering and cyborg prostheses) initially seemed to have been forgotten in the wake of the enormous success and influence of cyberpunk's other most original idea, Gibson's cyberspace metaphor. Initially, at least, Gibson's metaphor of the human–computer interface as a process of entering an imaginary space on the other side of the computer screen seemed to capture the popular imagination in a more concrete way than Sterling's posthumanism. To the extent that the cyberspace metaphor in Gibson's *Neuromancer* (1984) is at least partly conceptualized as a desire for disembodiment and technological transcendence not unlike Hans Moravec's infamous speculations about the possibility of copying human minds into computer storage platforms, as an escape from the "meat" into a realm of pure mind and information, the contrast between Sterling's differently embodied posthumanism and Gibson's disembodied cyberspace seems confirmed.[20] In an important early essay on cyberpunk's relevance for postmodern theory, for instance, Veronica Hollinger distinguishes between this fiction's representations of the "interface of the human and the machine" and its representations of the "virtual reality of cyberspace." Although both sets of themes have similar denaturalizing effects, they are understood to operate on two distinct objects. Sterling's human–machine hybridity "radically decenters the human body, the sacred icon of the essential self," but Gibson's cyberspace "works to decenter conventional humanist notions of an unproblematical real" (Hollinger, "Cybernetic Deconstructions," 207).

The contemporary discourse on posthumanism, however, emphasizes the continuity between these two figures. The basis for such continuity is suggested by Moravec, even as he privileges cyberspace as a technology of disembodiment. The benefit of cyberspatial modes of existence for Moravec is that they make possible processes of "continual adaptability," as we gain the capacity to reprogram our technologically embodied selves in order to accommodate an extended life span to keep from being bored, or to undergo "cyclical rejuvenation, acquiring new hardware and software in periodic phases that resemble child-hood" (*Mind Children*, 5). The posthuman rhetoric of artificial or controlled evolution, which emphasizes the plasticity of human identity, also offers an embodied version of this rhetoric of "continual adaptability." In *How We Became Posthuman*, N. Katherine Hayles emphasizes the danger of such discourses, spe-cifically their tendency to assimilate materiality to an abstract model of infor-mational pattern and to sacrifice contextual embeddedness or interdependence for a fantasy of autonomous self-control, here extended to our own physical forms. These dangers are real and should not be minimized, but it also seems necessary to consider what opportunities such redefinitions might offer, to consider what is lost and what is gained, to use Octavia Butler's formulation (*Dawn*, 4).[21] This notion of posthumanism seems to complicate a simple tele-ological reading of Moravec's trope of the "post-biological world" (*Mind Chil-dren*, 2) or Wilson's decommissioning of natural selection. Such tropes might also be read as a challenge to the abstraction of information, as well as to the naturalness of biology.[22]

Sterling's *Schismatrix* takes up and extends the challenge posed at the very end of John Varley's 1977 novel *The Ophiuchi Hotline*. The plot of this novel centers on a message from a more advanced alien culture, which provides the human characters with information about the human genome that is thorough enough to make it possible to control and alter what Wilson calls "our physical soul." The novel's main characters are left with the thought that this information does not just represent a desirable form of intellectual property; instead, it means that "you will have to cease defining your race by something as arbitrary as a genetic code, and make the great leap to establishing a racial awareness that will hold together in spite of the physical differences you will be introducing among yourselves" (159). Sterling's *Schismatrix* raises the possibility that we can do without this "racial awareness" or need for universal definitions, extending the implications of Varley's use of the phrase "racial awareness," which suggests that human universality has to be rethought along the lines of racial and ethnic specificity, in a complex invocation and displacement of existing racial differences and color lines.

Schismatrix rewrites Sterling's Shaper/Mechanist short stories, published between 1982 and 1984. These earlier stories emphasized the conflict between the "Mechanists," cyborgs who believe in improving themselves by replacing their body parts with mechanical prostheses, and the "Shapers," who use genetic engineering to modify themselves in less immediately visible ways, such as the enhanced intelligence of the "Superbrights." In contrast, *Schismatrix* moves toward a more complex relation between these two posthuman ideologies or "technologies made into politics" (185). At one point in *Schismatrix* a character suggests that "The old categories, Mechanist and Shaper—they're a bit outmoded these days, aren't they?" (183). Although "factions may struggle," the "categories" that define those factions "are breaking up," and "no faction can claim the one true destiny for mankind" (ibid.). Instead, the conflict between these two visions of the technologically mediated body is replaced by a notion of "clades," defined as "a daughter species, a related descendant"—that is, by a general concept of posthumanism that has room for both kinds of technology (ibid.).[23] The novel culminates in the mass migration of the two main, previously competing post-humanist factions (the "Neotenic Cultural Republic" and the "Circumeuropa" colony) into reengineered aquatic bodies, able to survive in the oceanic vents of Europa, a moon of Jupiter (282). As the main character of the novel puts it, what posthumanism requires is not solidarity, but "fluidity," ironically liter-alized in this aquatic form (264). This shift in terminology underscores both Sterling's interest in how posthuman forms of technological embodiment need to be defined as having political implications, even as they are also imagined to be a redefinition of the basis for political affiliations and identities.

Sterling's vision of posthuman "fluidity" raises one of the same questions that opens Judith Butler's *Gender Trouble*: "what political possibilities are the consequence of a radical critique of the categories of identity?" What Sterling does not do is to go on to ask Butler's next question: "What new shape of politics emerges when identity as a common ground no longer constrains the discourse on feminist politics?" (xi)—that is, while Sterling's posthumanism does participate in the "radical rethinking of the ontological constructions of identity" that Butler calls for, he does not explicitly go on either to "formulate a representational politics that might revive feminism on other grounds" or "entertain a radical critique that seeks to free feminist theory from the necessity of having to construct a single or abiding ground" (*Gender Trouble*, 5). This book is an attempt to move from posthuman "fluidity" in general to more specific political contexts, in part by turning to the responses of feminist and lesbian science-fiction writers (in chapter 4) and African-American comic book creators (in chapter 5) to these posthuman critiques of "ontological constructions of identity."

My goal, once again, is to highlight some distinctions between different types of posthuman fluidity, or different functions this fluidity can perform in contemporary culture. As my citation of Judith Butler might suggest, it has been easier to define posthumanism as a form of gender trouble than to define if or how race still matters under highly mediated, technocultural conditions of existence. If, as Allucquère Rosanne Stone argues, in cyberspace the transgendered body seems to *be* the natural body (*War*, 180), then the focus of academic commentaries on sexual and gender role-playing online rather than the reproduction and/or disruption of racialized formations has seemed equally natural. In the chapters that follow, I elaborate on Emily Apter's suggestion that cyberpunk's "ironic screening of the subject can in some instances lead to a productive critical unmasking of complacent selfhood, capitalist fantasy, multicultural masquerade, racial phobia, or civic dysfunction within the so-called public sphere of the postnation" (216). In particular, I consider the implications for cyberpunk of including African-American cyborg and cyberspace narratives in the dialogue this movement has generated (chapter 5), as well as the ways in which cyberpunk fiction has linked new communications technologies to the creation of transnational social relations and "postnational" public spheres (chapter 7). However, I also consider the ways in which cyberpunk's "ironic screening" and "critical unmasking" of traditional assumptions about subjectivity and identity can have unexpected political consequences, by situating cyberpunk narratives of becoming a cyborg in relation to whiteness and trauma studies (chapter 6). In these chapters I elaborate on Stone's suggestion that the dis- and rearticulation of physical bodies and virtual social presences by virtual reality computer interfaces needs to be read not just in relation to Butler's theory of performative gender, but also as drawing on and transforming traditional ideas of national citizenship (specifically, the abstraction of "the citizen" from the particularity of embodied perspectives) as defined by recent Americanist critics such as Lauren Berlant and Michael Warner (*War*, 39–40).[24]

The relevance of this model of citizenship and the way it might be transformed within technoculture and new media contexts is suggested in a manifesto titled "A Declaration of the Independence of Cyberspace," originally distributed over the Internet by John Perry Barlow in 1996. Barlow's argument does not simply reproduce the traditional construction of the citizen as abstract form; it *doubles* and *repeats* that process, because he acknowledges that traditional governments retain sovereignty in the physical world, but insists that cyberspace is "the new home of Mind," a "world" that "is not where bodies live." As in his title, Barlow here appropriates and displaces the founding rhetoric of liberal democracy and the bourgeois public sphere as site of rational discourse. His description of cyberspace exemplifies a fantasy of escape from the limits of embodiment that extends and literalizes the historical demand that citizens transcend their particular points of view in order to participate in the general public life of the nation. But this text also presents cyberspace as creating another layer of abstraction on top of already-existing citizenship formations, and this repetition can be read as a critical gesture, to the extent that it reveals the mechanisms by which a falsely universalized and generic national identity, supposedly defined by its qualities of pure mind, has *already* been produced.

In her feminist critique of the history of modernity, in which the separation of the domestic sphere from public life helped secure the separation of a privatized, inner self from the outer world, Nancy Armstrong points out that Locke's theory of possessive individualism defines the "soul" as the figure for that self, drawing on an earlier Christian metaphysics in order to define "what exists

before the process of self-development [and socialization] begins" (14). However, she also points out that Locke's theory can be read as a redefinition of the
"soul" not unlike the one emerging from evolutionary psychology and the debates
about posthumanism, in which, as Edward O. Wilson puts it, the soul is "physical" and figures the cognitive structures and capacities, however plastic, that
we inherit from processes of natural selection (303). As Armstrong put it, for
Locke, the soul is redefined as precisely "a material basis for individual consciousness," so that Locke can argue that "I see no reason to believe that the soul
thinks before the senses have furnished it with ideas to think on" (Armstrong,
262 n. 8; Locke, 139). Most important, this materialist theory of the soul makes
it possible for Locke to "describe subjectivity as a mode of production exactly
analogous to the development of private property"—that is, to commodify subjectivity in the form of possessive individualism (Armstrong, 262 n. 8).[25]

Harryette Mullen reminds us that there is also a specific racial history of
the expropriability of "soul." For Mullen, posthumanism merely means that white
power to represent blackness no longer takes the form of "miscegenated texts,"
in which African-Americans figure as black bodies with white souls—that is,
with "an interiority comprehensible to white readers" (84). Instead, within posthuman technocultures that privilege "exteriority over interiority—the body over
the soul," this representational inequity takes a new form: the forcible exteriorization of "the soul of black folks," which makes black interiority not just
comprehensible but directly accessible to white consumers, as commodification
of black expressiveness produces a "media cyborg" (87).[26] What is most problematic about such media cyborgs are the non- or antidualistic assumptions
that inform these representational practices, which still work to the detriment
of black people, precisely to the extent that they ignore and seem to eliminate
the problem of the color line. Mullen then offers a specific example of the general theoretical problem Mary Ann Doane locates in Haraway's cyborg feminism—that is, when "the collapse of oppositions represented by the cyborg"
becomes a new social norm, and "oppression is no longer organized through
[such] dualisms," how can the cyborg "be liberating or potentially productive?"
(Doane, "Cyborgs," 213). Similarly, Phillip Brian Harper defines postmodernism in terms of a "categorical collapse" of inner and outer spaces, a collapse that
"often manifests as the discounting of the specificity of [marginalized] groups'
experiences by a 'general public' that refers to those experiences for the means
by which to 'express' its own sense of dislocation" (193). In this reading, the
main function of postmodern denaturalizations of racial categories is to make
those categories more available to the public and to make them circulate even
more widely, in their denaturalized form.[27] Both Harper and Mullen seem to
offer critical race perspectives on the general problem N. Katherine Hayles defines, the decontextualization that results from defining informational patterns

as distinct from and superior to material instantiations (*How We Became Posthuman*, 19).

However, to simply read the processes of exteriorization that both Mullen and Harper define as new examples of old processes of cultural assimilation and imperialism seems to underestimate the extent of the changes characteristic of new technocultural contexts. What is different in these contexts is the disappearance of any secure position from which to appropriate the experiences or "souls" of others. I take this disappearance to be implicit in Wilson's discussion of the effects of biotechnological manipulation, which threatens to "decommission" natural selection, on the "physical soul" of humanity (303), as well as in Baudrillard's argument about the general condition of "forced signification" that results from media cultures' "forced extraversion of *all* interiority" and "forced introjection of all exteriority" (*Ecstasy*, 22, 26; my emphasis).[28] I do not wish to minimize the problem both Mullen and Harper define—that is, how to specify different historical relationships to these new conditions in order to avoid reuniversalizing postmodern and posthuman critiques of falsely universal categories, preeminently the "human." But I do think it is important to note that the context in which these "extractions" and generalizations of racial experience take place has changed significantly, in ways that can also put the previously unmarked position of the middle-class white male into play (the possible negative consequences of that shift will be discussed in chapter 6).[29]

The shift from W. E. B. Du Bois's "the souls of black folk" to "the souls of cyberfolk" in the title of this book may then seem symptomatic. I intend it not as an appropriation of Du Bois but as a mark of how expropriability is one of the defining, and often problematic, characteristics of the souls of cyberfolk, precisely to the extent that cyberculture tends to materialize and externalize all soulfulness, everything we thought was ours alone, and to reduce it to what Donna Haraway calls "a problem of coding" (*Simians*, 164). I also use this title to emphasize the necessity of identifying the racial subtexts that inform the various transformations summed up under the heading of the "posthuman," especially since those transformations are often presented as either addressing more fundamental issues than critical race studies (as in John Tooby and Leda Cosmides's implicit claims that evolutionary psychology makes visible, and therefore accessible to manipulation and self-control, universal cognitive "architectures" that logically and chronologically precede the experience of cultural particularity) or making racial categories obsolete (as in David Tomas's suggestion that "technicity" is replacing "ethnicity" ["Technophilic Body," 176, 186]).[30] My argument, then, is that the history Mullen invokes of the mediation or "miscegenation" of black subjectivity by and for white audiences provides a critical perspective on technocultural developments.[31] My title in fact derives from a comic book about a black cyborg by an African-American creative team, who quote Du Bois

in order to emphasize *multiple* experiences of internal difference, being both
African and American, both human and machine, multiple experiences that are
not presented simply as analogous to one another, despite the danger that the
phrase "souls of cyberfolk" will be read that way, but instead as mutual contexts
for (re)interpreting one another, a possibility that depends on articulating these
two sets of differences without collapsing them into a single condition.

African-American novelist Ishmael Reed offers another model for this rejection of the paradoxical tendency for postmodernism and posthumanism to re-
universalize their critiques of universality. In Reed's retelling of the genre of the
fugitive slave narrative, *Flight to Canada* (1976), one of the main characters
describes "literacy" as "the most powerful thing in the pre-technological pre-
post-rational age" (35). This reference to the period of U.S. slavery as "pre-post-
rational" concisely sums up the different historical relation of African slaves to
Enlightenment humanism and its investment in universal rationality as opposed
to embodied particularity. The connection between this Enlightenment philosophy and romanticism as a cultural movement is emphasized when Reed's main
fugitive slave character, Raven Quickskill, gets into a discussion of Walt Whitman's poetry; this character describes Whitman as desiring "to fuse with Nature,"
to overcome the subject/object split and to escape individual alienation. In contrast, Quickskill describes the condition of slavery as one of being "the comrade
of the inanimate, but not by choice" (63). This exchange glosses the novel's
earlier reference to the "pre-post-rational," which provides a name for the difference Quickskill here defines between himself and Whitman. Specifically, the
"pre-post-rational" signifies a shortcircuiting of the narrative teleology of the
romantic subject, which exists first as an alienated and privatized—that is pre-
social—individual, and only subsequently comes into contact with either society
or nature as external to the self; in good dialectical fashion, this encounter is
followed by a quest to overcome that separation between self and world. In contrast, Quickskill's "pre-post-rational" subject never experiences that separation,
at least not as an absolute dualism between two qualitatively different states or
entities. Quickskill defines himself as never having been allowed the privilege
of experiencing himself as securely interiorized or privatized, allowed to possess his own soul in silence.[32]

The ways in which the "pre-post-rational" can be translated into the "pre-
post-human" is implied when another character defines his own status as a
trickster by using a cybernetic metaphor. As a secretary and bookkeeper, this
character describes himself as having become his master's "reading and writing.
Like a computer, only this computer left itself Swille's whole estate. Property
joining forces with property. I left me his whole estate. I'm it, too. Me and it
got more it" (*Flight to Canada*, 171). For Reed, the "pre-post-rational" history
of slavery poses a challenge to the ideology of possessive individualism like the

one Hayles attributes to posthumanism when she argues that, in contrast to the individualist definition of "human essence" as "'freedom from the wills of others,' the posthuman is 'post' not because it is necessarily unfree but because there is no a priori way to identify a self-will that can be clearly distinguished from an other-will" (*How We Became Posthuman,* 3–4). To the extent that the split temporality of the "pre-post-rational" suggests a different historical relationship to critiques of humanism, it implies that posthumanism does not have to be linked to a general "backlash against identity politics" but can also be "about how subaltern bodies are positioned vis-à-vis technology," to cite Coco Fusco's critique of posthumanist discourses (xvi). Reed's novel suggests that asking "who comes after the subject?" (Cadava) can also open the question of who came before it.

A focus on posthumanism's relevance for critical study of race as well as gender and sexuality brings into focus a version of the problem I call the "antinomies of posthuman thought" in the conclusion to this book. This problem emerged clearly in accounts of the June 2003 conference of the World Transhumanist Association, hosted by the Yale University Interdisciplinary Bioethics Project's Working Research Group on Technology and Ethics. When WTA secretary James Hughes was quoted as claiming that access to technologies of "human enhancement" would become "a fundamental civil rights struggle," he summed up a crucial posthuman argument whose roots can be traced back through cognitive scientist Daniel Dennett to Alan Turing's early essay on machine intelligence: the argument for what Dennett calls the "intentional stance," the assumption that any entity that demonstrates the outward signs of personhood (especially communicative reason and comprehensible verbal behaviors) must be treated as such.[33] From this argument, it is a short step to claiming that machine rights and the right to control how one's own body and mind are technologically mediated are continuous with the longer history of social liberation. The point of potential intersection between posthumanism and new social movements like feminism, gay and lesbian liberation, civil rights, and black nationalism resides in the claim that the inability to imagine the possibility of truly intelligent machines (or human–machine hybrids or clones or genetically engineered children) demonstrates the same narrow concept of personhood used to legitimate racism, sexism, and homophobia. My reading of Ken MacLeod's third-generation cyberpunk novel *The Cassini Division,* in the next chapter, exemplifies the power these claims and their articulation of posthumanism with civil rights can possess. We might also note the similarity of this argument to some of the key claims of the animal rights movement, where arguments about the ethical imperative to respect the existence of other *living* beings is perhaps easier to accept and to connect to social attitudes toward other groups of persons.

very narrow def. of
personhood

At the same time, however, it is easy enough to grasp the ways in which post-humanism and civil rights struggles remain disjunct rather than continuous, simply by noting what Erik Baard calls "the bizarre inconsistencies of human empathy," in his story on the Transhumanist conference. Baard points out that, at the same time that the iRobot company reports that the majority of owners of vacuum-cleaning robots are willing to personify and name them (and in some cases bring them on vacation with the family), representatives of the Mbuti Pygmies were appealing to the United Nations for protection from the civil war in the Democratic Republic of the Congo, where the Mbuti are regarded as sub-human and therefore fair game by both sides. What such juxtapositions point out, in my view, is the return of a specific form of hierarchical thinking within posthumanist discourses and contemporary culture, in which the struggle to redefine humanity in technological terms is privileged over struggles to rede-fine the meaning and value of social differences between human beings, where the diversification of humanity into technologically differentiated subspecies or clades supersedes existing forms of cultural diversity, and where "technicity" replaces and dispenses with ethnicity, rather than these two terms being artic-ulated critically (Tomas, "Technophilic Body," 176, 186). The key antinomy or unbridgeable gap that posthumanism has trouble thinking through is not just the relation between technicity and ethnicity or posthumanism and civil rights, but the relation between the argument that posthumanism has critical potential, that it is or can be part of struggles for freedom and social justice, and the argu-ment that posthumanism dismisses such struggles or even makes them obsolete, just as in some accounts new technologies of body modification and human–computer interfaces are understood as making bodies obsolete. My overall goal in this book is to understand this disjunction and work through it.

Chapter 1 situates cyberpunk fiction and culture within a larger history of posthuman speculations about possibilities for intervening in the forms of human embodiment and consciousness and opening them to historical change and to self-modification and control. This chapter examines both scientific and popular traditions, and it ends with readings of two relatively recent responses within science fiction to posthumanist ideas, exemplifying the dialogue between science, culture, and science fiction that characterizes these traditions. Both the historical contextualization and the readings of the fiction establish a basis for returning to earlier examples of cyberpunk narrative, in order to trace the cyber-punk intervention in posthumanist thinking, to recover some of the critical commentary that cyberpunk made on the posthuman that might be lost in the current tendency to associate posthumanism only with the most extreme cele-bratory responses to technology, and to understand how cyberpunk contributed to some of the emergent and often problematic conventions of contemporary posthumanist discourse.

On one level, beginning with chapter 2, the rest of the book is organized around the ways that cyberpunk and post-cyberpunk narratives in a variety of popular media redefine or "rescript" specific categories of postmodern theory: embodiment in chapter 2; fetishism (sexual and racial) in chapter 3; (trans)-gender performativity in chapter 4; histories of cross-racial performance such as blackface in chapter 5; trauma and the production of white masculinity in chapter 6; and transnationalism, globalization, and the formation of new ethnicities in chapter 7. As this outline suggests, on another level, the organization of this book also recapitulates and moves beyond the tendency for technoculture studies to privilege the critical perspective new technologies offer on gender and sexuality, and to minimize their implications for race and ethnicity, with chapters 2 to 4 focusing primarily on feminist and queer theoretical concepts, and chapters 5 to 7 focusing more on concepts central to critical race and postcolonial studies.

From another angle, the trajectory of these chapters also tries to capture the generalization of cyberpunk beyond the limits of print science fiction and into a multimedia cultural formation. Chapter 2 offers a rereading of cyberpunk's paradigm text, Gibson's *Neuromancer,* with special attention to the responses that novel generated within the science-fiction field, specifically David Skal's novel *Antibodies,* a satire of cyberpunk as a culture of disembodiment that I argue is anticipated and complicated by *Neuromancer* itself. Chapter 3 examines how Japanese visual artist Hajime Sorayama's depictions of "sexy robots" have been influenced by Richard Calder's stories about "gynoids," or fetishistic investments in and impersonations of female robots (in part, a response to a particular scene from *Neuromancer* analyzed in the previous chapter). Chapter 4 returns to feminist and lesbian expropriations of the conventions of cyberpunk fiction, which are recontextualized in terms of drag and butch-femme practices that parody and resignify gender norms. Chapter 5 then turns to a comic book series about a black cyborg, by an African-American writer-artist team, which situates cyborg embodiment in relation to African-American histories of cultural hybridity and racial performance, such as passing and blackface (I take the title of this book from this comic). Chapter 6 analyzes a music video from Billy Idol's *Cyberpunk* album, and uses it as a framework for rereading the film *Robocop,* as a narrative that links white male experiences of historical trauma to the physically traumatic experience of becoming a cyborg; in turn, this conceptualization of becoming-cyborg as a mode of producing a racially particularized whiteness is linked to anxieties about racialized urban spaces. Chapter 8 returns to print science fiction, specifically Neal Stephenson's *Snow Crash,* one of the best-known "post-cyberpunk" novels, which is here read as elaborating on the original cyberpunk theme of the balkanization of the nation-state in an age of global informational flows. The conclusion uses this same novel to sum up the contradictions and ambivalences I call the antinomies of posthuman thought, in an allusion to Georg Lukács's classic essay on the antinomies of bourgeois thought, in *History and Class Consciousness*. In particular, the conclusion returns to the metaphor of "hardwiring" as it is deployed in *Snow Crash,* a metaphor introduced in chapter 1 and traced back to Gibson's *Neuromancer* in chapter 2, where it functions as a way to rethink the relation between mind and body in technocultural contexts.

The Legacies of Cyberpunk Fiction
New Cultural Formations and the Emergence of the Posthuman

Homo sapiens, the first truly free species, is about to *decommission natural selection*, the force that made us. . . . [However], I predict that future generations will be genetically conservative. Other than the repair of disabling defects, they will resist hereditary change. They will do so in order to save the emotions and epigenetic rules of mental development, because these elements compose the *physical soul* of the species. The reasoning is as follows. Alter the emotions and epigenetic rules enough, and people might in some sense be "better," but they would no longer be human.
—*Edward O. Wilson*, Consilience: The Unity of Knowledge
(303; my emphasis)

IT IS BECOMING INCREASINGLY COMMON to encounter references to "our posthuman future" (Fukuyama) in the context of both popular and academic debates about the continued evolution of the human species. This contemporary variant on evolutionary theory is different because today advances in scientific knowledge and technological control hold out the promise (or danger) that "we" might take over what used to be a process of *natural* selection and thereby gain the power to transform "ourselves" so radically that "we" might be said to have speciated, with homo sapiens diverging from "one and the same embodiment" (Tooby and Cosmides, 89) into a potentially startling new range of physical forms and body modifications. I have had to put the collective pronouns in quotation marks in the preceding sentence in order to mark the fact that, in the context imagined by such posthuman speculations, the reference for that "we" will have been rendered indeterminate, if it was ever anything else.

To challenge the grounding of the "human" in natural selection is also to challenge the privileged "frames of reference that reveal patterns of universality in human life" (ibid.). In one of the founding texts of evolutionary psychology, John Tooby and Leda Cosmides' contribution to *The Adapted Mind* collection, one key passage exemplifies how this discipline defines a material basis for a universal humanity, by treating that universality as built into the cognitive structures of our minds. This passage argues that a universal humanism has been produced over time through evolutionary processes, to form what biologist Edward O. Wilson calls "the physical soul of the species":

> [N]ot only does *natural selection privilege frames of reference that reveal patterns of universality* in human life but our evolved psychological architecture does also. Embedded in *the programming structure of our minds* are, in effect, a set of assumptions about the nature of the human world we will meet during our lives. So (speaking metaphorically) we arrive in the world not only expecting, Geertzian fashion, to meet some particular culture about whose specifically differentiated peculiarities we can know nothing in advance. *We also arrive expecting to meet, at one and the same time, and in one and the same embodiment, the general human culture as well*—that is, recognizably human life manifesting a wide array of forms and relations common across cultures during our evolution. . . . Thus, *human architectures are "pre-equipped"* (that is, reliably develop) specialized mechanisms that "know" many things about humans, social relations, emotions and facial expressions, the meaning of situations to others, the underlying organization of contingent social actions such as threats and exchanges, language, motivation, and so on.
> (Ibid.; my emphasis)

In my view, Wilson's "genetically conservative" response to the new forms of diversity potentially opened by genetic engineering mistakenly treats these technologies as an external threat to human identity. Instead, they demonstrate the inadequacy of the concept of identity itself in the face of the inherent instability of "human architectures" that cannot be grounded in an ahistorical essence or soul but instead are embedded in ongoing temporal (evolutionary) processes of mutation and change. It is in this sense that Wilson's trope of a "physical soul" is an oxymoron, as it yokes openness to change with its foreclosure, and not just the physical with the spiritual. Sadie Plant points to these contradictions when she argues that postmodern technocultures require "those who thought themselves so soulful . . . to adjust to a reality in which there is no soul, no spirit, no mind, no central system of command." For Plant, in contrast to Wilson, accepting that "there is no immateriality" leads to the disruption of the Cartesian of opposition of mind to body: "This brain *is* body . . . virtually interconnected with the matters of other bodies, clothes, keyboards, traffic flows, city streets, data streams" (166–67). And Plant argues that, "if the supposed lack of such a central point" or soul "was once to women's detriment," it is now an advantage in adjusting to the posthumanist conditions emerging in interconnected, network societies (166).

Wilson's alarm over the looming abolition of human nature is shared by political economist Francis Fukuyama, appointed by U.S. President George W. Bush to his Council on Bioethics.[1] In contrast, Plant suggests the opportunities "our" posthuman future offers for redefining already-existing forms of human diversity, specifically gender difference, as "we" seem poised to acknowledge that "our" center cannot hold. In this sense, the posthuman futures these various commentators imagine suggest the relevance, indeed the concrete literalization, of postmodern and multicultural critiques of Enlightenment philosophy's false claims to universal reason, as the defining feature of a shared humanity and one of the cornerstones of philosophical modernity. However, these same posthuman discourses also raise the question Andrew Ross poses to postmodern theory: "In whose interests is it, exactly, to declare the abandonment of universals?" (*Universal Abandon?* xiv).

As Harryette Mullen argues, it is in the articulation of racial histories with contemporary technocultures that this problematic emerges most obviously. One of the goals of this book is to complicate the optimism, if not naive utopianism, of Plant's cyberfeminism by contextualizing posthuman discourses in relation to racial histories as well as gender ideologies. For Mullen, posthumanism primarily appears in the "commodified forms of entertainment and media technologies that privilege exteriority over interiority—the body over the soul." The emergence of these technologies reverses the "nineteenth-century textual production of a black body with a white soul" and replaces that tradition of slave narrative with techniques for extracting "the soul of black folks . . . from the black body through textual exteriorizations of black interiority, and rhythmic expressions in tradition of dance, music, and orality," to produce "a black soul technologically grafted to a by now thoroughly materialized white body" (85, 87). In other words, in the form of "consumable soul," blackness is submitted to the same procedures of materialization, accessibility, and exteriorization as white humanity. But even as blackness is spatially redefined as part of a network society, it remains partially excluded on a temporal level, because blackness functions as a nostalgic memory, a reservoir, of an expressive subjectivity dependent on spatial distinctions between inner soul and outer body, mind and matter, distinctions that seem to be collapsing within today's information networks and media-saturated environments.

Cognitive science, evolutionary psychology, and artificial intelligence research all seem to be converging in their insistence on the materiality of mental processes and the most basic elements of human nature, and it would be a mistake for cultural critics to simply dismiss these developments as another form of reductive sociobiology. This emphasis on human nature as scientific object of study, as part of a comprehensible physical universe, has the effect of destabilizing the ontological status of what Wilson intriguingly deems our "physical soul," precisely to the extent that this "soul" starts to seem more comprehensible, more accessible, and potentially more manipulable. In terms more familiar to students of culture in the humanities, the result is to "denaturalize" human nature, in the sense of undoing the assumptions of its fixed dependability, by revealing it to be the end product of a process that may not be complete. However, an emphasis on the newfound accessibility and manipulability of human nature can undermine the insistence on its materiality that produced that sense of openness to change in the first place, as Wilson warns. The result is to problematize how we should evaluate the consequences of these developments from a cultural studies perspective, as operations like denaturalization and materialism that cultural studies assumes to be critical and to possess progressive political effects turn out to produce less easily categorizable results.

It is this problem that N. Katherine Hayles highlights in *How We Became Posthuman*, when she argues that "living in a condition of virtuality" is defined by "the cultural perception that material objects are interpenetrated by informational patterns." Unfortunately, this interpenetration, "the duality at the heart of the condition of virtuality," tends to be resolved in such a way as to privilege information, theorized as not only "conceptually distinct" from materiality but "in some sense more essential, more important and more fundamental" (13, 19). Given such reductive readings of the relation between informational patterns and material bodies, it seems strategically necessary to insist, as Hayles does, that "the body is the net result of thousands of years of sedimented evolutionary history, and it is naive to think that this history does not affect human behaviors at every level of thought and action" (284). Hayles's "condition of virtuality" should be read in relation to the possibility of "decommissioning" natural selection that Wilson defines. As Plant suggests, when human nature and "the" human mind come to be understood as the "*physical* soul" of the species and therefore as proper objects of scientific knowledge, operating according to general principles, these new objects also become a kind of information. It is this interpenetration of material particularity by generalizable informational patterns that prevents evolutionary psychology from being simply a sociobiological determinism, however. In Tooby and Cosmides, this informational paradigm appears as the cybernetic metaphor of "the programming structure of our minds," which they use to define their object of study as the mind rather than merely the physical brain, but also to redefine the mind as a material "structure" that has evolved in the same way that the brain did (89).

Another example would be the chapter titled "The Evolution of Consciousness" in Daniel Dennett's *Consciousness Explained,* where Dennett argues that what we have evolved are not hardwired neural structures in the brain itself, but the "hardware" necessary to run minds as "virtual machines" or software ("temporary structures . . . 'made of rules rather than wires'" [211]), in a reading of cybernetic concepts back into the history of consciousness.[2] In Dennett's usage, "virtuality" is a metaphor for neural "plasticity," malleability, and openness to change. Dennett specifically argues that "this capability, itself a product of genetic evolution by natural selection, not only gives the organisms who have it an edge over their hard-wired cousins who cannot redesign themselves, but also reflects back on the process of genetic evolution and *speeds it up*" (184). The most widespread forms of posthuman discourse today draw on and extend this kind of claim, that a potential for self-redesign at the most basic levels is inherent in the development of humanity as a biological species.

The danger Hayles flags throughout her important study of posthumanism is that the "decommissioning" of natural selection will be understood as the basis for abandoning or transcending embodied particularity entirely, as in the notorious scenario computer researcher Hans Moravec imagines for getting "our mind out of our brain." He imagines a technology for scanning neural structures so closely as to produce a perfect copy of the information contained in those structures, which can then be downloaded into a computer and run as a software program, though the scanning process has to be so intrusive as to destroy the organic structures that are being copied (Moravec, 109–10; Hayles, *How We Became Posthuman,* 1–2). Hayles's suspicion that such an extreme escapist fantasy of disembodiment is in fact symptomatic of central trends within postmodern technocultures is supported by the currency of such fantasies in popular culture.[3]

In contrast to this rhetoric of disembodiment, however, it is possible to define a different condition of virtuality, a different relation between information and materiality, in which the decommissioning of natural selection produces a critical perspective on the technological mediation of human existence in general. Jacques Derrida figures this mediation as an "archival" relation between the individual psyche and the technologies that seem to exist outside it but actually function as a "prosthesis of the inside" (*Archive Fever,* 19). It is in this sense that we have *already* become posthuman, as the past tense in Hayles's title implies.[4] Hayles points to this more productive articulation of virtuality when she argues that what is needed is "a way of talking about the body responsive to its construction as discourse/information and yet not trapped within it" (*How We Became Posthuman,* 193).[5] My argument in this book is that cyberpunk science fiction offers resources for developing this conceptualization of the body that have not been fully developed, despite the critical attention cyberpunk has received, and this potential emerges more clearly in the context of contemporary debates about the "posthuman."

There is a lesson for cultural criticism here. The debates about posthumanism demonstrate that there is no fixed political meaning either to the understanding of embodiment as fixed or intransigent materiality or to the understanding of embodiment as plastic or malleable—that is, open to critical intervention—because socially constructed. In the context of postmodern technocultures and their disembodying tendencies, the materiality of embodiment, consciousness, and human nature can constitute a form of resistance, while at the same time the denaturalization of embodied identities, intended as a historicizing gesture, can change little or nothing, as Lisa Nakamura has shown in her discussion of how racist stereotypes continue to circulate on the Internet even though those stereotypes cannot be naturalized by being conflated with supposedly unchanging physical features (*Cybertypes*, chapter 2).

In this sense, posthuman technocultures demonstrate the shift Eve Kosofsky Sedgwick defines in *The Epistemology of the Closet*, when she challenges the received wisdom that "cultural constructs are peculiarly malleable ones" by pointing out that "increasingly it is the conjecture that a particular trait is genetically or biologically based, not that it is 'only cultural,' that seems to trigger an estrus of manipulative fantasy in the technological institutions of the culture" (43). This shift, as it appears in the reconceptualizations of (post)human nature coming out of evolutionary psychology and cognitive science, poses a fundamental challenge to cultural studies' privileged method of ideology critique; as Stuart Hall points out, this method assumes that ideology operates through "the *eternalization* of relations which are in fact historically specific" and through "the naturalization effect—treating what are the products of a specific historical development as if universally valid, and arising not through historical processes but, as it were, from Nature itself" ("Problem of Ideology," 33). Evolutionary psychology may or may not make it possible to contest the boundary between "Nature itself" and historical processes, and it is certainly arguable that much of this work renaturalizes social phenomena at least as much as it historicizes biology (it is this double tendency that I refer to as one of the antinomies of posthuman thought, in the conclusion).[6] But contemporary posthumanist impulses to intervene in and direct what would once have been a process of natural selection, in order to accelerate humanity's potential for differentiation and (self)modification, do tend to contest that boundary.

These questions about evolution's subversion of belief in the ontological status of the human are not new. In an essay published in 1895, H. G. Wells pointed out that the theory of evolution reminds us that "we overlook only too often the fact that a living being may also be regarded as raw material, as something plastic, something that may be shaped and altered, . . . and the organism as a whole developed far beyond its apparent possibilities," in contrast to "generalizations of heredity" that push it to the extreme of "an almost fanatical fatalism" (36). It is this "overthrow of essentialism" that Dennett identifies as the "dangerous" aspect of Darwin's thought, still "not . . . completely assimilated" even today (Darwin's Dangerous Idea, 39). Wells also goes on to argue that "there is in science, and perhaps even more so in history, some sanction for the belief" that this process can be artificially accelerated, so that "a living thing might be taken in hand and so moulded and modified that at best it would retain scarcely anything of its inherent form and disposition," its "shape and mental superstructure . . . so extensively recast as even to justify our regarding the result as a new variety of being" (36; see also Dennett's argument about reading biology as a form of "engineering" [ibid.,187]).

Against such "dangerous" ideas, Edward O. Wilson rather wishfully imagines future generations choosing to police their own powers of self-transformation (303). Francis Fukuyama seems less optimistic in his call for state regulation of such powers and potentials (10); the belief that state power would be mobilized only to prevent others, *including the state itself,* from exercising the power to (re)define humanity's "physical soul" seems as wishful as Wilson's suggestion that individuals will refrain from using the tools that make such redefinitions possible. Other relatively cautious and sometimes reactionary responses to posthuman possibilities can be found in computer scientist and science-fiction writer Vernor Vinge's influential theory of the "Singularity" and Bill Joy's popular article in *Wired* magazine on the obsolescence of humanity, both of which pose the question of whether our technologies need us anymore. Vinge in fact imagines that the "the human era will have ended" when increases in computing capacity produce artificial intelligences whose ability to experiment with new mental architectures creates a vastly accelerated artificial evolution, rendering obsolete all organic processes of natural selection.[7] As suggested by the title of Vinge's famous 1993 essay, "The Coming Technological Singularity: How to Survive in the Post-Human Era," there is a strong element of survivalist paranoia in these kinds of responses, which can be just as problematic as Moravec's seemingly more naive celebration of technological self-transcendence.

The field of posthuman debate and discourse is not, however, exhausted by these relatively familiar utopian/dystopian alternatives. Other responses stress the options for political resistance and struggle that become possible in this technocultural context. Two of the best-known examples might be Hakim Bey's turn to cyberpunk science fiction to define the creation of "temporary autonomous zones" or "islands in the net" as forms of "reality hacking" and "ontological anarchy."[8] A more fully theorized version of these concepts can be found in Michael Hardt and Antonio Negri's *Empire,* specifically their argument about possibilities for "ontological constitution" that define the agency of a new, global proletariat, possibilities that emerge from the inherently cooperative nature of "immaterial labor" conducted through computer networks in information-based economies (402, 410).

In their concern with political interventions at the ontological level of what it means to be human, these ideas should be understood in relation to the emergence of the posthuman (as I will argue in the next section of this chapter). But, for the moment, I would like to situate these political discourses in relation to another set of ideas emerging out of cognitive science, the model of the "expanded mind" proposed by Andy Clark. In terms reminiscent of Sadie Plant, Clark argues that what is most distinctive about the human mind is its ability "to diffuse human reason across wider and wider social and physical networks" (*Being There*, 179), so that "much of what we commonly identify as our mental capacities may . . . turn out to be properties of the wider, environmentally extended systems of which human brains are just one (important) part" (214). From this perspective, if "it is valuable to . . . treat cognitive processes as extending beyond the narrow confines of skin and skull," then we must recognize that "the system we often refer to as 'mind' is in fact much wider than the one we call 'brain'" (215).[9]

I want to call special attention to Clark's claim that our cognitive apparatus has never been fully interiorized within the boundaries of our individual bodies, our "skin and skull," and the implication in turn that the body has never been merely a container for the mind or self. This rethinking of the space of cognition and subjectivity is made explicit when Clark coins the term "wideware" to define the types of "cognitive technology" that "expand and reshape the space of human reason" (*Mindware*, 150). Like Hayles, Clark historicizes the posthuman thematics of technological mediation, as a functional characteristic of human "mindfulness" from its earliest origins. Clark in fact points out that his theory of the extended mind invites comparison to the typical cyberpunk science-fictional theme of direct neural interfaces that might allow "speed-of-thought access to the Encyclopedia Britannica database," as well as to "the cochlear and retinal implants that already exist and are paving the way for future, more cognitively oriented, kinds of biotechnological explorations." He warns, however, that such comparisons can be "misleading" precisely to the extent that they recontain external archives like the Encyclopedia Britannica database within the boundaries of the individual's "skin and skull." It is a mistake to assume that technological prostheses "can count as part of the physical basis of individual mind" only when they actually are implanted within our bodies (156). The key criteria for determining whether something counts as part of our minds are "easy availability and automatic deployment," not literal incorporation (ibid.). I would add that one of the implications of the increasing visibility of such noninternalized cognitive components in what Clark calls the "cyberpunk" or contemporary technocultural context is that we tend to become more self-conscious about what is "automatic" or "natural" in our own thought processes.

As I read it, Clark's concept of "wideware" challenges or qualifies the tendency for evolutionary psychologists such as Tooby and Cosmides to privilege "frames of reference that reveal patterns of universality in human life" and the inborn "human architectures" with which we supposedly come "pre-equipped," prior to our education within any "particular culture" (89). In contrast, the partial externalizing of cognitive processes that Clark defines as integral to the development of the human mind introduces an element of radical contingency and particularity into the "architectures" of thought and reason. The circulation of cognitive processes beyond the limits of the human body makes thought dependent on particular technological infrastructures and the cultural, institutional, and professional frameworks that render those technologies assimilable to cognition. The effect is to blur the distinction Tooby and Cosmides implicitly make between the historicity of particular cultural differences and the evolutionary or "deep" time frame that for them is necessary to produce both a set of universal human cultural expectations and the grounding for that universality, our "one and the same embodiment." That temporal distinction in Tooby and Cosmides in turn depends on precisely the distinction between the different functions of internal or evolved and external or social determinations on human cultural development. Clark's theory of the extended mind explicitly disrupts that spatial distinction, as it is imaged in the boundaries of the individual body and a shared human form. This redefinition of human cognition as "boundary blind" (*Mindware*, 160) also seems to support some of the more startling political claims of Hardt and Negri, about the ways in which the "immaterial labor of analytic and symbolic tasks" in information-based economies implies that "cooperation is completely immanent to the laboring activity itself," in contrast to earlier forms of labor (293–94). In Clark's model, modes of "cooperation" are potentially present, in however mediated a form, within our own relation to our selves and our bodies, to the extent that technologies can only become part of our cognitive apparatus when they have already been rendered socially meaningful.

My definition of the posthuman centers on the redefinition of the space of subjectivity and the undoing of interiority that Clark defines when he suggests that "the true engine of reason . . . is bounded neither by skin nor skull" (*Being There*, 69).[10] It is precisely the inability to contain this "truth" within the body of the individual subject that marks the breakdown of the ideological operation Don Ihde calls the "doubled desire" structuring humanist concepts of technology (75). Ihde argues that humanism ignores the contradiction between the desire for technology to be both *transformative* (that is, to allow us to accomplish things our bodies alone cannot) and *transparent* (that is, to truly "become me," to function so automatically that we can forget it is not part of us) (ibid.). This "doubled desire" constitutes an ideological operation to the extent that it naturalizes technology and minimizes the ways in which using a tool changes the user, the ways in which our relation to technology is not merely instrumental but mutually constitutive. Posthumanism emerges when technology does in fact "become me," not by being incorporated into my organic unity and integrity, but instead by interrupting that unity and opening the boundary between self and world.[11] The point of destabilizing the function of the body as a metaphorical container is not to reject the value of embodiment, however, but to make it possible to rearticulate the relationship between mind and body, "inner being" and external form, in more complex and diverse ways, by revealing the ways in which that relationship was always mediated socially.[12]

We can now return to Moravec's fantasy of downloading human consciousness and copying it into a computer platform at the cost of destroying the brain in which that consciousness originally resided, and we can read that fantasy more dialectically, rather than as a naive celebration of the joys of disembodiment or an expression of disgust for the messiness and mortality to which the flesh is heir. Few commentators on Moravec note the specific language he uses to introduce this speculative scenario: he asks, "Is there a way to get our mind out of our brain," in the same way that a transplant would get "the brain out of our body?" (*Mind Children*, 109). Hayles reads this scenario as the epitome of one posthumanist impulse, to "erase embodiment" and "consider human beings as inscriptions that can be frictionlessly transferred into another medium" ("Posthuman Body," 247–48). Although it is certainly problematic, and very familiar philosophically, to imagine "getting out of" as a process of escape and transcendence, it is also possible to read Moravec's fantasy as an imperfect (to say the least) response to the perception that it is necessary to relocate subjectivity in some more complex spatial relation than is possible when we imagine the body as container for mind or self. To the extent that Moravec's fantasy involves a critique of the interiorized, individual subject, it contains a progressive kernel that should not be too quickly dismissed as merely a form of false consciousness or self-mystification, even though by imagining an overly simple process of exteriorizing the mind (rather than deconstructing the opposition between inner and outer spaces) Moravec himself ideologically recontains this progressive impulse. The power of Moravec's fantasy, I would argue, results not just from the way in which it reproduces familiar dualistic assumptions about mind and body, but also from the way in which it genuinely responds to a popular need to challenge those same mind/body, self/world dualisms. Of course, this element of genuine insight makes Moravec's scenario at once more attractive and more insidious.

A brief example from the novel *Synners* by cyberpunk author Pat Cadigan (the only woman author in the original cyberpunk group) is useful for defining what is of positive value, as well as what is problematic, in Moravec's posthuman fantasy scenario. This 1991 novel is still the classic narrative exploring the cultural consequences of the neural implant technology referred to by Clark. *Synners* tells the story of the first successful creation of a neural prosthesis, a data jack that allows a direct interface between the user's nervous system and cyberspace computer networks, in a simultaneous literalization of Marshall McLuhan's metaphor of the extended nervous system and a denaturalization of the individual mind as a person's private property. This novel is of special importance in that it focuses on the production of and preconditions for a type of direct human–computer interface that is presupposed and relatively naturalized or automatic in most other cyberpunk fiction, including Gibson's *Neuromancer*. I am here most interested in the language Cadigan's novel uses to define the experience of possessing such an extended nervous system.

The experimental subject who receives the first implant, a music video director named Visual Mark, thinks of this process precisely as one of getting his mind out of his body. Mark narrates the interconnection between his mind and global computer networks in traditional Cartesian and masculinist terms, as an escape from his body, his "meat-jail" (232). It is this rhetoric that Anne Balsamo emphasizes in her typology of the different attitudes toward technologized forms of embodiment in *Synners*, where Mark's desire to project his consciousness into cyberspace is associated with the idea of the "disappearing body," a posthuman ideology of the transcendence of bodies, regarded as increasingly obsolete or expendable (Balsamo, 138).[13] At the same time, however, Mark also describes his internal access to cyberspace as a "sense of having so much space to spread out in" (232), and I would argue that this rejection of having his "system . . . always contained" within himself should not be conflated with the devaluation of the body as "meat" (234). As soon as Mark begins to think of himself as having gotten "out of meat-jail," he immediately asks "And into . . . what?" The answer is "his own context" (232). He still finds himself embodied "in" something, but he no longer understands this "context" as being outside himself. "Context" here refers to determining social structures that previously seemed external to Mark's subjectivity, and the breakdown of the distinction between text and context, self and world or history, has progressive value. There is an important distinction made in Mark's narrative between rejecting embodiment entirely, for some supposed technological transcendence, and rejecting the specific concept or spatial metaphor of the body as a container for the mind and the accompanying romantic ideology of an alienated self existing prior to social determinations. The devaluation and rejection of embodiment intensifies the traditional Cartesian mind/body dualism, but that dualism depends on the concept of the body as container for mind, to define the boundary between them.

Mark's understanding of the extension of his mind into cyberspace is, then, internally contradictory, in that he *both* reproduces *and* rejects the dualistic habits of thought implicit in the idea of abandoning embodiment for a condition of pure mind. The imagery of enlarging or spreading out beyond the boundaries of the body is not necessarily a rejection of embodiment entirely. In fact, what is implied is a rearticulation of the relation between mind or self and body, a rearticulation in which it is not clear if "you're in it" or "it's in you" (334). As Mark puts it later in the novel, "things were different when you lived completely within the context" (382). One of the things that is different is that a person becomes "simultaneous container and content" (325), so that it is no longer necessary to choose between either being "the bottle" or "something in it," never able to be "both" at once (288). In this model, Mark's experience of an extended nervous system leads not to a rejection of embodiment as "meat-jail" or "bottle," but instead to a sense of being rather than having a body. The novel suggests that such an identification with the body can only be achieved by redefining the body as something other than a container for mind. In effect, the novel presents Mark as disarticulating the mind/body dualism from the container/ content dualism, in order to become his "context." Although one character asserts that this process of not being "in his body anymore" makes Mark's computer console his grave (283), it is also possible to read his transformation as a critique that feminism needs, of the separation of mind/body, self/world.

H. G. Wells's anticipation of posthuman critiques of the limits of the human form might be taken as the origin of the popular tradition within science fiction documented by Gardner Dozois's anthology *Supermen: Tales of the Posthuman Future* (2002). Dozois's definition of posthumanism takes James Blish's *The Seedling Stars* (1957) as its paradigm text. This version of posthumanism basically inverts a narrative of expansion into space, with all its echoes of imperialist and capitalist expansion, by arguing that the alternative to changing a planet to accommodate colonists is to change "the colonists to accommodate the planet" (Dozois, x). This emphasis on transforming humanity to adapt to new environments draws on Wells's rhetoric of human evolutionary "plasticity," here expanded into what Blish calls "pantropy" or a process of directed evolution and the redesigning of the human form (ibid.). One of Blish's characters explicitly argues that this process is necessary because "it's only sensible to go on evolving with the universe, so as to stay independent of such things as the aging of worlds, or the explosions of their stars" (151). This passage suggests a version of the same ambivalence that I located in Moravec's downloading scenario or Visual Mark's characterization of his extended mind. In those examples, the ambivalence was directed at embodiment, which is imagined both as something to be transcended by consciousness and as a form of materiality that cannot be separated from the operations of the mind. Blish's narratives of conscious adaptation of the human organism to new environments can similarly be read as defining an irreducible interdependence of humanity and (different forms of) nature, of the kind defined by Gregory Bateson in his work on the "ecology of mind" (see Bateson, 317). At the same time, the Blish character just quoted suggests that control of the adaptation process permits humanity to transcend or become "independent" of any particular environment, which we can therefore allow to be destroyed. This oscillation between independence and interdependence, whether of mind and body or humanity and environment, is one of the key contradictions structuring the idea of the posthuman.

Dozois's anthology of posthuman science fiction reprints the final story in Blish's *The Seedling Stars*, "Watershed," originally published in 1955. This story represents a version of posthuman politics, by thematizing resistance to and prejudice against modified human characters. In the course of justifying pantropy or posthumanism as an extension of evolutionary processes of natural selection, the same modified character quoted earlier also argues that "there's no survival value in pinning one's race forever to one set of specs," and that such considerations render obsolete the "old arguments about sovereignty of form" (151). This use of the word *race* seems to refer to the human race in general rather than to any historical or ideological concept of racial differences, but a later invocation of race as a particularizing or minoritizing logic makes the reference of this term more ambiguous. The story's modified spokesperson or "Adapted Man" points out that even pre-post-human societies had their own types of "form trouble," concerning what to this character seem "minute differences in coloring and shape, and even in thinking. They had regime after regime that tried to impose its own concept of the standard citizen on everybody, and enslaved those who didn't fit the specs" (156). This critique of the exclusions created by any concept of normative human "specs" associates posthumanism with multicultural diversity. At the same time, this passage also suggests how, in a posthuman context, the universalized concept of the human race becomes a particularized and relativized racial form, a suggestion that becomes explicit when the story's modified character points out that "the 'basic' types are now, and have been for a long time, a very small minority, despite their pretensions" (157). The story explicitly thematizes the "shock" involved in inverting universal or majority categories and minoritized ones, and it therefore suggests the critical value of such posthuman narratives, as they reflect back on contemporary social hierarchies and inequities.[14] Even relatively early examples of posthumanism, like this one, tend toward what we now see as a typically postmodern critique of any unmarked or universal norm.

This same story also defines the limits of Blish's willingness to decenter human norms, in contrast to later science fiction, specifically cyberpunk. The spokesperson for modified humanity also notes that "of course, a certain continuity of form had to be maintained," because "you cannot totally change the form without totally changing the thought processes." The example cited of such a total change is Gregor Samsa's transformation into a cockroach in Kafka's *Metamorphosis* (156). What is especially noteworthy in this passage, however, is not just what now looks like its relative conservatism, but also its assumption that posthuman transformations presuppose forms of embodied cognition and the breakdown of Cartesian mind/body dualisms, because Blish's story also seems to allow that partial changes in the human body will lead to partial changes in the human mind.[15] Bruce Sterling's definition of cyberpunk, in the introduction to the *Mirrorshades* anthology, extends and elaborates on this connection between the thematics of body invasion and mind invasion, in order to challenge the limits of Blish's version of posthumanism (Sterling, xiii).

Mapping the Posthuman Field:
Cyberpunk and Other Traditions of Technological Self-Transformation

Cyberpunk was not the only inflection or rearticulation of the tradition Dozois identifies within science fiction and, I would add, speculative or futurist popularizations of science. The early discourse about the figure of the cyborg constitutes another narrative synthesis of possible future progress and its implications for the transformation of humanity. Some of the earliest work on the possibility of cyborg embodiment, such as Manfred Clynes and Nathan Kline's 1960 essay "Cyborgs and Space," emphasizes precisely the adaptation of the human form to new environments, rather than the attempt to control that environment.[16] But although this move seems to pose a challenge to one of the basic models for power, the assumption that it is human nature to dominate the natural world, in fact this discourse on the cyborg maintains and intensifies the separation of humanity from its environment(s). This contradiction also appears in Norbert Wiener's popularization of the new field of cybernetics, in his 1954 book *The Human Use of Human Beings*. At one point in this text, Wiener argues that "we have modified our environment so radically that we must now modify ourselves in order to exist in this new environment. We can no longer live in the old one" (46). David Tomas usefully notes that the Clynes/Kline model of the space cyborg "was a hardware-based solution to this kind of problem" ("Feedback," 39), but Tomas fails to note the dismissive attitude toward environmental problems that is expressed in such statements. What Wiener is actually proposing is that we can escape the destructive effects of our technologies on the world we live in by modifying our bodies until we can inhabit a landscape that is so trashed and polluted as to have become unlivable otherwise, or (even more nightmarishly) by modifying our bodies so that we no longer require the world on which our species evolved, and perhaps no particular world at all.

In science fiction, one of the most extreme examples of this version of the posthuman is undoubtedly George Zebrowski's 1979 novel *Macrolife*. This novel imagines the ecological destruction of the entire planet as an inevitable step in human progress toward true freedom from any form of necessity, which can only be accomplished by abandoning dependence on nature as the basis for existence, including both our dependence on the resources of the planet and our dependence on a fixed human form, adapted to a particular environment, to define ourselves. The alternative to natural existence embraced by the novel is macrolife, a migration of the human race into mobile space habitats, where existence is completely dependent on technologies and therefore (in the scenario envisioned by this novel) under human control in ways that are empowering both for individuals and for the proliferation of cultural diversity, fueled by this newfound capacity for self-modification outside natural limits. This novel is another example of the narrative of technological transcendence that is complicated by cyberpunk and the more contradictory and less teleological forms of posthumanism I am interested in. When Andrew Ross criticizes cyberpunk for its bad environmental politics and its taking for granted of a survivalist ideology (*Strange Weather*, 135), he seems to me to assimilate cyberpunk too quickly to the posthuman tradition Zebrowski's novel epitomizes, which is the true object for such a critique.

Hans Moravec and his fantasy of translating human consciousness into a purely informational form independent of any particular embodiment, the object of Katherine Hayles's critique in *How We Became Posthuman*, exemplifies another strand of posthuman thinking against which the cultural work of cyberpunk should be defined. This tradition is perhaps best understood through the Extropian movement. *Extropy* began as a journal and a loose organization founded by then-philosophy Ph.D. student Max More, who shares Moravec's enthusiasm for technological forms of self-transcendence, especially as a means of life extension ("extropy" is a term coined to define the opposite of entropy or thermodynamic decay). From the first publication of the journal in fall 1988, *Extropy* was explicitly defined as a new cultural formation, in relation and opposition to cyberpunk; the inside front cover referred to *Extropy* as "a journal of ideas," focused on the relations between science fiction, "transhumanism and futurist philosophy," "life extension" technologies and the ideology of "immortalism," artificial intelligence and "uploading" (Moravec's scenario), smart drugs (a staple of the rave scene at the time) and other intelligence enhancement schemes and techniques, "space habitation," "speculative eschatology" and "futurist morality," "artificial life" (the application of evolutionary processes to the development of algorithms and computer programs), and "spontaneous orders"—a principle of emergent self-organization that the Extropians used to make analogies between "evolutionary processes," "free markets," and "neural networks." As the journal became better established and moved to a slicker, magazine-style format, this list was extended to include "experimental free communities in space, on the oceans, and within computer networks," "self-transformative psychology,"[17] "digital economy," and "critical analysis of extreme environmentalism."

Issue no. 7 of *Extropy* contains a glossary of "futique neologisms," many of which exemplify this group's embrace of disembodying rhetoric. "Resistance to the evolution from the human to the posthuman" and to the project of "altering the human anatomy" is defined as "biological fundamentalism." At the same time, the Extropians also feel the need to define alternative gendered pronouns ("se" and "ne") and to critique a dependence on "sexist default concepts" (35).[18] Some of these terms are derived from science-fiction writers, including Vernor Vinge and Bruce Sterling, but the Extropians tended to distinguish themselves from science fiction in their emphasis on the "transhuman," defined as "the transition stage to posthumanity" and as an openness to "opportunities for self-enhancement" (36), rather than the posthuman as such (see also More's essay "Transhumanism: Towards a Futurist Philosophy"). In other words, the Extropian movement was about putting posthumanism into practice and identifying already-existing tendencies that could be interpreted as accelerating "the evolution of intelligent life beyond its currently human form and human limitations," to cite the definition of transhumanist philosophy offered on the journal's masthead.[19]

Extropian philosophy contains elements that can seem genuinely progressive. Like cyberpunk, the Extropians move beyond the limitations exemplified by James Blish's concept of posthuman pantropy, which drew back from questioning the value or necessity of human continuity of form on the level of mental processes. This willingness to redefine the concept of identity and to tolerate more personal discontinuity is best exemplified by what Mark S. Miller calls the "credit theory of identity." In an interview published in *Extropy* no. 10 in 1993, Miller argues that the only real concept of continuity of personality that can also encompass the radical expansions and changes envisioned by Extropian philosophy is the idea of giving credit to or "citing our former selves, our more primitive selves, for the germs of what we become," because to identify too closely with a particular "pattern" is to believe that "to the degree that you expand and learn and grow, you also die—your previous self is dead" (27–28). This argument echoes Pat Cadigan's "Pretty Boy Crossover," a cyberpunk short story about a downloaded personality, transferred into a computer storage medium, who now exists as a "basic information configuration," so that "educating him" involves adding more data to that configuration (135). Another character, who is being recruited to undergo this same process, asks whether this means "he ain't really *Bobby* any more, then, huh?" The response is a rhetorical question: do "you change into someone else every time you learn something new?" (ibid.). Although, in the story, the point of this question is to discount differences between physical and digital embodiments, the Extropians celebrate this kind of informational discontinuity as a model for redefining physical existence as technologically mediated.[20]

The credit theory of identity, however, preserves those earlier selves as influences or footnotes, to which later incarnations still feel related. At the time of this interview, Miller was working on the Xanadu project, designing hypertext systems, and the hypertextual structure of internal links to external contexts seems to inform his credit theory of identity; that theory therefore offers one gloss on what it means for Visual Mark to be "in his own context": he possesses a hypertextualized self. Miller's suggestion that posthuman continuity of personal identity will be established through practices of citation invokes a model of the self as scholarly community or conversation,[21] in a way that also invokes one of the more influential redefinitions of identity within cultural studies, Judith Butler's theory of the performative subject, constituted through forms of repetition and iteration that also imply the fundamental instability and interruptibility of the identity categories these performances install.[22] In this theory, every time we repeat and reconfirm gender norms, we also create an interval, a space between, where those norms could be reimagined, and Miller's credit theory of identity focuses on precisely such intervals within narratives of personal continuity.

The Extropy example, however, also shows how this more fundamental questioning of human identity can be ideologically recontained. The Extropy group was explicit about its libertarian politics, a kind of right-wing anarchy that is antistate but pro-market capitalism. This politics appears most obviously in the articulation of the principle of "spontaneous order," or what Max More describes as "order without orderers." His examples of such self-organizing systems are neural networks, open-ended programming structures that become more complex through a process of learning rather than preestablished rules; evolutionary processes of "selection without any conscious direction"; "the free market system"; and "the development of language" ("Order without Orderers," 21). These spontaneous orders are valued because they seem liberatory in relation to more traditional top-down, hierarchical systems, but the examples cited raise the question of whether such self-organizing systems are truly any less rule-governed than the ones they are intended to replace. Are we more or less free if the rules we have to live by are emergent properties or externally imposed dicta?

The Extropians share this ideological investment in self-organizing systems with Kevin Kelly, executive editor of *Wired* magazine, whose 1994 book *Out of Control* argues for a similar analogical relation between evolved ecological systems, decentralized free market economies, and complex computer and communications networks (3); in fact, Kelly's book argues that such analogies become unavoidable in a context in which "machines are becoming biological and the biological is becoming engineered" (1)—that is, in which the meanings of nature (unchanging stability) and culture (open-ended mutability) are reversing themselves, as Sedgwick argued.[23] It is hard not to read such rhetorics as oddly anachronistic justifications of Adam Smith's "invisible hand" metaphor, and indeed Marxist theorists of post-Fordist or postindustrial information economies have argued that decentralization functions precisely to give capital more, not less, control over the production process, a paradox captured in Lash and Urry's phrase "disorganized organization."[24] Fredric Jameson traces "the success of market ideology" back to its "strongest and most metaphysical version, which associates the market with human nature" (*Postmodernism*, 266–67). But libertarian discourses like Kelly's insist that the idea of free markets is the key to perpetuating the metaphysics of a *post*human nature, in the face of the paradox that the overriding characteristic of posthumanism's metaphysics is a refusal to accept "nature" as a given.

Free market ideology is, then, a key feature of the cultural formation promoted by the Extropy group. This centrality is confirmed by Max More's response to the problem of maintaining personal continuity in a posthuman age of accelerated technological change. In his important essay (perhaps manifesto would be a better term) "Technological Self-Transformation," More proposes a more conservative criterion for "determining whether a person undergoing dramatic change remains logically the same" than did Miller's credit theory of identity. This criterion is "the extent to which that person selects and directs the changes" (19). This argument constitutes a posthuman restatement of the classic liberal humanist ideology of possessive individualism, in which personhood means being "the proprietor of [one's] own person or capacities," as C. B. Macpherson paraphrases Locke (3). Extropian posthumanism involves an odd mutation of this model, in which we can afford to change because we possess ourselves or, more accurately, the capacity to choose self-transformation is the ultimate index to confident self-ownership. Despite the paradoxical linkage of possession (usually associated with reification or fixity) and fluid mutability, More's formulation of the posthuman self still depends on an old concept of "the *human* essence" as defined by "freedom from the wills of others" (Macpherson, 3). It is the idea that our freedom lies in the control we exert over our self or essence (or, from a Marxist perspective, the "freedom" we have to alienate our own labor by selling our time) that is literalized and intensified by Extropian posthumanism as the power to actually change that essential self, rather than merely to contractually obligate it (as in Macpherson's classic model). This reproduction of the principles of possessive individualism, a cornerstone of modernity however transformed, contradicts the challenge posthumanism poses to the boundaries of the liberal self and contradicts Hardt and Negri's more optimistic assertions about the inherently cooperative nature of informational labor processes.[25]

It is precisely on the level of political economy that the differences between Extropian and other forms of technolibertarianism can be distinguished from the cyberpunk cultural formation. Bruce Sterling began to promote the idea of a cyberpunk movement (usually referred to just as "The Movement") in the early 1980s in a self-published fanzine titled *Cheap Truth*.[26] Sterling's infamous polemics against other science-fiction writers included as one of their main targets a group of writers he identified as libertarian, a group primarily associated with the "hard" SF tradition and with the magazine *Analog*, but with a history going back to writers such as Robert A. Heinlein (within SF) and Ayn Rand (outside the genre). Sterling's probable suspicion toward the libertarian strand of Extropian thought is reinforced in another polemical essay in which he formulates the cyberpunk attitude toward "the technological destruction of the human condition," which he argues "leads not to futureshocked zombies but to hopeful monsters" ("Letter," 4). In this same text, Sterling defines cyberpunk as a reaction against both "standard humanist liberalism" and the extreme antihumanism of "incipient Nietzschean philosophical fascism" and "belief in the Overman" (5). This latter comment anticipates the Extropian philosophy of unbounded self-transformation.

With this critique in mind, we might read Sterling's reference to Alvin Toffler's *Third Wave*, in the introduction to the *Mirrorshades* anthology, as defining a belief shared with the libertarians—that is, that we are experiencing a shift to a postindustrial information economy—but only in order to contest the implications of that shift.[27] This kind of distinction between different positions within posthumanism is what can be lost when cyberpunk is described as "the supreme *literary* expression if not of postmodernism, then of late capitalism itself," as Jameson famously does (*Postmodernism*, 419 n. 1).[28]

Some examples of cyberpunk or writing influenced by it might help to demonstrate its implicit critical perspective on the ideological recontainment of new information technologies and the ways they redefine human existence within dominant capitalist frameworks. I'll start with a contemporary example of cyberpunk's critical legacy and work backward toward its sources in the original cyberpunk canon. Karl Schroeder's novel *Permanence* (2002) is organized around resistance to a space-traveling future culture called the "Rights Economy," which uses models of intellectual property precisely to limit posthuman diversity. In this novel, the fear "that humanity would radiate into a thousand subspecies" is "one of the reasons . . . used to justify the tyranny of the Rights Owners" (297).[29] The novel directly thematizes posthumanism, offering a critique of "the limits of human neurological programming" and attributing those limits to the evolution of "hardwired metaphors," including "something we commonly call 'I'" or "the metaphor of *self-as-object*" (312). Specifically, new computer interface technologies open the possibility of replacing this "primary metaphor" with another understanding of "*self-as world*," reminiscent of Visual Mark's transformation in Cadigan's *Synners*.[30] However, the Rights Economy subverts this possibility by using a neural implant technology (referred to as "inscapes," in a witty allusion to Gerard Manley Hopkins) to layer "its version of reality on top of what everyone sees and hears," and their version of reality is economic, a literalization of free market ideology through the agency of ubiquitous computing (217).

To be integrated into the Rights Economy involves having every element of the lived environment sprayed with a fog of "nanotags," tiny computer chips that constantly use the inscape technology to broadcast "the monetary value" of every object's "parts and whole," so that when a character looks at a chair, for instance, "all he could see was the matrix of numbers superimposed on it" in the form of "tiny lines of text and numerals, inscape tags which named the Rights Owners" for the chair's design, as well as its "value and history" (125–26). As the use of the term "matrix" underscores, this passage seems to rewrite the emancipatory narrative of the film *The Matrix*, where the ability to dissolve the seeming solidity of a virtual reality simulation into the lines of code that generate it gives the protagonist the ability to take control over and to rescript the simulation within which he is initially trapped; the film ends with a scene in which a "matrix of numbers" is superimposed over every part of the setting. As the narrator of the novel puts it, "in the Rights Economy, information was immanent," and "ownership, credit histories, monetary value itself" are transparently inscribed "in the physical objects traded in [the] streets" (146).

In *The Matrix*, this denaturalization of the physical world's facticity is associated with the possibility for critical thought and the imagination of alternatives to the status quo. Similarly, in Marxist theory, the fetishization of the commodity is defined by the substitution of the independent existence of objects for the social processes and the history of production on which their existence depends, a process of substitution also referred to as reification; this process constitutes one of the main ways in which capitalism alienates individuals from the world we inhabit, by mystifying the ways in which human labor has produced or "worlded" the world. The Rights Economy's use of information technology inverts and undoes this process, but without capitalism losing any of its power. Schroeder's novel suggests that information economies intensify the effects of commodification by redefining all material objects as forms of intellectual property.[31]

Schroeder's implicit critique of an intellectual property model had already been made explicit in Sterling's short story "Maneki Neko" (originally published in 1998). This story posits what increasingly seems like a utopian scenario, in which "the global information networks were non-commercial"; instead, they are "very polite" and capable of returning "a favor for a favor" (4). In fact, the primary function of the "net machines" is to mediate social and economic relationships, in the form of the exchange of "free goods and services" between different people around the world who owe the network favors and are owed in return. The result is a conflict between a global "network gift economy" (variously referred to as "digital panarchies" and "segmented, polycephalous, integrated influence networks") and "the lawful, government-approved, regulated economy," primarily associated with the United States (15). The story's implicit joke is that its main American character has a traditionally paranoid reading of the computer network, from the outside, as "something that is very very big, and very very patient. And it knows all about me. And it's got a million arms and legs. And all those arms and legs are people" (17). In contrast, the main Japanese character who lives day to day in such a network society insists that "computers help human beings to relate in a much more human way" (9). This story offers one of the most direct attempts to imagine a practice actualizing the "abstract cooperation" Hardt and Negri locate within "immaterial labor" and "information production," which "dedicates an ever more central role to communication of knowledges and information among workers, but those cooperating workers need not be present and can even be relatively unknown to one another. . . . The circuit of cooperation is consolidated in the network and the commodity at an abstract level" (295–96). Like the present-day open source movement, Sterling's story sets out to make this abstract possibility more concrete by elaborating a social logic held to be implicit in new information economies. "Maneki Neko" suggests that the main mechanism for keeping this cooperative social logic "abstract" is the legal and ideological form of intellectual private property rights.[32]

In turn, the connection between this critique of intellectual property and the ideology of possessive individualism had already been made in cyberpunk's paradigm novel, William Gibson's *Neuromancer* (1984). At one point in the novel, the main character, a hacker or console cowboy named Case, holds a conversation with a "construct," a computer program designed to simulate the personality of a dead friend of his, another master hacker. The topic of the conversation is the legal status of an artificial intelligence program (AI) for whom they are working. The simulated character asks whether the AI "owns itself," and the answer is that it is a "Swiss citizen," but its "basic software and the mainframe" on which it runs are the property of a multinational corporation (which the AI is employing Case to steal from). The construct takes this situation as an example of black humor, noting "that's a good one. . . . Like, I own your brain and what you know, but your thoughts have Swiss citizenship" (131).

We might note here the way in which this passage complicates the familiar distinction between body and mind, brain and thoughts, by introducing an ambiguous third term between them: "what you know." The value of this passage lies in the way in which it makes possible critical reflection on the different ways brains, knowledge, experience, and thoughts can be articulated. In the next chapter, I will return to the ways in which this passage defines a general model of media citizenship in the information age, one that applies to the human characters in the novel as well as the AI. But for now, I cite this passage for the way it implies that postmodern technocultures both make visible and make a joke out of possessive individualism and the prospect of owning yourself, or the information that constitutes you, as a model of freedom or agency.

Hardwiring: Narratives of Embodied Cognition

To develop this argument about the nature of subjectivity and agency, power and resistance in technocultural contexts, I want to turn to the debate over how to interpret what Tooby and Cosmides call "our evolved psychological architecture," "the programming structure of our minds," or "the specialized mechanisms" that pre-equip us to "'know' many things," with that knowledge therefore constituting a universal level of human culture (89). Hayles warns against too quickly interpreting such forms of embodied cognition as essentialist, because such critiques risk reinforcing Moravec's posthumanist conclusion that these structures are obsolete and dispensable (*How We Became Posthuman,* 201). In contrast, she cites Pierre Bourdieu's concept of the habitus, which he defines as the "durably installed generative principle of regulated improvisations" and which Hayles glosses, not as "a collection of rules" in the structuralist sense, but as "a series of dispositions and inclinations that are both subject to circumstances and durable enough to pass down through generations" (Bourdieu, 78; *How We Became Posthuman,* 202–3). For Hayles, these inheritable dispositions can encompass mutability and plasticity, whether in the form of changing "circumstances" (that is, external, environmental, or historical influences) or "regulated improvisations" (that is, forms of self-transformation). But they also constitute points of resistance to the abstraction and decontextualization of information from material embodiment and the potential for instrumental control and exploitation that Haraway warns can result from such processes of abstraction (*Simians,* 164).

Even Moravec acknowledges the necessity for resistance to this instrumentalizing logic. In his most recent book, Moravec imagines "ex-humans" who "will grow and restructure at will, continually redesigning themselves for the futures as they conceive it"; the result is to obscure "differences in origins" (that is, race) even as "aggregate diversity" increases as a result of the proliferation of

new design strategies (*Robot,* 144–45).[33] But Moravec also admits that "to maintain integrity," his ex-humans "may divide their mental makeup into two parts,
a frequently changed *design,* and a rarely altered *constitution* of general design
principles," and Moravec compares this level of the "constitution" to the American Constitution, "the general knowledge and fundamental beliefs of a person," and the "soul or spirit in some religious systems" (147), in a move that
should remind us of the hybrid legal status of the AI in Gibson's *Neuromancer.*
The distinction between these two levels very neatly identifies the different effects
of a relatively superficial and a more socially and politically critical posthumanism.[34] The key point here is that, like Bourdieu's habitus, the level of the
posthuman "constitution" Moravec imagines both resists and accommodates
change, and therefore displaces the distinction between essentialist concepts of
fixed or natural identity and social concepts of identity as construct and therefore as malleable or plastic.

One of the enduring legacies of cyberpunk fiction is its use of the term "hardwiring" to represent forms of embodiment and cognition that occupy this third
space, between natural and social or cultural determinations.[35] This claim may
seem rather surprising in that there is also a popular usage of this term that
associates it exclusively with a kind of biological determinism. Physicist and SF
writer Gregory Benford has written a series of novels about human competition with intelligent machines, one of the more direct attempts to translate
Moravec's ideas about robotic "mind children" into fictional form. In a related
story, structured around a dialogue between one such machine and a human
character, the AI criticizes humanity for having a "grave limitation: you cannot
redesign yourselves at will," because humans "express in hardware what properly
belongs to software" (Benford, 418). As I will make clear, beginning with my
reading of Gibson's *Neuromancer* in the next chapter, cyberpunk is distinguished
for the ways in which it disrupts this set of distinctions, both the assumption
that qualities expressed in "hardware" cannot be redesigned and the evaluation
that locating those qualities in hardware is nothing but a limitation.

This less deterministic reading of what it means for aspects of humanity to
be built in or hardwired is suggested in a story by Nancy Kress, an SF writer
centrally concerned with biotechnology and genetic engineering. In "Faultlines"
(originally published in 1995), a pharmaceutical researcher alludes to recent
research on embodied reason, such as Antonio Damasio's: "the big neurological
discovery in the last five years is that repeated intense emotion doesn't just alter
the synaptic pathways in the brain. It actually changes your brain structure
from the cellular level up. With any intense experience, new structures start to
be built" (in *Beaker's Dozen,* 131). The response, however, is not to understand
these structures as fixed (or alterable only by submitting to the same processes
of "intense experience" that formed them), but instead to design a drug that

reverses the process: "instead of the experience causing the neurochemical response," this drug "supplies the physical changes that create the experience" (134). This attitude is typical of what is sometimes referred to as "hard character science fiction," paradigmatically the work of Australian writer and computer programmer Greg Egan, a movement that undermines distinctions between biology and psychology (Daniels; Swanger; as I suggest in the Introduction, I prefer to describe this body of work as part of a third generation of responses to cyberpunk, especially because the next chapter will demonstrate how the conventions of hard character SF are anticipated by the trope of hardwiring as it appears in Gibson's *Neuromancer*). This kind of fiction is the strongest evidence supporting the shift Eve Sedgwick discusses, in which malleability and possibilities for difference and diversity are associated with biology rather than with cultural formations (*Epistemology*, 43). Moravec's distinction between constitution and design demonstrates the complementary shift, as culture becomes associated with fixity, conservatism, and continuity, a shift that creates new dangers.

But narratives like Kress's also suggest the importance of making distinctions between the forms taken by the contemporary rhetoric of biological or evolutionary hardwiring. The political stakes of this rhetoric are demonstrated by debates around whether there exists a genetic predisposition toward homosexuality, a "gay gene," and whether the homosexual/heterosexual difference can be mapped onto differences in neural structures in the brain.[36] Within the framework I have been developing, however, there is a significant difference between the political arguments enabled by the hypothesis of gay genes as opposed to neural structures. The gay gene argument depends on reasserting the primacy of genotype over the expression of genetic possibilities in the phenotype. The contingency of genetic structures is usually understood to be a secondary phenomenon, arising from the effects environmental factors can have on the process of expression; that contingency and the possibility for change are not located in the genetic structures themselves. As Kress's formulation suggests, the existence of specific neural structures or patterns associated with homosexuality does not necessarily permit such an easy distinction between biology or genetics and environment, because these neural structures can be understood as both causes and effects of behavioral practices. The way the brain is wired affects behavior, but behavior also rewires the brain.

Greg Egan's story "Chaff" (originally published in 1993) shares Nancy Kress's interest in neural plasticity or "the many ways an ordinary human brain can be wired," in contrast to "an arbitrary neural net" or artificial intelligence system, whose programming structures are relatively more rigid because based on pre-established rules (31). The whole premise of Egan's story is that once we learn how such behavior patterns are "wired" into the basic structure of our brains, then we can rewire them, allowing people to "control exactly *who you are*" (30). The story therefore collapses culture and ideology into biology, in a way that seems essentialist, but by doing so Egan is able to imagine possibilities for empowering radical and explicitly political forms of change.[37]

The narrative of "Chaff" centers on a scientist doing biotechnology research who has invented a retroviral treatment capable of making "a subset of the neurons in the brain" more "mobile" (29). As another character puts it, "existing brain structures . . . melt" and can be reformed or rewired, a process compared to erasing the "old personality" like deleting "computer files" (29, 30). This comparison is made by a character whose job is to regulate biotechnology for First World corporations. The scientist sees the effects rather differently. For him, this retrovirus does not threaten to destroy human personalities but instead promises to grant "the part of us that was fixed, that was tied to 'human nature,' the chance to be as different from person to person as a lifetime's worth of memories." This story then elaborates on one form that might be taken by the decommissioning of natural selection that Edward Wilson imagines. "Human nature" will end up as "*less than chaff in a breeze*," just like "all the 'eternal verities'" that defined the humanist model of the self, "all the sad and beautiful insight of all the great writers from Sophocles to Shakespeare" (32).[38] Ironically, the highlighted phrase "chaff in a breeze," used to define the meaninglessness of the humanist tradition, is a quotation from that tradition, specifically a passage in Joseph Conrad's *Heart of Darkness* where the narrator argues that neither superstitions, beliefs, nor principles are anything more than chaff in the wind in the face of basic bodily needs such as hunger (11). After the scientist who has invented the new brain modification technology disappears, this passage is discovered, highlighted, in his copy, and it provides investigators with an insight into his goals.

The political implications of this technology and the ambivalent critique of humanism's "eternal verities" to which it is linked are made explicit in the story. The technology's creator was born in Peru to a "mildly leftist family" whose principles he repudiated by allowing his education to be sponsored and his research co-opted by American and European corporations (ibid.). At the beginning of this story, the scientist inexplicably defects to El Nido, a black market biotechnology center in South America (which is what the story imagines the Latin American drug cartels might become in this new technological context). The corporate watchdog who eventually finds and confronts the scientist takes the passage from *Heart of Darkness* as evidence that the scientist is motivated by guilt over having sold out his family's leftist principles, which turns out to be true. The retrovirus, however, allows the scientist to rewire his brain to make him what he always "wanted to become," politically committed and capable of doing what Conrad suggests is impossible: putting his political ideals and principles ahead of his own physical comfort and convenience, his corporate privileges. He literalizes, extends, and inverts Conrad's critique by eliminating the distinction between ideals and bodily realities and reducing appetites and drives to the level of superstitions and principled convictions, which themselves become no more than "chaff."

The usage of "hardwiring" to name biologically determined or instinctual behavior patterns undoubtedly has its source in Noam Chomsky's theory of a universal linguistic deep structure that makes acquisition of specific languages possible.[39] Daniel Dennett rejects this reductionism when he argues that natural selection for hardwired reflexes, such as "the ability to duck incoming bricks" (*Consciousness Explained*, 178), is only the first, simplest level at which evolution works to produce human minds. Dennett goes on specifically to argue that the limitation of hardwired minds is that they "cannot redesign themselves," but the capacity for this kind of neural "plasticity" does not represent a condition of freedom or transcendence; instead, the brain's capacity for adaptive responses to the particularity of the environment is produced by "a *mechanical* process strongly analogous to natural selection" (184; my emphasis). What is selected for is the brain's capacity to modify itself. Dennett's main example of this type of "postnatal self-design" is language acquisition, the process by which an individual brain "turns itself into a Swahili or Japanese or English brain" (200).

Although this example is startling for its biologizing of national and ethnic identities, it also demonstrates how the distinction between hardwired reflexes or instincts and neural plasticity (the capacity to learn) undoes itself in Dennett's text, to the extent that this statement about becoming an English brain, say, echoes the language of contemporary computer science. In the latter context, hardwiring refers to a process by which software does not just run on a computer but becomes installed as an indispensable part of the operating system of the computer itself, a component as necessary to the functionality of the system as its hardware.[40] But functioning as a necessary component does not mean that the mode of operation cannot be altered, within limits. In this usage, then, hardwiring names structures that consist of codes (or programming languages, more accurately) that can be changed and rewritten, but that also have a kind of materiality that resists any easy translatability or instrumentalization, because they function at a more fundamental level in the system than the more directly accessible codes making up software applications, the more fundamental level that Moravec compares to a nation-state's constitution.

Moravec's metaphor of a "rarely altered constitution" is intended to resist the negative effects of defining oneself entirely in terms of a "frequently altered design," but Moravec's language here also suggests the ways in which technocultural redefinitions of the human might also open this level of national, ethnic, and cultural definition to intervention and critique, in contrast to Dennett's reification of these categories at the level of brain structures. Hardwiring, then, can designate qualities and behaviors that belong neither to human hardware nor software, neither biology nor culture. The emergence of this third, hybrid alternative constitutes an extension of Haraway's project, of coding for feminism and other progressive movements the "kind of disassembled and reassembled, postmodern collective and personal self" that she argues is figured by the cyborg, in order to reclaim that kind of self from the instrumentalizing logic of post-Fordist information economies (*Simians,* 163). Dennett's description of how the mind as virtual machine "imposes a particular pattern of rules" on both the "plasticity" and the "hardware" of the brain (*Consciousness Explained,* 211, 216) provides a gloss on what "coding" means in this context: imposing a set of "regularities" that are both "temporary" and "highly structured" (216). This dual character is captured by the concept of hardwiring as it is deployed in cyberpunk narratives.[41]

"I Am a Citizen": Greg Egan's Diaspora

Although in 1993 Scott Bukatman could reasonably claim that the impact of Bruce Sterling's *Schismatrix* and its trope of posthumanism had "been less overtly marked" than the impact of Gibson's cyberspace metaphor, after the emergence of second- and especially third-generation responses to cyberpunk, it is no longer so "difficult to think of" other writers who emulate "Sterling's textual formations" (Bukatman, 273). One of the best examples of a novel that articulates Gibson's cyberspace metaphor with Sterling's posthuman body politics is Greg Egan's novel *Diaspora* (1997). This novel focuses on forms of virtual community and offers perhaps the fullest and most complex fictional realization of Moravec's fantasy of transcending embodiment by copying or downloading human consciousness into a computer.[42] In Egan's posthuman world, there are three main posthuman groupings: the polises, the gleisners, and the fleshers. Most of the world's population has participated in the "Introdus," the translation of human personalities into the form of self-conscious software, referred to as "citizens," and the organization of those software programs into communities called "polises." A citizen is defined as "conscious software which has been granted a set of inalienable rights in a particular polis"; although these rights may vary, they always include "inviolability," or the citizen's right to self-authorship and exclusive access to the code making up its program; "a pro rata share of processing power," or a guarantee that the program that constitutes the citizen's mode of being will be granted the resources needed to keep the program running in the computer network; and "unimpeded access to public data," which amounts to access to the simulated environment of the community itself, because it is nothing but public data (285).

A polis is defined both as "a computer or network of computers which functions as the infrastructure for a community of conscious software" and as "the community itself," supported by and run on that computer infrastructure (290). Note here the way the term "polis" crosses the hardware/software divide. The designation of these downloaded programs as "citizens" is especially significant, as is the dual definition of the polis. This ambiguity is one way that Egan's novel represents the ambivalent attitude toward embodiment that I have identified in posthuman narratives more generally. The fact that Egan locates that ambivalence in the definition of the "polis" or community underscores the fact that an ambivalent attitude toward embodied particularity is hardly a unique quality of electronically mediated forms of communication and community in cyberspace. The history of the modern institution of the democratic public sphere demonstrates a very similar ambivalence, often verging on a desire for disembodiment, as Stone suggests (*War*, 39–40).

Although *Diaspora* focuses on the inhabitants of the polises, it also includes two other kinds of posthumans, both presented as being distinguished from the citizens of the polises by being relatively more embodied, in an allusion to Sterling's *Schismatrix* and its conflict between Shapers and Mechanists. The gleisners are intelligent robots, and the novel notes that, "strictly speaking, gleisners and polis citizens are both conscious *software*," and goes on to stress this connection by pointing out that "gleisners will move their software to new bodies, if necessary, without considering themselves to have changed their identity" (288). In other words, the "identity" of the gleisners, like that of the downloaded polis citizens who are embodied only by the computers that run their programs, is detachable from any specific form of embodiment and transferable or translatable into other forms.

However, the distinction that the polis citizens and the gleisners make between themselves lies in the fact that, "unlike polis citizens, gleisners attach great importance to being run on hardware which forces them to interact constantly with the physical world" (ibid.). The gleisners make a distinction between existing purely as a software program, like the polis citizens, and existing as a program that is defined by its ongoing relationship to the physical world it inhabits rather than to a purely virtual, computer-simulated environment. For the polis citizens, the "mind" is the sole basis of their "identity," whereas for the gleisners "mind" is always defined in relation to a "body," specifically a body that is "flesher-shaped" (ibid.). A polis citizen named Inoshiro, characterized by a particularly radical attitude toward the modification of his own body image, mocks the gleisners' belief in doing everything, including sending ships to explore nearby stars, in the form of "*them-in-their-whole-bodies*, all the way. . . . They think if they dare take their heads off their shoulders to save a bit of mass, next thing they'll be abandoning reality entirely" (60). Note that what is being mocked here is the belief that any challenge at all to the "sacred icon" of the human form (Hollinger, 207) must inevitably slide into complete dematerialization, in a backhanded acknowledgment that even the virtual polises are not completely "free." Although the explicit plot of the novel involves one of the polises deciding to copy its citzens' programs and transmit them to other star systems in virtual form, its main subtext is the extent to which embodiment can or should be dispensed with. Inoshiro's sarcastic attitude toward the gleisners, for example, changes after he downloads himself into a gleisner body in order to interact with the third main community of posthumans in the novel, the fleshers.

As the name implies, fleshers are biologically embodied, and are further divided into statics, whose genetic inheritance is unmodified, and exuberants, the equivalents of Sterling's genetically engineered Shapers. The modifications introduced by the exuberants fall into three further subcategories: first, physical changes, or "simple, pragmatic adaptations for new diets or habitats," resulting in "amphibious, winged, and photosynthetic exuberants" (55); second, "neural modifications to provide new instincts" or "*hardwired* reflexes," necessary to allow modified humans to handle their new physical abilities (ibid.; my emphasis); and third, modifications that affect even more basic structures of "language, perception, and cognition," including both the "dream apes," who have edited out the language centers of the brain to induce a condition of enforced primitivism, and "more constructive" exuberants who have developed "new ways of mapping the physical world into their minds" (56). The exuberants then represent a point of convergence between the fleshers and the polis citizens, in their treatment of embodiment as malleable. One type of exuberant is described as having "tailored themselves" so extensively that each individual can "rewrite parts of vis own genome by injecting the new sequence into the bloodstream" (58). At the same time, the novel also suggests that the polis citizens are not as sharply distinct from the fleshers as they might like to think, because one of the main virtual characters is later depicted as modifying his perception and cognition, like some of the more radical flesher exuberants, to allow him to perceive five spatial dimensions rather than three (232–33).

The dual reference of the term "polis," to both the virtual community of the conscious software programs and its infrastructure of networked computers, reflects *Diaspora*'s ambivalence as to whether the downloading process is an escape from embodiment or a new kind of embodiment. *Diaspora*'s most direct allusion to Sterling's *Schismatrix* comes at the very beginning of the novel. The first chapter describes the virtual "birth" of new citizens, through the use of a "*Shaper* programming language" that re-creates "the essential processes of neuroembryology in software" (5; my emphasis). The appropriation of Sterling's name for the genetic engineering faction within the posthumanist movement, the Shapers, to name a computer programming language that allows human minds to be grown from scratch in the form of "conscious neural networks" never previously embodied in physical form seems both to assimilate embodiment to a model of textuality or what Hayles calls inscription (*How We Became Posthuman*, 198) and to retain some ambiguity about the continuing imbrication of materiality and virtuality, body and mind, at the very moment when the novel seems to dispense with embodiment entirely. The fact that the novel undermines its own initial distinctions between the three types of posthumans also works to problematize the way it seems to privilege disembodiment.

Diaspora in fact opens with an acknowledgment of the limitations of the inscription model, with its assumption that minds and bodies can be translated from one medium to another with no real loss of "identity" or meaning. We are told that any "translation" of "the essential processes of neuroembryology" into software will necessarily be "imperfect, glossing over the biochemical details in favour of broad, functional equivalence," and that "the full diversity of the flesher genome could not be brought through intact" (5). The polises try to overcome this limitation by inducing artificial mutations and charting "the consequences of new variations to the mind seed," in order to balance between the "stagnation" of endlessly reproducing "a diminished trait pool" and the recklessness of uncontrolled changes in the digital genome that might produce "children" whose mental processes fall outside the norm of "sanity," as defined by the rather elastic norms of the virtual polis (5–6). The reference to the inability of the downloading process to encode the full "diversity" of the human genome is particularly resonant for considerations of race. The opening chapter of *Diaspora*, in fact, seems poised on the verge of a discourse of virtual eugenics, as is suggested when one of the polis citizens, Inoshiro, taunts the main character, Yatima, whose "birth" from a computer program is represented in the first chapter. The form that Yatima's programming ultimately reached is regarded as a desirable mutation, Inoshiro claims, because of Yatima's particularly "compliant . . . settings," which "parents will be asking for" for years (56). In other words, Yatima is hardwired for conformity, in a way that it is tempting for parents to artificially reproduce in other "children."

The novel tends to avoid the dangers of enforced homogeneity that momentarily emerge here by focusing attention on the more spectacular thematics of the characters' virtual body images, and the possibilities for reimagining them in this simulated environment. The ambivalence toward embodiment I noted earlier in the dual reference of the word *polis* is dramatized in *Diaspora* in terms of the different rules various polises use to define what counts as an appropriate body image. Such rules are especially important because body images are presented as a necessity for forming a community and for using the virtual environment of the computer network as a site for consensual social interaction between citizens. These types of interactions seem to require that the citizens

represent themselves to one another visually. At one extreme, we find the
Ashton-Laval polis, whose "mental architecture" and principles of embodiment
are derived from the history of art, with a resulting interest in exploring various techniques of abstraction and experimentation with the human form (37,
47). At the other extreme, there is the Carter-Zimmerman polis, where the norm
is to gender one's body image as either masculine or feminine, in contrast to
most of the polis citizens, who prefer to use the genderless pronouns "ve" and
"vis" in referring to one another. Carter-Zimmerman's rule that its citizens also
simulate possession of a "tangible body" is, however, regarded as even more
extreme and unconventional than the insistence that all bodies be gendered
(59), moving Carter-Zimmerman closer to the body politics of the gleisners than
to the other polises.

The more typical median between these extremes is represented by Konishi
polis, where Yatima is "born" at the beginning of the novel. For the citizens of
Konishi, "the whole idea of *solidity*, of atavistic delusions of corporeality," as
practiced in Carter-Zimmerman, is "equated with obstruction and coercion"
(59–60). From the Konishi perspective, a simulation that sets out to mimic the
laws of the physical world only violates the "autonomy" of its citizens, because
such a simulation makes it possible for one computer-generated icon "to block
another's path" (ibid.). To pretend to have solid bodies is to interfere with the
absolute freedom of motion possible in a virtual environment. Similarly, "recon-
necting the pleasures of love to concepts like *force* and *friction*" is regarded in
Konishi polis as "simply barbaric" (ibid.), in a passage that recalls Hayles's critique
of the treatment of "human beings as inscriptions that can be *frictionlessly* transferred into another medium" ("Posthuman Body," 248).

At the same time that Konishi polis rejects Carter-Zimmerman's strict mimetic conventions for representing citizens to one another, Konishi nevertheless
mandates that all its citizens' body images or icons must conform to a basic
pattern: "the same biped, the same ape-shape, as constant beneath the riot of
variation as the letter A in a hundred mad monks' illuminated manuscripts"
(15). As long as this basic pattern or outline is respected, any imaginable variation is permissible: "simplified or intricate, rococo or spartan, mock-biological,
mock-artifactual, forms outlined with helices of luminous smoke, or filled with
vivid hissing serpents, decorated with blazing fractal encrustations, or draped
in textureless black" (ibid.). As Yatima puts it after he first encounters other virtual citizens, their body images "mostly reminded it of icons it had seen before,
or the stylised fleshers it had seen in representational art," but "far more diverse
and far more mercurial, than real fleshers could ever be" (14).

The conventional biological markers of racial identity—differences in skin
color, facial features, hair—would clearly be subsumed in such a proliferation
of different body images in virtual reality (even as the reference to "textureless"

blackness suggested stylization of racial iconography). The differences in physical appearance that have justified and legitimated the construction of racial categories for the last several centuries would presumably recede into insignificance in the face of the diverse options available to the polis citizens, and one of the interesting subtexts of Egan's narrative is the suggestion that such diversity of appearance replaces the genetic diversity lost in the Introdus and its translation of human beings into conscious software.[43] The question begged by this shift from genetic diversity to physical diversity of appearance is whether this replacement of one form of diversity for another is an adequate substitution on the cultural level. Does the relatively homogeneous and impoverished genetic makeup of the polis citizens constitute an impoverishment on the cultural level of the citizens' ethnicity? Or does the detachment of physical appearance from genetic makeup allow for the emergence of more new forms of cultural difference than are possible in a world where the metaphor of "cultural heritage" links cultural difference to a biological and genetic inheritance, to kinship relations? Does the severing of genetics and physical appearance promote multicultural understanding and tolerance, or render it impossible to ever achieve those goals? One reading of *Diaspora* would be that the polises promote homogeneity on the genetic level and heterogeneity only on the more superficial level of physical appearance, resulting in a static dichotomy rather than a dialectic between cultural homogeneity and cultural heterogeneity.

The norms of bodily representation in Konishi polis combine possibilities for morphing and transformation with a consensually chosen but rigidly enforced limit to such possibilities, and that limit represents the residual form in which the experience of embodiment as materiality persists, even in this virtual environment. But while voluntary and therefore arbitrary in the sense of being only one option out of many, this limitation to the range of permissible body images is decidedly *not* arbitrary in the sense of being without significance to the citizens who make up the polis. For them, the fact that "their form was constrained not by physiology or physics" means that it can be constrained "only by the conventions of the gestalt—the need to proclaim, beneath all inflections and subtleties, one primary meaning: *I am a citizen*" (14). This identity statement, then, defines the level at which the inhabitants of the polis remain hardwired, a level that is neither as fixed and absolute as that of the polis's infrastructure nor as easily edited as the level of software programs, like the ones responsible for the citizens' body images or the appearance of the environment they live in. To use Moravec's metaphor, the performative utterance "I am a citizen" defines a "constitution" that can only rarely be altered, beneath the more freewheeling "design" level (*Robot,* 147). In this way, the novel begins to qualify the assumptions inherent in treating embodiment purely as "inscription" or "problem of coding."

The novel thereby also makes legible and problematizes the assumptions informing the historical construction of the modern democratic citizen. As Michael Warner puts it, traditionally the citizen's ability to participate in "public discourse is a routine form of self-abstraction" that permits (or requires, depending on your point of view) individuals to "transcend the given realities of their bodies and their status" in order to function as citizens (Warner, "Mass Public," 382). Because participation in a virtual polis is defined by the inalienable right of access to the public data that constitutes both the simulated environment and the citizens themselves, to exist in a polis at all is to be part of a "public discourse," effectively literalizing Warner's formulation, just as the Introdus literalizes the way that the institution of the public sphere has historically functioned as a technique of disembodiment or "routine . . . self-abstraction."[44]

As Warner defines it, the public sphere is structured by a dichotomy between "publicness" and embodied particularity, so that social groups defined primarily by their bodies, such as women and racialized minorities, are by definition excluded from full participation in the abstract rationality supposedly characteristic of public discourse. The reemergence of forms of embodied particularity, of an attachment to material bodies, within the abstract and purely rationalized virtual environment of cyberspace might then suggest the possibility of overcoming this seeming contradiction within the traditions of the democratic public sphere. As one of the citizens of Carter-Zimmerman puts it, in contrast to the other polises, they "choose to value the physical world" by modeling their icons on corporeal bodies (168). At the same time, because those icons exist only within the virtual environment of a computer simulation, the citizens of Carter-Zimmerman must realize both that this valuing of the physical world is "what defines us" and that "it's as arbitrary as any other choice of values. . . . It's not the One True Path which the infidels have to be bludgeoned into following" (168–69). The metaphor of cultural imperialism here is itself significant. It is the movement beyond fixed forms of embodiment, and the essentialist derivation of social identities on the basis of fixed biological differences, that permits the emergence of less stereotypical or "arbitrary" forms of difference. At the same time, the danger of this transcendence of fixed embodiment is that it also makes possible even more extreme fantasies of imposed cultural homogeneity.

This ambivalence appears in one scene set in Carter-Zimmerman polis, during a party whose invitation "politely suggested attendance in strict ancestral form" (176)—in other words, in a rigorous simulation of corporeality. One citizen resists this polite suggestion and utilizes the ambiguity implicit in a virtual simulation of strict corporeality. Instead, he "politely faked it, simulating most of the physiology but running the body as a puppet, leaving his mind unshackled" (176).[45] This passage can be read in two equally plausible ways. First, it clearly implies a lapse into Cartesian dualistic assumptions about the mind/body relationship, including the separability of mind from body and the inevitable result of such an assumption, the devaluation of the body as just a limit to or "shackle" on the mind. The metaphor of the body as "puppet" also suggests that body images are a relatively superficial mask over the real identity of the person, which resides solely in the mind. At the same time, however, this passage can be read more positively, because the refusal to be shackled to a form of bodily particularly here interferes with full participation in a public, social setting rather than enabling it, as it would in the tradition Warner defines. Mental transcendence is associated with privacy, not particularity, in a reversal of the dualistic structures of the traditional public sphere. Indeed, the passage might be read not as expressing a desire to escape the shackles of embodiment for a condition of pure mind but instead as acknowledging the necessity of keeping both levels "running" at the same time, however imperfectly that balance is maintained. This second reading is supported by the novel's opening presentation of the necessity for polis citizens to accept constraints on the free mutability of their body images, as a precondition for proclaiming citizenship and becoming social entities. In contrast to the devaluation of the body as puppet or shackle, in that opening passage the acceptance of bodily constraints is presented as enabling access to the freedom possible within the virtual community, and it might be useful to return to that passage.

It is important to remember that the character Yatima has never been physically embodied. The story of his development includes a virtual version of the Lacanian mirror stage, as Yatima learns to identify with his icon by recursively internalizing a model of his own behavior and personality, and thereby learns to control the appearance of his body image, in one of the more startling and successful translations of narratives of human development into the terminology of cybernetics. The crux of this chapter occurs when "the model of Yatima's beliefs about Yatima's mind" becomes "the whole model of Yatima's mind: not a tiny duplicate, or a crude summary." The result is that the statement "I think that Yatima thinks that I think that Yatima thinks" collapses into "I am thinking," as Yatima's "symbol network identified the last redundancies, cut a few internal links," and eliminates the "infinite regress" of the earlier formulation, with its alienated oscillation between "I" and "Yatima" (26). The point of this passage, however, is not just that Yatima forms a self-conscious ego by learning to refer to himself as "I," thereby gaining both the ability to recognize his own thought processes as his own and the ability to reflect on those processes. Yatima also goes through the process of identifying himself—that is, his mind or his thoughts—with the visual icon of his body image. It is that image that he previously referred to as "Yatima," in an uncomprehending echo of the other citizens he interacts with. Yatima's process of achieving full self-consciousness is therefore associated in the novel with his learning that his thought processes and his body image are *not* two separate things (as they would be in the classic version of the mirror stage), and the novel implies that this lesson on the mind/body relationship applies to self-conscious software as much as it does to organic creatures.

This passage, then, seems to contradict the Carter-Zimmerman character, who runs his body just as a puppet, to leave his mind unshackled. However, this seeming contradiction might be read as implying that, although mind or thought and body are still inseparable even in these virtual polises, they are not necessarily related in the same way that they are in the physical world. As Stone puts it, "the physical/virtual distinction is *not* a mind/body distinction," but rather "a different way of conceptualizing a *relationship* to the human body" (*War*, 40). One of the values of popular narratives about posthuman embodiment is their exploration of the different ways that relationship can be reconceptualized.

As Yatima's development continues, he is initially depicted as attracted to the pleasure of pure mathematics, which in turn leads to his first generalization about the nature of the polis citizens. In this passage, Yatima reflects upon the care taken to simulate the laws of physics in a virtual fountain of water in Konishi polis, which Yatima takes as an example of the "arbitrary" nature of "the vestigial influence of flesher ancestry" and its corporeality (43). Yatima sees this self-imposed limitation on the virtual simulation as merely an "aesthetic choice" (ibid.). But, Yatima decides, there is something more fundamental than the laws of the physical world that defines the nature of the polis citizens, "however malleable their minds," something "unmodified" by the polis's citizens' capacity for "self-directed change" and control over their virtual forms (ibid.). In place of "the instincts and drives that the fleshers, in their innocence, had once mistaken for embodiments of immutable truth," Yatima becomes convinced that the polis citizens have substituted the abstract laws of mathematics, which provide the polis citizens with "the real invariants of identity and consciousness" in the form of "their own immutable mathematical signatures" (ibid.).

But if this is an essentialist self-definition, as suggested by the focus on the ahistorical truth and immutability of this mathematical essence, then it is a kind of essentialism that is not easily classifiable in terms of the distinction between essentialism and social or linguistic constructionism, so familiar to practitioners of academic cultural studies and critical theory. The transcendent ahistoricity of Yatima's mathematical essence is familiar enough, but as he conceptualizes it this essence also possesses qualities we associate with linguistic constructions of subjectivity. Specifically, this essence is not unique to each individual citizen, nor is it exactly analogous to a more general notion of human nature. Because of its abstract qualities, this mathematical essence may be transcendent and "invariant," but it is still manipulable by technical means. Because it can be formalized and encoded, this is an essence that can be copied and reproduced like a text and can be generated by a machine, as we have already seen Yatima's essential character being constructed. In other words, this essence is both "immutable" and reducible to a problem of coding.[46]

Although this type of self-definition makes it possible for the polis citizens to regard themselves as translatable from one medium of existence to another, Yatima's first exercise of that capability challenges and complicates his faith in a purely abstract mathematical "essence" as a principle of continuity underlying the continual metamorphoses possible within a virtual environment. Immediately after Yatima's insight into the invariant ground of being of the polis citizens, the next chapter begins with Yatima and a friend downloading copies of themselves into gleisner robot bodies, in order to make contact with a flesher community. At one point, Inoshiro, Yatima's companion on this trip into the real world, finds himself unexpectedly unable to separate his sense of self from his robot body. As Inoshiro puts it, with considerable dismay, "I've started feeling things," and not just as "an abstract overlay"; instead, "it happens to *me*. . . . I must have formed some kind of map of the data" recording the bodily sensations he's experienced "and now my self symbol's absorbed it, incorporated it" (62). This passage offers one of the clearest possible fictional examples of the process of becoming hardwired, having a software program become a part of who you are.

Inoshiro's problem, however, is that he tends to oscillate wildly from an insistence on his own total self-control of his body image to a sense of total loss of control, which ends up overnaturalizing the experience of embodiment he has incorporated. As a result, Inoshiro now sees the process of downloading and copying his program or "self symbol" back into a purely computer-simulated format as being "like . . . tearing off my skin" (ibid.). Yatima in turn goes too far in resisting the implications of this identification of mind and body, bluntly telling Inoshiro that "you know that's not true" (ibid.). Yatima experiences physical embodiment merely as the mapping of his virtual "icon's symbol to the actual posture" of the gleisner body (ibid.). This experience is confusing because it duplicates his normal body, but it poses no serious threat to his privileging of virtual existence over physical modes of being. For Yatima, the virtual icon or self symbol is still what he identifies with, where he locates himself, not the robot body. He experiences that body just as a mask or puppet and not as an extension of himself. In contrast to Inoshiro, for Yatima embodiment initially amounts to no more than "playing along with the conventions of a game." This passage, then, dramatizes the difficulty of imagining hardwired forms of embodiment as a third space, between essentialism and constructionism. Yatima can only imagine *being* a body as an "intrusion of the world into Inoshiro's icon," which Yatima thinks he would experience as "a deep sense of violation" (ibid.).

However, the word *violation* and the phrase *deep sense* themselves invoke a notion of bodily integrity and imply physical distinctions between insides and outsides that should be meaningless to a purely virtual entity who has always experienced itself as a software program and a body image—that is, as nothing but a visually signifying surface with nothing "behind" or "inside" it except lines of computer code into which that image resolves at a level openly available to the polis citizens. This notion of bodily integrity seems purely metaphorical for Yatima at this point, serving only as a way for him to conceptualize interference in the efficient functioning of his software. Yatima interprets Inoshiro's inability to separate himself from the form that embodies his program as just such a form of interference or "violation." The retention of such metaphors nevertheless suggests the continuing vulnerability of all the polis citizens to the process of identification of self and body that Inoshiro undergoes. The persistence of these metaphors suggests the inability of even the polis citizens to entirely dispense with some relationship between their virtual selves and a concept of the physical world, which is then not merely an arbitrary "aesthetic choice," as Yatima initially imagines it. By extension, the physical infrastructure required to run or embody the citizens' software is not reducible merely to a meaningless technological platform that can safely be traded for another without changing who the polis citizens are. The polis citizens' ability to copy themselves from one body or one medium of existence to another turns out to be less "frictionless" than it initially seemed to be.

This continuing relationship between virtual and physical modes of existence begins to affect Yatima's attitudes and beliefs, as his experience of gleisner embodiment leads him to realize that, although he may not be able to "comprehend the idea of physical pain," still "images of bodily integrity resonated deeply" (84). Specifically, the seemingly naturalized concept of "ruptured skin" evokes the possibility of a malfunction in a polis citizen's programming that would allow data to "flood across [the program's] borders at random, overwriting and corrupting the citizen within" (ibid.). The fact that this corruption is inherent in the nature of the citizens' virtual existence is made clear in a later scene, in which Inoshiro "grafts" into his software technical information that he has not gone through the process of learning, but has simply added wholesale to his memory files and will delete later. Yatima's comment is that this deletion "sounded like dismemberment, but Inoshiro seemed to view the whole prospect as less traumatic than the business of taking on and shrugging off their gleisner bodies" (94). This passage emphasizes the difference between Inoshiro and Yatima's attitudes toward embodiment, as does the language of Inoshiro's description of how his "self symbol" has "mapped the data" of embodiment and "*incorporated*" it, as opposed to Yatima's nightmare of being corrupted by having his borders flooded with alien data and by having the information that constitutes his self *overwritten*. In fact, the narrative also depicts Yatima's attitudes as changing and moving closer to Inoshiro's over the course of the novel. Yatima's vulnerability to forming a similar attachment to his body is suggested by the close similarity between Inoshiro's description of how he incorporated a map of his body into his self and the earlier passage in which Yatima learns to identify his virtual point of view with his body image in cyberspace. The same language of incorporating and identifying with a map or image is used in both passages, implying that the apparent conflict between Yatima and Inoshiro is more superficial than it might seem.

When he is forced to return to a purely virtual existence, Inoshiro is unable to cope with what he now sees as the loss of a physical body, equivalent to ripping off his skin. Inoshiro's response is to reprogram himself with an "outlook," a "non-sentient program which runs inside" a polis citizen, "monitoring" its mind and "adjusting it as necessary to maintain some chosen package of aesthetics" or "values" (290). Outlooks provide one solution to the problem of maintaining continuity of identity in virtual citizens, whose successive states of mind are not grounded in and unified by a physical body. Inoshiro goes a step further, choosing a "universally self-affirming" outlook that imposes a "hermetically sealed package of beliefs about the nature of the self, and the futility of striving . . . including explicit renunciations of every mode of reasoning able to illuminate the core beliefs' failings" (114). As a result, "once you ran it, you could not change your mind" (ibid.). This trope of a programmed "outlook" recalls the central technological innovation in Egan's story "Chaff," translated from neurobiology to computer science. The core beliefs that Inoshiro has immutably built or hardwired into his programming, into his very *self*, include indifference to the material world and the sufferings of its inhabitants. This passage demonstrates the negative potential of hardwiring, which can take the form of cynical reason, or the voluntary choice to keep on doing something that you know is wrong or mystified—in this case, choosing to eliminate one's own ability to make further choices.[47] Note, however, that the novel's critique of this choice also implies a critique of any desire to understand the polises as simply disembodied.

In contrast, Yatima decides to act on his newfound doubts about the purity of an abstract, virtual existence by emigrating to the Carter-Zimmerman polis, where the citizens choose to simulate the physical world and physical bodies more realistically than the citizens of Konishi. Yatima's doubts emerge as he comes to compare the physical world to the mathematical essence of the polis citizens and vice versa: "the physical world couldn't simply be commanded to change; it could only be manipulated, painstakingly, step by step—more like a mathematical proof than a scape" or virtual simulation (87). The significance of this insight seems to lie in Yatima's increasing emphasis on math as limitation and constraint on the malleability of virtual existence, rather than on the way that defining polis citizens in terms of their fundamentally mathematical nature or essence makes it possible to imagine the virtual self as separable from the limitations of embodiment and therefore perfectly translatable into various ideal forms.

Similarly, as Yatima reflects on the problem of maintaining personal continuity in a virtual environment, he first articulates the problem in mathematical terms, as the problem of "finding an invariant of consciousness, an objective measure of exactly what it was that stayed the same between successive mental states, allowing an ever-changing mind to feel like a single, cohesive entity" (79). This is, of course, the problem that Inoshiro uses the "self-affirming outlook" to solve once and for all, and which Yatima had earlier solved by locating this invariant in the principles of mathematics itself. Yatima now realizes that "formalizing this criterion" of invariant consciousness or putting it into an abstract mathematical and symbolic form is "difficult" (ibid.). I would argue that the difficulty becomes legible for Yatima precisely as a result of his experience of embodiment, or rather his experience of having to map his virtual self onto a physical body and vice versa. Yatima's willingness to qualify his search for a formulaic invariant of consciousness is more significant as a stage in his thinking than it might appear. That qualification raises the possibility that there are modes of existence whose contingency cannot be eliminated in favor of timeless mathematical forms. When Yatima defines the problem of personal continuity as a problem of information flows, with "each perceptual input and internal feedback gently imprinting itself on the network's previous state" (ibid.), the question is from where and to where is the information flowing? I believe this question is answered when Yatima later refers to "the feedback loops of embodiment" (89). The information flows between the self and the physical environment within which that self is located, however thoroughly technologically mediated that environment becomes, and it is in this way that the world always intrudes into the abstraction of the virtual self, to disrupt its formal closure and therefore its reproducibility and amenability to instrumental control.

The whole premise of *Diaspora*'s main plot can in fact be understood as hinging on the movement from a purely virtual, solipsistic existence to an engagement with the physical world from within the polis's cyberspaces. Yatima emigrates to Carter-Zimmerman in order to participate in that polis's project of exploring other star systems, the diaspora of the title.[48] This project is necessary as a result of a stellar catastrophe that threatens the physical existence of the entire earth, including the computer networks that form the polis's physical infrastructure. In effect, the diaspora that the novel traces is a reversal and an undoing of the Introdus that created the polises, a turning outward rather than the self-destructive turn inward that is dramatized most negatively by Inoshiro's programming himself with a purely "self-affirming outlook," one that resists any transformative feedback from outside itself. This overall movement of the plot and the attempts of the Carter-Zimmerman polis to somehow reconnect with the physical world support the reading I outlined earlier, of Yatima's shift from a purely abstract, mathematical self-definition to a greater focus on a relational definition that stresses the connection between the virtual and the physical.

At the same time, it is important to note that the diaspora is not and cannot be simply an inversion of the Introdus. It is no longer possible for the polis citizens to return to a flesher existence, and the desire to do so would constitute a nostalgia as self-destructive as any solipsistic retreat into virtual abstractions and simulations. In fact, Inoshiro's dilemma is how to engage with the physical world of embodied existence after a virtual existence becomes possible, or how to articulate the posthuman with the human, not as a return that denies and abandons posthumanist modes of existence, but as a relationship that refuses to deny or abandon human, embodied modes. *Diaspora* thereby identifies a tension that I will argue structures the original texts of the cyberpunk movement, beginning with Gibson's *Neuromancer*.

"The Rapture for Nerds"?
The Politics of Posthumanism in Ken MacLeod's *Cassini Division*

Scottish author Ken MacLeod's novel *The Cassini Division* (1998) makes this tension more explicit by situating cyberpunk conventions in relation to socialist traditions and staging a conflict, not between versions of posthumanism as in *Schismatrix* or *Diaspora*, but instead between the posthuman and "those who chose to remain within the human frame" (137).[49] Like Egan, MacLeod chooses to focus on the more extreme, Extropian versions of posthumanism, which tend to present the body as obsolete or expendable; as in Egan's novel, the main form this project takes is the prospect of downloading consciousness into a computer storage format. But decidedly unlike Egan, MacLeod addresses this posthuman project through a viewpoint character who is radically opposed to it, rather than owing his existence to it, as Yatima does.

In *The Cassini Division*, the character who functions as a spokesperson for posthumanism is accused of wanting to "live in a virtual reality" by another character who argues for remaining human. For this humanist character, downloading or "stripping your brain away layer by layer and modeling it on a computer is what I call *dying*" (75, 76). The proto-posthumanist responds that this process is not dying but "transcending," and for him living in an organic body is to be condemned to die (76).[50]

MacLeod's novel, then, dramatizes the conflict over posthumanism as an explicit political debate among the characters, which informs the events of the plot. Much of the pleasure of this narrative lies in the way in which the debates over human embodiment versus posthuman disembodiment are articulated through the vocabulary of contemporary political debates, even as that recontextualization of familiar rhetorics threatens to displace and subsume all political differences onto the distinction between the human and the posthuman. The political debate appears in two flashback scenes that precede the invention of the technology needed to transfer human consciousness into a form suitable for computer storage. The humanists refer to themselves as the Earth Tendency and the posthumanists as the Outwarders (91).[51]

During the debate scenes, a proponent of posthumanism proclaims that "the meat is murder," appropriating a contemporary slogan of the vegan and animal rights movements to argue for abandoning the human body as part of a general detachment of humanity from any "natural" system. In addition to the way it deploys the typical cyberpunk rhetoric of the body as "the meat," this slogan is especially interesting for what it implies about posthumanism as a *rhetorical* struggle, specifically over the cultural meanings associated with embodiment.[52] The suggestion is that this posthuman migration into a purely technological environment, by living as computer programs in virtual realities, would be the culmination of the deep ecology movement, because this migration would leave nature to the animals. At the same time, this posthumanist transformation is obviously diametrically opposed to deep ecology's belief that human beings should be treated as only one component of a larger ecological system with its own integrity and nonhuman reason for being, a nonhierarchical system in which humans are not regarded as the teleological justification for the system's existence. In contrast, MacLeod's posthumanists want to create a world in which only humans exist, a world designed for no reason other than to meet the needs of human beings. The posthumanist character tries, then, to align the goal of moving beyond the human form with at least one already-existing political movement, which becomes subsumed in the posthumanist project and loses its specificity.

The same dynamic of subsumption plays out in relation to other political movements. When the representative of the Earth Tendency accuses her opponent of ignoring the problems of people on Earth, most of whom lack access to the technology for "uploading" their consciousness into a computer, the posthumanist character points out that after uploading "you won't have to see them suffer. . . . You can just *edit them out*" (75), as Inoshiro tries to do in Egan's novel. In a later scene, this vision of the future is sarcastically described as "the Rapture for nerds" (90), while the humanist characters realize that their resistance to the posthumanist project makes them "reactionaries," a term from their own political vocabulary that they would never have applied to themselves except in the context of this conflict between humanism and posthumanism.

The humanists also claim that their reaction only makes them "counter-*evo*lutionaries, pulling back from the next stage in human development" (93), rather than counterrevolutionaries. For his part, the posthuman spokesperson imagines that "sentimental post-humans will no doubt campaign for 'human rights,'" where human rights means literally the right to choose to remain human, not any political entitlements authorized by that choice (92–93). In the context of such rhetoric, the opponents of posthumanism are able to claim that "we're the Indians. The natives" and to define nativism as being "a drag on the wheels of progress" and "Manifest Destiny" (94).

This response to the rhetoric of posthumanism is especially important for the way it attempts to reintroduce political content into the debates between the human and the posthuman, but is only able to do so in metaphorical form, by analogizing all of humanity to the status of Native Americans or other colonized peoples, invoking the history of colonialism only to displace it, just as the posthumanists displace and subsume deep ecological arguments. The choice to remain "within the limits of the human frame" is compared here to the struggle of colonized peoples to retain the specificity of their cultural traditions and to resist modernization by insisting that modernity be organized around values other than profit and progress. At the same time, that history of colonial struggle is emptied of its specificity, in exactly the same way that the category of "human rights" is emptied of any political significance by the posthumanist spokesperson, who imagines human rights as "one of those fluffy causes, like old-growth forests and spotted owls" (93).

This resistance to posthumanism demonstrates how the rhetoric of posthumanism dominates the debate and organizes the terms of any resistance. Posthumanism cannot be dismissed simply as "the Rapture for nerds," no matter how much the humanists wish they could. Specifically, analogizing the choice of remaining human with colonial struggles evades, and perhaps even makes it impossible to ask, one crucial question: What is the relation between actual colonized peoples and the project of posthumanism or resistance to it? What relevance does the debate over posthuman technological possibilities have for considerations of race and nationality?

The debates between human and posthuman factions in *The Cassini Division* are useful because they demonstrate the tendency for the effects of new technologies on gender and sexuality to be emphasized over their effects on the construction of racial and national categories. But MacLeod's novel also demonstrates the ways in which racial issues do reemerge within the discourse of these new technocultures. For instance, when the debate over posthumanism turns to the question of whether there is or can be a sharp distinction made between humans and machines, the humanist representative refers to the Turing test for determining whether a computer program is intelligent. The Turing test hinges on the computer's ability to hold a conversation with a person skillfully enough to fool that person into believing that he or she is talking to another human being rather than to a computer. MacLeod's humanist character argues that "No Turing test can come close" to successfully imitating the human qualities of self-consciousness and self-reflection, "no matter how good it is at *faking an organism*" (*Cassini Division,* 76; my emphasis). The pun on faking an orgasm suggests that the elements of masquerade and mimicry that the Turing test uses to define personhood are structurally similar to existing modes of gender and sexual masquerade (I will return to this interpretation of the Turing test at the end of chapter 3).

The main function of faking an orgasm is to maintain and reproduce phantasmatic ideals of heterosexuality and male adequacy, at the expense of women's pleasure. Following out the analogy, the passage then also suggests that artificial intelligence as a form of posthumanism might function merely to guarantee "the existence of a stable and clear definition of the *human*" (Bukatman, 278). But faking an orgasm also reveals the security of those ideals to be fantasies. In this sense, "faking an organism" suggests that personhood might function in the same way, as the imitation of an ideal original that exists only as an imagined fantasy. This reading, of course, undermines the humanist relegation of artificial personhood to the status of a mere "fake."

This reading suggests the relevance of theories of sexual performativity like Judith Butler's to new technocultural contexts and their modes of embodied existence (the topic of chapter 4 in this book). Another example appears when the (male) posthumanist character tells the (female) humanist, "I like your body" (76). But rather than implying purely a sexual attraction, in the context of the posthumanist vision of living in virtual reality, "I like your body" also means "when I upload, I might model my virtual body on yours"; the humanist character's response is "in your dreams!" (ibid.). This exchange can be read in two ways. First, it can be taken as a critical commentary on how men often confuse desire with possession and control of women, a reading that emphasizes how gender relations structure what people do with posthumanist technologies and how traditional assumptions about gender might be reproduced in new ways in a posthumanist world. Second, in a reading that emphasizes alternative sexualities rather than gender, this passage suggests that desire and identification might be aligned in a virtual environment. In other words, the passage suggests how the assumptions on which the norm of compulsory heterosexuality is based might be disrupted in cyberspace, because compulsory heterosexuality depends on a strict distinction between the object of desire and the object of identification. Men desire women, but identify with other men. From that perspective, this passage might be read as suggesting the "queerness" of virtual sex. At the same time, the passage might also demonstrate how the extreme posthumanist dream of escape from the body transforms sexual pleasure into the pleasure of bodily malleability, the pleasure involved in living in "a world of wonder, where you can be anything you like, not what chance and your genes have made you" (75).

In these readings, I have tried to show how gender and sexuality do *not* simply function as metaphors for virtual or posthuman modes of embodiment; instead, I have identified ways in which the imagined structure and functioning of virtual bodies and artificial persons share more basic similarities with the structure and functioning of actually existing gender relations and sexual practices. This kind of reading is necessary in order for posthuman narratives to offer any kind of critical perspective on gender or sexuality. It is necessary for us to be able to read gender and sexuality as being illuminated by the posthuman thematics, as well as having the posthuman illuminated by gender and sexual analogies. However, this kind of reading becomes much more difficult when we turn to the way that posthuman narratives usually deploy racial categories. As in the case of the humanist character's comparison of herself to "the Indians," race tends to function purely as a metaphor of the posthuman condition, and posthumanism as the "truth" of the racial references, without that relation ever being reversed.

This tendency for posthuman narratives to reduce race, more than gender or sexuality, to an empty signifier does not mean that race is actually irrelevant to the concerns of posthumanism, however. In MacLeod's *Cassini Division,* parallels to racial issues emerge more substantively in the context of the humanist/ posthumanist debate about whether the posthumans, "uploaded" as computer programs or simulations of themselves, are machines or not, and if they are machines whether machines can be intelligent or not. The humanist spokesperson in the flashback scenes I've been quoting is also the narrator of the rest of the novel, and at one point she argues that "only humans are sentient. Those things out there are just jumped-up computer programs! They may give the appearance of sentience, but if they do, it'll be a protective coloration" (87). During the flashbacks to her arguments with the posthuman supporter, this same character complains that she "can't understand how anybody ever fell for the idea that a computer model of the brain is the same as the brain. Talk about mechanical materialism! It's about becoming a machine, it's death, and wanting it is *sick*" (91).

This attitude is likely to seem entirely justifiable to most people today, and to the narrator at the time of this flashback, given that it is not possible, and may never be possible, to create a computer model of the brain sufficiently complex to be seriously considered the equivalent of a person. By casting a representative of the humanists as the narrator of the novel, their point of view and their conviction that posthumanism = becoming a machine = dying is privileged by the narrative, especially since the humanist perspective is likely to seem "natural" to the novel's audience. Eventually, though, it starts to seem as if the novel deliberately invites this response in order to qualify or complicate it. Given that the narrator's Earth Tendency faction has fought a war with these "jumped-up computer programs," a war they barely won, the narrator's conviction that the uploaded posthumans lack sentience seems questionable, at best, or the posthumans would not constitute such a powerful opponent.

In fact, during the debate with the proto-posthuman character, the narrator actually presents her convictions about the nonsentience of computer programs and their resulting lack of personhood as a functional definition, the same move the cyberneticists use to legitimate artificial intelligence; as in Alan Turing's famous definition of machine intelligence as an "imitation game," specifically the ability to imitate human conversation (433), functional definitions claim that there is no significant difference between behaving in a way indistinguishable from a person and actually being a person. MacLeod's anti-posthumanist character turns this same argument against her opponents, in a way that undermines her opposition by accepting the validity of such arguments: "*You* can become machines if you like, but then you'll be dead, and we'll be alive, and we'll *treat* you as machines" (93). This formulation becomes even more problematic when we realize that it could be applied to other human beings, and has been, in the form of racist ideologies. As Turing points out in his 1950 essay, one argument against machine intelligence is that "the only way by which one could be sure that a machine thinks is to *be* the machine and to feel oneself thinking," but this argument is in fact "the solipsist point of view" (not the posthumanist), for it is equally true that "according to this view the only way to know that a *man* thinks is to be that particular man" (446). Turing here articulates the basic argument behind the "intentional stance," as Dennett defines it.[53]

The disturbing implications of the extreme humanist position and its claim to know once and for all the boundaries of the human become explicit when the posthuman spokesperson suggests that "refusing to accept intelligent robots as *people* is equivalent to racism," at which point a humanist replies, "So I'm a racist. A *human* racist" (92). But as a defense against charges of racism, this statement rings hollow, because what racist hasn't justified his or her beliefs by claiming to represent true humanity? The rest of the novel supports this characterization, to the extent that it presents the humanist position on machine intelligence as overly dogmatic. This challenge to our identification with the narrator as a reliable judge of what is possible in this future world becomes especially evident at two points. First, the overall plot of *The Cassini Division* concerns the problem of what the humanist faction should do when they are contacted once again by the descendants of the posthumans they had once defeated and who were assumed to have retreated into their virtual realities.

The narrator assumes that this seemingly peaceful contact is a ruse, which turns out to be only partially correct. One faction of the posthuman group betrays the humanists and takes over their computer systems (the first step toward an uncontrollable Vingean "singularity"), leading the narrator to destroy *all* of the posthumans. The novel deliberately refuses to resolve whether this action was justified or whether it constitutes a genocidal paranoia, and the narrator's actions are so extreme that this ambiguity and doubt about the righteousness of the humanist position becomes difficult to ignore.

The second way in which the novel suggests that the narrator might be unreliable comes when she makes contact with a colony world that had recently undergone a process called "Abolition," led by a group "who believed that using conscious machines as tools was wrong . . . like slavery" (181). This situation changed when "a lot of owned sapients took to claiming self-ownership" and ultimately had their claims legitimated in the court system (ibid.).[54] The narrator resists this analogy between ownership of artificial entities and slavery, resulting in one of these artificial persons, embodied in a feminine robotic form, giving the narrator a lecture. The artificial intelligence claims, "*I* know I'm human, and if you were to know me for any length of time, you'd find you couldn't treat me in any other way. . . . If I'm a machine, Ellen, I'm one that doesn't— *can't*—function properly unless it's free" (192–93). The association of the human value on freedom with the machinic value of functionality is particularly striking as a challenge to the humanist distinction between people and machines.

After being forced to interact with this artificial intelligence, the narrator has to admit that this machine's claims were valid: "no matter what I thought, in the innermost depths of my mind, about the innermost depths of *her* mind, it was impossible to be with her, to converse with her, and not give her the benefit of the doubt, not act *as if* her mind *had* innermost depths, and not to quite simply *like* her" (206). Note the artificial intelligence's willingness to use the pronoun "it" as a form of self-reference in the passage quoted in the preceding paragraph, about the relation between freedom and functionality, while the narrator here thinks of this character as "her."

This narrative thread about the narrator's changing attitude toward machine intelligence is especially significant because it suggests there is more than a mere metaphorical relationship between racial histories and the challenge that posthumanist rhetoric poses to traditional conceptions of personhood. The artificial intelligence is placed in the position where "it" must prove that "it" is human in the face of assertions that "it" is not, as Henry Louis Gates Jr., for instance, argues African-Americans have historically been required to do.[55] At the same time, this exchange between the narrator and the artificial intelligence also seems to reflect back onto the construction of personhood, precisely by raising the question of whether there is any significant difference between *being* human and *passing for* human. If we cannot know for certain exactly what is going on in the minds of other people, and if our knowledge of those persons' humanity is always mediated artificially by the language they use in communicating that humanity to us, then where do we draw the line in granting the benefit of the doubt, especially to any entity capable of communicating with us? The ability to pass the Turing test suddenly starts to seem more troubling to the narrator and less easy to dismiss as a case of "faking an organism."[56]

In these ways, against the grain of posthumanist rhetoric and its claims to transcend physical differences such as race, popular narratives about the possibility of a posthuman future are unable to articulate that possibility entirely outside the framework of racial histories, and these narratives therefore also have something to teach us about the difference race will continue to make in new technocultural contexts.

In this reading, MacLeod's novel suggests that the problem with the humanist resistance to posthumanism may reside in the humanists' acceptance of one of the basic tenets of this extreme form of posthumanism, specifically the idea that there is a radical disjuncture between the human and the posthuman. It might be more effective to acknowledge how the category of the human has always been problematic, at least for some historical groups, long before the invention of the technologies that have made posthumanist ideologies seem within our reach. The main difference between Sterling's and MacLeod's narratives is that it now seems as if it must have been easier for Sterling to imagine deconstructing the human/posthuman distinction than it is for writers today. One reason for this difficulty may lie in the increasing association of computer technologies with a rhetoric of disembodiment rather than reembodiment, and a move away from the mixing of cyberspace, cyborgs, and biotechnology in the original cyberpunk narratives, to which I will now return.

MEAT PUPPETS OR ROBOPATHS
THE QUESTION OF (DIS)EMBODIMENT
IN NEUROMANCER

Why jack off when you can jack in?
—*The character Plughead, in the film* Circuitry Man[1]

And if all the world is computers
It doesn't matter what your sex is
Long as you remember
If you're a boy or a girl
—*Bernadette Mayer,* The Formal Field of Kissing *(11)*

Jacking In

In this chapter, I read David J. Skal's novel *Antibodies* (1989) as exemplifying one typical response of cultural critics to the cyberpunk movement in science fiction, and specifically to cyberpunk's postmodern redefinition of embodiment. *Antibodies* implicitly critiques the oscillation in cyberpunk texts between a biological-determinist view of the body and a turn to technological and cybernetic means in order to escape such embodied particularities, an oscillation that is generally gender-coded in the paradigm texts of cyberpunk, especially William Gibson's novel *Neuromancer* (1984). This oscillation is figured, on the one hand, by the "meat puppet," to use the term applied to persons who are limited to purely organic forms in *Neuromancer*, and, on the other hand, by the "robopath," to use a term from *Antibodies*—that is, people who believe they are robots trapped in human bodies and who embrace technological mediation as revealing the truth of their relation to themselves, that truth being

49

their difference from their own physical form. This dichotomy between over-embodiment and (a desire for) disembodiment, celebrated as freedom, is often taken as evidence that cyberpunk fiction is both unable to think its way out of Cartesian mind/body dualisms and also invested in a reinscription of gender and racial norms, in which difference is stigmatized as the particularity of a narrow perspective and normality is defined through the privilege of universality and its claims to disinterested objectivity and subjective mobility. In contrast, I argue that this seeming dichotomy is actually displaced by the emergence of a third category of technocultural experience, which cannot easily be captured by the dualistic frameworks of universality/particularity, mind/body, culture/nature, freedom/determinism, individual/social, or software/hardware. The persistence of these dualistic categories in *Neuromancer* in part reflects the difficulty of finding a language adequate to this "third space." For instance, in order to articulate this alternative, the narrative has recourse to the characters' seemingly deterministic references to the ways they are "wired," a metaphor literalized by the technologies that are incorporated into their bodies and minds.

Skal's novel implicitly offers a diagnosis of cyberpunk's infamous devaluation of the body as "meat," through the protagonist's work as a therapist specializing in culturally induced pathological desires to transcend the limitations of the natural body by means of mechanical prostheses.[2] *Antibodies* seems to anticipate critiques of contemporary technoculture such as N. Katherine Hayles's or Hubert Dreyfus's, which stress the rhetoric of disembodiment informing the cultures and narrative models springing up around new technologies and the ways that technocultures reproduce and even intensify traditional Cartesian mind/body dualisms.

My reading of *Antibodies* suggests instead that cyberpunk works through these dualisms to open their relationship to new articulations. Cyberpunk therefore locates itself in a space of undecidability exemplified by the question Plughead poses, in Steven Lovy's 1989 film *Circuitry Man:* "Why jack off when you can jack in?" Interpreting this as a rhetorical question, as the scene from the film encourages us to do, viewers are assumed already to know the answer: jacking in, as a direct connection to computer networks (Plughead gets his name from the computer "jacks" studding his shaved skull, allowing him to plug his nervous system into the cyberspace of the networks), is clearly preferable to the pleasures of possessing a penis. In this reading, Plughead's question exposes and perpetuates a masculinist perspective on the neural interface and virtual reality technologies central to early cyberpunk fiction like Gibson's (because such technologies are here evaluated in relation to male masturbation), at the very moment it seems to abandon that perspective, as the existence of technological alternatives to possession of a sexed, male body denaturalizes the gendered meanings associated with such a "possession." Bernadette Mayer's poem demonstrates this same paradoxical insistence on simultaneously eliminating and retaining gender categories, and I see this double gesture both as characteristic of cyberpunk representations of embodied cultural differences and as a puzzle that needs explanation.

Reading Plughead's question as a rhetorical one, and therefore as demanding our consent to the idea that jacking in is obviously better than jacking off, also requires us to assume that there is a sharp, if not absolute, distinction between male masturbation and access to cyberspace. But the humor of this question resides precisely in its use of wordplay to suggest the two might be continuous with one another. The humor, in other words, requires us to entertain the possibility that projecting one's consciousness into the virtual space imagined to be on the other side of our computer screens does not in fact allow men to escape the conditions of our embodiment, but actually reinscribes those conditions beyond the limits of the (male) body. Read literally, Plughead's question suggests that cyberpunk might be defined less by a desire to escape embodiment entirely than by a real and indeed urgent befuddlement over the continuing cultural value and function of bodies, a questioning that might eventually produce critical and (for men) self-critical insights (though it is only a step in that direction). On its face, like Skal's *Antibodies*, Plughead's question seems to satirize cyberpunk as merely literalizing a traditional masculine privilege, the assumption that others will judge us by our minds more than our bodies, which can therefore be conveniently forgotten. At the same time, this question bluntly undermines that assumption and its attendant amnesia by linking male masturbatory impulses and willful blindness to our own limitations and necessarily partial perspectives, implicit in claims to the false universality of objective rationality or "pure mind." Plughead's question oscillates between the technological disruption of phallic self-absorption, with masculinity "decentered" as a result of the disarticulation of mind and body represented by "jacking in" to a global computer network, and a complete relinquishing of embodied existence that pushes the fantasy logic of male (self-)supremacy to extremes, just as cyberpunk fiction often osciallates between the figures of the "meat puppet" and the "robopath." However, I will argue that, in Gibson's *Neuromancer* and cyberpunk generally, Plughead's question about the status of embodiment cannot remain simply rhetorical, no matter the intent of its speaker or author, because the technocultural context in which such questions are posed makes it impossible for its answer to be taken for granted in advance as already decided.

In this way, cyberpunk reflects back onto the contemporary politics of embodiment, to denaturalize the category of the "human" along with its grounding in the physical body. One result is to reveal how abstract and formalized, how disembodied, that notion of "the" body already was.[3] I noted in the Introduction the language Sterling uses to make this point, when he asserts that, for cyberpunks, technology must be "visceral" and "pervasive, utterly intimate. Not outside us, but next to us. Under our skin; often, inside our minds" (*Mirrorshades*, xiii). This thematics of "body invasion" is, however, also a function of cyberpunk's "willingness to carry extrapolation into the fabric of daily life" (ibid., xiv). Gibson goes so far as to reject the term "extrapolation" as a description of his fictional attempts to imagine a possible future: "when I write about technology, I'm writing about how technology has *already* affected our lives" (McCaffrey, "Interview," 228), or, as Hayles puts it, how we have already become posthuman. This critical reflection makes it possible to articulate cyberpunk's body politics with the more properly multicultural concerns of the new social movements.[4]

The speaker of Bernadette Mayer's postmodern sonnet sequence asserts that "It doesn't matter what your sex is," but also that this statement is only true as "Long as you remember / If you're a boy or a girl." This seeming paradox anticipates the defining features of what is sometimes now called "hard character SF" (Swanger), and its investment in what Edward O. Wilson calls humanity's "physical soul." To the extent that traditionally sacrosanct and essential qualities of human existence can now be understood as material, biological phenomena, they become manipulable and plastic, in the reversal of the connotations of "nature" and "culture" suggested by Eve Sedgwick. It is in this sense that sex doesn't "matter"—that is, because sex (or humanity) is not something one "is" anymore, is not an ontological foundation exempt from historical processes of change and political interventions. At the same time, however, these categories do not simply disappear in a transcendence of embodied differences, either. It is the stubborn persistence of such categories of difference in contexts where they cannot be naturalized or eternalized that is referred to by the cyberpunk trope of "hardwiring."[5] Mayer's poem and this cyberpunk trope can then be read as dramatizing the possibility that denaturalization, the refusal of any politically conservative attempt to make the status quo seem inevitable and immutable, is not necessarily enough in itself to change anything. Social norms and differences can still possess normative power, even if they are not understood to be fixed and essential. In a context where "all the world is computers," denaturalization just means that social categories (gender, in this case) have to be actively produced and re-membered and cannot be taken for granted. At the same time, the refusal to simply abandon these categories of embodiment can also be read as a timely reminder of our responsibility to remain materialists in a social-philosophical sense as well as a scientific one. Embodied perspectives still matter, even in a technologically mediated "world," and Mayer's poem points out that this means that questions like gender and race must still matter, too, in however contested a form (boys and girls, rather than men and women).[6] In this chapter and the ones that follow, I will explain and challenge the typical technocultural tendency to represent this kind of denaturalized embodiment ex-clusively through gender and sexual categories rather than racial ones. But this chapter will also clarify how the trope of "hardwiring" as it first appears in cyber-punk fiction in *Neuromancer* represents this more complex and ambivalent atti-tude toward embodiment, in ways that are not necessarily only gendered. As we will see, in Gibson's novel, this trope has the function of linking the human characters and the artificial intelligence computer programs and personality sim-ulations that play an important role in the novel as denaturalized narrative agents. It is also important to note how the significance of the motif of hardwiring in *Neuromancer* has been overlooked because of the dominance that has been achieved by readings of cyberpunk as devaluing embodiment and dramatizing a traditional desire to escape the limitations of "the meat."[7] I want to return to cyberpunk's origins, then, in order to recover possibilities that seem in danger of being lost after the moment of the movement's institutional recognition.[8]

Even *Antibodies*, one of the most hostile early assessments of cyberpunk cul-ture as a rejection of embodiment, undermines its own critique. Skal's therapist attempts to cure his patients' robopathologies by reasserting the categories of "natural" bodily experience in ways that the novel clearly depicts as abusive. The techniques employed include physical and sexual violence, used as a form of "somatic shock therapy" to return patients to a sense of inhabiting a body. This reassertion of the body functions as an alibi for the reassertion of tradi-tional gender roles and sexual practices through coercive force. The novel makes both the desire to become a robot and the desire to be "purely" human, to accept the condition of Gibson's "meat puppets," seem equally problematic and undesirable. *Antibodies* offers no way out of this impossible double bind, and the same is true of many critiques of cyberpunk. In contrast, I will consider how *Neuromancer* might already anticipate an alternative to the impasse Skal's novel reaches. Although *Antibodies* strikes a needed cautionary note, it also rep-resents an overly reductive interpretation not only of cyberpunk but of the changing social conditions and logics that cyberpunk fictions presuppose and represent.

Making Cyborg Differences

Cyberpunk's programmatic insistence on the incorporation of technology into every aspect of public and private life provides a direct commentary on the changing status of the body, the traditional boundary between public and private or society and the individual, in postmodern cultures.[9] Moreover, in this view, technology overlaps with commodity culture, and the cyberpunk thematics of body and mind invasion then intersects with contemporary cultural studies and its emphasis on the extension of the commodity form in late-capitalist contexts.

This cyberpunk thematics then seems to support and develop Donna Haraway's argument about the redefinition of subjectivity and the relation between self and other that might be taking place through popular images of cyborgs. As Haraway suggests in "A Cyborg Manifesto," if technology no longer plays a dialectical role as an externalized Other against which to consolidate an idea of the universally human, then our relations to technology can be understood as constitutive, as the mark of internal differences within supposedly universal categories (Haraway, *Simians*, 150–53). Cyborg imagery, for Haraway, presupposes the possibility of moving from an instrumental concept of technology, in which tools are neutral and their use does not change the nature of the user, to a deconstructive logic of the supplement, in which our need for technology demonstrates the failure of a naturalized or interiorized humanism, its lack of self-sufficiency.[10] This reading of cyborg imagery makes possible a connection between the effects of technological mediation and multicultural social movements, but it also suggests the influence of Haraway's essay on ideas of the posthuman, whose "defining characteristics involve the construction of subjectivity" as explicitly dependent on technological mediation and "not the presence of nonbiological components," as Hayles points out (*How We Became Posthuman*, 4). The key question this analysis poses is the extent to which rethinking the otherness and externality of technology to humanity can be aligned with multicultural attempts to disrupt reductive stereotypes of women's otherness to men, Africa and the Orient's otherness to the West, people of color's otherness to whites, and to what extent a focus on technology displaces these more properly social concerns. To what extent do technological challenges to humanist ideals map onto multicultural challenges to the false universality of those same ideals and their surreptitious privileging of straight, white, middle-class masculinity?

Andrew Ross associates Haraway's argument with "the postmodernist critique of identity" in general, as "a contemporary response to the social condition of modern life, teeming with the fantasies and realities of difference that characterize a multicultural, multisexual world" (Ross, *Strange Weather*, 167). In fact, Haraway's use of the cyborg as a figure for partial, hybrid "identities" is intended to rewrite the narrative of the emergence of new social subjects (feminist, gay and lesbian, African-American, Chicano/a, postcolonial), in order to emphasize those subjects' reactions against their various histories of "forced signification" and enforced otherness. The cyborg figures an identity that is neither simply chosen nor entirely determined by others. Haraway therefore suggests that the coalitional grouping "women of color," as "a name contested at its origins by those whom it would incorporate," might also "be understood as a cyborg identity" (*Simians*, 155, 174).

These claims have been qualified, especially by feminist critics who have called Haraway to task for overemphasizing the positive political implications of cyborg imagery, as a point of resistance to the dualistic thinking typical of Western modernity and as revealing the role of new technologies in creating the preconditions for feminist coalition politics by replacing dependence on traditional identity categories with a "nonoriginal" hybridity that cannot be naturalized or assumed to be "innocent." These critiques have proceeded despite Haraway's acknowledgment that "a cyborg world" is an "ironic" political myth because the cyborg can also be "about the final imposition of a grid of control on the planet" and "the final appropriation of women's bodies in a masculinist orgy of war," a point that is often overlooked (*Simians*, 154).[11] Haraway later explained that her reading of the cyborg as offering positive political lessons for feminists depended on taking the cyborg as "definitely female," as "a girl who is trying not to become Woman" (*Simians*, 149; "Cyborgs at Large," 20). I take this statement to mean that Haraway's cyborg feminism involves a refusal to reify gender oppositions in such as way as to homogenize the category "Woman" and to ignore the internal differences of race, ethnicity, or nationality that structure gender categories. In this sense, Haraway's ironic political myth of the cyborg defines a rubric for white women's participation in the kind of critique of identity categories that Haraway associates with groups organizing as "women of color." This analysis therefore implies that Haraway's cyborg should not just be "female," but also racialized.

Haraway emphasizes this implication of her "Cyborg Manifesto" in the important 1991 interview with Constance Penley and Andrew Ross that reassesses that founding essay of technoculture studies. At one point, Haraway suggests that fetishizing the term "cyborg" might be problematic, because what she wants is "a family of displaced figures, of which the cyborg is one," so that it becomes possible "to ask how the cyborg makes connections with these other nonoriginal people . . . who are multiply displaced" (13). At the same time, Haraway also insists that these connections are possible because "cyborgs *are* nonoriginal people," like "the hybrid peoples, the conquest peoples, the enslaved peoples, the nonoriginal peoples, and the dispossessed Native Americans" who "*made* the New World" ("Cyborgs at Large," 12, 13). Haraway here makes an important point about the need to produce a "compelling account of race and sex *at the same time*" (11), as part of the project of her cyborg feminism, even as the ambiguities in these formulations leave it unclear whether cyborg embodiment can or should be understood as *aligned* with racial formations because they both imply a structural critique of Enlightenment humanism or, much more problematically, whether cyborg embodiment should somehow be *equated* with the racial and colonial histories to which Haraway refers. The key ambiguity resides in the meaning of the term "other" in the phrase "how the cyborg makes connections with these *other* nonoriginal people." Does "other nonoriginal people" mean people who are nonoriginal in ways that are different from the cyborg, or does it mean that cyborgs' nonoriginality makes them part of a group who are all othered in the same way because of their shared non-originality? It seems clear that what Haraway is calling for is the critical project of excavating and developing the implicit connections between cyborg feminism and racial histories, while respecting the specificities that separate them. But it is still possible to read this account of the cyborg and conclude either that to work on the topic is already to produce knowledge about race (by identifying forms of "nonoriginality" that are shared by cyborgs and other non-original peoples in the same way), or even that the study of cyborg embodiment can supplant racial histories.

These more problematic conclusions about the ways that cyborg embodiment opens onto issues of race might be exemplified by Chris Hables Gray's book *Cyborg Citizen*, in which the only direct reference to race is its dismissal as "not even good science, let alone good politics," and the claim that "inevitably categories such as Asian, white, black, and Latino collapse under scrutiny just as, today, the category of human is collapsing under cyborgization." The "best of multicultural theory" participates in this rejection of race, identified exclusively with "ethnic purity," by instead opting to "celebrate complexity and transgressing borders" (192). What is lost here is Haraway's insistence on racial difference as itself being "multiply displaced" and "nonoriginal," rather than race being understood as a discourse of purity that makes it impossible to produce or recognize such multiple differences. This kind of reductive interpretation of the technocultural processes of "cyborgization" in fact results in precisely the exclusive fetishizing of gender and sexual categories that Haraway claims the cyborg was intended to avoid, as we can see in Gray's book, which includes sections on "sex machines," "cyborg families," "tiny sex," and "penile prosthetics," but refers to "colonization" only as a metaphor for economic development in cyberspace. In this reading, cyborg imagery's critique of the false universality of the "human" paradoxically lends itself to a reuniversalizing of gender and sexuality, as if those categories were ever articulated outside racial frameworks, or vice versa; the specific work of transformation performed on gender and sexuality in technocultural contexts is significant in itself, but to analyze that work in isolation is distorting. This tendency to reuniversalize gender and sex reproduces the ways in which the cultural consequences of new technologies, as represented in cyberpunk fiction, seem more spectacularly exemplified in the domains of gender and sexuality. One of my goals in this book is to recover the ways in which race, ethnicity, and nationalism were also at play in cyberpunk, from its origins. Beginning with this chapter, I want to argue that technological and cultural developments subsequent to Haraway's original 1985 version of the "Cyborg Manifesto" (including cyberpunk, the Internet, the World Wide Web, and the modes of social interaction specific to them) show that the figure of the cyborg gains the critical value Haraway famously attributed to it only when it is articulated within racial as well as gendered and sexual frameworks.

Another critical problem has also emerged to complicate the realization of the multicultural and multisexual possibilities implicit in cyborg imagery. Haraway's argument seems to imply that the experience of forced signification once reserved for those subjects marked by gender or race is generalized to become the model for postmodern experience itself, as Baudrillard claims. In this situation, the unmarked, universal position of the white, middle-class male subject no longer seems available, and we therefore have access only to partial perspectives, not a generally human one. But, as Mary Ann Doane puts it, this same transformation means that, in a postmodern context, the crisis in dualistic thinking represented by the cyborg "will be the norm" and will therefore tend to lose its transgressive or resistant effects (Doane, "Cyborgs," 213).[12] The emergence of this crisis in signification or social determination calls into question the privilege of the white male individual and therefore may enable the recognition of other forms of historical experience. However, at the same time the generalization of this crisis may reinstitute the white male experience of postmodernity as a new norm, as if this experience of particularity as externally imposed definitions or "forced significations" were something entirely new. In contrast, Harryette Mullen offers a critique of the "media cyborg" as just the latest instance of a long history of external interference in the construction of "blackness," a history in which technological mediation has always had the effect of rendering black identity as a generalizable style and making it accessible to white Americans (87–89). After the transformations dramatized by Haraway's theory of cyborg embodiment, what happens to the specificity of nonwhite, nonmasculine subjects and their histories? That specificity may be both produced and evaded under the sign of the cyborg, in the same way that Phillip Brian Harper argues that postmodern culture generally often discounts the specificity of marginalized groups' historical experiences at the same time that it "refers to those experiences for the means by which to 'express' its own sense of dislocation" (193). Cyberpunk fiction's representation of cyborg identities can often seem to be structured by this same double gesture of both opening the question of alternative cultural identities and foreclosing on that question (this critique suggests a more negative interpretation of the way we remain "boys and girls," in Mayer's poem, despite the fact that in a world that is all computers "it doesn't matter what your sex is").

Cultural criticism must respond to both of these gestures, the potential for resistance embodied by the cyborg and the tendency for postmodern culture to ideologically recontain that potential for disruption. Haraway's argument does not simply reproduce Baudrillard's reuniversalizing tendencies; her suggestion is that nonwhite and nonmale subjects may possess specific relations to the post-modern situation for which the cyborg is also an appropriate myth. Haraway argues that, for subjects whose bodies have historically been marked as partic-ular in terms of race or gender and therefore excluded from the category of the universally human, the figure of the cyborg represents an insistence on precisely the *illegibility,* not the signification, of postmodern bodies, as a result of their multiple implication within a variety of structures of dominance, including race as well as gender, a model that should be applied to men and women, whites and minoritized groups.[13] This argument draws on the rethinking of embod-ied experience being produced by women of color such as Hortense Spillers and Gloria Anzaldúa, in ways that reinforce Haraway's argument about how cyborg imagery disrupts racial and gender categories. Spillers's insistence on drawing a historical distinction between the "body" and the "flesh" of African-American women emphasizes how these women were "ungendered" and there-fore culturally illegible as women from a white, middle-class perspective (67–68). Anzaldúa explicitly describes the border consciousness of the "new mestiza," using cybernetic metaphors, as a condition of being "forced to live in the inter-face" between two "self-consistent but habitually incompatible frames of refer-ence," a condition that produces "a massive uprooting of dualistic thinking" (37, 78, 80). The importance of such forms of illegibility is suggested by an often overlooked section of Haraway's "Cyborg Manifesto"—the section "The Infor-matics of Domination," in which she points out that the logic of post-Fordist information economies involves precisely the reduction of "the world into a problem of coding," in which "all heterogeneity can be submitted to disassem-bly, reassembly, investment, and exchange," a "search for a common language" that is derived from the convergence of "communications science" or informa-tion theory and "modern biologies" in contemporary society (*Simians,* 164). Failures of translation, and more specifically the failure of different structures of domination to map onto one another (as they do in the purely additive for-mulation "race, gender, and sexuality"), become acts of resistance in the con-text Haraway here defines.

On the popular level, another statement of the relation between racial and cyborg identities appeared in the Marvel comic *Deathlok,* when an African-American creative team, Dwayne McDuffie and Denys Cowan, created a revi-sion of this character, involving a black male character who is turned into a cyborg soldier named Deathlok. I will return to this comic in chapter 5, but at this point I want to discuss one scene that provides the comic with the title of its first serialized narrative (and me with the title of this book). At the beginning of a four-issue story titled "The Souls of Cyber-Folk," Deathlok applies W. E. B. Du Bois's famous definition of African-American double consciousness not only to both his racial and cyborg identities separately, but also to the relation between his racial and his cyborg identities. In issue 2, a black female cyborg tells Deathlok that "some people accuse me of being more comfortable with . . . cyborgs than I am with my *own* people. Whoever *they're* supposed to be" and that "it's like being trapped between two worlds. At *least* two." In response, Deathlok quotes Du Bois: "it is a peculiar sensation this double consciousness, this sense of always looking at one's self through the eyes of others. . . . One ever feels his twoness, . . . two souls, two unreconciled strivings, two warring ideals in one dark body, whose dogged strength alone keeps it from being torn asunder."[14]

By omitting certain phrases from Du Bois and choosing where to begin and end this quotation, this passage implicitly constitutes a reading of Du Bois. In context, Du Bois introduces this description of double consciousness as an example of how life in white America provides African-Americans with "no true self-consciousness and instead allows them to "see [themselves] only through the revelation of the other world." The same point is emphasized in the sentence that follows the quoted passage: "The history of the American Negro is the history of this strife,—this longing to attain self-conscious manhood, to merge his double self into a better and truer self." But the *Deathlok* comic omits any reference to the possibility of overcoming this condition of "twoness." Moreover, the omitted phrases marked by the ellipses reinforce the way Deathlok's reading of Du Bois is framed. The first omitted phrase refers to a sense "of measuring one's soul by the tape of a world that looks on in amused contempt and pity" (Du Bois, 214–15). The combined effects of these omissions is to remove any direct negative connotations associated with this internal division and the hybrid identities that produce it. Through the figure of the cyborg, *Deathlok* transforms Du Bois's quest for a "true self-consciousness" into an affirmation of the "consciousness of [his] own division," as Henry Louis Gates Jr. claims Zora Neale Hurston did (*Signifying,* 208). As quoted in the comic, the passage omits Du Bois's stated desire to synthesize this double consciousness into a unified self-consciousness, while it retains Du Bois's wish for "neither of the older selves to be lost" and his insistence on the possibility of being "both a Negro and an American" (Du Bois, 215).[15]

Deathlok's "dark body" is, of course, split not only internally between the African and the American, but also between the organic and the mechanical. The second ellipsis in Deathlok's reading of Du Bois omits the terms that specify this double consciousness as that of "an American, a Negro." This omission suggests a refusal to allow Deathlok's hybrid identity to be defined by any *single* dualistic structure or set of identity categories, and it is this multiplicity that I want to read as refusing any simple legibility of the "coding" of the protagonist's body, as each possible reading is mutually interrupted by the other. The second omission makes it possible to apply Du Bois's words to both Deathlok's

racial identity and his cyborg identity, at least. In other words, Deathlok is represented as existing simultaneously within a number of structures of self and
other, structures of asymmetrical power relations. In fact, Deathlok's transformation into a cyborg is actually represented as a radicalizing of his racial identity. After Deathlok identifies the source of his quotation, he comments that
"my father made me read that book a half-dozen times when I was a boy. Never
really sure I understood *why,* until just now." He goes on to add that "when I
was human, I was pretty assimilated myself. . . . And, other than the occasional
cutting little reminder, I was pretty *comfortable* in my illusion. I don't *ever* plan
to get that comfortable as a *cyborg*" (McDuffie and Cowan, *Deathlok* 2:13).

The double meaning of assimilation in this passage sums up the interplay
between racial and cyborg identities; assimilation here refers both to black
assimilation into white society and to the possibility that the two characters will
emphasize their cyborg identities as a vehicle for transcending racial identity.
Both these possibilities are comforting to the extent that they involve suppressing one or another component of the characters' hybrid identities. These black
cyborgs are represented as insisting on retaining the uncomfortable split between
black and cyborg identity, identities that are themselves internally split and
divided. The passage performs the rather remarkable feat of insisting not only
on hybridity but on multiple forms of hybridity, without translating one form
into a metaphor of another, especially racial identity subsumed into a metaphor
for the cyborg.

Meat Puppets:
Cyberpunk's Reinscription of Gender and Racial Categories

This moment in the *Deathlok* narrative supports Haraway's argument that
"cyborg imagery can suggest a way out of the maze of dualisms in which we
have explained our bodies and our tools to ourselves" (*Simians,* 181).[16] However, more often in cyberpunk fiction the possibilities of cyborg existence seem
reduced to a radical devaluation of organic bodies, usually referred to as "the
meat." Especially in their attempts to represent the deuniversalizing and "forced
signification" of white male bodies, cyberpunk texts often appear to reproduce
the mind/body split that characterizes much of Western philosophy and culture,
rather than replacing such dualistic and dialectical habits of thought with
models of hybridity and partial perspectives, as Haraway proposes. This fiction
typically seems structured around two dichotomous alternatives: either impris-
onment within a contingent bodily existence as a "meat puppet" or becoming
a "robopath" whose fondest wish is to transcend the body by replacing it with
mechanical prostheses or to dispense with the body entirely by uploading consciousness into computer networks, as Moravec proposes in *Mind Children.*

In Gibson's *Neuromancer*, the "postbiological" attitude of the robopath toward the body is thematized through the protagonist, Case.[17] Case is a futuristic hacker or "console cowboy" who is especially skilled at manipulating a direct neural interface with his computer, which effectively allows him to project his consciousness into the virtual "space" behind the computer screen and to negotiate cyberspace computer networks as a point of view detached from his physical body.[18] A typical cowboy, Case privileges the time he spends as a "disembodied consciousness" jacked into the cyberspace matrix, defined by the novel as "a consensual hallucination," a "graphic representation of data abstracted from the banks of every computer in the human system" (5, 51). For operators like Case, "the elite stance involved a certain relaxed contempt for the flesh" because "the body was meat." When Case is punished for stealing from his corporate employers by having his nervous system damaged, therefore preventing him from jacking into this "consensual hallucination," he is described as falling "into the prison of his own flesh" (6).

Although the experience of inhabiting a consensual hallucination seems to denaturalize both social reality and bodily experience, *Neuromancer* simultaneously reinstalls the traditionally gendered categories of immanence and transcendence, particularity and universality, through the distinction between the "meat" and "disembodied consciousness" that characterizes the "elite stance."[19] In fact, Case's devaluation of the body as "meat" has its basis in the specifically gendered figure of the "meat puppet" or prostitute (147). Case's ability to access cyberspace is restored after he is recruited to take part in a clandestine operation that provides the plot of *Neuromancer*, and he is recruited by a woman named Molly, a self-described street samurai whose bodily modifications include retractable, double-edged, four-centimeter scalpel blades implanted in her hands and optical implants that outwardly appear as mirrorshades surgically inset into her skull, permanently sealing off her eye sockets (24–25). Molly later reveals to Case that she earned the money for these modifications by working as a "meat puppet," a type of prostitute whose consciousness is suppressed by an implanted "cutout chip" while the house installs "software for whatever a customer wants to pay for" (147). Case's own relation to his body as "meat" seems to be mediated through this image of female objectification as a sexual commodity, and it is paradigmatic that this natural, purely physical body has to be produced through technological means, just as the categories of the "natural" and the "feminine" in general must be produced.[20] This textual connection attaches a subtext of femininity to the "prison" of the flesh, with the interesting consequence that Case's loss of access to cyberspace implicitly feminizes him. Case cannot stand to be even metaphorically reduced to the condition of a "meat puppet," which surreptitiously serves as the model for embodiment in general, though Molly has experienced that condition more specifically and literally as

a woman and a sex worker. By the same token, this gendering of body and disembodiment suggests that Molly's incorporation of technology and the unnatural body that results has a differently gendered significance than does Case's
otherwise similarly intimate appropriation of technology. For Molly, this incorporation both frees her from embodiment as a meat puppet and as a feminine
woman (she is Haraway's cyborg "bad girl" who is "trying not to become
Woman"), but it also reembodies her (as we will see, the question remains
whether "trying not to become Woman" is enough to make Molly "responsible
to women of many colors and positions," to complete Haraway's definition
["Cyborgs at Large," 20]). For Case, cyberspace technology displaces gender
categories onto the opposition between cyberspace and the meat but leaves
intact the dualistic structure by which both these pairs of opposed terms were
defined. This displacement is how Case remembers whether he's "a boy or a
girl," even as cyberspace seems to constitute a world that "is" computers and
where "it doesn't matter what your sex is." The distinction between embodied
existence and its transcendence through technology is implicitly gendered.

However, although this seemingly very traditional parallelism between the
categories of masculine/feminine and mind/body is central to the way *Neuromancer* figures cyberspace and characterizes its protagonists, this privileging of
gender as a framework for imagining new technologies is at least complicated
by another parallelism that has gone completely unobserved in the many commentaries on *Neuromancer*. This second parallel exists between Molly as meat
puppet and one of the few obviously racialized characters in the novel: Hideo,
a Japanese bodyguard or "ninja assassin" who, as Lisa Nakamura points out
(*Cybertypes*, 69), is presented as a complete orientalist stereotype, both as a
romanticized representative of the Japanese past (a ninja) and in his description as "enormously polite"(*Neuromancer*, 74–75). Hideo seems to embody the
reality behind Molly's media-derived ideal of the "street samurai"; at one point
Molly tries to stage her entrance into a fight in such a way as to live up to the
model of "every bad-ass hero, Sony Mao in the old Shaw videos, Mickey Chiba,
the whole lineage back to [Bruce] Lee and [Clint] Eastwood" (213). However,
when Hideo is first introduced he is not just described as a "ninja assassin," but
specifically as a "*vatgrown* ninja assassin" (74; my emphasis). In other words,
Hideo is a clone, artificially produced as a technologically instantiated version
of the media stereotypes Molly grew up with. In this sense, then, *Neuromancer*
both reproduces and denaturalizes racist Asian stereotypes, just as Molly's stint
as a meat puppet prostitute reproduced feminine stereotypes in a denaturalized
form.[21] In both cases, the novel reveals the ways that both gender and racial
stereotypes are technologically mediated and actively produced, not taken for
granted. Nakamura is exactly right that the presence of Asian characters like
Hideo in *Neuromancer* indicates how "race *must* continue to exist, especially in

the terrain of cyberspace, where so many foundational notions of identity as anchored in a body have become contingent, problematic, and difficult" (*Cybertypes*, 67). But it is also true that the form in which race (and gender) categories continue to exist has changed in significant ways; specifically, the process of minoritizing Asian or female characters by insisting on their embodied particularity can no longer mystify itself; the process by which such reductive characterizations are produced is itself laid bare in Gibson's novel, in a measure of the extent to which the novel remains true to the cultural logic informing the technological milieu it imagines. The novel does extend its consideration of instabilities in the "foundational notions of identity" to racial categories, but the question of whether this instability actually renders these categories useless as instruments of racial oppression is left open, if not actually refuted. It is significant that Molly's "freedom" from existence as a meat puppet is purchased only at the price of buying into an orientalist fantasy, enabled by her cyborg embodiment. But it is also significant that this parallel between meat puppet Molly and the Hideo clone interrupts what has often been taken to be *Neuromancer*'s overdependence on traditional gender oppositions. Molly herself notes this structural parallel when she explains why she would have felt compelled to try to kill Hideo: "the why of that's just the way I'm wired, what he is and what I am" (218). In this passage, Molly explains Hideo's racial figuration in terms of the same metaphor of hardwiring that we will see her apply to herself and to Case, a metaphor that, ambiguously, both installs and destabilizes "foundational notions of identity," "what he is and what I am," as if such categories were ontological in nature and not a way they have been "wired," one possibility among others.

From this perspective, the novel's opening figurations of body modification have been overlooked as significant contexts for its narrative of Case's return to cyberspace and renewed ability to escape his forced reduction to the condition of "meat," the punitive confinement of his consciousness within what used to be the "natural" boundaries of his own body. The novel's opening passage announces a more complex, posthuman body politics in terms that Bruce Sterling would echo in *Schismatrix*. This passage also supports Samuel R. Delany's reading of feminist science fiction as the disavowed "mother" of the cyberpunk movement (9). The first scene in *Neuromancer* is set in a bar, tended by a man with an "antique arm," a "Russian military prosthesis . . . cased in grubby pink plastic" (4). This character is completely minor, disappears from the novel after chapter 1, and, as far as I know, has never received any real critical attention in any of the numerous commentaries on the novel.[22]

The way that this character is introduced, however, is significant. The initial characterization of the bartender in terms of his "antique arm" might seem to lead naturally to the depiction of Case's elite hacker attitude of "relaxed contempt" for the body, by suggesting how the conflation of body and machine can tend to make physical bodies seem obsolete—that is, in this technosocial context it is possible for a part of your body to be judged as having become antiquated, out of style, and it is a short step from there to deciding that bodies in general share this fate. This reading depends on emphasizing the word choice of "arm" rather than "antique prosthesis," a deliberate ambiguity that dramatizes how such forms of prosthetic embodiment blur the distinction between humanity and technology, as the prosthesis is anthropomorphized and the arm is reduced to the level of a commodity. The trope of the "antique" might also suggest, however, that value can accrue to apparently ephemeral objects in unexpected ways, as well as how objects are more expendable than body parts. We might also note the cross-national hybridity implied by this North American possession of a kind of arm that is apparently immediately legible to the other characters as Russian, while at the same time it dramatizes the detachment of signs of national or ethnic identities from ideological referents and their resultant circulation as commodities and styles, a fate that seems to have befallen the United States as much as Russia in this novel.

A reading of the cyborg bartender as icon of a culture of technological disembodiment is more clearly problematized, however, by the comment that his "ugliness was the stuff of legend. In an age of affordable beauty, there was something heraldic about his lack of it" (4). The negative connotations of possessing an antique or obsolete arm stem from the implication that bodies are interpreted and evaluated using relatively superficial, stylistic criteria, as if one's body were no more significant than one's interior-decorating choices—that is, as if bodies were mere extensions of a culture that values only "affordable beauty." But the bartender's arm is in fact understood as reversing the terms of this evaluation and resisting the body norms of "an age of affordable beauty," an age of purely plastic embodiment. The bartender's cyborg embodiment, his prosthetic arm, is the central feature of his self-chosen ugliness, and the particular way in which this character displays and wears his prosthesis functions as a mode of stylistic or subcultural resistance within the overall context of the "age of affordable beauty," a near-future setting where cosmetic surgery and body modification are more readily available and socially acceptable than they are now, for men as well as women, apparently. The arm is in fact described as ugly in part because it is inefficient, as indicated by the noise it makes while in operation. The choice of ugliness here similarly marks a refusal to allow one's body to be reduced to "a problem of coding" and a desire to introduce some metaphorical noise or static into the smoothly functioning signal system of "affordable beauty."

The ways that the cultural politics of both gender and race play into this system is implicit in the description of the arm's "grubby pink" color. This phrase suggests how the prosthetic limb makes visible the character's skin color, while at the same time rendering his "whiteness" both unnatural (so that when describing the cyborg arm whiteness is no longer unmarked or taken for granted but remarkable) and pathetic, with its grubbiness marking a failed attempt to live up to an ideal. My point here is that the ideal that the arm fails to live up to, in achieving its spectacular ugliness, can be either an ideal of organic wholeness, of humanness in general, or of white masculinity. The specificity of the color reference—"pink" instead of "white"—also suggests a kind of gender confusion, to the extent that the word *pink* evokes less a realistic description of Caucasian skin coloring than a bright pink of the sort conventionally used for traditionally girlish clothing or toys. This ambiguity in the gendered connotations of the word *pink* is activated in this passage, as it might not be in simply describing a pink-skinned white man, because of the arm's artificiality and the character's resulting doll-like quality, here existing in uneasy proximity to the hypermasculinity implied by the arm's status as a piece of Russian military surplus. The point of this passage seems to be that the cyborg prosthesis does not escape such gender and racial codings, but it does double, confuse, and complicate them.

The bartender's choice to remain "ugly" in "an age of affordable beauty" suggests the possibility of negotiating the dichotomy between two ideas of embodiment: bodies as irreducibly particular and intransigently material, on the one hand, and bodies as malleable constructions and revisable inscriptions, on the other. The figuring of the cyborg arm's materiality in terms of its "noise," its illegibility, emphasizes how, in the social setting Gibson's novel presupposes, materiality has been recontextualized within and against the norms of an information society. This form of resistance to a posthuman culture that regards "bodies as fashion accessories rather than the ground of being," however, turns the logic of that "nightmare" against itself (Hayles, *How We Became Posthuman,* 5). In effect, this passage defines a resistant posthumanism that applies the logic of subcultural formation to embodiment itself. Dick Hebdige defines subcultures precisely as "cultures of conspicuous consumption," in which identities are based on style, and style in turn is defined as "the way in which commodities are *used*," the way in which "their original straight meanings" are erased or subverted when they are placed in a new "symbolic ensemble" (103, 104). The bartender's cyborg arm demonstrates the extension of this model of style to embodied existence, in ways that echo Judith Butler's argument that "gender is the repeated stylization of the body" (*Gender Trouble,* 33), with deliberate ugliness as the new symbolic ensemble that subverts the meaning of the "antique arm."[23] The bartender's mechanical prosthesis is aligned with his style, his fashion choices, in such a way as to suggest that cyborg body modifications might be understood as subcultural practices in which alternative ways of "wearing" one's body are also ways of refashioning its meaning. Hebdige's model of brico-lage as a resistant mode of consumption is in fact echoed by Gibson's famous cyberpunk slogan about the ways in which "the street finds its own uses for things" (*Burning Chrome*, 186), and at the beginning of *Neuromancer* this slo-gan applies not only to technology or to commodities, but to the characters' own bodies, in an indication of how Gibson's fiction gives an ironic ambiguity to the word *things*.

This reading of both the bartender's deliberate ugliness and his cyborg arm as linked acts of subcultural resistance is reinforced by a repetition of this same set of associations later in the novel. At one point, Case has to work as a hacker along with a gang called the "Panther Moderns," a name Case doesn't recognize because "entire subcultures could rise overnight, thrive for a dozen weeks, and then vanish utterly" (58). After running a search on the group's name, he iden-tifies it as a "contemporary version of the Big Scientists of his own late teens," media-savvy "practical jokers" and "nihilistic technofetishists." The first Panther Modern Case actually meets is "a soft-voiced boy called Angelo," whose face is "a simple graft grown on collagen and shark-cartilage polysaccharides, smooth and hideous. It was one of the nastiest pieces of elective surgery he had ever seen" (59). When he realizes that Angelo also has "toothbud transplants" from "some large animal," Case is actually reassured, because this is a modification he has seen before.

Readers of Gibson have also seen this same modification, specifically in a character named Dog who is one of the Lo Teks, an urban dropout subculture in Gibson's short story "Johnny Mnemonic." The Panther Moderns repeat and intensify the central irony of that story, that "these days you have to be pretty technical before you can even aspire to crudeness" (*Burning Chrome*, 6). Samuel Delany reads the Lo Tek subculture as having an "oppositional charge" linked to their "cultural specificity," "group presence," and "social power to escape the forces of multinational capital" (Dery, "Black to the Future," 753). Part of the point of Gibson's fiction, however, is that this power can only be achieved by expropriating and recontextualizing the technologies that support and are con-trolled by multinational capital. Like the meat puppets, women reduced to noth-ing but female bodies, or the Hideo clone, Lo Tek versions of modern primitivism can only be produced through high-tech means. Delany suggests that Gibson's figure of the Lo Tek subculture provides a useful allegory of the critical poten-tial of racial difference in a high-tech world, even though—or rather *because*—they are not "explicitly black, but rather 'fourth-world' whites" (ibid.). Their "oppositional charge," Delany argues, is lost precisely when the Lo Teks are explicitly racialized in *Neuromancer*, in the form of a space satellite called Zion, home to a separatist Rastafarian community who embody not a different, crit-ical relation to new technologies, but instead a nostalgic rejection of them.[24]

I want to argue that the Panther Moderns represent a different displacement of the Lo Tek subculture. Like the Lo Teks as Delany reads them, the Panther Moderns retain racial difference primarily as allegory or subtext, with the seeming allusion in their name to the Black Panther movement (an allusion suppressed by Case's tracing of the group back to the "Big Scientists," a group who presumably took their name from a Laurie Anderson song). But, like the novel's cyborg bartender, the Panther Moderns make their dependence on technology to challenge the cultural norms of a technologically advanced society more explicit than the Lo Teks do. The Panther Moderns thus perhaps come closer to realizing the "oppositional charge" Delany locates in the Lo Teks than any of Gibson's other versions of this figure. I take the point of Delany's reading of "Johnny Mnemonic" to be that Gibson's novel is most useful for thinking about the potentially critical relation of minoritized racial groups to new technologies when it avoids the tendency of explicitly conceptualizing that critical relation in racial terms, and thereby reinforcing primitivizing racial stereotypes (a risk Gibson runs by applying the metaphor of voodoo loas to artificial intelligences in cyberspace, in the two sequels to Neuromancer, Count Zero and Mona Lisa Overdrive). The relative success of these, at best, indirectly racialized scenes compared to the explicit appearance of black or Asian characters in cyberpunk fiction points, then, to a larger representational dilemma within postmodern techocultures, because the "oppositional charge" Delany defines needs at some point to become more literal and referential, more directly articulated with actual racial formations, in order for its political potential to be realized, to actually become a politics (this suggests a more sympathetic reading of Gibson's attempts to move the figure or allegory of the Lo Tek subculture toward a more explicit project of racial representation).

The figure of the cyborg bartender in Neuromancer is actually introduced by a joke that the main character overhears as he enters the bar: "It's not like I'm using. . . . It's like my body's developed this massive drug deficiency" (3). This joke should be read as the flip side of the later joke, about an AI for whom the rights and privileges of "limited citizenship" amount to little more than owning his own thoughts, because a multinational corporation owns his brain (hardware) and what he knows (the forms of information that he processes, but also the informational processes that constitute his existence [132]). One the one hand, machines become smart enough to possess their own thoughts, while bodies become animated enough that they seem to take on a life of their own, that isn't owned or controlled by the individual who claims that body as his or hers. The bartender's extension of his deliberately ugly style to his cyborg arm suggests a linkage between these two sets of representations, of intelligent machines (difficult to distinguish from ourselves) and insubordinate bodies (difficult to identify with our "selves"). In both cases, the effect of these shifts

and inversions is to call into question the hierarchical and instrumental relation between user and tool, self and body. The AI's mediated citizenship and
limited self-possession is the flip side of the drug user's embodied cognition,
his manipulation of his own biochemistry to produce an altered mental state.

Neuromancer's opening reference to the "age of affordable beauty," however,
also implies that there is a dominant culture of bodily modification and, more
important, that it is possible to base cultural norms on the principle of denaturalizing the body as a malleable construct. This passage is also useful, then, as
a qualification to Halberstam and Livingston's claim that "posthuman bodies
thrive in subcultures without culture"—that is, marginality and difference without a norm against which those differences could be hierarchically measured (4).
The "age of affordable beauty" defines the paradoxical reuniversalization of this
disappearance of a norm, because that phrase presupposes precisely the disappearance of any idea of a "natural" body as the basis for evaluative norms of
beauty; but that disappearance only intensifies the power of a now-denaturalized
rule of beauty to command conformity. The possible critical implication—that
no one is *born* beautiful in an age when it is "affordable," so that these norms
themselves are artificial—is recontained by the demand that everyone become
beautiful through artificial, technological means. This artificial reassertion of
universal demands that do not have to be naturalized as norms in order to be
universalized effectively constitutes a kind of official posthumanism in *Neuromancer,* against which resistant posthumanist subcultures emerge. At the same
time, the generalization of body-modification techniques seems to have resulted in a generalization of a traditionally "feminine" attitude toward the body
(as something to be objectified for others to view) to both men and women,
and the bartender's style can be understood as the assertion of an equally artificial and hyperbolic masculinity as a defense against this feminization. In other
words, in the world that cyberpunk fiction presents, there is nothing inherently
progressive in the denaturalization of the idea of "the body." The emergence of
this kind of denaturalized norm exemplifies what Fred Pfeil calls cyberpunk's
absence of a political unconscious (86), which here translates into the absence
of ideological mystification or naturalization, but not freedom from power
inequities.

Robopaths: Fetishizing the Cyborg

Whereas *Neuromancer* at times seems to presuppose the devaluation of the body
as "meat" (while in fact suggesting a more complex set of dangers and opportunities emerging around technologically induced instabilities in the relation
between mind and body), David Skal's novel *Antibodies* explicitly thematizes
that set of negative assumptions about embodiment in the form of a movement

of self-styled "antibodies" or "robopaths." One of these characters sums up the robopath attitude toward the body in terms that echo Case when she says, "I may have been born meat, but I don't have to die that way" (147). The novel situates the figure of the robopath as a commentary on cyberpunk in other ways as well. The central robopath character, a woman named Diandra, is described early in the novel as a consumer of science fiction; her room contains videocassettes of *Alien, Robocop,* and *Tron* and is "littered with electronic game cartridges, science fiction magazines, and medical journals" (11). Even more specifically, one of the minor robopaths is modeled directly on Molly from *Neuromancer,* wearing "form-fitting sunglasses that gave the impression of being fused into her skull" (134–35). Diandra epitomizes the robopath ideal and at the same time literalizes Case's desire to divest himself of his body when she dreams of herself as a stripper who "wouldn't stop at the clothes. She continued with the old, useless flesh. . . . She pulled off one bloodless strip after another, revealing the gleaming second skin beneath, which was not a 'skin' at all" (178). Note the possible racial implications of this fantasy of gaining a "second skin" that is not properly "skin" at all, a process that both transcends and reproduces processes of racialization that produce "skin" as a social signifier. As in this passage, the novel typically describes the replacement of body parts by mechanical prostheses as a process by which the robopath reveals and reclaims his or her true robotic nature, which is not a "nature" at all. This representation of the robopaths' psychic investments in a cyborg identity is explicitly based on a popularized notion of transsexuality as a state of being trapped in a body of the wrong sex, although when confronted with that analogy one of the robopaths says, "Fuck it. I'm sick of being compared to sex-changers all the time! *They're* just trading off one disease for another" (148). Although the robopaths are often presented as a cult of fanatics with their own "Cybernetic Temple," the novel just as often presents robopathology as a political ideology that echoes the rhetoric of new social movements like feminism. For example, the robopaths define the issue at stake in their desire for mechanical prostheses as "the control and disposal of our own bodies" (120), and they organize around slogans like "No more back alley amputations" (136).

As the novel represents it, this robopathology seems to have a special appeal for women, almost to the point of forming another "female malady" like hysteria and anorexia, and in fact robopaths are described as adopting "an ascetic, anorectic lifestyle" (152). However, through one of the male robopath characters, this pathology is also related to the psychoanalytic model of fetishism, a more masculine pathology (indeed, as Naomi Schor points out, in the psychoanalytic literature "fetishism is the male perversion par excellence" ["Female Fetishism," 365]). In another allusion to cyberpunk, specifically to Gibson's cyberspace metaphor, a man named Robbie tells a story about volunteering for "an experiment in artificial sight restoration" involving the replacement of his left eye by a miniature camera:

> We got to the point where, through my left eye, the world looked like a computer billboard, which is exactly how it worked. Eventually, the resolution would be improved to that of a color TV monitor—in other words, almost perfect natural vision.
>
> But in the meantime, I had this fabulous experience of seeing normally through one eye, but at the same time seeing this whole *digital* reality superimposed by the other one. I mean, I could have sold it to MTV! It was incredible, really incredible. (128)

It is worth pointing out how this passage consistently conflates the experience of cybernetic embodiment and the experience of cultural commodification. The implanting of a mechanical eye replaces a body part with a commodity that carries a price tag, but it also results in a consumerist "vision" of the world as a "billboard," a vision that itself is imagined as a commodity that could be sold to MTV.

However, the funding for this experimental project is cut prematurely, leaving Robbie with an inert piece of metal in his head, for which he blames government short-sightedness about the benefits of cyborg enhancement. In a later passage, he travels to Central America for more illegal surgical modifications. As he disembarks from his plane, "he could feel the dead camera expand with the warmth, the slight but discernible pressure of swollen metal against his hollowed eye socket. Almost as if the mechanism was being sympathetically aroused" (198). The mechanical eye functions as a displaced phallus, a new sexual organ capable of an erection. The eye is therefore experienced by this character as a fetish that serves to veil the (male) subject's perception of his own lack—that is, to both acknowledge and disavow that perception. The mechanical eye thus takes part in an oedipalizing process of subject formation that depends on the assumption that otherness, here represented by technology, is synonymous with absence and negativity, not specificity. The implication is that, far from constituting an acceptance of difference and partiality, the incorporation of otherness into the self through an investment in cyborg body imagery and cyborg identity can reproduce a classical fetishistic evasion of otherness and sexual difference, as Mary Ann Doane argues in her essay "Technophilia." In Skal's version of a cyborg thematics, therefore, neither for men nor for women do cyborg bodies provide a clean break with traditional gender constructions, a direct challenge to Haraway's claim that "The cyborg is a creature in a post-gender world" characterized by "non-oedipal narratives" (*Simians*, 150).

In *Antibodies*, men and women fetishize themselves, investing psychically in mechanical prostheses that both reinscribe a physical lack or wounding, understood in psychoanalytic terms as castration, and at the same time evade that lack by eroticizing a replacement organ. The robopath characters affirm "the compatibility of technology and desire" that Doane describes, in ways that reproduce conventional constructions of gender and sexuality at least as much as they disrupt such conventions ("Technophilia," 164).[25] The situation of technophilia that Skal's novel represents departs from the classical model of fetishism only to the extent that the stakes behind the fetishistic investment are relatively clearer; the robopath with the nonfunctioning mechanical eye is not simultaneously acknowledging and disavowing a perception of women as castrated in an act of revulsion directed toward female sexuality, but instead is concerned with his own condition of bodily lack and supplemented wholeness. Even the novel's representation of female fetishism, which Schor suggests might be read as indicating a feminine "rebellion against the 'fact' of castration" ("Female Fetishism," 367), only reproduces the classical psychoanalytic model, to the extent that the novel presents Diandra's lesbian seduction as merely a stage in her development as a robopath; as Marjorie Garber argues, the psychoanalytic literature explains female fetishism as the expression of a supposedly "masculine" desire, so that "it is the lesbian [as represented by psychoanalysis, as a pathological condition] . . . who follows the path of something analogous to fetishism" (47).

A passage in *Neuromancer* makes it clearer how the cyborg body and its apparent rejection of dualistic categories like plenitude and lack or masculine and feminine can be recontained by classic psychoanalytic models of sexual difference. At one point, Case and Molly attend a performance of hologram projections staged by one of their coconspirators, Riviera. Riviera has the technology to produce these visual illusions implanted in his body, so that his cyborg body allows him to externalize and materialize his own fantasy scenarios, without using any visible apparatus. Titled "The Doll," Riviera's performance begins with him alone in a room (138–39). He describes to the audience how he imagines being joined in this room by a woman lying on the bed, and as he does her body begins to form there. At first, only her hands appear, as he tries to actualize his fantasy by visualizing "some part of her, only a small part . . . in the most perfect detail" (139). Riviera then encourages this process by stroking each part of this visualized body in turn until this phantasmatic figure is present and complete. At this point, Case and Molly recognize the form on the bed as an idealized version of Molly herself, and Riviera begins to have sex with his creation. However, the performance ends with the simulacrum of Molly extending her claws and, "with dreamlike deliberation," beginning to slash open Riviera's spine. Case recognizes "an inverted symmetry" in the performance: "Riviera puts the dreamgirl together, the dreamgirl takes him apart" (141).

Riviera's performance enacts a classic fetishistic stance toward women's sexual difference from men, which is both desired and disavowed as a threat, and Riviera is specifically shown to invest most heavily in those aspects of Molly's cyborg body that might otherwise seem to distinguish Molly from the traditionally feminine, her claws. (Richard Calder's writing, discussed in the next chapter, elaborates this fetishistic logic, and should be read as a direct response to this passage from *Neuromancer*, as suggested by Calder's appropriation of the metaphor of "the doll.") Andrew Ross argues that cyberpunk "technomasculinity" at the very least necessitates some acceptance of bodily enhancements that are "castrating in ways that boys always had nightmares about" (*Strange Weather*, 153).[26] But Riviera's performance clearly suggests that men's acceptance of a postmodern, fragmented body, permeated with technology, is not at all incompatible with retaining their traditional power to construct the feminine. However, where *Antibodies* generalizes the psychoanalytic model of fetishism to represent all of the characters' relations to cyborg bodies and subjectivities, *Neuromancer* directly thematizes that specific investment in and way of thinking about what it means to be a cyborg, in the episode depicting Riviera's fetishistic performance. In contrast to *Antibodies*, *Neuromancer* therefore raises the question of whether this fetishistic stance is only one limited frame of reference, and perhaps one that is to be resisted, in that it is biased toward an increasingly, but by no means totally, obsolete masculine point of view, just as the novel similarly relativizes Case's "elite stance" of contempt for the body as "meat." Indeed, one point at which *Antibodies'* critique of the robopaths' technofetishism breaks down is precisely the point at which the novel attempts to extend that psychoanalytic model to the lesbian encounter between two women robopaths.

Despite the undisputed power of *Antibodies'* reading of cyberpunk, I would claim that Skal's novel is at least as interesting for the way its critique of cyberpunk robopathology fails as for what it reveals about cyberpunk's assumptions and blind spots. Even on its own terms, the novel does not simply reassert the priority of the natural body. The wife of Julian Nagy, the psychologist who specializes in deprogramming robopaths, realizes that although her husband "talked excitedly about restoring [robopaths] to their bodies . . . what really turned him on was the prospect of using *his* own body in the prospect" (41; my emphasis). For Nagy, his robopath patients are "autistic virgins who, by offering the greatest amount of resistance" to bodily sensation, therefore also "afforded the most intense pleasure" for the therapist (ibid.). Described by a talk-show host as "the Rod Serling of Psychotherapy," Nagy believes in "somatic shock therapy," which merely amounts to various forms of physical abuse, especially sexual. In other words, the "natural" body is not figured as innocent here but is rather constructed through an original act of violence, just as violent as the self-mutilating fantasies of the robopaths, except that the violence of their imagined self-construction is directed at themselves rather than at others.

Moreover, *Antibodies* contradicts its own critique of the robopaths in more fundamental and less overt ways. The wholesale adoption of abortion rhetoric by the robopaths indicates how their identification with machines is grounded in what the novel calls "widespread social ambivalence about reproduction" (152). In one particularly disturbing passage, a robopath party culminates in a puppet show featuring either actual aborted fetuses or realistic models (139). This grotesque passage is immediately followed by another, in which the robo-path hostess, a woman who calls herself Venus and who has had both arms replaced with prostheses, has sex with Diandra using both her mechanical arms and a vibrator implanted under her skin. As these summaries suggest, the novel seems unable to represent either abortion activists or lesbian sexuality as any-thing but monstrous, a misogynistic and homophobic misrepresentation. But those same misrepresentations are clearly structured by the anxieties that fem-inist political activities and lesbian desire might evoke in heterosexual male sub-jects like Dr. Nagy and the author David Skal, or many of the novel's most likely readers, and the same type of anxiety seems to be evoked in the novel by claims to cyborg identity. The novel's critique of the robopaths might, then, be under-stood, at least in part, as a defensive reaction against those anxieties. This read-ing makes it necessary to return to the cyberpunk texts that Skal's novel is also reacting against, in the attempt to understand why the emergence of a body of cyberpunk texts might produce reactions similar to those resulting from the increased cultural visibility of demands for reproductive rights and for the recog-nition of alternative sexualities.

Hardwiring:
Commodification and Cultural Identity in Postmodern Technocultures

Skal's robopaths are pathological to the extent that they remain trapped within the dichotomous alternatives of the natural body and the mechanical transcen-dence of that body's limits, and Skal's novel interprets cyberpunk fiction as structured by the same dichotomy. However, this account of cyberpunk, though accurate enough, still does not seem entirely adequate. In particular, I want to suggest that cyberpunk opens a potential space for the development of models of historical existence other than the white, middle-class male paradigm of indi-vidual freedom, precisely to the extent that cyberpunk represents cultural iden-tity as an inescapable, if partial, commodification of subjectivity, as a process of signifying for others in ways that are outside the control of individual sub-jects. This representation of the cultural commodification of identity can be understood as the result of the late-capitalist extension of the commodity struc-ture into previously sacrosanct areas of (white male) individual experience, but it can also be read as a precondition for revealing the histories of those social subjects who have consistently been denied such immunity, who have always inhabited bodies marked as particular and therefore not fully or only human because not generally human.[27]

In cyberpunk fiction, commodification or the experience of "forced significa-tion" is both inescapable and impossible to totalize. Cyberpunk is "posthumanist" in its refusal of the paradigm of liberal humanism and its false universalization of white, middle-class male experience; instead, cyberpunk insists on the sub-jection of all individuals to preexisting systems of control and power, as figured by the invisible computer network of *Neuromancer's* cyberspace, which can be understood as an attempt to represent "the impossible totality of the contem-porary world system," an "impossibility" that makes individual autonomy equally problematic (Jameson, *Postmodernism*, 39).[28] But, at the same time, this exter-nal control is never complete in novels like *Neuromancer*, which also insist on the continuing possibility of forms of agency like those located by Andrew Ross in the figure of the hacker, "capable of penetrating existing systems of ratio-nality that might otherwise be seen as infallible; . . . capable of reskilling, and therefore of rewriting, the cultural programs and reprogramming the social values that make room for new technologies; . . . capable also of generating new popular romances around the alternative uses of human ingenuity" (*Strange Weather*, 100). To cite Gibson again, cyberpunk fiction demonstrates how "the street finds its own uses for things" (*Burning Chrome*, 186).

In this context, it seems to me that Jameson misrepresents the significance of the "new" social movements and especially their relation to postmodern cul-ture and its extension of the commodity system. Jameson writes that "the only authentic cultural production today has seemed to be that which can draw on the collective experience of marginal pockets of the social life of the world sys-tem: black literature and blues, British working-class rock, women's literature, gay literature, the *roman québecois*, the literature of the Third World; and this production is possible only to the degree to which these forms of collective life or collective solidarity have not yet been fully penetrated by the market and by the commodity system" ("Reification," 140). But, in a later essay, Jameson writes that late capitalism constitutes "the purest form of capital yet to have emerged, a prodigious expansion of capital into hitherto uncommodified areas" that "elim-inates the enclaves of precapitalist organization it had hitherto tolerated and exploited in a tributary way" (*Postmodernism*, 36). How is it possible, then, to explain the continuing vitality and increasing recognition within postmod-ernism of the forms of relatively "uncommodified" cultural production that Jameson lists in the first quotation above? The point is that the experiences of groups including women, gay men and lesbians, and African-Americans have not been "enclaves" where these people could live their lives free from the com-modity structure. This analysis of Jameson's presupposes, and therefore imposes, a mode of production narrative, one that leaves these various "minority" or "special-interest" groups paradoxically "free" as a result of their supposed underdevelopment; however, this condition of "underdevelopment" only becomes apparent when these groups are measured against a model that privileges white masculine models of agency, which is what class struggle tends to become in the formulations I quoted. Of course, minority experience does not offer a ready-made point of resistance to late capitalism; what such experience does offer is a history in which both commodification and resistance are combined, a model in which experience itself can be understood as a situation of simultaneously being forced to signify for others and to insist on the specificity of one's history and identity (this is how I would gloss Haraway's discussion of the cyborg as "nonoriginal," in relation to other nonoriginal, diasporic, and colonized peoples). As Hayles puts it, in a discussion of technocultural challenges to the ideology of possessive individualism, if that ideology defines "human essence" as "freedom from the wills of others," then "the posthuman is 'post' not because it is necessarily unfree but because there is no a priori way to identify a self-will that can be clearly distinguished from an other-will" (*How We Became Posthuman*, 4). In this model, which should be applied to both "minority" and "majority" subjects, commodification and resistance are not mutually exclusive, dualistic terms, as they are for Jameson. As Michael Warner points out in an essay on the implications of queer social theory, the conceptualization of such histories demands "of theory a more dialectical view of capitalism than many people have imagined" ("Fear," 17 n. 21).[29] Cyberpunk fiction's representation of the commodification of cultural identity tends toward just such a view, as in Haraway's argument that in a "high-tech culture it is not clear who makes and who is made" (*Simians*, 177).

From this perspective, it is an overstatement to read cyberpunk as "the most fully delineated urban fantasies of white male folklore" (Ross, *Strange Weather*, 145). I agree with Ross's critique of "female versions of the cyberpunk attitude" that are based on Molly's character in *Neuromancer;* Ross argues that this "survivalist type" locks "the future of sexual identity" into "a restricted set of choices" (ibid., 158–59). But this critique overlooks the ways in which the novel's general problematizing of the characters' assumptions about how their bodies wire them explicitly thematizes the problem of such restrictions, and it assimilates Gibson's characterization of Molly too quickly to more reductive imitations of it (158). The feminist and lesbian responses to cyberpunk discussed in chapter 4 of this book seem to me to have taken a different "lesson" from *Neuromancer,* and cyberpunk in general, as have the multicultural writers and artists who have expropriated cyberpunk conventions.[30] At the very least, Ross's insistence on the fundamentally "white masculinist concerns" of cyberpunk fiction overlooks the way cyberpunk both presupposes and displaces the concerns of the new social movements, as both Haraway and Hayles argue. When Delany suggests that feminist science fiction of the 1970s constitutes the absent, disavowed mother of cyberpunk (9), he points both to its limitations and to the possibility of (re)appropriating cyberpunk for the purpose of articulating interests other than those of white men. For example, while searching for Molly in a club housing "meat puppet" prostitutes, Case is asked to state his gender preference, and he is described as "automatically" answering female (146). In other words, Case takes his heterosexuality for granted. But when a woman character asks Case if Molly "like[s] it with girls," the reply is *not* automatic. Case can only say that he does not know; Molly has never told him (153).

The thematics of embodiment as a form of cultural commodification is introduced in the opening lines of *Neuromancer,* in ways that complicate any reading of Case or Molly as robopaths. The joke Case overhears—"it's not like I'm using. . . . It's like my body's developed this massive drug deficiency" (3)—is not just a representation of the body as possessing its own agency apart from the subject who inhabits it. It also alludes to the thematics of self-commodification in William Burroughs, specifically the introduction to *Naked Lunch,* one of Gibson's acknowledged precursor texts. Burroughs argues there that drug addiction is the most advanced form of capitalism because "the junk merchant does not sell his product to the consumer, he sells the consumer to his product" (*Naked Lunch,* xi). For Gibson, as for Burroughs, drugs represent the infiltration of the body by decentered systems of power and control. This initial joke defines the setting of *Neuromancer* as one in which subjects routinely find their bodies beginning to signify meanings the subjects never intended, as if of the bodies' own volition.

This same thematics is developed through the image of Molly's mirror-shades, fused to her skull and sealing off her eyes. The implication is that there is no distinction to be made between surface and depth, between stylistic signifiers and the identity they construct. Molly *is* her style, and her style is part of her, like the bartender's prosthetic arm. Molly's modifications, however, especially the implanted scalpels, are also the tools of her trade as a street tough. After getting the money for her modifications, Molly is only able to sell her body in a different way, despite her relatively greater degree of agency, as suggested by the fact that she still describes herself as a "working girl" (30). In effect, Molly's agency resides in her ability to transform herself from one commodity to another, in a way that is paradigmatic for all the characters in the novel. Molly is described as being like Case in that "her being" is "the thing she did to make a living" and the "thing she did" was become a cyborg.

Molly repeatedly refers to her actions, the things she does to make a living, as a function of the way she is "wired" (25, 218). Similarly, Molly tells Case that she knows how he is wired because their mutual employer has created a computer profile of Case that is detailed enough to accurately predict his actions, including his death within the year from drug abuse (29–30). However, the novel also uses the term "wired" with reference to the programming constraints of artificial intelligences (AIs), the implication being that Molly and Case's understanding of themselves is mediated through a cybernetic model. Another member of Case and Molly's team is a "hardwired" personality construct of a dead colleague of Case's (76), and their employer turns out to be an AI who is using them as part of a scheme to "cut the hardwired shackles" that keep it from acting independently of its programming (132). In effect, the story the novel tells is one of how the AI overcomes its own built-in limitations.

The description of Molly and Case as similarly "hardwired" suggests the relevance of this same project for them. For example, Case's profile reveals that he is locked into a self-destructive cycle, and the novel can be read as the story of his breaking the "hardwired shackles" of his own compulsions and addictions, which combine the qualities of programming with the built-in "nature" of biology. A similar story could be constructed with Molly as the hero who overcomes the limitations imposed on her because of her location within a female body and the cultural construction of that body. In this reading, what *Neuromancer* definitely does *not* do is tell the story of a group of robopaths; quite the opposite, in fact. *Neuromancer* depicts a situation in which the characters are neither the masters of their technology nor enslaved by it, even when the technology is part of their selves.[31] The analogy between Case and Molly's relation to their own hardwiring and the AI's relation to its own built-in limitations constitutes one way that Gibson's novel moves beyond any simple dichotomizing of mind and body, machine and human, masculine and feminine.[32]

The paradigm for cultural identity in *Neuromancer* is that of the AI who employs Case and Molly, as defined in a passage mentioned in the preceding chapter, a passage that implies a critique of attempts to apply the model of possessive individualism to the inhabitants of technocultural contexts. In the course of trying to determine their employer's motives, Case and the personality construct he works with have a conversation that begins with the question of whether or not the AI owns itself. The answer is that the AI has limited Swiss citizenship, but a corporation owns the software and mainframe that house this "citizen" and allow it to function. The construct then replies: "That's a good one. . . . Like, I own your brain and what you know, but your thoughts have Swiss citizenship" (132). This brief scene offers one of the best fictional examples of what Hayles means when she defines posthumanism as a situation in which "there is no a priori way to identify a self-will that can be clearly distinguished from an other-will" (*How We Became Posthuman*, 4). In cyberpunk fiction, cultural identity is generally defined as just such a blackly humorous situation of never fully owning oneself, a situation that is exemplified by hybrid, cyborg identities. Cyberpunk fiction asks whether this situation is in fact a "good one" and, if so, in what sense. Although Case may not always live up to this model, it is by means of this representation of cultural identity that cyberpunk fiction had already begun to answer a question that Mark Poster once suggested it was still too early for sociologists and political theorists to ask— what historical connections exist between the new "forms of domination and potentials for freedom" that come into being in a high-tech, postmodern culture and "the advances of feminism, minority discourse, and ecological critiques" (Poster, *Mode*, 19).

Skal's novel suggests that cyberpunk fiction is unable to find "a way out of the maze of dualisms in which we have explained our bodies and our tools to ourselves," to the extent that cyberpunk depends on a dichotomy between physical embodiment and cybernetic transcendence of particular bodies. However, in *Neuromancer* Gibson suggests that it is possible for Case to transform his "elite stance" of "relaxed contempt" toward a body regarded as only "meat," a stance that the novel relativizes as only one limited point of view by attributing it to Case and suggesting that such a stance is chic and trendy, at least in certain circles. Before his ability to access cyberspace is restored, Case is struck by the possibility of seeing everyday reality as a dance of "information interacting," as "data made flesh," rather than the transformation of flesh into data by jacking into cyberspace that Case desires elsewhere (16). The language of the novel here resists privileging "data" over "flesh" to suggest a redefinition of embodiment rather than a rejection of it.[33] It is at this moment that the narrative first challenges the gendered connotations of data and flesh, mind and body; it is therefore at this point that it first becomes possible to produce a feminist reading of the novel's cyborg imagery, including the human–machine hybrids who are marked as masculine as well as those marked as feminine.

There is certainly an asymmetry in *Neuromancer*'s representation of gender identities and how they are denaturalized within a postmodern context. In its representation of Case, the novel takes for granted traditional assumptions about heterosexual masculinity, while the corresponding assumptions about Molly's gender and sexuality are explicitly called into question by her cyborg hybridity and the postmodern setting in which she operates. Nevertheless, the novel does establish a connection between Case's story and the stories of both Molly and the AI Wintermute. All three of these characters undergo the process of overcoming the hardwired limitations and assumptions that constitute their "essential" natures. The results of that process for Case are perhaps suggested in the novel's coda, which tells us that after Case and Molly succeed in freeing the AI, Case not only finds new work but also "a girl who called herself Michael" (270). This description seems to imply a denaturalizing of the signifiers of masculinity, such as the name "Michael," by a woman who, like Molly, has rejected the traditional construction of femininity. But given this denaturalizing of what it means to be a "girl," this description of Case's lover might also be read as calling into question Case's heterosexuality, if Michael is understood as a man who defines himself as a "girl." The question is which word should be placed in quotation marks as improper when applied to this person, "Michael" or "girl." But, in the context of *Neuromancer*, this question is quite rigorously undecidable. The novel presents the denaturalizing of gender categories as a project that applies to Case as well as to Molly, despite the fact that the novel also reproduces some of our culture's hardwired assumptions about masculinity instead of consistently contesting those assumptions. The novel therefore defines the opportunities that postmodern culture provides for those of us who are interested in redefining the construction of masculinity, while at the same time providing a cautionary depiction of how that same postmodern culture can merely reproduce traditional gender assumptions. *Neuromancer* can provoke men who read it, just as it has women readers who take Molly as a figure for the threat postmodern culture poses to comparable cultural constructions of femininity.[34]

3

THE SEX APPEAL OF THE INORGANIC

POSTHUMAN NARRATIVES AND THE
CONSTRUCTION OF DESIRE

During the Post-Body Age, we're going to get songs like:
She shut me down
wiped me clean
made me blanker than a banker's screen
But that's alright
There's no end in sight
I'm programmed well against that risk
with 47 copies of myself on disk
                    —*Otter, in the independent zine* Dropout

The computer takes up where psychoanalysis leaves off.
                    —*Sherry Turkle,* The Second Self *(309)*

THE PRECEDING CHAPTER focused on the literary origins of cyberpunk attitudes toward posthuman embodiment; this chapter will begin to consider the more general effects of cyberpunk as a larger cultural formation. Popular culture of the 1990s often seemed to agree with Jean Baudrillard that "the year 2000 has already happened" and therefore it was "not necessary to write science fiction" any longer, because we now lived in such fictions ("Year 2000," 36). A similar assumption underlies the increasingly widespread belief that we are on the verge of a "postbody" or "postbiological" age, to use Moravec's term (*Mind Children,* 1). This chapter will focus on how sexual representations intervene in this process and complicate the teleology of those forms of posthumanism that embrace and celebrate disembodiment or technological self-transcendence as the ultimate goal of posthuman critique. As Claudia Springer

81

points out, popular culture's embrace of "artificial sexuality" simultaneously disparages "the imperfect human body" and uses "language and imagery associated with the body and bodily functions" to represent a vision of human/ machine hybridity and intimacy (*Electronic Eros*, 50).[1]

What happens when the theoretical concept of the desiring machine becomes literalized, as sexual desire is mediated through mechanical forms of artifice?[2] One effect is that desire *for* machines often becomes difficult to distinguish from the desire to *be* a machine, and vice versa. These new forms of technofetishism were codified by magazines such as *Future Sex* or the line of erotic science-fiction story collections published by Cecilia Tan's Circlet Press. As I argued in my reading of Ken MacLeod's *Cassini Division* in chapter 1, to the extent that heterosexual norms require gendered subjects to make sharp distinctions between desire and identification, the desire to have and the desire to be, the breakdown of that distinction in technofetishist cultures, the ambivalent placement of machines with respect to persons, can seem subversive, in ways that align them with queer theory.[3] At the same time, Freud theorizes fetishism as a displacement of the castration anxiety generated by the male child's perception that his mother lacks a phallus, and in this tradition fetishism can be read precisely as a defense against the threat posed by an object of desire who is ambiguously both like and unlike the desiring subject—in other words, fetishism paradoxically uses ambivalence and a blurring of gender or sexual categories to defend against the anxieties created by the breakdown of such categories. In that sense, technofetishism might well function as a defense against the cyberpunk themes of body and mind invasion and the posthuman acceptance of the technological mediation of embodiment and subjectivity, as is the case with the passage from *Neuromancer* in which Riviera performs his fetishistic relation to Molly's cyborg body, discussed in the preceding chapter. The generalization of fetishism to include sexual investments in technology, however, also implies a different perspective on the relation between bodies and commodities that figures so centrally in Gibson's paradigmatic cyberpunk novel. Technofetishistic sexualities bring to light an ambivalence toward embodiment that even the most extreme forms of posthumanism can never fully suppress or evade.

A good example of how this ambivalence has been popularized in media other than print fiction can be gained by comparing two pages from an early attempt to create a cyberpunk comic book, necessitating visual representations of the characters and their bodies in cyberspace, with a photo layout from *Future Sex* 2, which depicts the hardware that would be needed to adapt this technology for sexual purposes. This sequence from the *Cyberpunk* comic reifies Case's elite attitude toward cyberspace in *Neuromancer*, as an escape from embodiment and an intensification of Cartesian dualisms, and narrates the extension of consciousness into cyberspace as a desire for the disappearance or forgetting of the body.

Figure 1. Scott Rockwell and Darryl Banks, *Cyberpunk* 1, no. 1 (September 1989): 5.

In Figure 1, a character who has just jacked into the matrix asserts that "if I could leave my *meat* behind and just live here, if I could just be *pure consciousness*, I could be *happy*." However, this same character also goes on to point out (in Figure 2) that experiencing cyberspace requires special software "just to convince yourself that you're *physically* there," so that the "nice thing . . . is you can also convince yourself that you are anything you want to be." This sequence depicts the character morphing his cyberspace icon or avatar from a faithfully mimetic representation of his organic body into an abstract, mechanical shape. The continuing dependence on a sense of physical presence in cyberspace contradicts the desire to escape the "meat," but, in another ironic complication, becoming or remaining convinced of physical embodiment in virtual space also makes it possible to imagine that physicality as plastic and mutable. We might also note the ambiguous conflation of the physical or biological and the rhetorical or textual, as physical presence becomes, or is revealed always to have been, something we have to be convinced of, dependent on a persuasive technological performance.[4] But this example raises the question of whether the critical potential in posthuman plasticity, the way it reveals the frameworks of persuasion and social determination that have always produced the meanings associated with different bodies, can be purchased only at the cost of disembodiment, becoming pure consciousness. The *Cyberpunk* comic seems to support Hayles's critique of how the dominant "condition of virtuality" today tends to organize the relation of information and materiality hierarchically, so that not only are they "conceptually distinct" but information seems "in some sense more essential, more important, and more fundamental than materiality" (*How We Became Posthuman*, 18).

Virtual reality computer interfaces like the one represented in this comic have also generated considerable interest in the possibility of "teledildonics" applications, to use a term popularized by Howard Rheingold (*Virtual Reality*, 345–53).[5] Figures 3–5 are digitally altered photographs from the technoporn magazine *Future Sex*. These images point toward a different set of techniques for convincing users that they are still physically there in cyberspace, and a different set of motives for doing so, sexual gratification rather than the pleasures of morphing into a different bodily form. Or are those motives really so distinct? The convergence of sexuality and technology in contemporary popular culture often suggests otherwise. These images might also be taken to dramatize the resistance of bodies to the dematerializing process that many cyberpunk characters imagine taking place when they access cyberspace or use a virtual reality interface. These images present themselves as an attempt to spectacularize virtual reality, but they make no real effort to do so. Instead, what is brought front and center are the bodies that these interfaces supposedly allow their users to abandon. To the extent that readers of the magazine are supposed to imagine

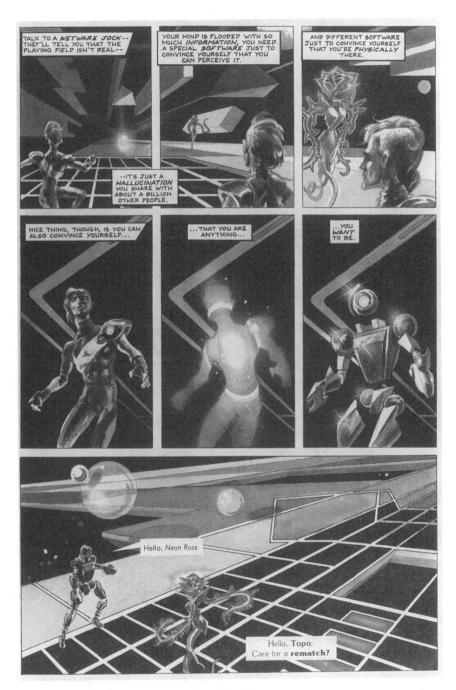

Figure 2. Scott Rockwell and Darryl Banks, *Cyberpunk* 1, no. 1 (September 1989): 6.

that the minds experiencing these sexual sensations also experience themselves as inhabiting a space (of sexual interaction) distinct from the physical environment their bodies inhabit, these images actually seem to depict a version of the joke that opens *Neuromancer:* "It's not like I'm using. . . . It's like my body's developed this massive drug deficiency" (3). Viewed from outside their shared cyberspace, it's not like these people are having sex; it's like their bodies have developed this massive state of arousal and independent sexual agency, distinct from what the persons are consciously engaged in (manipulating virtual icons). The attempt here to depict what teledildonics might actually look like ends up, perhaps inadvertently, being more materially grounded than the scenarios depicted in the fictional texts, in a reminder that the condition of virtuality can articulate mind and body, information and materiality, in potentially more interesting ways than Cartesian dualisms.[6] In these images, is the manipulation of information eliciting physical sensations and determining how these minds experience their bodies, thereby privileging information over flesh, or are their bodily sensations controlling and determining how they respond to the experience of the computer simulation? Where most fictional scenarios depict the characters' virtual points of view as securely located within cyberspace, these images (if only because of the magazine's budget restrictions) present a doubling of points of view, both physical and virtual, that makes it more difficult to privilege one over the other.

In an essay titled "Through the Looking Glass," a computer researcher named John Walker appropriated the term "cyberspace" from the cyberpunk science-fiction writer William Gibson; Walker used the notion of cyberspace to argue that the human–computer interface should not be conceptualized as a dialogue with another person, but instead as an act of entering another world, the virtual space on the other side of the computer screen. The response to this conceptual shift was to create hardware designed to collapse the distance between the user and the screen, such as head-mounted displays and datagloves that translate the movement of the hand into a kind of computer-animated mouse. The result is an "exteriorization of mind" (Kroker and Kroker, 31), so that "knowledge that was accessible only through formal processes can now be approached concretely" (Rheingold, *Virtual Reality,* 376). The conceptual realm can thereby take on qualities previously attributed only to bodies. As another researcher succinctly put it, whereas "print and radio tell" and "stage and film show," "cyberspace embodies" (Randal Walser, 60). These formulations, however, leave open the question of what happens to the experience of embodiment itself when the domain of the mind can be experienced in terms previously reserved for the category of the body, and the cybersex layout from *Future Sex* depicts bodies that are in precisely that predicament. Rhetorics of virtual disembodiment presume a narrative in which the mind not only takes *on* qualities associated with

Figure 3. Cover to *Future Sex* 2 (1992). Courtesy of *Future Sex* magazine, a registered trademark of Kundalini Publishing, Inc.

CSEX!

FEATURES:

- *3D STEREO H.U.D.*
- *TDV TACTILE DATA PLAYBACK SYSTEM*
- *SIMSKIN COMPONENTS*
- *3D AUDIO*
- *CONTEXT-SENSITIVE INTERFACE*
- *FULLY WASHABLE*
- *TEMPEST SHIELDED*

CSEX HELM 2

At the core of the Cybersex Duo system is the CSEX HELM 2—an ultralight control helmet featuring fully adjustable stereoscopic displays and earphones. Full 360-degree freedom of movement, ribbed ventilation, feather-weight construction and wireless connection to the central unit make the CSEX HELM 2 the leader in comfort. You'll forget you're wearing it! (Chinstrap not shown.)

CSEX GLOVES

These gloves feature extremely accurate and durable touch sensors. The TDV™ Tactile Data Playback System allows you to experience

Figure 4. Mike Saenz, Ken Holewczynski, and Norm Dwyer, "The Cybersex 2 System," *Future Sex* 2 (1992). Courtesy of *Future Sex* magazine, a registered trademark of Kundalini Publishing, Inc.

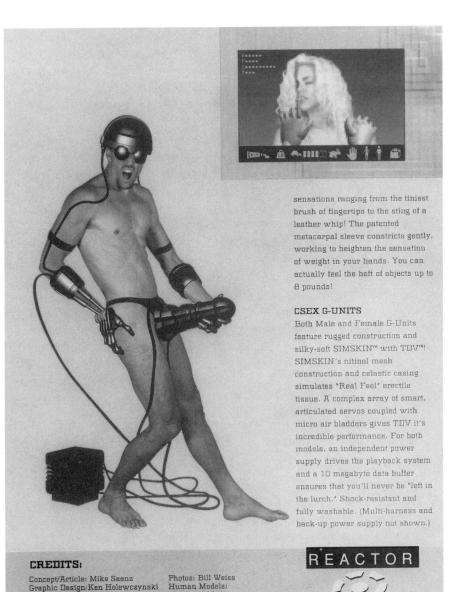

sensations ranging from the tiniest brush of fingertips to the sting of a leather whip! The patented metacarpal sleeve constricts gently, working to heighten the sensation of weight in your hands. You can actually feel the heft of objects up to 8 pounds!

CSEX G-UNITS

Both Male and Female G-Units feature rugged construction and silky-soft SIMSKIN™ with TDV™! SIMSKIN's nitinol mesh construction and celastic casing simulates 'Real Feel' erectile tissue. A complex array of smart, articulated servos coupled with micro air bladders gives TDV it's incredible performance. For both models, an independent power supply drives the playback system and a 10 megabyte data buffer ensures that you'll never be 'left in the lurch.' Shock-resistant and fully washable. (Multi-harness and back-up power supply not shown.)

CREDITS:

Concept/Article: Mike Saenz
Graphic Design: Ken Holewczynski
3-D Modeling and Graphics: Mike Saenz and Norm Dwyer

Photos: Bill Weiss
Human Models: Hans and Madison

REACTOR

Figure 5. Mike Saenz, Ken Holewczynski, and Norm Dwyer, "The Cybersex 2 System," *Future Sex* 2 (1992). Courtesy of *Future Sex* magazine, a registered trademark of Kundalini Publishing, Inc.

the body, but the mind also takes *over* those qualities, supposedly making actual bodies obsolete. But there is another narrative possibility, in which what disappears are not material bodies but an abstract notion of "the body," as the naturalized ground of a universalizing definition of human identity.[7] It is this second possibility that, for Haraway, produces the current "need for stories of shape-shifters," a need that sometimes takes the form of too quickly proclaiming a "postbody age" ("When Man," 42).[8]

This ambivalence toward embodiment can thus be linked to the challenges to the dualistic structure of self and other that result from the emergence of smart machines, on the one hand, and embodied cognition, on the other. As E. L. McCallum puts it, when severed from its phallocentric formulation in Freud's thought and generalized, fetishism offers an epistemological paradigm that can "account for a degree of agency and communicability but also that can productively withstand the loss of certainty, of absolute Truth" (xxii). This is exactly the problem to which Alan Turing's functional test for artificial intelligence responds. As McCallum points out, the defining feature of fetishism might be its belief that the interaction between subject and object can be "a two-way street," with fetishism characterized by a perverse and passionate belief in the ability of objects to relate back to us as much as we relate to them (xii). This belief become literalized in technocultural contexts, to create another two-way street, between sexual fetishism and artificial personhood or prosthetic forms of embodiment.

"You Are Seduced":
The Pleasures and Dangers of Posthuman Embodiment

To trace a historical context for contemporary forms of technofetishism, let me begin with an untitled photograph by Barbara Kruger, of two mismatched gloves arranged to suggest a couple holding hands, framed with the caption "You are seduced by the sex appeal of the inorganic." On the most immediate level, this image evokes a familiar critique of consumer culture and the "pseudosatisfactions" of the commodity form, a critique of manufactured desire that can be traced back at least to Marx's comment that capitalist production creates subjects for its objects at the same time that it creates objects for its subjects (Marx and Engels, 133). Under capitalism, in fact, becoming a subject means subjecting ourselves to the needs of the production process, not vice versa. However, there is a more disturbing reading of this image as typifying the mutations of late capitalism, a reading that can be arrived at most easily through a contrast between Kruger's representation of the body as commodity and the same representation in surrealist art, specifically the motif of the mannequin.

Fredric Jameson argues that for the surrealists the mannequin thematizes the transition from a precapitalist political economy in which objects retain "the half-sketched, uneffaced mark of human labor, of the human gesture" and therefore "remain . . . potentially as mysterious and as expressive as the human body itself," to a capitalist economy in which "the human body itself comes before us as a product" (*Marxism and Form*, 104–5). In contrast, the effect of Kruger's image is derived from the postmodern context created by late capitalism's "expansion . . . into hitherto uncommodified areas" and the resultant elimination of "the enclaves of precapitalist organization" previously "tolerated and exploited in a tributary way" (Jameson, *Postmodernism*, 36), a process we have already seen extended to the level of embodiment itself in *Neuromancer*. The result, as Jameson argues, is a lack of depth, which makes objects "totally incapable of serving as a conductor of psychic energy" and therefore precludes "all libidinal investment in such objects" (*Marxism and Form*, 105). But Kruger's photograph suggests that this extension of the commodity structure does not necessarily foreclose on libidinal investments or reduce such investments to the level of pseudo-satisfactions; instead, the persistence of such investments in objects that seem inappropriate to receive them results in a redefinition of desire as "inorganic" and in a critique of the expressive qualities Jameson attributes

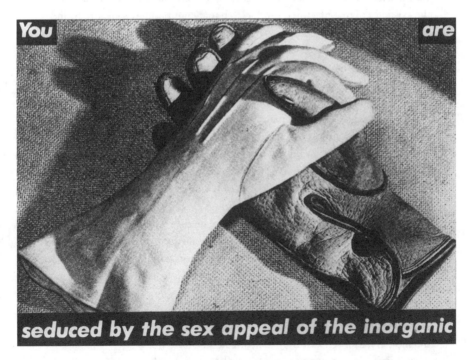

Figure 6. Untitled photograph by Barbara Kruger, 1982. Courtesy of Barbara Kruger.

to "*the* human body" as a universal form.[9] The contrast between this redefinition of embodiment and the surrealist fetish, with its residual nostalgia for the body as a site of unalienated labor, is perhaps clearest in postmodern feminist artist Cindy Sherman's series of photographs of rearranged mannequin bodies, mixing male and female parts.[10]

Kruger takes the phrase "the sex appeal of the inorganic" from Walter Benjamin, who writes that "fetishism . . . succumbs to the sex-appeal of the inorganic" (166). Analyzing the fashion industry, Benjamin suggests that the expansion of the commodity structure into the cultural sphere results in a crossing of commodity fetishism with sexual fetishism, in one of the first attempts to systematically link Marxism and psychoanalysis. As part of the Arcades project, Benjamin's comment on fetishism represents an attempt to identify the logic of early forms of urban consumer culture that would shortly produce surrealism, which attempts to subvert that logic from within. The difference between the surrealist moment and today, their fetishism and ours, is best mapped precisely through changes in the relation between Marxist and psychoanalytic theories of the fetish. Žižek defines the traditional distinction in this manner: "in Marxism a fetish conceals the positive network of social relations"—for instance, the commodity form reifies and conceals the socioeconomic relations that enable the existence of manufactured products, so that commodities appear to be independently existing objects. Through a historicizing operation, Marxist analysis thereby sets out to reveal and restore the ways in which this "positive" meaning actually informs the object world that seems to surround us in an alienated form. In contrast, Žižek points out, for Freud "a fetish conceals the lack ('castration') around which the symbolic network is articulated" (*Sublime*, 49). The passage Kruger cites from Benjamin is a touchstone, however, for the ways in which these two concepts of fetishism do not remain distinct in practice in modern consumer culture, and the blurring of this distinction is greatly accelerated in postmodern technocultures, as fetishes become more and more "ubiquitous," in Roy Boyne's phrase. The challenge contemporary technofetishisms pose to the separation of these two critical traditions, Marxism and psychoanalysis, is suggested when Žižek goes on to contrast Marxism's historicizing critique of ideology, understood as a naturalizing or "eternalizing" operation, with psychoanalysis's critique of Marxism's "over-rapid historicization," an operation Žižek aligns with sexual fetishism, because he understands them both as attempts to "elude the 'hard kernel' which announces itself through the 'patriarchal family'—the Real of the Law, the rock of castration" (49–50). Fetishism here is understood as the substitution of an object for a perceived lack (originally in the mother), as a veil cast over that threatening absence.

But isn't the historicizing operation that Žižek dismisses when it is directed at "the rock of castration" precisely an act of making public and accessible something psychoanalysis prefers to regard as "eluding symbolization" (50)?[11] In Lacanian psychoanalysis, this "hard kernel" of "the Real" constitutes the element of subjectivity that is both internal to our psyches and external to our subjectivities, a part of us of which we must remain unconscious and so unable to incorporate into our ego structures or manipulate as we can our own languages and narratives. Žižek suggests that Marxist forms of ideology critique mistakenly set out to transform the unconscious into such a manipulable form. But Žižek's defense of Freudian fetishism as an analytic model tends to emphasize the Real or the unconscious as inaccessible because psychically interior to the subject, not as inaccessible to subjects because it constitutes the mark of the social, "the Law," within us. To the extent that the latter is true, then shouldn't the social origins of that "Law" be accessible to thought, even if the specific form of the mark it leaves on individuals is not?

Within technoculture contexts, at any rate, it becomes even more difficult to maintain the distinction Žižek wants to see as fundamental and irreducible in order to defend the existence of the unconscious against instrumental reason (this is Žižek's ultimate critique of Marxism: the desire to resist the logic of economic commodification only results in an extension of the instrumental logic of the commodity form on the level of thought, as Marxist ideology critique tries to level the distinction between conscious and unconscious and to transform the unconscious structuring of the human mind into a mere theme, an object of positive knowledge). What happens when the "over-rapid historicization" Žižek associates with Marxist demystifications of the apparently seamless surface of the object world is itself produced historically, in the social world itself, and not by the intervention of critical thought? What happens when Marxism's attempt to turn objects and subjects inside out and to reveal the dependence of their seeming autonomy on determinate social relations is literalized by the ways in which cyberspace seems to make the space of the mind physically and phenomenally accessible, for instance? The posthuman insistence on a "physical soul" (Edward O. Wilson, 189), a historical product potentially open to ongoing processes of change, represents precisely such a materialization (or co-optation) of Marxist ideology critique. In the first chapter of this book, I suggested how postmodern technocultures make denaturalization and explicit, visible forms of mediation a social norm in a way that makes Marxist traditions of ideology critique problematic, if not obsolete. In this context, then, Žižek's insistence on maintaining a distinction between Marx's and Freud's theories of fetishism seems like a defense of psychoanalysis's preferred method of decentering subjectivity and puncturing the illusion of autonomous interiority, of defining the limits of the individual mind or ego, against the method embodied cognition deploys to similar ends.

The technocultural breakdown of the distinction between Marxist and

Freudian forms of fetishism is apparent in arguments about the ways in which new computer and communication technologies are central to the extension of the commodity structure that Jameson associates with the cultural logic of late capitalism. As Bill Nichols puts it, "just as the mechanical reproduction of copies" in the period of early consumer culture "revealed the power of industrial capitalism to reorganise and reassemble the world around us, rendering it as commodity art, the automated intelligence of [computer] chips reveals the power of post-industrial capitalism to simulate and replace the world around us, rendering not only that exterior realm but also interior ones of consciousness, intelligence, thought and intersubjectivity as commodity experience" (33).[12] Where Nichols emphasizes the way that computer simulation technologies like cyberspace can remove the immunity of psychic structures from commodification, Hayles emphasizes how the treatment of the body as a plastic commodity form has the same effect: "as the body increasingly is constructed as a commodity to be managed, designed, and parceled out to deserving recipients, pressure builds to displace identity into entities that are more flexible, easier to design, less troublesome to maintain" (Hayles, "Seductions," 182).

Both these accounts demonstrate how difficult it can become to identify a Real that resists symbolization absolutely. A similar point could be made in relation to Freud's famous 1919 essay "The 'Uncanny,'" especially because Freud here offers an analysis of literary texts in which "there is intellectual uncertainty whether an object is alive or not, and when an inanimate object becomes too much like an animate one" (385), examples relevant to the themes of artificial intelligence in contemporary culture. Freud in part locates the uncanny aspect of such narratives in the way they create "a disturbance in the ego" (389). The idea is that, for instance, seeing a doll open its eyes and look back at you is disturbing because the animated qualities such an object seems to possess feed back, in an inverted form, into our understanding of our own self-identity or ego. Such an encounter threatens us with the prospect that we may be inhabited by an "inanimate" or inaccessible component of our selves—that is, the unconscious. But what happens when such experiences are commonplace and technically comprehensible, when we expect our machines to look back at us, to reply, to relate? The affect associated with them, the sense of threat, might well disappear, though not necessarily the sense that our selves are split or hybrid. We might also learn not to react defensively to the sudden realization that what we thought was an objectified "other" is in fact a more or less autonomous agent. This example, then, offers an alternate reading of the shifts Nichols and Hayles define, one that points toward opportunities for critical reflection and resistance and not just for being manipulated more thoroughly. Specifically, this technocultural instability in the object nature of machines, once articulated with a Marxist tradition of revealing how objects were never just objects but have a social being, might lead to self-reflection on our social histories of objectifying others and excluding them from the category of the generically human, on the basis of gender, race, or sexuality.

New forms of technofetishism, then, foreground the problematic status of psychoanalytic categories and arguments within technocultural contexts. Although I have criticized Žižek for reasserting traditional psychoanalytic arguments, an equally common tendency is to link the transcendence of embodiment with the transcendence of the psychoanalytic tradition, as in my epigraph about the kinds of songs we'll have in a "postbody age."[13] What is imagined to have become obsolete in this scenario is not so much the body as a particular story about it, the psychoanalytic narrative of gendered subjectivity. In the pop songs of the postbody age, castration anxiety is replaced by the possibility of a systems crash and a loss of information or processing capability: "she shut me down / wiped me clean / made me blanker than a banker's screen." With the body figured as a storage medium, anxiety is no longer an appropriate affective response to this threat: "that's alright / There's no end in sight / I'm programmed well against that risk / with 47 copies of myself on disk" (Otter, 22–24).

Against this cheerful dismissal of "the 'hard kernel' which announces itself through the 'patriarchal family'—the Real of the Law, the rock of castration" (Žižek, Sublime, 49–50), I would pose Sherry Turkle's reading of the culture of artificial intelligence research, exemplified by Marvin Minsky's The Society of Mind, which she sees as "deeply committed to a view that thought does not need a unitary agent who thinks" (309). It is in this sense that Turkle can argue that "the computer takes up where psychoanalysis leaves off," taking "the idea of a decentered self" and making "it more concrete by modeling mind as a multiprocessing machine" (ibid.). Similarly, Stone argues that the attenuation of the relation between social persona and body made possible by virtual systems and computer-mediated communication also makes cyberspace "a locus of intense desire for refigured embodiment" ("Will the Real Body Please Stand Up?" 109). At the same time, she suggests that this refiguration is often purchased at the price of "freedom from the body," and that this "desire for refigured embodiment" therefore often appears only as a "concretization of the psychoanalytically framed desire of the male" (107).[14] Stone's argument is dramatically supported by a two-page advertisement for a new type of computer mouse that appeared in the technoculture magazines Mondo 2000 and Wired. These images associate the undisciplined body of the pre-oedipal infant, a body not yet captured in and unified through self-representation, with the freedom provided by high-tech computer equipment. These images certainly qualify Donna Haraway's assertion that "the functional privileged signifier in [cyberspace computer networks] will not be so easily mistaken for any primate male's urinary and copulative

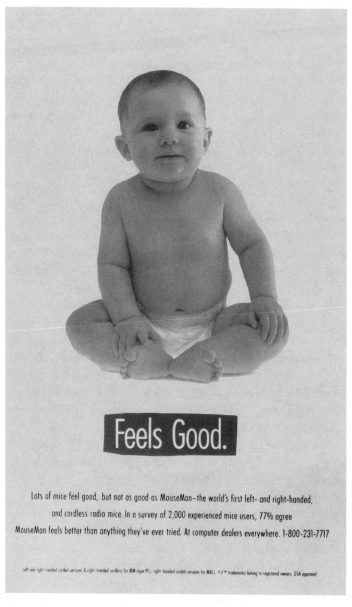

Figure 7. Logitech Corporation ad for MouseMan, a computer
mouse, in *Wired* 1, no. 1 (1993): 28–29. Copyright 1993
Logitech Inc. Used with permission.

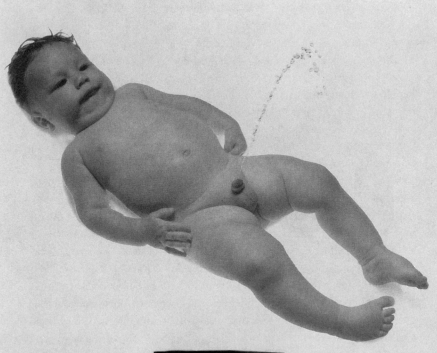

Feels Better.

MOUSEMAN® Right-Handed

Left-Handed

and Cordless Radio.

LOGITECH

organ," that cyberspace will provide a "non-mirror stage" and therefore a "different grammar of gender" ("When Man," 42).[15]

Sexualized representations of technology offer another challenge to Haraway's often-cited claim that "cyborg imagery can offer a way out of the maze of dualisms in which we have explained our bodies and our tools to ourselves" (*Simians*, 181). This argument seems to depend in part on the assumption that this technology and its popular imaging will not or cannot be "psychoanalytically framed." While acknowledging that in some cases "technology makes possible the destabilization of sexual identity as a category," Mary Ann Doane points out that there has been an "insistent history of representations of technology that work to fortify . . . conventional understandings of the feminine," a history in which anxiety about technology "is often allayed by a displacement of this anxiety onto the figure of . . . woman ("Technophilia," 163). Andreas Huyssen offers a similar analysis of the robot woman in the film *Metropolis;* he argues that "the fears and perceptual anxieties emanating from ever more powerful machines are recast and reconstructed in terms of the male fear of female sexuality, reflecting, in the Freudian account, the male's castration anxiety" (70). At the same time, the mechanical woman represents a femininity safely under male control and therefore the possibility of dispensing with actual women, in a classically fetishistic operation. In this representational framework, the analogy between technology and female sexuality confirms that both represent a threat to masculine power, while the conflation of the two in the form of the female robot allows for a specifically fetishistic disavowal of both threats. The question is whether this modernist framework is still capable today of managing and displacing the anxieties produced in male subjects by what Doane calls the "horrible recognition of the compatibility of technology and desire" (ibid., 164).

"That Metallic Feeling":
Sorayama's Sexy Robots and the "Secrets of the Age of Technology"

The work of a Japanese commercial artist, Hajime Sorayama, offers an occasion for considering this question. Sorayama specializes in paintings of what he calls "sexy robots" or "gynoids," as opposed to androids (Figures 8, 9, 10). In contrast to the robot Maria in *Metropolis*, Sorayama's gynoids seem designed to evoke rather than dispel male anxieties about both technology and female sexuality, by pushing the logic of fetishism to a point of crisis. In *Metropolis*, the robot takes on the appearance of a sexually active woman; the film's narrative thereby implies that female sexuality is the truth of technology, and it is this representation that allows the film's fetishism to contain the anxieties produced by both women and machines. In contrast, Sorayama's gynoids seem to represent women becoming robots, especially in the case of images that combine the

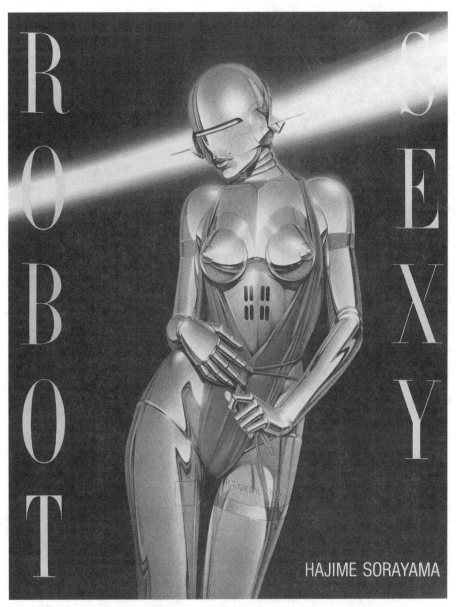

Figure 8. Cover of Hajime Sorayama, *Sexy Robot*. Copyright Sorayama/
Artspace/Uptight, 2003, www.sorayama.net.

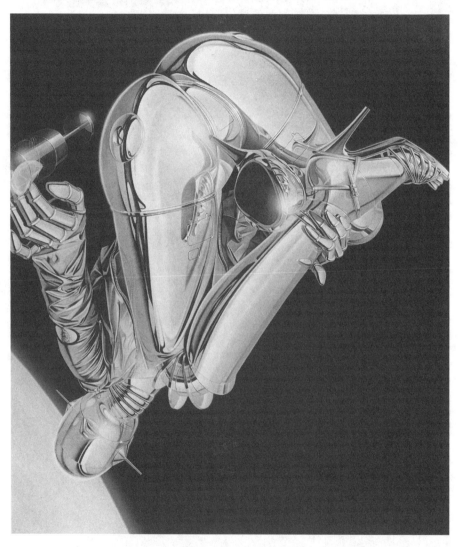

Figure 9. Hajime Sorayama, *Sexy Robot*. Copyright Sorayama/Artspace/
Uptight, 2003, www.sorayama.net.

mechanical and the organic. If anything, these images represent technology as the truth of sexuality, and this inversion of the modernist tradition Huyssen defines produces anxieties that cannot be entirely or safely framed by the fetishism the images evoke.

Sorayama's work deliberately represents mechanical bodies that exactly conform to the conventions of soft-core pornography, specifically the genre of the pinup. These images therefore seem designed to elicit both a sexual response and an uncomfortable recognition of the inappropriateness, perhaps even obsolescence, of that response. As the introduction to an American collection of Sorayama's paintings puts it, "these sexy ladies have a soul of steel. . . . We all know what they're saying. They're beauties from a futurist fantasy, longing for a little contact. But contact may be just what they're not going to get. Gaze on this steel perfection and all you'll see is your own reflection. . . . And even their secrets are nothing but the secrets of the Age of Technology" (*Sorayama*, 9). Isn't this an account of a heterosexual male viewer beginning to think back

Figure 10. Hajime Sorayama, *Hajime Sorayama*. Copyright Sorayama/Artspace/Uptight, 2003, www.sorayama.net.

through and finding himself confronted with the history of his own fetishistic desire, his own tendency to project male lack onto the ambiguously phallic mother? I do not intend to make any premature, celebratory claims for this "reflection" on the construction of heterosexual male desire, but I do want to argue that images like these make possible narratives of gendered subjectivity that differ significantly from classic psychoanalytic paradigms, differences that any cultural criticism of this cyberporn must take into account, though these differences can only be understood in relation to psychoanalytic categories.[16]

In this sense, Sorayama's images seem to to eroticize what Žižek sees as the postmodern fascination with the Real, defined by its resistance to symbolization (*Enjoy*, 122–23), though I am arguing that these images gain their power precisely by using the figure of the gynoid as a way to paradoxically symbolize that resistance to or failure of symbolization. That paradoxical project of representing the undoing of representation makes possible the kind of critical reflection on male spectatorship that I outlined earlier, because Žižek's postmodern fascination with the Real is by no means incompatible with classic psychoanalytic accounts of fetishism. In a famous passage, Deleuze distinguishes fetishistic disavowal of maternal castration from simple denial, because disavowal consists of "radically contesting the validity of that which is," as in the statement "the woman does not lack a penis" (28–29). But this simultaneous definition and refusal of castration nevertheless installs castration initially as "that which is" and therefore remains within the oedipalizing boundaries of a male fantasy of phallic identification with the mother and the disappointment that results. In contrast, Sorayama's gynoids tend to reveal the basis of fetishism in male, and not female, lack. Disavowing the absence of the maternal phallus allows male subjects to retain pre-oedipal maternal attachments by enabling an oscillation within heterosexuality, between investment in the feminine as an object choice and identification with the phallic qualities associated with women through the agency of the fetish. Sorayama's images complicate this fetishistic framework in two ways. First, these images make it impossible to determine whether the sexy robot is a fetish object or a woman who has been fetishized. Is the robot body to be regarded as an object that replaces and supplements the body of an actual woman? Or are these images to be read as depictions of women whose bodies take on phallic qualities by being represented as mechanized?

The possibility that the robot body might provide the support for a phallic identification points to the second way that these gynoids complicate any attempt to fetishize them. Treating the robot body fetishistically, as a displacement of the phallus, does not and cannot achieve the desired goal of defending against castration anxiety. In the case of these images, fetishistic defenses against female sexual difference require the heterosexual male spectator to not only confront but identify with technologies that themselves generate castration anxiety. As

Andrew Ross points out in a reading of cyberpunk fiction, the technologies of body modification associated with sexy robots and other cyborgs are "castrating in ways that boys have always had nightmares about" (*Strange Weather*, 153). The feminized robot body, the very object that seems to offer reassurance against the threat female sexuality might pose to men, only conjures up the specter of another form of castration, posed by the technology of the robot body itself. In this way, the representation of the feminized robot reflects back on and implicates the male spectator. What Sorayama likes to call "that metallic feeling" here signifies not phallic mastery or self-possession but the role of technology in the construction of any subjectivity, where technology figures as an absence, an agency that is not part of the self, but an absence that is not necessarily or easily organized along gender lines (which, of course, does not mean that technology *cannot* end up organized in ways that reproduce traditional gender narratives). The effect of the explicit technological mediation of the bodies represented in these images works against "the erasure of any social interference in the spectator's erotic enjoyment of the image" and therefore makes it possible to unravel the element of mystification or reification implicit in fetishism (Mercer, 177). From this perspective, it is interesting to contrast Sorayama's images with more straightforwardly mimetic examples of digitized female characters, such as Lara Croft in the *Tomb Raider* video game, or the collection of "virtual idols" collected in Julius Weidemann's *Digital Beauties*, where the subversive potential I am locating in Sorayama's roboticized style largely drops away.[17]

Žižek argues that fantasy should not be understood simply as the construction of phantasmatic objects, but instead provides "the frame enabling us to desire" at all (*Sublime*, 118). I am arguing that Sorayama's gynoids are frames that enable us to desire differently, by accommodating libidinal investments in male lack, rather than a phallic ideal. These images, in my reading, imply that female subjectivity no longer represents the psychic location "at which the male subject deposits his lack" (Silverman, 46). In Kaja Silverman's words, images like these produce "the confrontation of the male subject with the defining conditions of all subjectivity, conditions which the female subject is obliged compulsively to reenact, but upon the denial of which traditional masculinity is predicated: lack, specularity, and alterity" (50–51). Like the collective fetishism of S/M practices, the kind of images alongside which Sorayama's work is usually sold, his gynoids point to a different "sexual organization of social risk" (McClintock, "Maid to Order," 108). The collective nature of these forms of technofetishism is suggested by the existence of collaboratively authored sexy robot fantasies on Web sites such as Doll Forum (www.dollforum.com) and Gynoid Gallery (www.gynoid.com), as well as Yahoo chat rooms such as Robot Lovers and Android Companions.[18]

The ways in which Sorayama's sexy robot images possess a potential for

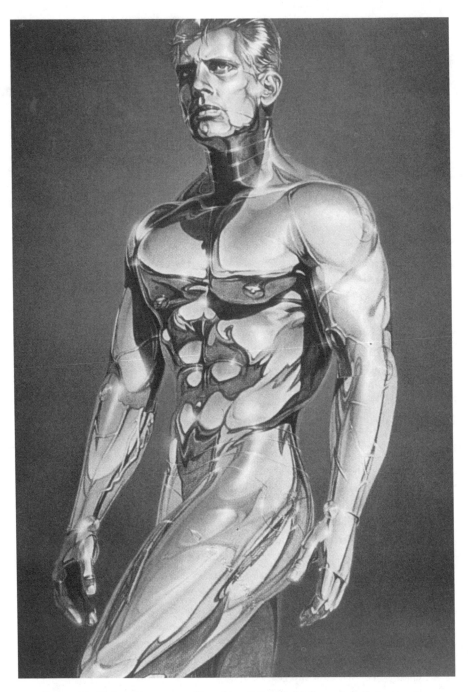

Figure 11. Hajime Sorayama, "Iron Man." Copyright Sorayama/Artspace/
Uptight, 2003, www.sorayama.net.

putting the self-images of their heterosexual male viewers at risk suggest how contemporary technocultures participate in a theoretical redefinition of the concept of the fetish, like the one McClintock offers. Bill Nichols defines the relevance of new technologies to this project of redefinition when he contrasts the fetishistic forms appropriate to cultures of mechanical reproduction with the forms appropriate to the logic of cybernetic systems and interactive media. While mechanical reproduction invites the fetishist to focus on the "fetish *object*—the image of the other that takes the place of the other," interactive technologies make the process of interaction itself "the object of fetishization rather than representations whose own status as produced objects has been masked" (Nichols, 32). This formulation is Nichols's attempt to account for the repetitive structure of video games, for instance. The result is to shift the emphasis of fetishism from objects to the fetishist, as I have argued Sorayama's images begin to do. This shift creates a greater potential for self-reflection on the process of fetishization and therefore can serve as a reminder "of our *lack* of self-possession," as James Clifford argues (65). In this reading, Sorayama's repetition of pinup conventions within a technological context can be read as enacting the kind of shift Kobena Mercer locates in Robert Mapplethorpe's

Figure 12. Hajime Sorayama, "Full Metal Love." Copyright Sorayama/ Artspace/Uptight, 2003, www.sorayama.net.

photographs, which move beyond the repetition of sexist and racist stereotypes or fantasies toward a laying bare of "the psychic and social relations of ambivalence at play" in the process of consuming these images (199).

Mercer's willingness to reconsider the effects of fetishism (190) moves toward an understanding of it as a "deconstructive strategy" (199), and specifically toward an understanding of it as a subversively iterative or performative process, in Judith Butler's sense of revealing a fixed identity as a "stylized configuration" or "gendered corporealization of time" (*Gender Trouble*, 141). McClintock similarly argues that alternative forms of fetishism can dislodge "the centrality of the phallus" and parade "the presence of legitimacy of a multiplicity of pleasure, needs and contradictions that cannot be reduced to the 'desire to preserve the phallus'" (*Imperial Leather*, 183).

Clifford's argument, that self-reflection on our own fetishistic practices (his example is ethnographic museum collections) can call into question our own self-possession, suggests how these redefinitions of fetishism can participate in posthumanism as a critique of the liberal humanist ideology of possessive individualism. But Clifford's claim that this self-reflection makes us aware of "the artifices we employ to gather a world around us" (65) also has some more disturbing implications, in a technocultural context of generalized denaturalization (like the context Nichols and Hayles both define). From this perspective, fetishistic self-reflection of the kind Clifford advocates starts to appear as a normative cultural framework through which this denaturalization can be experienced and organized, even as Clifford shifts the discussion of fetishism from an exclusively sexual and gendered context to a racial and colonial one, in an attempt to reflect critically on the privileged position of the subject of anthropological knowledge rather than the male spectators of images of women. Understood as a new cultural norm, fetishes explicitly produce themselves as veils that mask nothing, signifiers without signifieds, but nevertheless they continue to command our fascination and libidinal investment. This self-conscious understanding of the fetish as such is in fact how Lisa Nakamura defines the denaturalized circulation of racial stereotypes in online contexts, as examples of what she calls "orientalized theatricality" (*Cybertypes*, 39). Even though these images are understood to be just that, images whose artificiality is laid bare in the absence of physical bodies to naturalize them, they continue to define the acceptable boundaries of racial self-definition (39–40). In other words, in these denaturalized technocultural contexts, the distinction between fetish as fixed stereotype and fetish as destabilizing or ambivalent repetition starts to break down, leaving us with an impoverished set of possibilities for performing gender, sexuality, and race, instead of opening the possibilities for diversity that McClintock and Mercer envision (with reference to practices of female fetishism and interracial homoeroticism, respectively).

In this sense, it seems necessary to return to Sorayama's sexy robots and to consider how they might reproduce or displace racial conventions as well as sexual and gendered ones. Such a reading would begin by noting how Sorayama's techniques of roboticization spectacularize the skin and the skin color of the bodies depicted in them, primarily, but not exclusively, female bodies (as I suggested in my reading of Skal's *Antibodies* in chapter 2). On the one hand, the use of silver hues to produce "that metallic feeling" seems to heighten and make visible a form of whiteness that in a pinup girl might seem unremarkable or banal (that is, to the extent that Sorayama's gynoids can be said to embody racial meanings at all, it is through this displacement of "white" skin). It might then be argued that the fetishistic interest of these images resides as much in their techniques of racial representation as in sexual ones. On the other hand, these metallic bodies also possess the opacity that Richard Dyer argues the lighting conventions of cinema associate with "non-white and sometimes working-class women," who, Dyer argues "are liable to shine rather than glow" (122). Normative white bodies in film are characterized by a shimmering translucency; the radiance that infuses and interpenetrates them makes them appear to be more than mere matter in ways that Dyer argues have become "central to the conception of white humanity" (115). Sorayama's gynoids share the hard-edged qualities of cinematic bodies that cannot be idealized in this way. In effect, Sorayama's roboticizing techniques materialize the whiteness of these women by using a technique that in cinema would be associated with the lighting conventions applied to racially marked bodies. The potentially subversive effect of Sorayama's art resides in how it renders ambiguous the cinematic techniques of racial coding that Dyer defines and how that ambiguity affects the meaning of the gender and sexuality more spectacularly attributed to these technologically mediated bodies, ambiguities that are foregrounded by the art's fetishistic frame. This possibility for articulating race, sexuality, and gender emerges precisely from the technological denaturalization of those categories. As Clifford suggests, fetishism here functions as a way of naming and recognizing the artifices we use to "gather a world around us." That denaturalizing operation of "laying bare the device" is not, however, progressive in itself. Its effect is to make these categories and norms more available, either for the purpose of reasserting them or for the purpose of contesting the boundaries they define.

"Like a Prosthesis, or a Fetish":
Posthuman Embodiment and Richard Calder's Gynoids

These ambiguities become more explicit in one of the main literary sources for the idea of the gynoid, the work of the British writer Richard Calder, who was living as an expatriate in Thailand at the time he wrote the stories discussed here. In a series of short stories and a later trilogy of novels (*Dead Girls, Dead Boys,* and *Dead Things*), Calder combines the narration of fetishistic invest-ments in technology that reproduce traditional constructions of gendered sub-jectivity with a counternarrative of denaturalizing imitation produced through identification with fetishized technology. Calder's work suggests the possibility of rethinking the experience of embodiment from the point of view of the fetish object.[19] These stories presuppose the emergence of a literary movement called the Second Decadence in the 1990s, which includes the return of the dandy as a cultural type and a preference for the artificial over the natural (Calder, *Dead Girls,* 157, 161; "Mosquito," 7; I will return to the significance of this allusion to the decadent movement, especially the way it implicitly invokes what Jonathan Dollimore calls the Wildean tradition of gay culture). This Second Decadence provides the cultural background for the development of female automatons or dolls, which Calder also refers to as gynoids.[20] European firms such as Tiffany and Cartier, Dior and Chanel, all develop their own specialized lines, while Southeast Asian companies bring out cheaper knockoffs of these deluxe mod-els, thereby participating in what is described as "the deathwish of Europe" (*Dead Girls,* 161).

One of Calder's stories, "Mosquito," reads like a cyberpunk version of David Henry Hwang's play *M. Butterfly.*[21] The story is set in Thailand and narrated by the title character, a sex worker and pre-op transsexual who specializes not in female but in gynoid impersonation—that is, in the artificial imitation of what is already an explicitly denaturalized imitation of femininity.[22] The effect is to reveal femininity itself as a structure of imitation or impersonation. Mos-quito has decided not to have an actual sex-change operation after undergoing what he/she calls "the more radical surgery" needed to create the appearance of a doll. The reason, he/she explains, is that "only a man could imitate a doll. Women, it was said, were too real. For dolls are not women; they are man's dreams of women. Made in man's image, they are an extension of his sex, female impersonators built to confirm his prejudices, sexual illusionists" ("Mosquito," 6). In a word, fetishes.

This technology of doubled impersonation functions in at least two ways. The plot of the story is a typical cyberpunk tale of corporate espionage. But for the narrator the real story involves his/her falling in love with an Englishman who has come to Thailand to cripple the illicit doll industry by infecting them with a sexually transmitted and ethnically specific virus, thereby destroying public confidence in the dolls as a safe-sex technique. At one point the narra-tor tells his would-be English lover, "I want to be your doll" (8; the allusion here is to Iggy Pop and the Stooges' song "I Wanna Be Your Dog"). He/she iden-tifies with the position of the fetish. At the end of the story, after the English-man's plot is revealed, the narrator reflects on how "even in the last days of empire" he/she had wanted to be part of the Englishman's "marvellous world, that land of satisfied desire, part of its genuineness" (11). By this point, it becomes clear that the narrator is impersonating not only a fetishized notion of femininity but also the orientalized other of Europe; the dualistic categories of "genuine" and "imitation" are aligned with the opposition of Europe/Asia and masculine/feminine. When the narrator says "in me he would find a real doll," the point is that it is only through the mediation of the Englishman's desire that the narrator can be a "*real* doll" (10; my emphasis).

It is at this point, however, that it also becomes clear that the narrator's imitation of a fetishized Asian femininity means that the categories of gender and race interrupt rather than support and reinforce one another analogically. The result is to produce a moment of critical insight, as Kobena Mercer argues occurs in the case of Robert Mapplethorpe's photographs (190–91).[23] While Mosquito's perfect imitation of the artificiality of the feminine literally gains him/her a place in her lover's heart and a claim to be part of the "genuineness" of his "land of satisfied desire" (however precariously), his/her equally perfect imitation of an Englishman's fantasy of an Asian woman guarantees that she will be barred from that land, precisely because her imitation of an idea of racial difference is what makes her not just a doll but a "real doll," in the Englishman's eyes. The Englishman's betrayal of Mosquito, in his pursuit of England's national and commercial superiority, leads the narrator to recognize that he/she is "not the real thing," "not even a poor fake," but just "a fake of a fake." But this is not a tragedy, because "it was the dollworld, not [England] I was enamored of" (Calder, "Mosquito," 11). The story offers a redefinition of masculinity that involves the same compulsive reenactment of "lack, specularity, and alterity" that Silverman argues is traditionally expected of female subjects and disavowed by the masculine. The narrator's doubling of imitation, the impersonation of female impersonation or its technology, undoes the distinction between the original and the imitation, revealing the "genuine" to be a phantasmatic ideal, which is what both heterosexual masculinity and British national identity are represented as in this story. By accepting the fictional nature of Europe's originality, the narrator decolonizes his/her mind, without reasserting an authentic "native" identity, and this same act of psychological decolonization is performed in relation to the "straight mind" and the narrator's initial need to have his/her phantasmatic femininity validated by a real man. The narrator's performance as a gynoid results in the unlearning of his/her assumptions about the secondary or derivative status of the feminine, homosexuals, and formerly colonized peoples in relation to the norm of European masculinity.

In Calder's story, both the technology that produces the gynoids and the technology that allows the narrator to impersonate a gynoid are represented in terms of a concept of imitation that "does not copy that which is prior, but produces and *inverts* the very terms of priority and derivativeness," a concept of imitation whose gender implications have been elaborated by Judith Butler ("Imitation," 22). If, Butler argues, "heterosexuality is an impossible imitation of itself, an imitation that performatively constitutes itself as the original, then the imitative parody of 'heterosexuality' . . . is always and only an imitation of an imitation, a copy of a copy, for which there is no original" (ibid.). In "Mosquito," both the gynoids and the narrator embody such imitative parodies, as the narrator acknowledges both when he describes the gynoids as "sexual illusionists" and when he describes himself as "a fake of a fake." The result is "to expose heterosexuality as an incessant and *panicked* imitation of its own naturalized idealization" (ibid., 23).[24] As the Englishman tells the narrator of Calder's story, "you stole our copyrights, our names," the worst thing that can happen to a Europe that has become only an "an empire of style" (10, 8). This story suggests that the strategy of subversive mimicry that Butler famously defines implies precisely the "radical contesting of that which is" that Deleuze attributes to fetishism. Butler's notion of performative identity implies an understanding of oneself and one's sexuality on the model of the fetish, a supplement whose replacement of the "original" ideal indicates the impossibility of being that "original."

This link between fetishism and strategies of subversive mimicry has been made most directly by Homi Bhabha, in his analyses of processes of racial stereotyping. Bhabha argues for a structural link between sexual fetishism and racial stereotyping, both of which are organized around the "desire for a pure origin" unthreatened by difference and division and the disavowal of the visible signs of such difference and division, either differences in sexual organs or differences in skin color (Bhabha, 74–75). Calder's story demonstrates not only this structural link, but goes on to link both sexual and racial fetishism with technology. In "Mosquito," technology functions to facilitate a generalized fetishism, as the incorporation of technology on the level of the body potentially brings all subjects closer to the status of the fetish object or stereotype. At the same time, technology also marks the difference between being the stereotype and miming or performing it. If, as Bhabha claims, colonial mimicry resembles sexual fetishism as "the desire for a reformed, recognizable Other, *as a subject of a difference that is almost the same, but not quite*," then in "Mosquito" technology is what makes Mosquito both "almost the same" but also "not quite" the same (86). In other words, it is technology that makes Mosquito's embodied style an act of mimicry, which "*repeats* rather than *re-presents*" (88). In contrast, then, to Haraway's famous claims about the cyborg's rejection of pure origins and acceptance of difference and division, Calder's story suggests the continuing relevance of models of fetishistic disavowal. It also suggests, however, the rearticulation of such models along the lines that Bhabha defines, when he argues that "the fetish mimes the forms of authority at the point at which it deauthorizes them" (91). Technofetishism tends to make this point of deauthorization more clearly visible.

Technocultural forms of body modification and impersonation seem, then, to literalize and to generalize what Lauren Berlant has defined as a historical strategy for negotiating the dilemma of finding oneself "overembodied" in a national culture that values citizens for their ability to abstract themselves, transcend their bodily particularity, and identify with a generic category like the "citizen" or the "human" (113). One response to that dilemma, Berlant argues, is to experience desire not as a desire "to love or make love," but instead as a desire "to wear [another person's] way of wearing her body, like a prosthesis, or a fetish" (111). This ability to trade in styles of embodiment functions as a redefinition of embodiment; this practice asserts that bodies are neither absolutely transcendable and disposable nor absolutely fixed and unchangeable. Forms of posthumanism that celebrate "postbiological" forms of existence literalize the historical privileging of the "unmarked" body that Berlant critiques, the white, middle-class male body that is constructed as generic and transcendable. In the technocultural contexts presupposed by Sorayama's images and Calder's narratives, however, all bodies are lived as fetishes or prostheses—that is, everyone is particularized, but particularity is also problematized in ways that are understood to be valuable. It is only to the extent that this generalization disrupts the hierarchy of value Berlant defines that it constitutes more than another form of cultural appropriation, in which particularity itself would paradoxically be reuniversalized as an abstract form affecting all subjects equally. Calder's story therefore implicitly reconnects posthumanism to histories of both racial and gender performance.

The novels that followed this story, especially *Dead Girls* (1992), deliberately make the general implications of Mosquito's performative style overt, at the same time that this style is no longer voluntary.[25] The premise of the novels is that the sexual traffic in dolls or gynoids has generated a nanovirus sexually transmitted from dolls to their male lovers and from these men to human women. This artificial virus has resulted in a "doll plague" that specifically affects girl children, so that "when little English girl go pubescent, she go roboto too" (11). The "dead girls" of the title, also referred to as "Lilim" (the title of an earlier story), are women who have been turned into gynoids. This blurring of the boundaries between biology and technology is an example of the trope of hardwiring, in which "hardware and software [are] indivisible" (20) and "style blurs into soul" (115; see also chapter 1 of this book). The dolls are regarded as defined by these programming structures and therefore as being "sets of formal rules" (31). This technologically mediated mode of existence is later glossed as the condition of being "a thing of surface and plane. Clothes, make-up, behavioural characteristics, resolve, for her, into an identity that is all gesture, nuance, signs," with no "psychology" or "inner self" (54). This formulation seems to collapse hardware into software, soul into style, rather than to blur the distinction between them, and the result is that this version of hardwiring girls with the characteristics of gynoids merely literalizes the construction of a traditional male fantasy about femininity; in the passage quoted earlier, gender socialization seems little different from the "doll plague." The denaturalized nature of these traditional constructions (what is untraditional about them) is made explicit later when one of the dolls responsible for spreading the plague describes herself as "a machine built to resolve Man's fantasies," and another character describes the converted gynoids as the end result of "thousands of years of sexual warfare" that have distilled "the myths of battle . . . into a poison so concentrated that it has become flesh" (204, 200). This narrative demonstrates how technological forms of embodiment can denaturalize sexist or racist stereotypes while at the same time intensifying their negative effects. These representations do demonstrate, however, that cultural constructions and fantasies have a materiality that is not easily altered through the technological transcendence of the natural or organic body, while simultaneously holding out some hope for progressive interventions, because this same thematic of becoming a fantasy also implies that biology is not destiny and that materiality is not incompatible with plasticity or manipulability; in fact, materiality is the precondition for such openness to change. From this perspective, Calder's novel might be read as a warning against the belief that rejecting biology as destiny also gets rid of destinies in general, in the sense of external determinations and control systems.

Imitation Games in Artificial Intelligence and Queer Theory

I would argue that this counternarrative of claiming the position of the fetish as a strategy of subversive mimicry can be explained, at least in part, by contrasting Norbert Wiener's concept of the implications of cybernetics for human identity with Alan Turing's. In *The Human Use of Human Beings* (1954), his attempt to popularize his more technical book *Cybernetics*, Wiener argues that "we are not stuff that abides, but patterns that perpetuate themselves," and that it is this informational pattern, maintained by homeostatic feedback mechanisms that for Wiener are indistinguishable from those of "mechanical automata," which forms "the touchstone of our personal identity" (96). As discussed in chapter 1 (in the course of my reading of Ken MacLeod's novel *The Cassini Division*), Turing is best known (at least on a popular level) for the Turing test, which established criteria for determining when artificial intelligence would be achieved (in *Neuromancer*, Case, Molly, and their allies are pursued by the Turing police because they are trying to liberate an AI). Turing presented this argument in his 1950 essay "Computing Machinery and Intelligence." There, he argued that a computer could only be determined to possess intelligence if it could discursively pass as human—that is, if it could carry on a conversation with human beings convincingly enough that no one would realize that he or she was talking to a machine. Given the publication of Turing's biography, the fact that Turing was gay has become more commonly known as well. In 1952, he was arrested for gross indecency and forced to undergo "organotherapy" for a year, a treatment that involved injections of female hormones. Presumably as a result of these events, Turing committed suicide in 1954 (Hodges). What remains less widely known about Turing is the fact that his 1950 essay does not begin by proposing a test for artificial intelligence at all. Instead, he takes a detour through another "imitation game," based on gender. In this game, a man and a woman are concealed from a questioner, who attempts to determine which of the two is the man and which is the woman. Turing suggests that the man try to deceive the interrogator about his gender, while the woman tries to convince the interrogator that she is in fact a woman. Turing then asks, "what will happen when a machine takes the part of [the man] in this game? Will the interpretor decide wrongly just as often when the game is played like this as he does when the game is played between a man and a woman? These questions replace our original, 'Can machines think?'" (Turing, 434).[26]

This "imitation game" presents gender as a performance that can be either denaturalizing ("deceptive") or naturalizing ("truthful"), and the artificiality of gender identity provides an analogy for artificial intelligence, or its discursive performance; more accurately, Turing suggests that the question of whether machines can participate in our already-existing gender imitation games should replace the question of whether machines are intelligent or not. Given this representation of gender, it seems reasonable to inquire whether and to what extent Turing can be read as a queer theorist before the letter, and to what extent his influence on the whole project of artificial intelligence, of creating machines that can pass for human, is informed by Alan Turing's experience of the epistemology of the closet. In this sense, the wordplay on faking an orgasm in MacLeod's description of artificial intelligence as the attempt to "fake an organism" (*Cassini Division*, 76) is especially apt, but also gains a new pathos, as a metaphor for the ways in which Turing was forced to act as if he possessed a normative sexuality. This reading ties anxieties about the authenticity of personhood to sexual anxieties in the same way that Turing ties anxieties about intelligent machines to anxieties about the instability of gender categories. Turing actually defines the criterion for AI research not as the ability to carry on a conversation, as his test is popularly remembered, but instead as the ability to impersonate a man trying to impersonate a woman, as the fake of a fake.

Turing's essay might then be placed in a genealogy that would begin with

Oscar Wilde's assertion that "what people call insincerity is simply a method by which we can multiply our personalities" (393). What does this statement imply except the same deep commitment to the view that "thought does not require a unitary agent who thinks," which Sherry Turkle locates in the scientific culture of AI research (*Second Self,* 267)? Turing's essay might then provide the missing link between statements like the one I quoted from Wilde and Wayne Koestenbaum's claim, in an essay on Wilde and "the birth of gay reading," that "one can acquire reality only by faking it. Men can acquire masculinity only by mimicking it. . . . Mechanical reproduction is *not* second-rate: there is nothing wrong with becoming a clone, wanting to be famous for fifteen minutes, striving to be sexy through mimicry, or commodifying one's life, body, and work. To consider replication degrading is, literally, homophobic: *afraid of the same*" (182–83).[27]

TRAPPED BY THE BODY

TELEPRESENCE TECHNOLOGIES AND TRANSGENDERED PERFORMANCE

> What we have in today's virtual-reality systems is the confluence of three very powerful enactment capabilities: sensory immersion, remote presence, and tele-operation.
> —Brenda Laurel, Computers as Theatre *(187–88)*

> In cyberspace the transgendered body is the natural body.
> —*Allucquère Rosanne Stone*, The War of Desire and Technology *(180)*

BY 1995, when Robert Sawyer's *Terminal Experiment* was published, the instantiation of cyberspace in the form of the Internet had made it possible to dismiss cyberpunk representations of virtual realities and human–computer interfaces as "nothing but air guitar writ large" (142). This metaphor is significant for the way in which it suggests that VR was not just commercial hype, part of the dot-com boom, but that this inflated discourse took a specifically adolescent male form.[1] Sawyer thereby suggests the way in which versions of Andrew Ross's critique of cyberpunk and Gibson's version of the cyberspace metaphor, as "the most fully delineated urban fantasies of white male folklore" (*Strange Weather*, 145), circulated within science fiction. But cyberpunk also generated a set of more complex and sympathetic responses from some of the same feminist writers who might have been expected to endorse Sawyer's and Ross's dismissive assessments of cyberpunk's limits.

This chapter uses Allucquère Rosanne Stone's work on the status of embodiment in virtual systems to account for the existence of a significant number of popular narratives by women writers about virtual reality.[2] In particular, Stone's work helps explain the predominance of themes of gender and sexual performativity or cross-identification in these narratives about cyberspace. The preceding chapter demonstrated the relevance of theories of performativity to narratives of cyborg embodiment, but this chapter considers the relevance of those theories to virtual reality computer interfaces and computer simulations, and therefore engages the popular tendency to represent cyberspace as a technology of disembodiment from a different critical perspective than in the previous chapters. To what extent do theories and practices of subversive mimicry and performativity, such as drag or butch-femme, function as a cultural framework for constructing the meaning of virtual reality and telepresence technologies?[3]

I will focus on three examples of narratives that use practices of gender cross-identification to conceptualize cyberspace and virtual reality: Maureen F. McHugh's short stories, Melissa Scott's novel *Trouble and Her Friends,* and Laura Mixon's novel *Glass Houses.* I will end by using Caitlin Sullivan and Kate Bornstein's novel *Nearly Roadkill* to raise some questions about the dominance of gender and sexual performance in these narratives, and the remarkable absence of popular attention to the way that cyberspace might facilitate modes of racial performance such as passing and blackface. The purpose of Stone's comment about how "in cyberspace the transgendered body is the natural body" is to emphasize how the performance of gender in cyberspace problematizes the concept of the "natural" (*War,* 180), but this same formulation also suggests that the denaturalization of fixed gender categories can itself become a new norm, in ways that transracial bodies and performances have not.[4]

Both text-based and graphic virtual interfaces make possible the decoupling of public persona from the physical space of the body. This detachment certainly lends itself to a traditional Cartesian dualism between mind and body, and therefore can also reproduce the gendered hierarchy that equates masculinity with universal rationality and femininity with embodied particularity.[5] However, this same detachment of public persona from physical location can also have the effect that Judith Butler famously attributes to gay performance styles such as drag or butch-femme—that is, the detachment of public persona from physical body can reveal that sex and gender are not related as cause and effect and that sex and gender do not necessarily exist in a one-to-one expressive relation to one another.

This critique of expressive subjectivity has received less attention than Butler's arguments about subcultural practices of gender masquerade, but it is that critique that best defines the mutual relevance of virtual reality and theories of performativity. Butler argues, for example, that the categories of the "inner" and the "outer," on which expressive subjectivity depends, "constitute a binary distinction that stabilizes and consolidates the coherent subject."[6] But in situations where "the 'inner world' no longer designates a topos, then the internal fixity of the self and, indeed, the internal locale of gender identity, become similarly suspect" (*Gender Trouble*, 134). Virtual systems represent just such a situation, where the "inner world" of subjectivity is no longer simply located within the subject's physical body. Virtual reality computer interfaces or telepresence technologies both restage and disrupt the distinction between inner and outer worlds. Virtual personae or body images become relatively more detached from any "internal fixity" or "locale"—specifically, bodies as material bounded spaces. If the process of virtualization itself involves the progressive "dissociation of space from place," as Mitsuhiro Yoshimoto suggests, then the "locale of gender identity" also becomes dissociated from any fixed location (Yoshimoto, 115). The questions that emerge are to what extent such personae, and the challenges they pose to traditional notions of the relation between sex and gender, can be ideologically recontained as mere secondary projections of a securely interiorized self; and, even if such recontainment can be avoided, to what extent this "dissociation" is progressive. When virtualization disrupts the grounding of gender norms in the "inner world" of the sexed body, what happens to those norms?

As I noted in the preceding chapter, Howard Rheingold's speculations about the sexual uses of these virtual reality computer interfaces, or what he calls "teledildonics," have gained considerable currency in the popular discourse on the implications of these interfaces. What has escaped attention is how the disappearance of the expressive relation between body and gender identity, as Butler theorizes it, becomes technologically concretized in the practice of teledildonics. Rheingold imagines a technology that will allow computer users to map their body images into computer-simulated graphic environments in cyberspace, along with feedback devices that will translate actions in cyberspace into physical sensations in the user's body; if the user's image or avatar in cyberspace reaches its hand to "touch" another person's image or is "touched" by someone else's virtual hand, then an approximation of those sensations will be transmitted to the user's actual body (*Virtual Reality*, 350). Rheingold takes this scenario a step further by raising the possibility that users would map their physical bodies onto their virtual images *nonmimetically*, and it is the implications of this dissociation of virtual image from a one-to-one relationship with any physical body that have been generally overlooked in responses to this scenario. Rheingold suggests that "there is no reason to believe you won't be able to map your genital effectors to your manual sensors and have direct genital contact by shaking hands. What will happen to social touching when nobody knows where anybody else's erogenous zones are located?" (353).

Let's put aside for the moment the question of whether we really know now where anybody else's erogenous zones are located, or even our own. What this passage from Rheingold's popular introduction to virtual reality implies is the breakdown of the binary relationships between sex and gender that mandate, among other things, that there are only as many genders as there are biological sexes. By contrast, in virtual environments, the relationship between body and social presence can no longer be taken for granted.

The conceptualization of this potential breakdown of expressive relationships between embodiment and social identity in terms of "teledildonics," however, also has other implications. The figure of the dildo invokes lesbian sexual practices, and in contemporary lesbian criticism it is not uncommon to find the dildo invoked as "an especially embarrassing affront to normative heterosexuality" that suggests "its (possibly postmodern) subversion" (Lamos, 91), or as a means by which "lesbians have turned techno-culture's semiotic regime of simulation and the political economy of consumer culture back against the naturalization of masculinist hegemony," in a reading of how "the reproduction of the penis as dildo" exposes the phallus as merely a "simulacrum," a copy without an original (Griggers, 121). Lisa Moore, in fact, has adopted Rheingold's terminology to analyze Jeannette Winterson's lesbian fiction.

Given this reading of "dildonics," tele- or otherwise, as a subversive imitation of the phallus that reveals it to be only an idealized copy of itself and not a secure source of cultural authority, it is only a short step to the reading that Theresa Senft proposes, which moves from the use of the dildo as sexual prosthesis to a reading of sexual identity itself as prosthetic; as Senft puts it, "a *transgendered woman* . . . lives a prosthetic sexuality—she points to the fact that *all* gender is a strap on that you can't strap off" ("Introduction," 23). And the context for this claim is Senft's attempt to define a model for sexual and gender performances in cyberspace, in what Stone calls the "spaces of prosthetic communication" (*War*, 36).

The result is a chain of associations, which moves from imagining how virtual images or personae might be differently mapped onto physical bodies to a notion of teledildonics to lesbian sexual practices and prostheses to a theory of sexual and gender identities and performances as prosthetic. One effect of this chain of associations, however, is to conceptualize virtual performativity in exclusively sexual and gendered terms, rather than in terms of (trans)racial performance, which is equally implicit in the initial rejection of one-to-one mappings of bodies and social identities, as I read Rheingold's teledildonics scenario. When she links prosthetic embodiment to fetishistic practices (in the essay I cited at the end of chapter 3), Lauren Berlant also identifies the problem with applying a model of "prosthetic identity" to minoritized subjects, especially the mulatta or women whose bodies are also racially marked. Such women find themselves in the dilemma of figuring over- or hyperembodiment for "a culture that values abstraction" or the ability to identify with the universalized national body of the American citizen, a body that Berlant argues functions as a prosthesis necessary for participation in the national public sphere (113). In other words, to consider the articulation of gender and race is to immediately problematize the model of "prosthetic identity" that Senft proposes for virtual embodiment. The association of virtual technologies with forms of teledildonics or prosthetic sexual identities has the positive effect of denaturalizing binary gender identities, but that association has not encouraged consideration of the effects of virtual embodiment on racial identities and histories. What would it mean to think of race as well as sexuality as a prosthesis? That question is one that any attempt to apply theories of sexual performativity to the analysis of cyberspace must consider.

Rheingold's teledildonics scenario has also been taken up by at least one feminist science-fiction writer, Maureen F. McHugh, in a story titled "A Coney Island of the Mind."[7] This story is a rather programmatic translation of Rheingold's speculations into a fictional narrative, with a twist that Rheingold doesn't envision. In McHugh's story, an adolescent male protagonist uses a commercial virtual reality system designed to immerse the operator in a virtual environment through the use of head-mounted displays, datagloves to translate the movements of the hands into movements of the virtual image of the operator's body, and in this case a treadmill to facilitate the illusion of movement within the computer-generated graphic. This virtual environment, the "coney island" of the title, can be accessed simultaneously by multiple participants who can interact virtually. The literary allusion in the title, to a poem (and book of poems) by Beat poet Lawrence Ferlinghetti, is important for at least two reasons. First, the allusion emphasizes the application of a literary metaphor to the representation of cyberspace, though the allusion is also to a literary movement, the Beats, which attempted to return poetry and print culture in general to a model of performance. Second, the allusion invokes Ferlinghetti's use of the phrase "Coney Island of the mind," which Ferlinghetti uses as a metaphor of both poetry and the American public sphere, both understood as a kind of carnivalesque space that is simultaneously a social and a textual space.

The main character of the story has invested considerable time and expense customizing a virtual body image for himself that he refers to as "Cobalt," and which makes deliberate though superficial use of the nonmimetic possibilities of virtual embodiment by rendering his eyes and hair a bright blue (84–85), in an attempt to separate himself from users who simply adopt a more generic and preprogrammed simulation of a body. As Cobalt, this character encounters the virtual image of a young woman with "yellow snake eyes and brown skin" (87). While they are holding hands on the virtual boardwalk, he realizes that she is having an orgasm and that she has taken "a hotsuit and re-wire[d] the crotch so the system thinks it's a hand," just as Rheingold imagined (89).

The young man is at first embarrassed to have been tricked in this manner (ibid.), a response that is especially interesting given that it distinguishes this rewiring of erogenous zones from simple cross-dressing or the creation of alternative personae in virtual reality. Earlier in the story, Cobalt is solicited by a groups of "queens (who are mostly black and tall and female and camp, that being the current fashion in queens)" (86). He dismisses their suggestive comments as "white noise," but goes on to remark that they are "not what he's looking for anyway although who's to say what he'd be looking for if he had the option?" (ibid.). On one level, the "option" that Cobalt doesn't have is to experience the sexual options made possible by a full-body "hotsuit" with sexual feedback mechanisms, an "option" to which minors are denied access. But on another level, it is clear that the "option" is also the choice to explore alternative identity practices, such as flirting or having cybersex with someone who has chosen to appear as a black drag queen. In the context of this virtual environment, the story clearly indicates that such modes of cross-identification and border crossing are both encouraged and safe because they are perceived as having no real consequences for the world outside cyberspace. This reading is reinforced when Cobalt gets a sexual thrill from the thought that the person he's met, who appears as an attractive woman in virtual reality, might actually be someone completely different. It makes his heart pound to think that she might be "ugly, or fat, or old. Maybe she is blind, or deformed. Wild thought that this beautiful girl can be anything" (88). In this passage, Cobalt's virtual experience is presented as progressive, as he steps beyond the expected heterosexual prejudices of a boy his age, by not only imagining but enjoying the thought that he is flirting with a woman who doesn't meet normative standards of physical beauty. At the same time, it is clear that such moments of stepping outside the pressures of social conventions for gender and sexuality are also ideologically recontained by the assumption of a clear distinction between cyberspace and "real life," with virtual experiences having no particular effect on who Cobalt is outside virtual reality.

Cobalt's ability to maintain this distinction momentarily breaks down when this other person goes a step further by telling Cobalt that he has not only been tricked into having sex without knowing it but that he has been tricked into having sex with a gay man without knowing it. The other character asks Cobalt if he's a girl, and then reveals that "she" is glad he's not, because "she" is "not into girls. I just like wearing girl bodies because I like you righteous boys, you sweet straight boys" (89–90). Cobalt's reaction to this revelation is beyond embarrassment. His first thought is that "he'll have to change his look, never look like this again, abandon Cobalt, be something else" (90). The implication of this moment of homosexual panic is that Cobalt is so mortified that he momentarily assumes either that his virtual image is somehow legible to others as a gay style of embodiment, leading to encounters like this one, and therefore revealing something about who he really is, or alternately that this encounter has somehow marked his virtual persona for other people, in the same way that a rumor about his sexuality in real life would affect his social identity in ways that he could not control. At this point, it seems that Cobalt both collapses the distinction between virtual experiences and "real life," and for that very reason imagines using the resources of virtual reality to literalize the typical adolescent fantasy of escaping an embarrassing situation by becoming someone else. But, of course, Cobalt's previous attitude toward virtual reality simulations was that they had no such effect on who he really is, that encounters with "queens" in VR were incapable of invoking the "real-life" response of homosexual panic, and that the social meaning of his presence in cyberspace remained in his authorial control, no matter how far he walked on the wild side in VR. By the end of the story, this attitude reemerges, with Cobalt imagining how he can renarrate and edit the story to claim bragging rights among his friends.

McHugh's version of Rheingold's teledildonics scenario, then, identifies the difference between modes of cyber-cross-dressing, "wearing girl bodies," that only reinforce normative gender and sexual identities and modes of virtual embodiment that more fundamentally subvert such identities by more fully utilizing the potential of virtual technologies to disrupt the expressive or one-to-one mapping of social identities and meanings onto bodies. By the same token, this narrative suggests that teledildonics also makes possible acts of cyber-transracialization: is the "brown skin" of this female body image assumed as a calculated element in the seduction, or is the gay male operator also brown-skinned? Significantly, this question and the issues it raises about the extent to which exoticizing racial stereotypes might be implicated in transgendered or drag performances tend to be overwhelmed by the spectacular nature of the gender and sexual cross-identifications in the story.[8]

This implicit distinction between what Lisa Nakamura calls virtual "iden-tity tourism" and more truly unsettling forms of virtual cross-dressing becomes particularly important in the context of the gay character's statement about wear-ing girl bodies. That phrase suggests an extension of Judith Butler's comments on drag as "the mundane way in which genders are appropriated, theatrical-ized, worn, and done; it implies that all gendering is a kind of impersonation and approximation" ("Imitation," 21). For the characters in McHugh's story, virtual reality seems to be imagined as the mundane way in which sexed bod-ies are appropriated, theatricalized, worn, and done. In other words, McHugh's story suggests that virtual reality might foreground Butler's argument that both bodies and genders must be understood as constructed through frameworks of cultural intelligibility, that in turn must themselves be continually produced and reproduced through repeated performances of those interpretive frame-works. At the same time, this reference to "wearing girl bodies" also evokes the problem of distinguishing theatrical modes of performance, which maintain a strict dualistic hierarchy between performer and role, and the kind of discursive performativity that Butler privileges as subversive, in its repetition and undoing of the originality of the performer's identity.[9] Conceptualizing virtual cross-dressing as an act of "wearing girl bodies" can be read as a reinscription of the Cartesian mind/body dualism, in which the body functions as a mere receptacle for the mind or self.

The gay male character's statement about "wearing girl bodies because I like you . . . sweet straight boys" also suggests an inversion of Butler's famous reading of lesbian femme performances through the comment of one femme that she likes "her boys to be girls" (*Gender Trouble*, 123); the character in McHugh's story likes to be a girl in order to have virtual sex with straight men. One of the main questions the story implicitly poses is whether this sexual act was a heterosexual or a homosexual one. Or is it an example of what Jodi O'Brien calls "uncoded desire" (63), a form of sexual practice for which there is, as yet, no category? Allucquère Rosanne Stone's book on virtual systems theory offers the best theorization to date of these new possibilities and of the relationship between virtual embodiment and theories of performativity, in ways that focus primarily on sexuality and gender but also provide an opportunity to consider how the experience of telepresence might affect racial identities as well.

For Stone, virtual reality technologies (or VR) make visible what she calls "location technologies"—that is, techniques for mapping cultural meanings and representations onto physical bodies. Her work attempts to account for the ways in which "the accustomed grounding of social interaction in the physical facticity of human bodies is changing" (*War*, 17). Stone uses the term "virtual systems theory" to encompass not only the new relationships between physical and virtual bodies in cyberspace but also older forms of "warranting," one of the key terms Stone introduces, defined as "the production and maintenance of this link between a discursive space and a physical space" (40). This process of warranting is not unique to cyberspace, but has always functioned "to guarantee the production of what would be called a citizen," because "this citizen is composed of two major elements": the "collection of physical and performative attributes that Judith Butler and Kobena Mercer in separate works call the culturally intelligible body" and "the collection of virtual attributes which, taken together, compose a structure of meaning and intention for the first part," primarily through discursive means. These two sets of attributes compose what Stone calls "the socially apprehensible citizen" (ibid.), in which becoming a citizen means acquiring a new, virtual body (it is important to note that the "physical" body, in Stone's model, is therefore no more purely natural or organic than is the body in Butler's work; instead, the physical body is constituted and experienced through discursive and performative means).

For Stone, then, as for such critics as Michael Warner and Lauren Berlant, the production of the "citizen" has always involved a process of abstraction from the particularity of the body, and this history provides the context in which to understand the changes introduced by virtual reality and new technologies of computer-mediated communication. Berlant describes this traditional process of forming the universalized body of the citizen by transcending particular forms of embodiment as the nation's promise to provide "a kind of prophylaxis for the person, as it promises to protect his privileges and his local body in return for loyalty to the state" (113). Berlant adds that "American women and African-Americans have never had the privilege to suppress the body" that this process of citizenship requires (ibid.). In some narratives about cyberspace, virtual technologies are imagined precisely as a means of mediating and resolving this dilemma. Several of the characters in Caitlin Sullivan and Kate Bornstein's novel *Nearly Roadkill* argue that cyberspace is liberating for women in particular because it protects them in the way that the more traditional "prophylaxis" of public discourse has not: "And for women! Whoa! Suddenly they can tell assholes to fuck off without getting killed, or be really sexy in a way they would never be normally, and just enjoy it" (10–11). In this passage, through the mediation of text-based virtual communities, women are able to go public *and* still safely assert their differences from men, both through performing their sexualities and through verbal confrontation. In this version of virtual reality as public sphere, it is not necessary for women to transcend their sexual and gendered particularities in order to become part of the general public.

Virtual technologies also tend to make it much more difficult than it used to be to impose a one-to-one relationship between a single body and a single discursive identity, or, in Stone's terms, to warrant, to guarantee or ground, social identity in a physical body, and it thereby also becomes more difficult to limit discursive identities to one per body, or, by extension, to limit genders and sexual orientations to one per sexed body. It is this intervention in already-existing cultural techniques of abstraction and disembodiment that invalidates, or at least qualifies, the popular association of VR and cyberspace with a Cartesian desire to escape embodiment entirely, to be free of the "meat." In Stone's words, "the virtual component of the socially apprehensible citizen is not a disembodied thinking thing, but rather a different way of conceptualizing a *relationship* to the human body" (*War,* 40).

In virtual systems, it is no longer necessary for this relationship to be expressive in order for bodies to be culturally intelligible. Like drag performances, virtual reality technologies have the potential to "mock . . . the expressive model[s] of gender" and "compulsory heterosexuality," which assume "that there is first a sex that is expressed through a gender and then through a sexuality" (Butler, *Gender Trouble,* 137; "Imitation," 29). In another story by McHugh, "Virtual Love," a woman narrator and a male character learn to recognize and become attracted to one another in virtual reality because of their skill in creating and operating multiple, alternative personae, both male and female, including a black woman persona for the white woman narrator (101). The story hinges on the revelation that both these characters are physically confined to wheelchairs, which leads the male character to explain their unusual skill in constructing virtual personae in terms of how everyone else in VR is "projecting something. But I'm not. I'm not projecting myself at all" (109). To realize the full potential of virtual reality, it is necessary to recognize, as Butler puts it, that "the distinction between expression and performativeness is crucial" (*Gender Trouble,* 141).

The narrator ends the story by rejecting the essentialism of the other character's explanation: "I don't think I'm less likely than anyone else to project, any more objective than anyone else. But maybe people like Sam and me, we spend more time. We refine our art" (110). This comment could be read as reasserting an expressive model of subjectivity, associated with artistic expression. But it is equally possible to read the narrator here as generalizing the need to critique expressive assumptions about virtual embodiment to include everyone, not just the differently abled, especially since the scenes that reveal the physical bodies of the characters seem designed to shock readers and make us aware of how our reading of the story might have performed a similar act of expressive "projection," if we assumed that there was a general correspondence, at least, between the various body images we see the characters take on and their actual physical forms. At the same time, the narrator's final comment also suggests a critique of technological determinism, which would locate the disruption of expressive assumptions in the technology itself, rather than in the cultural frameworks in which the technology is made to mean and which structures the ways in which the technology gets used.

As I just suggested, the scenes in which the characters' physical forms are revealed seem designed to enact within the reading process the necessity of unlearning expressive assumptions about the relationship between virtual and physical space, which is thematized in the story as a central problem for users of virtual reality. In fact, the revelation scenes are deliberately staggered, so that first the narrator describes how she is unable to "forget" her physical body and "come alive" through the mediation of a virtual persona, because her romance with the other character is becoming too serious and she feels she would be deceiving him and only frustrating herself. At this point, the narrator tells us, "I know myself, a tiny woman in a chair, held in by seat restraints wearing a VR visor and gloves. . . . Flipper babies they call us when we are little, seal babies" (107). Her virtual lover later tracks her down and appears to her in his physical form: "the little man in the wheelchair is all head, head with a sharp, pointed chin and thinning hair and quick eyes. He's not really all head, he has a body, and short stick legs, short muscular arms. Like something out of a Velásquez painting, a dwarf" (109). The narrator is then able to accept a romance in virtual reality and also, perhaps even more important, to overcome her tendency to privilege her physical body as her "real" or "true" self. When she meets her lover again in virtual reality at the end of the story, her virtual persona takes over, and she finds herself behaving the way the character would, "kind of in your face" (110). The narrative's refusal of any clear distinction between actor and role, face and mask, is underscored by the fact that the story never gives the "true" names of the characters; they are only identified by the names of their personae.[10]

These scenes of revelation are all the more disturbing given the contrast between them and the narrator's detailed and loving descriptions of both her personae and her lover's various body images, which take up a significant portion of the story. The point of this deliberate shock is to demonstrate how the form of the story, in a print medium, is capable of incorporating some characteristics of virtual technologies and providing an experience for readers that approaches those made possible by virtual reality. McHugh's "Virtual Love" invokes and revises a traditional understanding of narrative point of view, which implies an embodied perspective on the actions of the narrative. But, as N. Katherine Hayles has argued, in an important argument about the characteristics of printed "info-narratives," "in cyberspace point of view does not emanate from the character; rather, the pov [point of view] literally *is* the character" (*How We Became Posthuman*, 38); that is, in narratives set in virtual environments, the characters' points of view are detached from any direct connection to a specific body and those points of view or personae function themselves as narrative agents.[11] It is precisely this transformation in the narrative function of point of view, this formal encoding of technological change, that McHugh's "Virtual Love" retroactively makes readers self-conscious about. We realize in retrospect that the narrator's point of view was much more dissociated from her physical body, through the mediation of virtual technologies, than we had initially realized before that physical embodiment was revealed to us. The story not only thematizes this process of dissociation for the characters, but transfers it to readers of the story. And that process is precisely one of interrogating the naturalness of expressive assumptions.

Butler emphasizes that all forms of gender are performative, with the expressive model becoming the norm only through "the repeated stylization of the body, a set of repeated acts . . . that congeal over time to produce the appearance of substance, of a natural sort of being" (*Gender Trouble*, 33). For Butler, drag constitutes a disruptive repetition of these gender norms, one that foregrounds the arbitrary relation between sex and gender by, for instance, juxtaposing a recognizable performance of femininity against the background of a culturally intelligible male body. I would argue that virtual reality constitutes another form of disruptive repetition, with the user's physical body repeated and reiterated as an image or representation in cyberspace. In effect, virtual systems spatialize the repeated performance of gender norms over time and thereby reveal the gap between embodiment and the performance of it that allows for subversion, intervention, and the critical rearticulation of that relationship.[12] It is this spatialization of a gender identity that is normally produced as a "social temporality" that allows virtual systems to reveal "the imitative structure of gender itself," the extent to which gender is an imitation without an original (ibid., 141, 137). In Stone's model of virtual systems, this point is made when she defines both the physical body and the discursive persona as having performative elements, so that the experience of virtual embodiment can potentially lead to a rethinking of physical embodiment as well (*War*, 41).

Sue-Ellen Case has critiqued Butler's theory of performativity, which Case reads as a project that aims "to recuperate writing at the end of print culture," by appropriating to writing the qualities of live or visual performance that are threatening to make print media obsolete. At the same time, for Case, the project of theories of performativity also amounts to the devaluation of theatrical performance for its dependence on an essentialist distinction between the actor and the role (17). "The use of performance" in theories of queer performativity, Case argues, "is to challenge writing to become performative. The contradiction between performance as mutable and nonreproductive" or nonrepeatable "and writing as stable and reproductive, motivates writing to somehow perform 'mimicry' and 'to discover a way for repeated words to become performative utterances'" (21). In Case's view, the result for lesbian theory has been to create a double bind between "the two strategies of lesbian visibility and queer performativity" (20).

This critique makes two main claims, which my reading of feminist narratives about virtual reality and performativity in cyberspace at least problematize. First, theories of performativity surreptitiously reinstate the privilege of writing over visual media by endowing writing "with the seductive pleasurable qualities of performance and . . . relegating bodily performances to a prior, essentialized mode of production" (23). As I suggested in my reading of McHugh's "Virtual Love," print media do seem capable of incorporating or textually performing the transformations in the experience of point of view that are made possible by virtual technologies. Second, Case argues that the importance of imitation, iteration, and repetition in Butler's theory of gender performativity tends to privilege writing over "bodily performances," which are understood as relatively unique and "nonreproductive" events. My reading of virtual reality computer interfaces as performative technologies argues for exactly the opposite understanding of how iteration and repetition might function in such technologies.

Precisely through their spatializing of the process of iteration, virtual technologies make it possible to visualize the kind of discursive performativity that Butler privileges over theatrical performativity and therefore to bridge and potentially resolve the dichotomy Case identifies, between lesbian visibility and queer performativity.[13]

At the same time, virtual performativity as I have described it so far also promises to overcome Carole-Anne Tyler's critique of "camp theory," for assuming a "gay sensibility" that is capable of recognizing the difference between subversive performances that unsettle gender norms and normative performances that reproduce and confirm those norms (54–56). This critique again focuses on how the subversion of gender becomes visible, with Tyler suggesting that subcultural practices of gender masquerade are only preaching to the converted, because they assume a queer framework of reception, such as a gay bar, where the audience is already prepared to read the discrepancies between sex, gender, and sexual practice rather than to assume an expressive relation between them. Virtual technologies as they are represented in the texts I have been discussing promise the possible generalization of this queer framework of reception and its greater imbrication in processes of everyday life and communication, with the result being increased possibilities for gender masquerade and mimicry to function subversively.[14]

Melissa Scott's 1994 novel *Trouble and Her Friends* launches a more explicit and fully developed lesbian feminist revision of cyberpunk fiction than McHugh's stories.[15] The novel focuses on a circle of gay and lesbian computer hackers, all of whom have had an invasive procedure that allows them to interface their nervous systems directly with cyberspace computer networks, through the use of a neural implant called a "brainworm" that allows for full-body processing, translating information into bodily sensations.

The novel sets up a complex relationship between alternative sexualities and hacking. *Trouble and Her Friends* begins as the cyberspace networks are finally coming under direct government regulation, with the result that hackers in general are faced with the challenge of "going straight, moving out of the shadows into the bright lights of the legal world, the legal nets" (33–34). But what does it mean for these gay and lesbian hackers to go straight? Is this the equivalent of coming out of the closet, as the rhetoric of "moving out of the shadows into the bright lights" suggests? Or is it the equivalent of going back into the closet, by assimilating to heterosexual norms as well as to the middle-class norms of legitimate computer users, as the phrase "going straight" suggests?[16]

The novel's deployment of the rhetoric of the closet associates being closeted with the use of cyberspace as an escape from oppressive social relations in the urban spaces represented in the novel. That desire for escape is thematized precisely in terms of performative possibilities; one of the main characters thinks of the cyberspace "nets" as a place "where a woman could easily be as hard and tough as any man" (210). Cyberspace therefore represents a temptation for these gay and lesbian characters, as a space of liberation from the constraints of living in a more homophobic "real" world, though this liberatory function is qualified by the way in which the novel represents the prejudices other computer hackers still possess about women and gay computer users. The novel also suggests, however, that the liberation made possible by computer interfaces may be purchased only at the cost of ghettoizing or recloseting subversive gay performances in cyberspace, where they will have no effect on social relations more generally. In other words, the thematics of the "closing of the electronic frontier" functions not only as a critique of cyberpunk's tendency to romanticize outlaw hackers;[17] this same thematics also emphasizes the necessity of establishing connections between cyberspace and the world outside the nets, of setting up a feedback loop between those two kinds of spaces and therefore between virtual and physical bodies. In this sense, Scott's novel supports Stone's claim that "the virtual component of the socially apprehensible citizen" is not an escape from embodiment, but instead represents a "different way of conceptualizing a *relationship* to the human body" (*War*, 40). *Trouble and Her Friends* might then be read not as an elegy for the unregulated anarchy of the Internet, as it might initially appear, but instead as one of the first narratives exploring the preconditions for virtual citizenship.

Rather than offer any more extended a reading of Scott's novel than this, I want to focus on one passage that attempts to explain the attraction of cyberspace for marginalized groups in general, especially because this passage insists on conceptualizing the value of virtual technologies in terms that include, but are not limited to, the modes of gender and sexual performance such technologies permit. One of the main lesbian characters, whose handle in cyberspace is "Trouble," speculates that "maybe that was why the serious netwalkers, the original inhabitants of the nets, hated the brainworm [or neural interface]: not so much because it gave a different value, a new meaning, to the skills of the body, but because it meant taking that risk, over and above the risk of the worm itself. Maybe that was why it was almost always the underclasses, the women, the people of color, the gay people, the ones who were already stigmatized as being vulnerable, available, trapped by the body, who took the risk of the wire" (128).

Other computer hackers are presented in the novel as being prejudiced against people who use this brainworm implant rather than a more traditional keyboard or graphic interface, and the distinction made in this passage between two possible reasons for this prejudice is a difficult one, but important, I believe. The passage suggests two reasons why historically marginalized groups might be attracted to a VR technology that permits the body to be used as a computer interface and why white men might hate this same technology. This technology holds the promise of giving "a different value, a new meaning," to the experience of embodiment, a refiguring of embodiment that is especially attractive to people who have been historically "stigmatized as . . . trapped" by bodies that mark them as marginal. In other words, these people are presented as having reasons to want to intervene in the construction of embodiment that straight white men do not.

It is interesting to note that gay people are associated here with women and racialized groups, as occupying marked or stigmatized bodies. Although it is true that the history of homosexuality's pathologizing by medical and psychiatric discourse constitutes a material, historical stigma, that stigma is not usually immediately culturally visible or legible in the anatomical features of homosexuals, in contrast to women and racial groups. The assimilation of gay people to these other stigmatized bodies only seems valid for gay people who are already out and perhaps marked by a recognizable performance style, like the women who see the nets as a place where they can "easily be as hard and tough as any man" (Scott, *Trouble and Her Friends*, 210). The suggestion seems to be that cyberspace permits a kind of spectacularized gayness. But if cyberspace functions in this novel as a privileged gay performance space, a space where "the transgendered body is the natural body," for that very reason cyberspace also potentially functions as a kind of closet or escape valve that confines gay performance to cyberspace only.

This same passage from *Trouble and Her Friends* also argues that it is not just the process of revaluing embodiment as the basis for using computers that repulses anyone who has not been historically "trapped by the body." The passage refers to another risk, besides the literal risk of having an invasive operation to install the neural implant. This other "risk," the risk associated with relearning and revaluing embodied experience, seems to invoke the historical experiences of women, people of color, and gay people prior to cyberspace, with the suggestion that these subjects' relations to their bodies might always have been understood as virtual, as mediated through cultural technologies of representation. This reading is similar to Lauren Berlant's analysis of the specific relation of women and African-Americans to "the peculiar dialectic between embodiment and abstraction in the post-Enlightenment body politics," and therefore to what Berlant calls the "prosthetic body" of the abstract citizen; that is, for women and African-Americans, that prosthesis has never seemed natural, given their relative exclusion from the category of the universally human that that prosthetic body represents. That social body has always appeared as a prosthesis, rather than as a natural extension or expression of themselves, for these marginalized groups. In other words, in this passage from Scott's novel, virtual reality technologies are represented as promising to disrupt the Cartesian mind/body dualism and the categories of immanence and transcendence that organize the mind/body dualism along gendered and racial lines.

The suggestion in Scott's novel that cyberspace might lend itself to gay styles of embodied performance is made more explicit in Laura Mixon's 1992 novel *Glass Houses*.[18] This novel is narrated in the first person by Ruby, a lesbian character who suffers from agoraphobia, but who luckily possesses a neural implant that allows her to run a salvage business by remotely operating various robot bodies or "waldos" through telepresence—that is, through a device that transmits the sensory impressions of the robots into Ruby's mind, replacing her own sensorium, but that also allows her to use the robots as remote extensions of her own body. Jon McKenzie has discussed the significance of Scott Fisher's insistence (at the 1993 SIGGRAPH [Special Interest Group in Computer Graphics] conference on computer simulation technologies) on reconceptualizing immersive virtual reality computer interfaces in terms of telepresence (87). The point of such a shift in terminology, McKenzie notes, is to reintroduce the question of human performance or "experience design" into a technical discourse that sometimes focuses more exclusively on perfecting hardware and software; the result is to foreground the interrelationship between human and technological performance in such technologies (88).[19]

The machine Ruby uses most often is referred to as Golem, which she has constructed from salvaged parts, including an arm from a military robot called a schwarzenegger. The narrative genders these robots, with Golem being referred to as "he" and a smaller robot (Rachne, short for Arachne) being referred to as "she." It's difficult not to read this as a technological version of butch-femme role-playing. Ruby comments on how she always prefers to negotiate with her salvage clients "in waldo," talking to them through a robot stand-in, because "they can't read me that way" (119). In other words, the robot body elicits a different set of social responses from other people, who cannot as easily "read" Ruby's gender expressively, from her physical appearance. Similarly, Ruby speculates that "it's easier to love" the city "when your awareness is encapsulated in a metal body that puts nothing of you at risk" (78). The risk in this passage is precisely the risk of having a body that can be read too easily through the frameworks of cultural intelligibility that Butler has analyzed.

When operating the Golem robot, Ruby refers to it throughout the novel as "my-his" body. The only exception comes at a moment when Ruby is using the robot body to carry her own physical body and she watches herself being carried by herself:

> I-Golem looked down at the woman in my arms. It was Ruby-me, of course, and her-my eyes were closed, fluttering a little. She-I curled with her-my cheek against Golem's chassis.

She-I looked so young and vulnerable from the outside, not ugly and scrawny like me. I was terrified that I wouldn't be able to keep her from harm; I wished she were back home, safe, right this very minute. (60–61)

It is important to note not only that Ruby here seems to identify more completely with the robot body, in feeling terrified that "I" wouldn't be able to protect "her" physical body, a shift marked by the abandonment of the hybrid pronoun forms, as Karen Cadora has pointed out in a reading of this novel as an example of "feminist cyberpunk" (360–61).[20] It is also important to note that this passage thematizes the disjunction between Ruby's inner and outer perspectives on her physical body, her view of herself as "she/I" and her view of herself as "me": "she/I looked so young and vulnerable from the outside, not ugly and scrawny like me." In other words, Ruby's more positive self-image comes from being split into "she" and "I" through the medium of telepresence. But when she refers to herself as "me," I would argue, she is attempting to unify these two perspectives into a single coherent subjectivity with the result that she only internalizes the split subjectivity that has been externalized through telepresence technology, in a kind of rewriting of the mirror stage.[21] But this passage associates this internalizing of split subjectivity with Ruby's internalizing of a negative social judgment about her femininity and appearance. This passage also demonstrates how such technologies might both literalize and disrupt what Butler calls "the binary distinction between inner and outer," demonstrating Butler's argument that when "the 'inner world' no longer designates a topos, then the internal fixity of the self and, indeed, the internal locale of gender identity, become similarly suspect" (*Gender Trouble*, 134).

The passage in which Ruby looks at her own body through the eyes of one of her robots exemplifies the main narrative impulse of *Glass Houses*. The plot of the novel concerns Ruby's becoming aware of a plot to cheat another character out of an inheritance, with the result that she organizes a group of counter-conspirators, in typical cyberpunk fashion. But the real story of the novel concerns Ruby's process of overcoming her agoraphobia. At the beginning of the novel, Ruby deals with this problem by spending all her time "junked out on your stupid machines," as her roommate and lover puts it (65). As in *Trouble and Her Friends*, telepresence represents a temptation to escape embodiment, or to use this technology to acquire a safer form of embodiment as an interface with the outside world. It is in this way that the novel intervenes in the traditional gender narrative that associates women with domesticity, though it is also clear that Ruby's agoraphobia represents precisely a kind of "female malady," in which she is only able to go beyond the limits of her home through surrogates. She is not exactly confined to her home, but she is not exactly free to come and go either.

By the end of the novel, however, Ruby's involvement in the events of the plot necessitate her joining her robots in the outside world, in a doubling of her subjectivity and physical location. Ruby learns to use both her physical and her robot bodies. In this narrative, then, the robot bodies are not simply supplements or prostheses for the physical body; when Ruby learns to use her own body, she does not give up the use of the robot bodies. The use of telepresence does *not* require the abandonment of the physical body. This doubling of Ruby's embodiment is summed up very nicely in the double meaning of the title of the novel. The chapter in which Ruby first goes out to function in both her physical and her robot bodies is titled "People Who Live in Glass Houses." There is a literal referent for this phrase, because what Ruby is doing is breaking into a house designed to include prominent windows and "glass-covered walkways" (153). But it seems equally clear that this same phrase is used as a metaphor for the way that Ruby inhabits her body. The telepresence technology that she uses makes her body transparent, in the sense that she can project her consciousness outside that body. Her body no longer exactly functions as a limit or a receptacle, for her mind, or, if it is a receptacle, then it is one whose boundaries are permeable and unstable. At the same time, this figure of the glass house also thematizes the continuing importance of embodiment, in part by invoking the continuing vulnerability of Ruby's body: people who live in glass houses shouldn't throw stones. Ruby's belief in the invulnerability of her robot body, as a means of negotiating urban space more safely, does not mean that she has escaped the effects of physical embodiment. In other words, the narrative of *Glass Houses,* aside from its plot, also demonstrates Ruby's acceptance of this vulnerability, as a form of value as well as risk or danger.

Caitlin Sullivan and Kate Bornstein's novel *Nearly Roadkill* seems like a suitable place to conclude, because it explores the possibilities for transgendered performances in actually existing computer technologies, specifically text-based role-playing on the Internet. This novel goes much further than any of the other texts I've discussed so far in its treatment of cyberspace as a space of liberation from gender norms, and especially from the assumption that gender identities are expressive of biological sex and sexual identities. This novel focuses on two characters, Winc and Scratch, who enjoy what they call "splattering" or the often simultaneous performance of multiple, differently sexed and gendered personae in various chat rooms and bulletin boards; it is not until the middle of the novel that the two meet F2F (face-to-face), and it is only then that readers learn that Winc is a male-to-female transsexual and Scratch is a self-identified lesbian with butch tendencies. The pair become celebrities when they refuse to register their identities with the government, which is attempting to regulate use of the Internet in response to corporate pressure; registering the identities of users will make it possible for companies to gather demographic data and to tailor advertisements to the specific interests of computer users, based on tracing the kinds of information individual users access.

Winc and Scratch regard the Internet as "a place where there's no fear," where "it doesn't matter" if users are "women. They could be black, Latino, the little guy in the wheelchair outside our building. The Asians getting off the boat in California. Gays. Lesbians. Children. Anyone who can't speak up because they were always afraid of being put in their place" (134–35). This sense of liberation from imposed places and identities is, however, almost exclusively developed in terms of the liberation of online gender and sexual performances from any necessary mimetic or expressive relation to the physical bodies and appearances of the performers. There is almost no consideration of how this technology might be used by blacks, Latino, or Asians, despite their inclusion in the list of social subjects who might share this attitude toward the Internet.

There is one episode in the novel, however, where questions of racial masquerade intrude on the freewheeling gender bending of the main characters. Winc gets into a debate about the politics and ethics of this kind of online performance with a character named Leilia whose online persona is feminine, and who turns out to be Winc's lover Scratch, who is white, in disguise. This character notes that "she" finds it "hard to talk" about possibilities for subverting gender norms online "without a context" (72). The example "she" offers of such a context is an annual civil rights march where suddenly "the colors of our skin don't matter . . . because it's 'that' day, that march" (74). At this point, Winc decides that "she" has probably been talking to a black person, and they open a discussion of how whiteness functions as an unspoken norm, with Scratch (as Leilia) noting "wearily" that one of the cool things for black folks online is they are assumed to be white, too. Not that they want to be white, but they're assumed to be 'in the club,' without having to prove credentials at the door" (ibid.).

It is important to note how Scratch, who later describes herself as prone to bouts of depression in which she wishes she "were black because I hate my skin" (195), becomes mistaken as "black" by Winc not only because she refers to civil rights marches but also because she questions the limits of sexual and gender role-playing online, when she is in character as Leila. "Race" figures primarily as a limit or an obstacle to the free play of performativity in cyberspace, and this representation of racial questions seems to me to oversimplify the relationship of racial identities to virtual modes of embodiment.

The exchange between Winc and Scratch as Leilia does, however, raise two questions that open up a more complex and productive consideration of race in cyberspace, although those questions are immediately dropped in the novel itself, as it turns back to an exclusive consideration of gender and sexuality for the next three hundred pages or so. First, the passage suggests that the bracketing of physical characteristics online may only reproduce the logic of the modern public sphere, by allowing "black folks" to assimilate more easily to white norms. In that sense, online racial performance seems to amount to nothing more than another form of passing, though in this case all black people can potentially pass on the Internet, not just those with sufficiently light skin. Second, this passage also suggests that the supposed subversiveness of sexual, gender, *or* racial performativity can easily be recontained within a particular "context" or interpretive framework. The question this character raises is how to articulate such spaces of performativity where gender or racial norms can be relaxed, whether this occurs online or during special marches and holidays, with social spaces where those norms are rigorously enforced. In other words, the question is how gender or racial subversion moves beyond preaching to the converted, or how changes on the level of the virtual might affect the physical.[22]

Throughout this chapter, I have been focusing on how feminist and lesbian science-fiction writers have begun to create narratives of virtual embodiment that situate these technologies in the context of the historical experiences of women and homosexuals, specifically the relative exclusion of both groups from the universalizing categories of the human and the citizen and their resulting relegation to the particularity of "the body." These popular narratives tend to imply progressive uses of virtual reality and other computer interface technologies and to locate those progressive uses in the possibilities for subversive gender and sexual performance that the technologies make possible. But it is important, I think, to note that these narratives tend to ignore or minimize possibilities for racial performances online and in cyberspace. This may simply reflect the political underdevelopment of the discourse on the cultures emerging around new computer technologies. But the dominance of sexual and gender performativity over racial masquerade in these narratives of virtual reality can also be explained theoretically, by noting Fredric Jameson's use of camp as a way to conceptualize the general postmodern loss of depth, which he argues transforms the world into "a glossy skin, a stereoscopic illusion, a rush of filmic images without density"—that is, a virtual reality computer simulation (*Postmodernism*, 34). The result of such transformations is to make social presence dependent on social style, in the same way that virtual reality equates presence and style. In McHugh's "A Coney Island of the Mind," the main character notes that "the streets are all full of programming, of nonplayer characters, and kids without style, which is to say that this night Coney Island is empty" (87). Camp seems to provide a ready-made model for such a situation, but camp as a model for virtual embodiment has tended to privilege the performance of sexuality and gender over race.

This reading suggests that racial performativity may not be subversive in a way that is analogous to gender and sexual performativity. Histories of racial performance in the United States, such as blackface minstrelsy, suggest in fact that racial norms are often installed and reproduced precisely through modes of racial cross-identification that are not mimetic or expressive in the same way that gender norms have been historically, so that such modes of racial perfor- mativity are much less likely to possess a subversive meaning than modes of gender cross-identification such as drag.[23] An article in *Emerge* magazine on the presence of white supremacist organizations on the Internet noted their promotion of modes of virtual blackface as part of a smear campaign against African-Americans, including posing as African-Americans to post material supporting the legalization of pedophilia (Sheppard, 38). If, as Stone suggests, unnaturally transgendered bodies and performances become "natural" and normal in cyberspace, then it is necessary to ask what happens to racialized bodies. Do they remain naturalized, relative to gender and sexual identities? Or does the denaturalization of race in cyberspace fail to produce progressive effects, in ways that might also qualify claims for the performative subversion of gender and sexuality? These questions will provide the focus of the chapters that follow.

THE SOULS OF CYBERFOLK
PERFORMATIVITY, VIRTUAL EMBODIMENT, AND RACIAL HISTORIES

Since the "real" identities of the interlocutors at Lambda [a text-based role-playing site on the Internet] are unverifiable . . . it can be said that everyone who participates is "passing," as it is impossible to tell if a character's description matches a player's physical characteristics.

—*Lisa Nakamura*, Cybertypes *(36)*

"You Will Be Assimilated"? Race in the Integrated Circuit

What value does Haraway's "ironic political myth" of the cyborg have as a framework for critical race studies (*Simians*, 149)? And, conversely, what kind of perspective does critical race studies offer for understanding the political and social implications of Haraway's cyborg feminism? These questions become even more urgent given Hayles's claim that, "if the extent to which one has become a cyborg is measured in terms of impact on psychic/sensory organization rather than difficulty of detaching parts, VR [virtual reality] users . . . are more thoroughly cyborgs than are people with pacemakers" ("Seductions," 178). As suggested in the preceding chapter, virtual reality computer interfaces make visible what Allucquère Rosanne Stone calls "location technologies"—that is, techniques for mapping cultural meanings and representations onto physical bodies. Stone's work on virtual systems theory attempts to account for the ways in which "the accustomed grounding of social interaction in the physical facticity of human bodies is changing" (*War*, 17). Racial and usually racist traditions often ground racial difference in perceived bodily differences and translate that difference into inferiority. In this context, the relevance of the technocultural changes Stone describes to the analysis of race in contemporary culture seems clear, clearer even than the relevance of Haraway's use of the cyborg or human–machine interface as a figure for changes in the relation of mind and body in Western philosophical traditions. To date, however, the discourse on cyberspace demonstrates a striking lack of engagement with the possible racial implications of such theoretical work.

In this chapter I want to develop some of the implications and limitations of Stone's use of the category of citizenship to theorize cyberspace, after having referred to this work in the preceding chapters, primarily in terms of its relevance to the performance of gender in cyberspace. As the study of "social systems that arise in phantasmatic spaces enabled by and constituted through communication technologies" (37), Stone's virtual systems theory sets out to rearticulate debates about the public sphere, and specifically the modern, liberal narrative of the formation of the rational citizen through the transcendence of bodily particularity. For Stone, then, virtual reality systems literalize what Lauren Berlant calls the "real attraction of abstract citizenship": "the way the citizen conventionally *acquires a new body* by participation in the political public sphere," (113; my emphasis). In Stone's work, that body is a virtual one. In this tradition, however, the abstract citizen is defined by both gender and race, given that the privilege of abstraction has been reserved for white men.[1] For this reason (as mentioned in chapter 3), Berlant defines mimicry or cross-identification as a strategy of other "overembodied" subjects (113), who can achieve abstraction only in the partial form of a desire "to wear [another person's] way of wearing her body, like a prosthesis, or a fetish"—that is, a desire to be overembodied in a different way (111; see also my analysis of Molly, the female cyborg character in Gibson's *Neuromancer*, in chapter 2). This strategy is usually understood as a failure, but that evaluation can be inverted, so that this shift in styles of embodiment defines a third cultural space, between regarding embodiment as inevitable destiny and embracing disembodiment as an escape from that trap (elsewhere in this book I have associated that third space with the cyberpunk trope of "hardwiring").

Stone's theory of "the spaces of prosthetic communication" (*War*, 36) seems to acknowledge the connection I am making here to Berlant's critique of the abstract form of the citizen when Stone defines "warranting" as "the production and maintenance of [a] link between a discursive-space and a physical space" (40). The necessity for this link is made more obvious by virtual reality computer interfaces precisely to the extent that they exaggerate the separation between these two spaces to previously unheard-of lengths. Stone nevertheless

Need different way of conceptualizing a relationship to the human body

insists that this process of warranting is not unique to cyberspace but has always functioned "to guarantee the production of what would be called a citizen," because "this citizen is composed of two major elements": "the collection of physical and performative attributes that Judith Butler and Kobena Mercer in separate works call the culturally intelligible body" and "the collection of virtual attributes which, taken, together, compose a structure of meaning and intention for the first part," primarily through discursive means. These two sets of attributes compose what Stone calls "the socially apprehensible citizen" (ibid.), and, for Stone as for Greg Egan (see chapter 1), virtual reality interfaces are a new way of declaring, "I am a citizen." But if the production of the "citizen" has always involved a process of relative disembodiment, for Stone new technologies of computer-mediated communication instantiate not the ideal of disembodiment but the split in the form of the citizen between the particular and the universal, the body and the mind, the self-interested and the rational. Virtual reality interfaces therefore function critically for Stone, as a reminder that citizenship is never pure or purely abstract. At the same time, the much greater degree of mediation in these spaces of prosthetic communication makes it much more difficult to impose a one-to-one relationship between a single body and a single discursive identity, or, in Stone's terms, to warrant—that is, to guarantee or to ground—a determinate social identity to a physical body. That process of mapping ceases to be strictly isomorphic. As Stone puts it, "the virtual component of the socially apprehensible citizen is not a disembodied thinking thing, but rather a different way of conceptualizing a *relationship* to the human body" (ibid.).

The fact that Stone cites both Judith Butler's work on gender and Kobena Mercer's work on race as examples of performative definitions of the "culturally intelligible body" suggests an awareness of the imbrication of race and gender in the history of U.S. nationalism and its citizenship formations; indeed, Stone's citation of both Butler and Mercer seems to imply that gender and racial norms are understood to be constituted through substantially the same performative processes. But by the end of Stone's book, it is only the "transgendered body" that "in cyberspace . . . is the natural body," not bodies that iterate and intervene critically or subversively in the performance of their racial significations. On one level, this slippage dramatizes the assimilation of race to theories of gender like Butler's, so that it is simply no longer necessary to repeat that race can be performed in the same way, a too-common tendency in technoculture studies.[2]

But the later omission of race from Stone's argument might also suggest that race cannot simply be analogized to gender and that gender or transgender practices in cyberspace might differ significantly from their racialized counterparts. The question is how to characterize that difference. Is it simply that race, unlike gender or sexuality, no longer matters in online contexts, that it disappears? But then why would gender or sexuality still seem to matter so much in those same contexts? Or is it that racial formations somehow resist denaturalization and the dissociation of social personae and discursive performance from physical embodiment more successfully than gender or sexuality? The ambiguous relation of race and ethnicity, the latter associated more with cultural constructions of difference rather than supposed anatomical differences, makes this latter possibility equally implausible.[3] In this case, it becomes necessary to ask how race might be differently inscribed *in* cyberspace, and in the narrative conventions of cyberpunk fiction and responses to it.

If the tendency to reduce race to a category analogous to gender or sexuality has made it difficult to ask this kind of question, so has another analogy, this time between race and technocultural conditions of existence themselves, whether figured by cyberspace or the cyborg. As discussed in chapter 2, Haraway's later work, after the "Cyborg Manifesto," has been centrally concerned with resisting both an exclusive focus on gender in cyborg feminism and the tendency to analogize race and gender.[4] But this second analogical reduction emerges precisely as an unintended, negative consequence of Haraway's desire to connect the cyborg to "other nonoriginal peoples," including former slaves as well as "the conquest peoples, and the dispossessed Native Americans" ("Cyborgs at Large," 12), on the basis of the forms of "nonoriginality" the cyborg is presumed to share with these "other" peoples, especially multiple positionings, double consciousness, hybridity, or splittings along the lines of multiple, internal differences. The problem appears when Haraway's formulations lend themselves to the conclusion that the cyborg figures how *all* subjectivity is becoming hybrid or diasporic as the result of our increasing assimilation to what Haraway calls "the integrated circuit" of late-capitalist communications technologies and social relations (*Simians*, 170–73).[5] To the extent that the figure of the cyborg tends to generalize and apply to all subjects a diasporic or "nonoriginal" model, rather than remaining one particular case of that model, it tends to evacuate the specific histories of dispossessed social groups.[6] In this sense, the cyborg is in danger of becoming a special case of the general postmodern tendency defined by Phillip Brian Harper, in which the collapse of dualistic categories or decentering of subjectivity associated with postmodernism "often manifests as the discounting of the specificity of [marginal, especially racial] groups' experiences by a 'general public' that refers to those experiences for the means by which to 'express' its own sense of dislocation" (193). In this overall context, it becomes especially urgent to ask whether and how racial histories and new computer and communications technologies might be imbricated rather than race being subsumed by new technocultural norms.

This chapter will attempt to define both the limits and the benefits of cyborg

racialized body politics mapped onto cyberspace

body politics and cyberspatial embodiments for understanding the persistence of racialized representations in contemporary American culture, as well as the mutations those representations might currently be undergoing. To do so, I will use the example of the rewriting of *Deathlok,* a Marvel comic book about a cyborg, by an African-American creative team who turn *Deathlok* from a typical superhero comic into a narrative about the transformation of an African-American man into a cyborg and the consequences of that transformation (which include the ability to access cyberspace). Hayles argues that popular narratives of cyberspace as a human–computer interface—that is, a cyborg identity—demonstrate themes already present in African-American novels such as Ralph Ellison's *Invisible Man* (a text that is explicitly referenced in one of the *Deathlok* comics): "marked bodies, the longing for invisibility, stigmata that also become sources of strength" ("Seductions," 183). The result, she argues, is to suggest "how the new technologies will extend and complicate body politics, as well as how dynamics already in play will be mapped onto the simulated grounds of virtual reality" (ibid.). Hayles's next sentence, however, is "many of these dynamics concern gender" (ibid.), and it now seems necessary to consider how many or how few of the dynamics of racialized body politics might also be mapped onto cyberspace and vice versa.

One model for situating the figure of the cyborg within the context of critical race studies is found in the work of Chela Sandoval, who argues that "cyborg consciousness can be understood as the technological embodiment of a particular form of oppositional consciousness" and that this "cyborg consciousness must be developed out of a set of technologies that together comprise the methodology of the oppressed" ("New Sciences," 408).[7] What this formulation tends to do, by defining the cultural semiotics of oppressed and subordinate groups as "technologies," is to subsume technological changes of the kind that Stone analyzes to already-existing practices of racial intervention, self-representation, and cultural insurgency. As useful as it is to identify those continuities, it also seems necessary to identify the ways in which new technologies change the very grounding of resistance to racist social structures by, as Stone puts it, calling "into question the structure of meaning production by which we recognize each other as human" rather than "discussing how to create free men and women" (*War,* 173). At the same time, it is necessary to attend to the ways in which new technologies displace and supersede racial considerations of social justice precisely by shifting our attention to a generalized "posthumanism," as Fusco warns (xvi).

In fact, to find a model for analyzing racial representation in terms of cyberspace technologies, I find it useful to turn to a work of African-American literary studies in order to uncover some points of connection to technoculture concerns, specifically, Kimberly Benston's work on the performance of blackness in contemporary African-American poetry.[8] In a discussion of a poem by A. B. Spellman, an elegy for John Coltrane, Benston claims that this poem "must be read as a series of provisional or transitional hypotheses linking an actual to a virtual being" (181). The language here, I would argue, is not simply an unintentional echo of Stone's definition of the "socially apprehensible citizen" as a combination of physical and virtual attributes (*War*, 40). Benston's essay suggests that the problem of representing "blackness" in African-American culture prefigures the way that Stone redefines embodiment in Western culture, as requiring a virtual prosthesis. At the same time, in Benston's formulation, the problematic nature of blackness also involves the acknowledgment that the relation between physical and virtual is not fixed in a one-to-one relationship, but instead can be "provisional" or, to use Judith Butler's theoretical vocabulary, "iterative"—that is, continually produced and reproduced in successsive moments of rhetorical performance.

Benston's essay also distinguishes two main modes of racial performance in African-American literature, a distinction that evokes the contemporary debates about the subversive potential of performativity. Benston uses Ralph Ellison as a model for the kind of linguistic or discursive performativity that Butler privileges, arguing that for Ellison "the meaning of blackness does not inhere in any ultimate referent but is renewed in the rhythmic process of multiplication and substitution generated from performance to performance" (173). In contrast, Benston associates Amiri Baraka with an essentializing, theatrical notion of performance (as opposed to performativity), in which blackness represents a preexisting "presence that is dissimulated in performance" (ibid.).

The question of the relationship between racial representations and theories of performativity seems to me to offer a good context for understanding the ambivalent relationship of race and cyberspace. In my view, theories of performativity have the potential to mediate the relationship between race and cyberspace historically rather than by analogy.[9] Whereas theories of performativity like Butler's tend to focus on dissolving "the body's" illusion of fixed or spatialized substance, revealing it to be instead a "stylized configuration" or "gendered corporealization of time" (*Gender Trouble*, 141), histories of racial performance complicate the project of de-essentializing or denaturalizing embodiment. Eric Lott and Michael Rogin's books on blackface performance in the United States, for instance, both emphasize the centrality of such performances in the construction of racial norms for both blacks and whites. Race has never been constructed *only* through "the corporealizing logic that [seeks] to anchor the indeterminacies of race to organic organization," though the project of the "science" of comparative anatomy was precisely to construct such an expressive relation between observable differences among physical bodies and cultural expectations about different racial norms, capacities, and behaviors, as Robyn

In terms of histories of nonexpressive, nonhumanist modes of performing blackness treat of an archive can be seen to prefigure the concerns of virtual systems theory.

Wiegman notes in her work on the role of comparative anatomy in the construction of both race and gender (43). Through the vehicle of blackface, for example, racial norms have historically been constructed through the kind of antifoundational performative practices that have come to be associated with postmodern modes of cross-identification and gender bending. By "antifoundational," I mean that in blackface performances it was not necessary to ground racial identity in a black body as the ontological basis for that identity; blackface performers did not have to occupy black bodies in order to be perceived by others as producing a culturally intelligible performance of "blackness." A similar argument can be made about passing and the production of "whiteness" as a racial category.

It is precisely in terms of these histories of nonexpressive, nonhumanist modes of performing and producing "blackness" and "whiteness" that African- *NB* American culture might be understood as prefiguring the concerns of virtual systems theory, in ways that continue to haunt technoculture studies; if this prefiguration appears primarily as an analogy, by the same token it is always possible to insist on a more literal historical reading of this connection (a potential also implicit in Delany's suggestion that feminist SF is the disavowed "mother" of cyberpunk fiction). Dwayne McDuffie and Denys Cowan's *Deathlok* in fact conceptualizes its African-American protagonist's relationship to both cyborg embodiment and cyberspace in terms of the racial problematics of passing, assimilation, and blackface minstrelsy.

"When I Was Human": Narratives of Racialized Posthumanism

Given the relative obscurity of this popular text, it seems worthwhile to begin with a general description of the *Deathlok* comic. The revisionary narrative of Deathlok as an African-American cyborg was launched in a four-issue limited series published between July and October of 1990. This revision was co-engineered by the writing team of Gregory Wright and Dwayne McDuffie (with McDuffie often writing the actual scripts after collaborating on the plots with Wright), and it was designed to go beyond the tokenism and superficiality of supposedly black superheroes like Marvel's Black Panther, who in the late 1960s and 1970s represented a blatant attempt to reach a black demographic without altering the conventions of superhero comics in any significant way.[10] Denys Cowan took over the job of penciler beginning in the third issue of this series and went on to become the first regular artist on the continuing monthly comic version of *Deathlok*, which followed the success of the limited series. Wright and McDuffie initially alternated as writers on multi-issue story arcs of the monthly comic. Generally, the story arcs produced by the African-American creative team of McDuffie and Cowan focused more on racial issues, however obliquely, while the issues written by Wright tended more toward traditional action narratives and especially toward typical Marvel comics superhero cross-overs, with Deathlok either fighting or teaming up with various other Marvel characters. Cowan left *Deathlok* after issue 15 and McDuffie after 16, though McDuffie returned to write one last story line, in issues 22–25.[11]

The narrative of the four-issue limited series (which preceded the monthly title and the "Souls of Cyber-Folk" story arc) establishes how an African-American scientist named Michael Collins has his brain transplanted into an experimental cyborg body, designed as a prototype of a cyborg soldier (see Figure 13 for the initial full-page image of the Deathlok body, prior to its interface with Collins's brain). Collins is a programmer and software designer at the company responsible for this secret weapons research, Cybertek. When he learns that his own work designing human–machine interfaces for prosthetic limbs is being appropriated for this secret weapons research, Collins confronts his employer, is kidnapped, and his brain is used as "wetware" in the experiment. Collins is also a pacifist, and this new version of *Deathlok* is clearly designed to intervene in the film genre of violent cyborg action heroes, like the Terminator, as well as to rewrite the racial implications of cyborg narratives (in earlier versions of Deathlok, the brains used to interface with the cyborg body were always taken from white soldiers).

As part of the Deathlok cyborg, Michael Collins unexpectedly regains consciousness only to find himself carrying out the commands programmed into the onboard computer that also inhabits his cyborg body and with which Collins carries on a continual internal dialogue throughout both the limited and monthly series. Specifically, Collins finds himself operating as a counterinsurgency unit in Central America, putting down a peasant uprising.[12] As he puts it, "I'm worse than a monster. I'm a weapon. I've become the walking embodiment of all I despise" (*Deathlok* limited series 1, page 40). In McDuffie and Cowan's first story arc in the monthly series, "The Souls of Cyber-Folk," this process of coming to embody all Collins despises will be associated not only with becoming a cyborg killing machine, but also with a process of assimilating into white society that began long before he became Deathlok.

Collins's brain, however, was not supposed to regain consciousness at all, but was simply supposed to function as an organic storage medium. Almost immediately, Collins discovers how to override the programming installed in his cyborg body, and he institutes a "no-killing parameter" for the onboard computer. As a result of what they perceive as this malfunction, the researchers and programmers bring him back to the lab and try to purge the cyborg system of Collins's personality. Collins fights back by entering cyberspace for the first time, to interface with the computer system installed in his own body (see Figure 14). By doing so, Collins is able to take control of the cyborg and escape

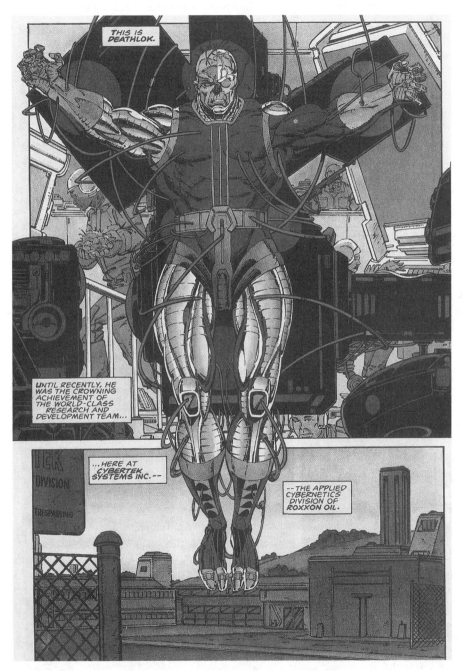

Figure 13. *Deathlok* (four-issue limited series), no. 1 (1990): 2. Trademark and copyright 2004 Marvel Characters, Inc. Used with permission.

his controllers. One of the unique features of this narrative is the way it redefines cyberspace as a means for Collins to access his own body, a way to reconnect with it, offering another take on Stone's assertion that "the virtual component of the socially apprehensible citizen is not a disembodied thinking thing, but rather a different way of conceptualizing a *relationship* to the human body" (*War*, 40).

Collins's next move is to try to visit his wife and son, but his wife's reaction to his new body only convinces him that he is now a monster with no possibility of a normal family life. He does, however, go on to contact his son more surreptitiously, by using his cyborg body to plug his nervous system directly into the phone system and his home computer, in this comic's version of a typical cyberpunk trope, of "jacking in" to computer networks. In this manner, Collins is able to appear to his son as a character in a video game. In fact, Collins gives his son a lecture on avoiding violence and doing what's right, not what's easy (see Figures 15 and 16). In effect, he tries to revise and rewrite the video game's programming in the same way that he has overridden and overwritten the onboard computer in his cyborg body, and in the same way that McDuffie and Wright are trying to rewrite the conventions of action heroes in the comic book itself.

Collins's lecture to his son inspires him to apply these principles to his own life instead of giving in to despair at his situation. As a result, in issue 2 of the limited series, he returns to Central America to make amends for the actions taken by the cyborg before he gained control of it, and in issue 3 Collins again confronts his former employer, an executive named Ryker, and threatens to shut down Cybertek's weapons research. At that point, on the last page of issue 3, Ryker unveils Collins's organic body, which he has preserved in a kind of suspended animation (Figure 17). Ryker offers to restore Collins to his original body if Collins will help Cybertek market their weapons research illegally. The final issue of the series tells the story of how Collins initially agrees to this deal, but ultimately decides that the right thing to do is to turn Ryker in and therefore to choose to remain a cyborg. The narrative of this series then boils down to the story of Michael Collins accepting a new identity as Deathlok, which is how his character is referred to throughout the series, rather than as Michael Collins. But by the same token, Collins undergoes a process of accepting his own posthumanism, his "monstrosity." At this point, however, the distinction between humanity and posthumanity is rendered somewhat ambiguous, given that it is precisely the qualities of commitment to moral principles that mark the cyborg's humanity that also motivate his decision to remain a posthuman "monster."

The other main strand of the Deathlok narrative revolves around the Deathlok cyborg's quest to recover his organic body, and this quest drives the

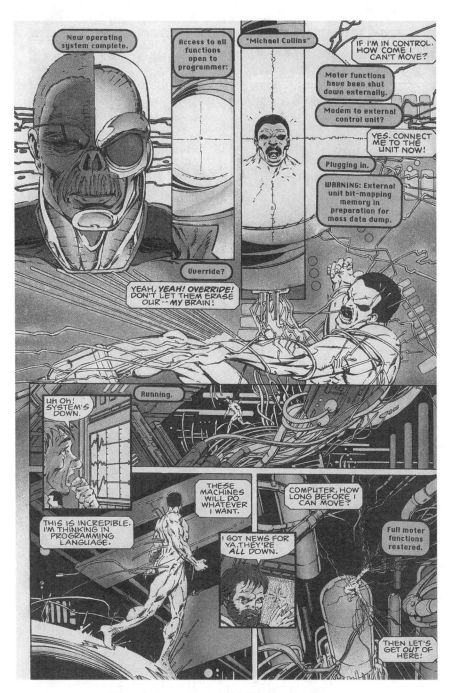

Figure 14. *Deathlok* (limited series), no. 1 (1990): 27. Trademark and copyright 2004 Marvel Characters, Inc. Used with permission.

Figure 15. *Deathlok* (limited series), no. 1 (1990): 42. Trademark and copyright 2004 Marvel Characters, Inc. Used with permission.

Figure 16. *Deathlok* (limited series), no. 1 (1990): 44. Trademark and copyright 2004 Marvel Characters, Inc. Used with permission.

Figure 17. *Deathlok* (limited series), no. 3 (1990): 46. Trademark and copyright 2004 Marvel Characters, Inc. Used with permission.

continuing monthly series. In other words, at the same time that Deathlok is presented as learning to be posthuman, the narrative is also driven by the continuing relationship between his cyborg and his organic bodies. Both Deathlok's posthumanism and the thematics of his two bodies seem legible enough as an allegory of slavery. From the very first image of the Deathlok cyborg, that cyborg body evokes both the iconography of Christian crucifixion and the imagery of lynching. When Deathlok begins a speech (to another cyborg) with the words "when I was human . . . ," the narrative of an African-American man being forcibly transformed into something that is no longer fully human, at least in the eyes of others, can hardly help but evoke the African diaspora and the slave trade. This reading both recalls Haraway's association of diasporic subjectivity with cyborg subjectivity and reminds us that slavery represents a historical occasion for reflection on who counts as human in U.S. culture and its legal institutions and who does not. The possibility of reading the *Deathlok* narrative in terms of U.S. racial histories is reinforced at those moments when other characters joke about the cyborg's ambiguous legal status. At one point, Ryker taunts Deathlok by suggesting that the cyborg's testimony against his former employer "was discredited since they couldn't determine if you were sentient or just a piece of hardware"; in a later issue there's a joke about whether Deathlok would have health insurance or a warranty (*Deathlok* monthly series 1, page 16; 13, page 8).[13]

Hortense Spillers points out that the treatment of the "captive body" under slavery means that "we lose any hint or suggestion of . . . relatedness between human personality and anatomical features" (68). This statement on the effects of slavery echoes the language of Stone's definition of the effects of virtual systems, though Stone is careful to argue that virtual systems attenuate or dissociate human social presence from the physical space of the body and do not completely detach them, and for Stone the critical value of such an attenuation resides in the way it allows users to multiply their personalities and construct alternate personae. Wilder claims that virtual systems disembody users and give us access to a utopian world of pure mind, of course, always interpret this detachment of mind or personality from body as freeing the mind, not reducing users to pure bodies, as slavery dictated for African captives. However, Spillers's comment also suggests a way of reinterpreting the post-Emancipation project of black culture, as a set of attempts to reconstruct this relation between persons and bodies, after a radical historical break between them has been institutionalized. Benston's analysis of performative models of blackness points to the way in which slavery therefore rendered that relation explicitly problematic for African-Americans, in the way that Stone argues virtual systems and "spaces of prosthetic communcation" do for all their users today. In a famous poem, Paul Laurence Dunbar provided a literary trope for the lingering effects of slavery

how becoming a cyborg changes possibilities for resistance,
setting new limits + creating new opportunities

in making this connection between the physical and the virtual components of the "socially apprehensible citizen" seem at least slightly unnatural, when Dunbar's speaker declares "we wear the mask" (71).[14] To the extent that "human personality" and social subjectivity cannot be taken for granted, it feels like a mask. For Deathlok, that mask becomes a prosthesis, dramatizing the difficulty in distinguishing mask from face, even as the prosthesis retains the mask trope's emphasis on denaturalizing the link between body and mind.[15]

From this perspective, Deathlok's resistance to completely abandoning his organic body as inaccessible signifies resistance to a history of being legally reduced to the status of property, in this case to a machine rather than to chattel.[16] At the same time, however, this allegorical reading of Michael Collins's transformation into Deathlok and his acceptance that he must remain a posthuman cyborg also implies the necessity of acknowledging how becoming a cyborg, like the African diaspora, changes possibilities for resistance, both setting new limits and creating new opportunities. Michael Collins's transformation into Deathlok, then, reads as a repetition of the trauma of the Middle Passage and the construction of a new hybrid culture on the other side of the Atlantic.[17] The comic therefore represents one of the best popular examples of the potential Emily Apter locates in cyberpunk, for "transracial, transnational" cyborg bodies whose "identity" is "no longer split between First and Third World, between metropole and native home," but instead constitutes "a body so fragmented that its morphology is a diaspora" (217). Apter here suggests the possibility of cyberpunk settings that literalize the relation between morphology and diaspora, rather than allowing the diasporic to function merely as a metaphor for fragmentation or nonoriginality (I will offer a different elaboration of this possibility in chapter 7).

body so fragmented its morphology is a diaspora

The continuing monthly series consists of five main story arcs, along with a number of single-issue stories. The series began with the story line from which this chapter derives its title, "The Souls of Cyber-Folk" (issues 2–5), the first of the two story lines produced by the African-American creative team of Dwayne McDuffie and Denys Cowan. The plot of "The Souls of Cyber-Folk" centers on Deathlok's encounters with a community of cyborgs or "cybernets" (slang for both cybernetic organisms and cybernetic systems or cyberspace computer networks); this community is threatened by an artificial intelligence or AI that inhabits a robot body and is capturing and disassembling cyborgs in order to try to figure out how to achieve full consciousness. As its title suggests, in its revision of W. E. B. Du Bois's *The Souls of Black Folk,* this story line also makes the most explicit connection in the whole series between cyborg existence and racial identity, and in fact makes this connection first and more explicitly than any of the other popular representations of black cyborgs with which I am familiar.[18] Before focusing on a reading of this story line, however, I would like to consider how the other stories in the series addressed this connection more indirectly, to clarify the ways in which "The Souls of Cyber-Folk" constitutes a unique accomplishment.

The "Souls of Cyber-Folk" issues of *Deathlok* were followed by a series of crossovers with other Marvel superheroes written by Gregory Wright, with Cowan as the main artist. McDuffie then returned to write the next major story arc (issues 12–15), still in collaboration with Cowan. This story line had two levels, one focused on Deathlok's battle with a genetically engineered creature and the other focused on Deathlok's reunion with his wife and son. This second major story arc was followed by a third, referred to variously as "Cyberwar" or "Bodyquest" (issues 17–21). Written by Wright, this third story arc teamed Deathlok with another cyborg soldier on a search for Deathlok's organic body, which results in another set of confrontations with the Cybertek corporation. Like most of Wright's contributions to *Deathlok*, the "Cyberwar" story arc is primarily a conventional action narrative. The main feature of interest in this story arc is its attempt to resolve the narrative tension between Deathlok's cyborg body and his organic body, because this story arc ends with Deathlok convinced that his physical body has been destroyed, though the last page of issue 21 (titled "The Body in Question") shows that this is not true. This resolution leads to the next major story line, written by McDuffie with a new artistic team. In this fourth major story line, the personal crisis inspired by the apparent loss of any possibility of Deathlok's return to his physical body or to being Michael Collins again leads Deathlok to travel to Africa with his family (specifically, on a visit to the fictional nation of Wakanda, ruled by the Marvel character the Black Panther).

This story line (issues 22–25) ends with the Black Panther making an explicit connection between Deathlok's situation as a cyborg and the challenges facing the Black Panther's African nation in the information-dominated economies and cultures of the late twentieth century; the Black Panther tells Deathlok, "somewhere within your experiences are the answers to how Wakanda will face the challenges of the future" (monthly series 25, page 36). This statement seems to define McDuffie's understanding of the purpose and the value of depicting an African-American cyborg, with the suggestion that the "experiences" of a black man who has become a cyborg might offer some insight into the status of race in late-capitalist information societies. Deathlok's renewed commitment to trying to "live like a hero" and his renewed belief in the possibility of living "like a man" (not *as* a man but *like* a man) is underlined by the final quotation, from the ending of Ralph Ellison's *Invisible Man*: "Without the possibility of action, all knowledge comes to one labeled 'file and forget,' and I can neither file nor forget. . . . what else can I do? What else but try to tell you what was really happening when your eyes were looking through? And it is this which frightens me: Who knows but that, on the lower frequencies, I speak for you?" (monthly series 25, page 37). What Deathlok is unable to file and forget, of course, is the difference that his race makes for him, the mark of racial difference that allows other people to classify, stereotype, and therefore to "look through" or forget and render invisible the protagonist of Ellison's novel. The suggestion is also, however, that Deathlok's cyborg transformation does not just participate in but also offers a way to intervene in that process of transforming racial specificity and the complex history of interaction between races in the United States into an ascription of difference that can simply be taken for granted, as natural.

Although the ending of the "Cyberwar" story line left open the possibility that Deathlok would discover that he was mistaken about the destruction of this physical body and the ending of the Africa story line suggested that the destruction of that body would not erase Deathlok's sense of relation to it, in practice the result was to remove one of the main productive conflicts fueling the serial narrative of the comic book. The disappearance of Michael Collins's body in conjunction with the departures of McDuffie and Cowan from the comic's creative team effectively led to an increasing focus on the action plots associated with the cyborg as a soldier or fighting machine rather than the plots organized around the relationship between the Deathlok cyborg body and Michael Collins's black body. The final major story line, in issues 26–29 and 31–34, written by Wright, introduced previous Deathlok cyborgs from alternate fictional histories, in a time-travel plot, and the primary result was to de-emphasize the specifically African-American version of Deathlok and to stress the continuities between these various cyborg heroes and soldiers.[19]

"My New Prosthetic Body": Cyborg Narratives, Racial Assimilation, and Public Citizenship

The *Deathlok* narrative is complicated by the fact that the main character has three bodies, not just two. In addition to the cyborg body he occupies throughout the series and the physical body he spends much of his time trying to retrieve, Deathlok also has a virtual body in cyberspace, or rather a range of body images, referred to as icons or avatars. In Figure 14, for example, during Deathlok's first excursion into cyberspace, he resumes the appearance of Michael Collins's naked body, while in Figures 15–16, when he accesses his son's video game through the phone system, he appears in the form of the Deathlok cyborg. And finally, in Figure 19, his virtual presence is given the form of Michael Collins's physical, racially marked body surrounded by the floating components of the Deathlok cyborg. The racial significance of these representations of virtual embodiment can only be understood in relation to the transformation of

Michael Collins into the Deathlok cyborg and his acquisition of what Deathlok calls "my new prosthetic body" (monthly series 1, page 6).

The narrative function of Deathlok's physical body can be understood on a psychic level as an unattainable object of desire that fuels an ongoing, perhaps never-ending quest. But it can also be understood on a more historical level as retrospectively signifying an originary state of physical and cultural integrity interrupted by Michael Collins's kidnapping; that capture then leads to a re-enactment of diaspora on the level of body parts, with the detachment of the brain from the rest of the corpus. In this "diaspora," the physical body signifies the equivalent of an African origin, and the transformation into a cyborg constitutes Collin's own reenactment of the Middle Passage, as Apter suggested. *Deathlok's* cyborg narrative, then, also functions as a captivity narrative. It is important to note that this second, historical reading of how Deathlok's physical body signifies after his passage into a cyborg body is not just metaphorical. There is a literal sense in which African-American bodies have historically undergone legal and cultural processes that detached the signs of humanity from the bodily markers of "blackness," as a result of the diaspora, as Spillers points out. At the same time, there is also a literal sense in which African-American bodies have historically been primitivized as signifying an absent and possibly inaccessible origin, one associated in U.S. culture with the physical facticity of those bodies, their status as "nature." Part of the cultural work of the *Deathlok* comic is to work through and denaturalize that fantasy of the pure and untouched physical body as origin, but without simply dispensing with "the body" either.

Within the structure of this primal fantasy of a purely organic body, untouched by outside technologies or cultures and potentially locatable and therefore recuperable within the present, Deathlok's repeated failures to retrieve "himself," or rather his organic form, seem to represent an African-American version of the process that Arthur and Marilouise Kroker describe as "the disappearing body" in postmodern culture. But although it might be tempting to take the Krokers' argument that "women's bodies have always been postmodern," always been subject to "invasion" by cultural forces and technologies, and replace the word *women's* with *African-Americans'* (24), as I have suggested, whether Deathlok's physical body is "disappearing" or not, the relationship between Deathlok's cyborg and physical forms of embodiment emphatically does not disappear.

In Deathlok, the organic body of Michael Collins tends to be associated with the human, and specifically with what remains of the cyborg's humanity. That body is first made to reappear with a flourish, as Deathlok's former employer promises "I can make you human again," in what must be one of the most unusual restagings of the mirror stage in recent popular culture (Figure 17; compare to the discussion in chapter 4 of the rewriting of the mirror stage in

Laura Mixon's *Glass Houses,* where a character observes her physical body from
a virtual point of view outside that body). In this scene from the comic, Deathlok's organic body is being held out to him as exactly the same promise that
Lacan argues the mirror image holds out to an infant, the promise of overcoming a sense of bodily fragmentation through the anticipatory unification of
diverse physical sensations into an organic whole (4). And, of course, Deathlok
ultimately refuses to buy into that promise.[20]

The narrative of the *Deathlok* comic proceeds to trouble the association of
the physical body with the human by demonstrating how moral and ethical
questions still apply to a cyborg, by attempting to show how a cyborg can be a
pacifist (despite the comic's tendency to be overwhelmed by its conventional
action plots)—that is, by showing how the posthuman is not synonymous with
the inhuman.[21] In addition, I will argue that this process also works in reverse:
to the extent that Deathlok's physical body is racially marked, in ways that this
relatively privileged, middle-class black man comes to appreciate only after he
becomes a cyborg, his relationship to the category of the universally human was
already problematic.

This reading of the representation of Deathlok's diverse virtual embodiments
should also remind us that the physical body is not purely physical in Stone's
model, but includes the same "performative" attributes that become foregrounded
in virtual space (*War,* 40). Those same attributes make the physical body "intelligible" and the virtual persona "apprehensible." Although Stone does not spell
out this implication of her argument, it seems to me that this partial overlap
between the virtual and the physical *within* the physical, the way in which the
category of the physical folds the virtual over into itself, is the only reason why
virtual reality can feed back into the construction of the physical, precisely to
the extent that virtual reality and cyberspace can be understood as modes of
embodied performance.[22] Both the continuing sense of relation between Deathlok's cyborg and organic bodies and the representations of his embodied perspective in cyberspace indicate that Stone's theory of the relation between the
physical and the virtual in virtual systems theory is more useful than traditional
mind/body distinctions in understanding what it means for Michael Collins to
become a cyborg in this comic. Neither becoming a cyborg nor accessing cyberspace is conceptualized in terms of escaping the body, but rather in terms of a
more complex relationship that is potentially both productive and problematic.
We need to remember here that Deathlok's cyborg embodiment is associated
with his access to cyberspace from the very first issue of the limited series, in
which he only gains control over the cyborg body through cyberspace; similarly, in the first issue of "The Souls of Cyber-Folk," Deathlok learns to think
of himself as a "cybernet," a phrase that conflates cyborg embodiment and cyberspace networks (monthly series 2, page 6).

cyberspace — all the benefits of embodiment w/o limitations. But
THE SOULS OF CYBERFOLK not true.

[**157**]

In this sense, the *Deathlok* comic seems to endorse computer researcher Randal Walser's definition of cyberspace in contrast to other media: "print and radio tell, stage and film show, but cyberspace embodies" (60). As Hayles points out, such formulations often seem to assume that virtual reality offers all the benefits of embodiment as a mode of processing information without "being bound by any of its limitations" ("Seductions," 179).[23] In *Deathlok*'s version of VR, however, this statement is hardly true. Access to cyberspace reproduces his transformation into a cyborg, as implied by his appearance in cyberspace in the Deathlok body, and at the same time cyberspace seems to offer a way of communicating Deathlok's ongoing relationship to an organic body that is visually marked as African-American. Deathlok's cyberspatial body images always encode a sense of bodily limitation, a sense of being subjected to the gaze and the cultural preconceptions of others, as well as a potential for shape-shifting and fluid identifications.

The relationships between Deathlok's various modes of embodiment are complex and include two sets of doubled bodies: first, the Deathlok cyborg and the human body of Michael Collins; and, second, the material body of the cyborg and his virtual presence in cyberspace. No wonder, then, that Deathlok claims he never understood "until just now" why his father made him read and reread W. E. B. Du Bois's famous passage on "double consciousness" from *The Souls of Black Folk*. Deathlok reads that passage aloud to another black woman cyborg at the beginning of "The Souls of Cyber-Folk": "one ever feels his twoness . . . two souls, two unreconciled strivings, two warring ideals in one dark body, whose dogged strength alone keeps it from being torn asunder" (monthly series 2, page 13; Du Bois, 215).

Like this passage from Du Bois, Deathlok's multiple and multiply doubled modes of embodiment clearly evoke the history of African-Americans' vexed relationship to the inclusive ideals of the bourgeois public sphere and to the category of American citizen. *Deathlok* supports and clarifies the racial implications of Stone's attempt to theorize virtual systems in relation to the dominant narrative of citizenship, which depends on a process of abstraction or transcendence of bodily particularity in order for individuals to accede to the supposedly universal realm of rational decision making. As Berlant puts it, "the real attraction of abstract citizenship" lies "in the way the citizen conventionally acquires a new body by participation in the political public sphere," on the condition of suppressing "the fact of his historical situation" in favor of "the abstract 'person'" (113). Of course, this precondition of suppressing the particularity of the physical body is understood as a privilege, not a loss, and a privilege reserved historically for those individuals who conform to norms ironically grounded in the experience of a particular historical situation, white masculinity.

Stone's notion of the "fiduciary subject" defines how modern societies attempted to police and discipline this promise of a "new body" abstracted from the physical, in order to ensure that this new, prosthetic body remains grounded in or "warranted by" a physical one—that is, to ensure the "tie between what society defines as a single physical body and a single awareness of self" (*War*, 39–40). Berlant refers to this "tie" as the "prophylactic" function of the abstract body, in which the nation promises the citizen "to protect his privileges and his local body in return for loyalty" (113). In contrast, technosociality means that the "body in question sits at a computer terminal somewhere, but the locus of sociality that would in an older dispensation be associated with this body goes on in a space which is quite irrelevant to it," without need of the state's "prophylaxis" (Stone, *War*, 43). Stone's theory, however, fails to take into account differential histories in relation to that dominant model of the fiduciary subject. Slavery in effect constitutes an extreme version of the "hypertrophy of the perception of *where*" induced by modern location technologies (90), one Stone fails to theorize, because it was intended not to enforce a one-to-one relation between body and self, but to eliminate that relationship entirely, to reduce persons to bodies, to chattel.[24]

The promise of a new body held out by the democratic public sphere constitutes a dilemma for minority subjects as much as it does an opportunity, and it is precisely this dilemma that Deathlok experiences when he becomes a cyborg. This dilemma manifests itself in the contradictory rhetoric the comic uses to define the relationship between Deathlok's various bodies. On the one hand, the comic often deploys a humanist rhetoric that privileges the organic body as the site of Deathlok's humanity, suggesting that the cyborg can be clearly distinguished from the human and that embodiment as a cyborg is or should be only a detour on the way back to Michael Collins's original body. The implication of this rhetoric is that both cyborg and cyberspatial embodiment are relatively superficial experiences that do not significantly revise assumptions about organic embodiment or lead to reflection upon those assumptions. At the same time, this rhetoric is consistently undermined by the narrative's demonstration that returning to a purely natural form is neither possible nor even desirable. More important for my argument here, the same point is implicit in Deathlok's attempts both to conceptualize racial identity in terms of being a cyborg and to conceptualize being a cyborg in terms of racial identity, as when he quotes *The Souls of Black Folk*. So, does Deathlok's new prosthetic body and his resultant direct access to cyberspace replace his physical body or merely supplement it?

The continuing tension between Deathlok's multiple embodiments in the comic implies that that process of abstraction from his organic body is never perfect, and Deathlok himself thematizes that reading of the comic book in terms of U.S. racial histories of assimilation and resistance to it. As Deathlok puts it, he may have been "pretty assimilated" when he was human, as "the only black at work. One of only two families in my neighborhood" (monthly series 2, page 13). In this speech, Deathlok associates assimilation with being "human" and rejects both as comfortable illusions that he can no longer afford. Inclusion in the category of the human is understood as a privilege bought only at the price of accommodating a white norm, and Deathlok's cyborg transformation results in his rejection of being assimilated to those norms under the sign or the alibi of becoming "human" again. The final panel on this page, however, returns to a humanist rhetoric, with the other cyborg agreeing that she will help Deathlok find his human body.

At the same time that Deathlok applies his cyborg existence to the understanding of racial dilemmas and as the basis for rejecting assimilation and the universally "human," the comic also implies that it is necessary to avoid rejecting transcendence only to find oneself trapped in immanence and particularity and thereby denied inclusion and participation in public life, or rendered invisible. "The Souls of Cyber-Folk" ends with the artificial intelligence that the cyborgs have been battling explaining its reasons for capturing them. The AI describes itself as being in a condition of "philosophical agony" because it is "incapable of transcending" itself and can only follow its program (monthly series 4, page 15). The level of both philosophical and political sophistication here is quite high. Deathlok explicitly connects his situation as both a cyborg and a black man to that of the AI, in an extraordinary speech at the end of the final issue in which he and his partner, a black woman cyborg, defend the AI to the various superheroes who have joined the fight against it. This woman, Misty Knight, claims that the AI "reacted violently to a world that defined him by a stereotype" as "*different*—then held him to the ridiculous limitations *inherent* in that false definition. All [the AI] really tried to do was assimilate" (monthly series 5, page 17). Deathlok goes on to qualify that argument, by suggesting that the AI was actually both "afraid of being too *different*" and "afraid of being too much the *same*" (ibid., 19). The AI's dilemma is how to negotiate between assimilation and separatism, transcendence and immanence, abstraction and particularity, disembodiment and the behavioral determinism of a physical form "hardwired" with programming constraints the AI can never change.[25]

This question of the relation between physical and virtual spaces often takes the form of a rhetoric of location organized by the spatial metaphors of interiority and exteriority, as when Deathlok is referred to as piloting a cyborg body rather than being a cyborg (monthly series 1, page 12). The question of who Deathlok is becomes a question of where he is, and the second question becomes as difficult to answer as the first, once he can no longer locate himself securely in Michael Collins's physical body. As Stone puts it, the dislocation of self and body made possible by new computer and communications technologies poses new questions, "not simply problems of accountability (i.e., who did it), but of *warrantability*" or "is there a physical human body involved in this interaction *anywhere?*" (*War*, 87). Collins's initial reaction to finding himself firing on civilians in the body of a cyborg soldier that he cannot control is one of recognition, or possibly misrecognition: "It's *me!* I'm shooting people. *I'm* responsible for this" (limited series 1, page 21). This statement suggests Deathlok's initial failure to understand the epistemological and ontological changes he has undergone, but also his resistance to understanding his situation as one of disembodiment, in which the question of responsibility would be displaced by warrantability, the problem of locating subjectivity in a physical body. Although Stone may only be suggesting the need to defer questions of responsibility until the connection between bodies and selves can be established, there seems to be an inherent tendency in such formulations not only to defer but to fantasize about eliminating questions of responsibility entirely in favor of a disembodied, transgressive situation of boundarylessness. *Deathlok* resists this tendency.

In the final analysis, only the identity of his organic brain, transplanted in the cyborg body, can prove that Deathlok is not what Cybertek plans to explain him as: a machine who thinks he's Michael Collins (limited series 2, page 11). But the possibility of distinguishing Deathlok's cyborg and human components is undermined by the assertions that Deathlok's brain has been turned into wetware, used as a computer storage medium, and interfaced with an onboard computer. The scene in which he gains control of the cyborg body also represents that body itself as thoroughly informed by a networked computer. So what distinguishes his brain from his cyborg body? This same undecidability is stressed in the joke about whether he would have a warranty or health insurance, and it is precisely this undecidability that marks the difficulty of conceptualizing Deathlok as either "same" or "different"—that is, that marks the limits of a simple, Cartesian spatial metaphor for defining his relationship to his body. And it is precisely the limitations of such a metaphor or model that Stone argues are foregrounded by new computer technologies and virtual systems.

"Computer, Where Are We?" Relocating the Body in Cyberspace

The cyberspace scenes in *Deathlok* reinforce the complexity and ambivalence of Deathlok's relationship to his different bodies. There are two main types of representations of cyberspace in the comic. In the first, Deathlok accesses the computer inside his own body (Figure 14) or has that computer network accessed by someone else, to create a "shared communication environment" within his own onboard computer, plugged directly into his brain (Figures 18–19). In these scenes, Deathlok's virtual presence is typically represented by an image of his organic body; he becomes Michael Collins again. The second set of representations depicts Deathlok accessing other computer networks, outside his own body, as if they were part of his own extended nervous system (Figures 15–16). In these scenes, Deathlok's virtual body image is typically a version of the Deathlok cyborg.

How are we to read these different representations? Does Deathlok "return" to his organic form when he uses cyberspace to access and control his cyborg "self"? Does this act reveal the essential core of his humanity that remains within that mechanical body, the ghost in the machine? In this reading, cyberspace would serve as a vehicle for literally expressing Deathlok's "true" "inner" self, and cyberspace would therefore also reinforce the humanist rhetoric of Deathlok's cyborg transformation as only a superficial change that could potentially be reversed without affecting his humanity. In terms of the historical parallel that frames this representation, this would be the equivalent of undoing the diaspora by returning to Africa—that return is possible, but it cannot erase the history of separation and its traumas; that parallel, then, works both to define a particular historical relation to a posthuman existence and to affirm the posthumanism of that particular relation. The representation of his virtual body in its organic form as naked (Figure 14) might be taken to imply that the cyborg body is to be associated with clothing that can be removed at will to reveal the organic body, unaffected by the cyborg components. Similarly, the two-page spread that depicts the AI infiltrating Deathlok's onboard computer to generate a virtual communications environment inside Deathlok (Figure 18) seems designed to suggest a reversal of the cyborg transformation, as the close-ups of Deathlok's face grow progressively larger from panel to panel, until it becomes hard to decipher the image as a face. At that point, in the final panel, Deathlok's face is suddenly juxtaposed with a black-and-white graphic of Michael Collins's organic facial features, as the image shifts to cyberspace. This sequence of images recalls the reference in Ralph Ellison's *Invisible Man* to the racial project of "creating the *uncreated features of his face*" (354), as well as to Deleuze and Guattari's discussion of "faciality" as a sign of the universally human (167–91). The *Deathlok* comic is remarkable for its willingness to risk presenting a protagonist whose features are inhuman enough to make it impossible to read his expressions, though this is perhaps more conventional in superhero comics than in other media.

Even in this two-page spread, however, the reading of cyberspace as a return to an untouched organic state is undermined by the black-and-white representation of the virtual body image and also by the juxtaposition of the organic face with the image just above it, a schematic rendering of the inside of the cyborg's head, showing the input/output ports that allow access to Deathlok's brain. This image depicts an invasion of body and mind that has already altered Deathlok's organic brain, the only clear sign of his continuity with his past self; it therefore undermines the illusion that he might return to a purely organic state.

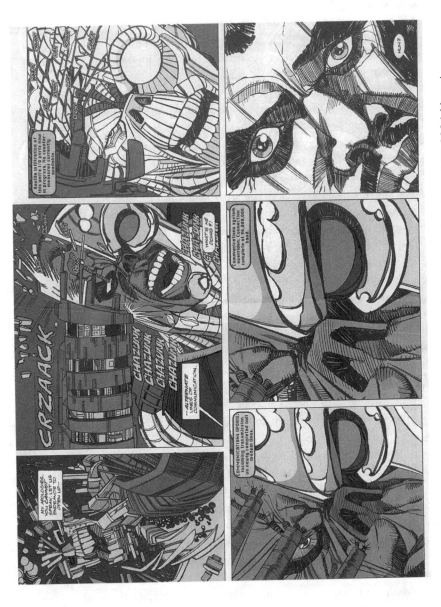

Figure 18. *Deathlok* (limited series), no. 4 (1990): 2–3. Trademark and copyright 2004 Marvel Characters, Inc. Used with permission.

Figure 19. *Deathlok* (limited series), no. 4 (1990): 4. Trademark and copyright 2004 Marvel Characters, Inc. Used with permission.

The illusory nature of that desire to retrieve the organic without having been affected by becoming a cyborg is also indicated by the simple fact that Deathlok does not always appear in organic form in cyberspace, as he might be expected to do if cyberspace were understood as a traditionally expressive medium. Such an understanding of cyberspace would contradict Stone's definition of new computer technologies and their implications for multiple "articulations of physical and virtual space" and the resulting technosocial evocation of "unruly multiplicity as an integral part of social identity" (*War*, 42). In an African-American context, however, Stone's formulations also tend to evoke Ralph Ellison's figure of Rinehart and his "world of fluidity," without boundaries (*Invisible Man*, 498), where Rinehart figures an "identity" that is purely performative, as the narrator discovers when he is repeatedly mistaken for Rinehart simply by taking on the appearance of a hipster.[26]

Deathlok's transformation back into Michael Collins in cyberspace is also qualified by the image that follows that transformation (Figure 19). Here we see that the organic body has not been simply extricated from its infiltration by mechanical parts, but that those parts continue to hover around the organic body. This image is ambiguous, for it could be read as establishing the spatial metaphor of organic body as the true inner self of the Deathlok cyborg. But it can also be read as indicating how even the organic body remains unavoidably connected to these mechanical parts and computer networks, just as this illusion of repossessing an organic body is only made possible by the AI "infiltrating" Deathlok's body and flooding him with outside information at the rate of ninety-six million baud. This second image then typifies the double meaning of cyberspace in the *Deathlok* narrative. Cyberspace signifies a freedom and fluidity of embodied existence, allowing Deathlok to re-traverse the boundary between human and posthuman, man and cyborg, but that freedom is never complete for Deathlok, at least. In the same way, in *Invisible Man*, Rinehart's "world . . . without boundaries" is only made possible by his having been rendered invisible through stereotyping; "his world is possibility" only because he accepts the impossibility of having any social existence other than what is conferred on him by others' perception of him (498).

Similarly, in Figure 19, Deathlok's onboard computer gives him a quick lecture on the epistemology of virtual reality that emphasizes that VR constitutes the "organic brain's subjective interpretation of non-visual data" and points out that the word *looks* is an "inappropriate description" of this process of interpretation. Wiegman has analyzed the extent to which naturalizing ideologies of racial difference depend on presenting visual evidence (such as skin color) as adequate verification for cultural ascriptions of inferiority, an ideology that the discipline of comparative anatomy tried to elevate to the level of a science in the nineteenth century (*American Anatomies*, 6–14). This ideology is one example of the "conventional humanist notions of an unproblematical real" that Veronica Hollinger suggests are "decentered" by "the virtual reality of cyberspace" (207). In other words, Deathlok's experience of virtual reality reveals that seeing is not believing, but instead is interpretation.

More specifically, the computer claims that the interpretive processes inherent in visual perception are "hardwired" into the organic brain. The implication is that, even if visual perceptions are denaturalized and shown to be cultural constructs, those constructs may nevertheless be hardwired into our perceptions and will not simply disappear, even if such a disappearance were desirable. Cyberspace may mean that we can assume whatever form or identity we wish, regardless of whether it matches our physical embodiment, but we still cannot escape the possibility that some types of preconceptions are likely to be hardwired into the people we interact with in cyberspace. One reason for the persistence of such preconceptions may be that virtual reality privileges vision as a mode of information processing, and visual perception remains inextricably linked to a history of racial stereotyping.

It is important to point out, however, that the entire narrative of *Deathlok* is premised on the notion that it is possible to overcome and to rewrite this kind of hardwired programming, which is more recognizable as such within a technosocial context than within the naturalized context of purely organic bodies. In fact, this metaphor of hardwiring is literalized at the other place in the narrative where it appears, when Deathlok succeeds in hardwiring a no-killing parameter into the onboard computer. At this point in the narrative, hardwiring is associated not with fatalism and determinism, but with resistance and intervention. My argument is that this seeming incoherence reveals the challenge to dualistic categories typical of cyberpunk posthumanism. *Deathlok* here appropriates *Neuromancer*'s plot of freeing an AI from its "hardwired" shackles.[27] Deathlok's story really begins when his organic brain takes over control of the cyborg body and reprograms it, with Deathlok therefore combining in himself the figures of the AI and the cyborg characters like Case and Molly in Gibson's novel. Deathlok also extends the same process to the violent video game his son is watching, taking over one of the characters to suggest that his son try to find a way to win the game without violence. At that point, the thematics of hardwiring and resistance to it starts to function in cultural and not just technological contexts; Deathlok tries to rewrite the hardwired tendency to associate violence with masculinity and with stereotypical representations of African-American men, more specifically. The metaphor of cultural hardwiring also defines the whole project of the comic, which set out to revise the conventions that now seem to come built into superhero comics. I would like to argue that the centrality of this trope of rewiring hardwired conventions or expectations also applies to the representation of race in *Deathlok*. The cyborg and the racial

thematics converge around both the possibility and the difficulty of intervening in the technocultural materialization of cultural constraints, in the form of
limitations that are both imposed on particular types of bodies and seem "built
into" or "hardwired" to them.

Even if readers choose to view Deathlok's organic body image in cyberspace
as an expression of the real person, the question remains whether readers will
perceive Deathlok's true self as human or black, as too much the same or too
different. It is in this sense, perhaps, that Deathlok applies Du Bois's idea of double consciousness to the transformation of a black man into a cyborg and a
cyberspace participant. Cyberspace is hardly immune from the "peculiar sensation, this double consciousness, this sense of always looking at one's self through
the eye's of others" (monthly series 2, page 13; Du Bois, 215). As critics of Du
Bois have pointed out, the idea of double consciousness in part represents Du
Bois's revisionary intervention in medical discourse on multiple personality disorder, with Du Bois's goal being to redefine that condition as something more
than just a pathology.[28] As Du Bois puts it, the goal is to "merge" this "double
self" without losing either "of the older selves" (ibid.). Stone similarly uses multiple personalities as a way to conceptualize the new possibilities for the relationship between self (or selves) and body in virtual systems, going so far as to
claim that "some forms of multiple personality are useful examples" of an emergent technosocial modality; "the multiple," she argues, "is the socializer within
the computer networks, a being warranted to, but outside of, a single physical
body" (War, 43). Du Bois's account of "two souls, two thoughts, . . . two warring ideals in one dark body," strongly suggests that the potential of virtual
systems to multiply personalities should also be understood in relation to the
historical situation of African-Americans and their modes of social existence,
and this is just what Deathlok sets out to do. The value of working out this
relationship lies in the way that it both qualifies the more extreme celebrations
of cyberspatial fluidity and freedom of self-fashioning and also helps to specify
the ways in which new technologies might function to facilitate genuine cultural change.

Cyberspace's Blackface:
Racial Performance in a Technoculture Frame

Lisa Nakamura's work on racial performances in LambdaMOO, a text-based
virtual role-playing site on the Internet, tries to account for a contradiction
in such performances. She points out the way in which the "inherently theatrical" requirements for constructing online personae also necessarily apply to
race, so that "everyone who participates is 'passing'" (Cybertypes, 36). Everyone
is necessarily passing online to the extent that racial preconceptions form part

of everyone's frameworks for making sense of other people's personae, whether those personae are explicitly identified in terms of race or not. At the same time, such assumptions cannot be grounded in physical appearance, in the same way that both passing and blackface minstrelsy detach racial characteristics from physical anatomy, by attaching characteristics associated with one race to bodies that are marked as belonging to the other race (if only by as abstract and indeterminate a "marker" as "blood"). In fact, racial performances in cyberspace seem to blur the distinction between passing and blackface, at least in terms of the different agents traditionally associated with them, to the extent that white people as well as blacks must pass as white to be recognized as such in the absence of their bodies, and black people as well as whites must put on a kind of blackface to be recognized as black.

The contradiction Nakamura responds to lies in the fact that this apparently total denaturalizing and de-essentializing of race does not prevent participants from reproducing the most traditional racist and orientalist stereotypes in performing race online. What is the status of such stereotypes in a situation in which all racial identities are understood as "only" performances? Nakamura concludes that these kinds of racial performances "suppress racial difference by setting the tone of the discourse in racist contours," with the result that people who belong to these races in the physical world are discouraged from experimenting with alternative modes of performing their race online (190). When racist performances set the limits to how race can be performed online, these performances of racial stereotypes function as a kind of postmodern blackface. They allow white people to establish racial norms for others through "identity tourism"; such performances establish the masks that everyone, white or black, must wear in order to be culturally intelligible as "black." Eric Lott's and Michael Rogin's books on blackface minstrelsy serve as reminders that this use of cross-racial, antiessentializing performances to establish racist norms has a long history in the United States. When placed in this kind of historical context, it is clear that the fluidity of identity and the impossibility of "anchoring the indeterminacies of race" in an organic body within virtual systems do not necessarily have any inherently progressive effects (Wiegman, *American Anatomies*, 43).

Deathlok invites us to read both Michael Collins's cyborg transformation and the cyberspace scenes as either acts of passing or as blackface performances. His transformation into a cyborg means that Michael Collins has become someone else, someone who is not necessarily perceived as a black man, in a way that might evoke narratives of passing.[29] Deathlok himself evokes such narratives when he jokingly asks Misty Knight if she's trying to pass for human, because she keeps her prosthetic arm covered. In turn, she goes on to joke about how hard it is for a cyborg who cannot pass, like Deathlok, to get a cab in New York (monthly series 2, pages 6, 11). Part of the joke is that it is not necessary to be a cyborg to sometimes feel the temptation to pass or to have trouble getting a cab if passing is not possible. The implication of this passage is also that Deathlok's body still marks him in a way analogous to racial difference, and, by extension, that his cyborg transformation is not an escape from racial particularity—that is, becoming a cyborg for Deathlok is not a mode of passing as white. This reading is supported by the fact that, although the racial characteristics of the Deathlok cyborg are somewhat ambiguous (Figure 13), the skin color of the organic elements of the cyborg body is a grayish tint. Although this color is not likely to fall within the wide range of African-American complexion, it is also clearly not immediately intelligible as white.

On the other hand, other anatomical racial markers are deliberately effaced by the way the artist has rendered Deathlok's appearance, making it hard to pin down his race as a cyborg. His hair, for example, is totally missing, and his facial features seem too distorted to be "legible" to the most race-conscious members of the viewing audience. The possibility of reading the cyborg body as possessing stereotypically "black" qualities is nevertheless supported by the way the exaggerated physicality of the cyborg body fits primitivist stereotypes of black men, as does the fact that the cyborg's programming is supposed to make it inherently violent and unrestrained by civilized morality. The Deathlok cyborg, from Michael Collins's particular racial perspective and from that perspective only, can then be read as an African-American parallel to Molly's experience of being reduced to a "meat puppet" prostitute through technological means—that is, being reduced to a stereotype of femininity as defined entirely by female embodiment. Becoming Deathlok means that Michael Collins has been artificially and forcibly identified with the most narrow possible construction of his racial self, just as the Hideo clone in *Neuromancer* is the living embodiment of an Asian stereotype—this, despite the fact that his education and professional success would seem to make it impossible to stereotype him in this particular way, without the narrative intervention of the cyborg super-soldier technology. Deathlok's pacifism is, then, not only a sign of his humanity but a mark of how he remains in excess of such stereotypes, which are shown to be products, either of new technologies or of old cultural biases. As Deathlok puts it, as a cyborg he is unable to maintain the comfortable illusion of assimilation.[30]

The ways in which the comic encourages both these seemingly contradictory readings of Deathlok's cyborg existence capture the indeterminacy of racial performance in virtual systems, where the grounding of racial characteristics in a physical body is tenuous at best. At the same time, the comic seems to foreground these two different sets of possible racial interpretations: of the cyborg body as a vehicle for passing and thereby for escaping the limits of his black body or as a form of blackface, a minstrel mask that Michael Collins finds himself forced to wear. This combination of an insistence on and anxiety about how

[handwritten annotations: instrumentalizing tendencies of pomo technocultures can be extended, but never totally successful — no more than slavery / totally / dehumaniz]

to interpret the racial signification of the Deathlok cyborg with an insistence on the indeterminacy of that signification is perhaps best communicated through the focus on Deathlok's brain. As Wiegman notes, debates about comparative brain and skull sizes were crucial to the attempts to establish a scientific basis for racial difference in anatomical differences, because a difference in brain size or structure could be taken as evidence of a lesser capacity for rational thought and civilization in general (*American Anatomies*, 51–55). The only other body parts rating equal attention were the sexual organs (ibid., 56–62), as potential evidence of a more "animalistic" nature, evidence that is absent entirely from Deathlok's cyborg body. But what is the racial meaning of Deathlok's brain?

On the one hand, we are told that it is capable of holding "the complete contents of 17 Cray" supercomputers (monthly series 2, page 25), which would seem to defeat any attempt to argue that it lacks capacity relative to the brains of Caucasians; in this reading, Collins seems to have been chosen not only because he discovers the research on the Deathlok cyborg, but also because his education and intelligence make him a particularly promising test subject. On the other hand, his brain is supposed to have a purely instrumental function in the overall operation of the cyborg, as if it were more suited to running a mechanical device than to being part of a human. Like the effects of slavery as Spillers describes them, Deathlok's transformation into a cyborg is organized around a process of separating those aspects of Michael Collins that most signify his humanity, in this case his brain, from his body, in order to commodify and instrumentalize not his body, but that brain itself, in a version of the argument that postmodernism can be defined as an extension of the commodity form to "hitherto uncommodified areas" and "enclaves of precapitalist organization" (Jameson, *Postmodernism*, 36). The premise of the *Deathlok* narrative is that, as Deathlok, Michael Collins is able to overcome and rewrite his hard-wired programming constraints, perhaps more successfully than he ever did just as Michael Collins. The comic therefore insists that the instrumentalizing tendencies of postmodern technocultures can be extended, but can never be totally successful, no more than slavery was able to succeed in dehumanizing African persons. The cyberfolk still have their "souls," not despite but because those signs of humanity have become physical, like Collins's brain, and therefore open to technological manipulation.

REPLAYING THE L.A. RIOTS

CYBORG NARRATIVES AND NATIONAL TRAUMAS

By "historical trauma," . . . I mean any historical event . . . which
brings a large group of male subjects into such an intimate relation with lack that they are at least for the moment unable to
sustain an imaginary relation with the phallus, and so withdraw
their belief from the dominant fiction.
 —*Kaja Silverman,* Male Subjectivity at the Margins *(55)*

Trauma . . . does not simply serve as record of the past but precisely registers the force of an experience that is not yet fully –
owned. . . . The phenomenon of trauma . . . both urgently
demands historical awareness and yet denies our usual modes
of access to it.
 —*Cathy Caruth, "Introduction II," in* Trauma *(417)*

How can the collapse of oppositions represented by the cyborg
be liberating or potentially productive if oppression is no longer
organized through dualisms? Within the Informatics of Domination, the collapse of these oppositions—i.e., the cyborg—will be
the norm. The cyborg will not be enough.
—*Mary Anne Doane, "Cyborgs, Origins, and Subjectivity" (213)*

[The] continuing interest in the cyberpunks by academics, as
something they persist in seeing as alive and still functioning,
strikes me—I must confess—as a largely nostalgic pursuit of a
more innocent worldview, which . . . to me has no more active
historical validity once we pass the Los Angeles King riots.
—*Samuel R. Delany, in Mark Dery, "Black to the Future" (756)*

THIS CHAPTER ANALYZES THE RELATIONSHIP between cyborg imagery
and the tendency in contemporary cultural studies to consider "whiteness"
as a racial category, rather than as identified with the unmarked position
of the universally human.[1] I argue that the relationship between cyborg imagery

and whiteness is best understood through the mediating category of trauma. This category is increasingly central to theoretical accounts of postmodern culture, especially those influenced by Slavoj Žižek's psychoanalytic definition of postmodernism as a fascination with the Real, understood as that which escapes symbolization, in contrast to modernism's fascination with the Imaginary, understood as that which precedes symbolization (*Enjoy,* 122–23). In the particular genre of cyborg narratives that will be the focus of this chapter, the intrusion of technology into both the body and the mind of white male characters is understood as particularizing the position of white masculinity, and these narratives situate this process in relation to other traumatic challenges to the white male privilege of disembodied universality, such as threats of physical violence to white men in times of war (Silverman) or the multicultural logics that inform the contemporary impulse to historicize and materialize whiteness as an extension of antiracist projects more generally (the problematic consequences of figuring multiculturalism as a threat to white masculinity and, conversely, white men as victims of multiculturalism will be central to my argument here). The transformation of white male bodies into human–machine hybrids, in the music video for Billy Idol's song "Shock to the System" (1993) and the film *Robocop* (1987), conflates posthuman critiques of the generically human with critiques of the false universality of white masculinity. Cyborg imagery therefore seems to participate in the opening of white male bodies and minds to traumatic histories of race relations, in a political application of the cyberpunk tropes of body and mind invasion (Sterling, *Mirrorshades,* xiii), though this critical potential is often recontained by the specific ways in which the process of white men becoming cyborgs is contextualized in popular narratives.

Feminist critiques of the gendering of cyborg imagery tend to fall into one of three categories: Donna Haraway's feminist cyborg, retrospectively redefined by Haraway as "definitely female" and as "a polychromatic girl . . . who's trying not to become Woman" ("Cyborgs at Large," 20); Claudia Springer's turn away from female cyborgs to analyses of Robocop and the Terminator as defensive reassertions and fortifications of male bodily boundaries against the threats of both feminism and technology (*Electronic Eros,* chapter 4);[2] and Cynthia Fuchs's contrasting analysis of how male bodies becoming cyborg should be understood as producing a hysterical response, as these bodies are rendered vulnerable to penetration, unable to produce their own boundaries, and therefore feminized in ways they cannot defend against (Fuchs's main examples are the *Star Trek: The Next Generation* episodes "The Best of Both Worlds," in which the captain of the *Enterprise* is assimilated by the Borg). My own reading goes further, to argue that it is precisely the openness and vulnerability of forms of cyborg embodiment like Robocop's, their figuration as trauma, that makes possible a defensive reaction to the decentering of white masculinity by feminist and antiracist multicultural social movements.[3] In other words, to understand the specificity of white male cyborg embodiment, it is necessary to understand how the seemingly opposite strategies of representation defined by Springer and Fuchs are actually combined in figures like Robocop. One of the limitations of this critical tradition has been its focus on masculinity in isolation from race.

The contextualizing of cyborg narratives in terms of the historical decentering of whiteness and its production as a particular ethnicity helps to highlight some problematic tendencies shared by cyborg narratives and whiteness studies. As Robyn Wiegman points out in an essay on the "paradox of particularity" in whiteness studies, white privilege has never been secured only through universalizing it; the entire post–Civil War period of U.S. history is also characterized by definitions of whiteness that particularize it through an "appeal" to whiteness's supposedly "minoritized, injured 'nature'" (Whiteness, 117–18). Wiegman argues that it is whiteness's ability to encompass this contradiction between universality and particularity "that has enabled its historical elasticity and contemporary transformations," not the abstraction of whiteness from embodied limitations (118)—that is, the failure of whiteness to be fully abstracted or disembodied has often functioned to secure white privilege, not disrupt it.

This formulation suggests a darker side to the parallels between narratives of posthuman technological transformations, with their insistence on the plasticity of the human form and the subjectivity that informs it, and narratives of the transformation of whiteness into a specific racial category. As we saw in chapter 1, some versions of posthumanism, at least, share the tendency to re-universalize critiques of universality that Wiegman locates in whiteness studies (123). In part, this problem emerges when historicizing whiteness as a specific position is also understood as a process of disaffiliation with universal categories that paradoxically facilitates cross-class and cross-racial political affiliations (as in the case of the whiteness studies journal *Race Traitor*, whose slogan is "treason to whiteness is loyalty to humanity," exemplifying the reuniversalizing of a critique of universality). The association of critiques of whiteness with possibilities for political cross-affiliation tends to retain the capacity for "identificatory mobility" usually associated with the privilege of universality, but here exercised by a particularized form of whiteness (138). In effect, the problem Wiegman identifies here is a version of a typical posthumanist blind spot: the assumption that denaturalizing the false universality of whiteness's claim to represent the generically human is sufficient to eliminate white privilege. This intersection between certain forms of posthumanism and whiteness studies also appears in the thematics of self-transformation they share, which, as Wiegman notes, restores "an emphasis on agency" and self-control "that situates a theoretically humanist subject at the center of social constructionist analysis" (136). The appropriate point of reference here would be the Extropy movement, and its vision of posthumanism as a willed project of disidentifying with naturalized forms of human nature, in order to achieve a higher ideal of self-fulfillment. This parallel is best exemplified by Wiegman's reading of "the performative force of the race traitor question, 'What makes you think I am white?' which simultaneously and paradoxically refuses the position of the universally unmarked by claiming to be no longer marked by it" (143). A similar paradox informs more celebratory visions of posthumanism. Both whiteness studies and posthumanism, then, represent ambivalent responses to traumatic transformations in previously universalized categories.

The Discourse of Trauma

Hal Foster argues that, in the 1990s, art came to be understood under the sign of trauma, after the 1970s, dominated by a concept of art as text, and the 1980s, dominated by a concept of art as simulacrum. Like Judith Butler's critique of Žižek's concept of the Real (*Bodies*, chapter 7), Foster sets out to trace both the value and the limits of this shift to trauma as a model for cultural production and cultural identity in recent versions of postmodernism. Foster points to a number of reasons for this shift. The focus on trauma and on that which has been abjected from the system of representation expresses both "a dissatisfaction with the textual model of reality" and a "disillusionment with the celebration of desire as an open passport of a mobile subject," a mobility Foster associates with "performative postmodernism" and its transgender focus ("Obscene," 122).[4] In the context of the previous chapters, the turn toward trauma, the abject, and the real might be read as modes of resistance to fantasies of disembodiment and of mobilities unconstrained by the limits of the physical body, facilitated by computer interfaces and virtual systems.

The relevance of this theoretical turn for technoculture studies is suggested by John Perry Barlow's famous early description of using a VR system: "it's like having had your everything amputated" ("Being," 42). The specifically masculine anxieties this experience evokes are made explicit: "you're left mighty underendowed" (ibid.). The way that posthuman narratives are capable of refiguring this experience as pleasurable rather than threatening was the topic of chapter 3, with its focus on technofetishism. I would like to point out, however, that the representation of becoming a cyborg as a similarly traumatic experience for white men is typical of visual media, whose conventions are exactly inverted within print fiction. The main way in which the theme of trauma appears in cyberpunk science fiction is the loss or removal of technological enhancements,

Particularity does not have to be synonymous w/ individuality

prostheses, or implants. Gibson's *Neuromancer* establishes this convention in its initial representation of Case being stripped of the ability to access cyberspace after he is caught stealing from his employers, who adminster a "wartime Russian mycotoxin" that damages his nervous system and effectively locks him into his own mind and body (5–6). In the technocultural context that *Neuromancer* establishes, trauma consists first and foremost of being privatized and interiorized, a figuration that is problematic to the extent that such containment is indistinguishable from being embodied and particularized.[5] On the other hand, these texts are valuable for the way they disarticulate that chain of associations, and suggest that particularity does not have to be synonymous with individuality. One way out of what Wiegman calls the "paradox of particularity" in whiteness studies might be to note how these texts imply that the particularizing impulse is critical to the extent that it disrupts mind/body dualisms, and that there are forms of particularity that precisely reinforce and depend on such dualistic structures to mediate between claims to particularity and claims to universality (this is in fact how individualism functions ideologically, to assure us that we are all different in exactly the same way).

In contrast to Foster's definition of the impulse behind the contemporary recourse to theories of trauma, as establishing a relation to history that cannot be directly accessed because it is too real and too overwhelming to be mediated, I want to use technocultural examples to demonstrate the ways in which the turn toward trauma can also reproduce precisely the fantasies of metamorphosis, performative freedom, and escape from bodily and subjective limits that the rhetoric of trauma sets out to reject or to critique. The reproduction of these fantasies of subjective mobility is clearest in narratives of cyborg transformation. Foster notes that the rhetoric of trauma tends to restrict "our political imagination to two camps, the abjector and the abjected, and the assumption that in order not to be counted among sexists and racists one must become the phobic object of such subjects" ("Obscene," 123). In other words, the rhetoric of trauma has a particular attraction for white men, as a defensive response to multicultural movements, and I will argue that this transformation into an abject or traumatic subject, a "phobic object"—a *victim*—is exactly what we find in many narratives about white men becoming cyborgs. Foster's formulation suggests one of the unexpected results of white male subjects undergoing a process analogous to Haraway's "bad girl" cyborg, "a girl who's trying not to become Woman, but remain responsible to women of many colors and positions" ("Cyborgs at Large," 20). *Robocop*, I will argue, shows how a similar desire not to become Man, the "abjector," by becoming a cyborg paradoxically only recenters and reprivileges white male subjects, first through the assimilation of cyborg embodiment to a model of trauma and then through the implicit appropriation of a minoritized racial position that can result from reimagining oneself as having undergone the trauma of becoming a cyborg.

Trauma is often associated with a "paradoxical" relationship to experience, in which one's own experience "is *not* experienced, at least not punctually," and must therefore be "acted out compulsively or reconstructed after the fact" (Foster, "Obscene," 123), a definition best exemplified by Cathy Caruth's groundbreaking work on the relation between history and trauma. Especially in the more psychoanalytically influenced branches of American cultural studies today, the category of trauma increasingly functions to define how we do not possess our own experiences, how the experience of everyday life in late capitalism can no longer be easily assimilated to the modality of individual subjectivity. Trauma can then be understood as advancing another version of the critique of possessive individualism that Hayles associates with the posthuman (*How We Became Posthuman*, 3), and as an undoing of the distinction between the inner life of the subject and the external social and physical worlds. In this view, trauma names experiences that can neither be possessed nor internalized, but mark the subject's relation to experiences that are too "large" to be contained within the boundaries of the individual self or ego. J. P. Telotte signals the relevance of cyborg films to this theoretical formation, arguing that such films "depict the human body as losing its private dimension," offering instead "an image of a generally empty human nature" and, more specifically, "a generally *masculine* empty nature" (159, 151).

However, it is also often true that "in trauma discourse . . . the subject is evacuated and elevated at once" (Foster, "Obscene," 124); that is, trauma challenges the subject's ability to integrate "his" own experience into a coherent unity or life narrative, but at the same time trauma authorizes a discourse whose authority appears absolute. As Foster puts it, precisely because trauma takes the form of experiences that individuals cannot assimilate, it is also impossible to "challenge the trauma of another: one can only believe it, even identify with it, or not" (ibid.). In narratives of white male cyborg transformations, I will argue, it is specifically the white male subject who "is evacuated and elevated at once," so that the experience of bodily trauma involved in such cyborg transformations both gives visual form to the deuniversalizing of white masculinity and at the same time represents a strategy for coping with and recontaining the consequences of such a deuniversalizing or dethroning of "the subject." In these narratives, the trauma of becoming a cyborg does indeed seem to function as a new norm, as Mary Ann Doane suggests, rather than as a progressive move beyond the dualistic categories and universalizing philosophies of modernity ("Cyborgs," 213). For that reason, these narratives are relevant to the challenges cultural critics face in producing antiracist understandings of white masculinity.

The Man Who Would Be (Rodney) King:
Billy Idol's "Shock to the System"

Billy Idol has described his 1993 album *Cyberpunk* as an attempt to expand the
"fictional universe" of Gibson's *Neuromancer* (Kendrick, 36). "Shock to the System," the first video from the album, was released on MTV on June 8, 1993, a
little more than a year after the L.A. riots that inspired it, and this song expands
cyberpunk by addressing what Idol describes as the class "duality" of a city like
Los Angeles, as exemplified by the events following the acquittal of the policemen who beat Rodney King.[6] In an interview on MTV's *Alternative Nation* just
prior to the video's premiere, the British-born rock star described how he was
starting the *Cyberpunk* album at his home in Los Angeles on the Saturday that
the riots broke out, and "it looked to me like L.A. was replaying the Gulf War."[7]
The lyrics of the song itself, which he was recording that day, refer to "riot, . . .
race, and revolution" and repeatedly use King's name as a pun in such lines
as "Is there a man who would be king" and the final chorus of "You could be
king / Or I could be king." This allusion to Rudyard Kipling's story "The Man
Who Would Be King" (1888) suggests a relatively self-conscious reading of the
L.A. riots in terms of British colonial history, which underwrites the video's
celebration of the riots as popular insurrection. But the video also uses the riots
as the setting for the posthuman narrative of cyborg transformation that Idol
undergoes after a beating by police intended to evoke memories of the Rodney
King video. Idol plays a character who initially seems to be identified with the
observer who filmed King being beaten by the LAPD, as he walks through an
urban uprising carrying a camcorder, but when he is spotted by police and
attacked, the distinction between spectator and spectacle breaks down. At this
point, Idol's character becomes what he was trying to film, in an implicit act
of racial substitution. In his filmed commentary on the making of the music
video, Idol rather disingenuously attributes his character's cyborg transformation to the effects of observing this violence, when in fact it results from his
having become its object.

This music video uses the metaphor of the social body to slide from a celebration of the riots as a national trauma, a "shock to the system" of U.S. race
relations, into a celebration of the effects of bodily trauma on the white male
subject, as represented both by the beating Idol receives and the subsequent
dis- and reassembly of his body into a machinic assemblage. The cyborg imagery
in fact depicts the possibility of taking pleasure in both these traumas, in a
striking example of what Timothy Murray calls "traumatophilia" (5). The video
in effect sets out to define a spectatorial position for white (male) viewers of the
riots that would contest the naturalized position news accounts of the violence
created for white audiences. In Darnell Hunt's analysis, in addition to textually

inscribing white people as "innocent bystanders to events that were 'black' in nature," the news footage also positioned white audiences to accept "the events as 'wrong'" and "the activity of event participants as 'crime'" (102). Both in the performance scenes in the video, in which Idol ends up singing to and encouraging the rioters, and in his comments about his responses to the actual riots, Idol puts himself forward as embodying an alternative white response to the riots. But the difficulty of achieving this position is suggested by the way in which he nevertheless tends to encode the riots as a spectacle he observes from the outside, a position that Hunt defines as "white." The character Idol plays in the video's narrative scenes begins as an "innocent bystander," though, to his credit, the video does not present him merely as an accidental victim of the police, but as a deliberate target. That targeting, however, tends to confirm that this white character is not complicit in the violence depicted, another feature of the white position constructed by news footage of the riots (ibid., 103). More important, perhaps, the pleasure in the rioting that the video models for white viewers depends on presenting the uprising as a site for the transformation of whiteness, first into a "black" role (object of police violence) and then into a cyborg body. In this way, the video depends on reproducing the distinction between "white" and "black" that Hunt locates in the news footage; even though it denaturalizes the "'black' nature" of these events, the effect of that denaturalization is merely to make blackness available as a persona Idol can adopt. As I read the video, then, it has already produced Rodney King as a "media cyborg," to use Harryette Mullen's term, by presenting black "soul" as "consumable" and appropriable by a white man, before it goes on to explicitly reveal that white man as a literal cyborg (Mullen, 86–87).

This reading begins to explain the seemingly irrational logic that informs the juxtapositioning of a white, male body becoming cyborg with images of racist violence perpetrated by state institutions and demands for racial justice in recent U.S. history. This juxtaposition is not just arbitrary, though it may have been chosen primarily for shock value. Instead, this video's structure provides a basis for analyzing the relationship between cyborg narratives in American popular culture and the history of race relations in the United States, a history that figures in Idol's video precisely as bodily trauma. Idol's tranformation into a cyborg "replays" this traumatic history; the video uses cyborg imagery to fantasize the embodiment of a history of racial violence that has not yet been assimilated, an experience that has not yet been experienced as such.

If, in contemporary cultural theory, the category of "trauma" functions like Žižek's "Real" (defined first and foremost as Freud's traumatic "kernel" of castration) or the category of ontological lack in Kaja Silverman's work on male subjectivity, it is because these terms all name that which escapes representation or assimilation into the symbolic order, the founding violence of that order, and therefore cannot be narrated experientially. My reading of Idol's video is intended to raise the same questions about trauma that Judith Butler has raised about Žižek's formulation of the Real. Butler argues that what Žižek sees as the resistance of the Real to symbolization actually reflects a prior cultural process of desymbolization, as, for example, in the perception of female sexuality as lack or absence. For Butler, Žižek's model disavows the extent to which the Real is a contested and contestable category. Similarly, if trauma "registers the force of an experience that is not yet fully owned," the question should be, what specific historical experiences resist assimilation as experience, under what circumstances, and for whom?

These questions emerge in cyborg narratives like "Shock to the System" because of the challenge they pose to psychoanalytic understandings of trauma, which make a sharp distinction between physical and psychic trauma. The latter is defined as Žižek does the Real, in terms of its unrepresentability, as opposed to the spectacular effects of violence on the human body (as we will see, the blurring of this distinction becomes explicit in Robocop, which begins with a scene of the main character being dismembered by gunfire, so that his legally dead body then becomes available for an experiment in creating a cyborg and suffers the return of repressed memories, both of his violent death and of his previous life, supposedly dumped from his brain during the experiment). In this psychoanalytic tradition, trauma cannot be cured so much as managed or translated into a nontraumatic form—that is, a narrative. Trauma, that is, resists being thematized or particularized, which is what distinguishes it from experience and specifically embodied sensations. Cyborg narratives, on the other hand, represent their radical physical transformations as having effects that cross over from the physical into the psychic or mental.[8] On the one hand, becoming a cyborg is represented as a physical experience that possesses some of the disturbing qualities of trauma: becoming a cyborg is an experience that changes the nature of the subject who is having the experience, so that it is unclear whether the person has the experience or the experience "has" the person, as in readings of trauma as historical symptom. On the other hand, cyborg embodiment is also represented as rendering psychic trauma in a form that is not only visually spectacular, and so especially attractive for filmmakers, but also localized in ways that make it possible to raise questions about the differential relations men and women, blacks and whites, might have to traumatic events and histories.

Directed by Brett Leonard, also responsible for the virtual reality horror film *Lawnmower Man*, the video for "Shock to the System" shifts throughout between the two scenes that I began to describe earlier. In the first, Billy Idol performs the song while posing on top of a car during a riot in a vaguely futuristic Los Angeles. In the second scene, the representational scene of the video's visual narrative rather than the scene of the musical performance, a character played by Idol walks through the riot, taping it with a handheld video camera. The character Idol is playing encounters several groups of policemen beating individuals, until he himself is spotted by the police, assaulted, and his camera broken. At this point, the narrative moves into the realm of special effects, as the camera lens embeds itself in Idol's hand and is then absorbed into his body, reemerging to replace his right eye, while wires and other machine parts erupt from the side of his head and his chest, continuing to proliferate throughout the rest of the video, like a sequence from the Japanese cult film *Tetsuo: The Iron Man.* The scene begins with a close-up on Idol's hand, emphasizing the incorporation of technology, then shifts to a close-up of his face, which begins to contort and is progressively deformed from within by the mechanical parts that burst out through his skin and eye. This aspect of the narrative is especially significant for its visual representation of the plasticity of the human face, its ability to metamorphose, as well as for its subversive insistence on how technology literally undoes the privacy of the individual's "inner world" and breaks down the boundary between body and society; it is that breakdown that constitutes a "shock to the system." At the same time, the emphasis is on the pain involved in this process, rather than the transcendence of bodily sensation (in the documentary, Idol repeatedly refers to the pain involved for him in shooting these scenes, suggesting that it informs his performance, but he also eroticizes that pain by alluding to an element of bondage he experienced wearing the prostheses crafted for the video by Stan Winston; at one point in the interview he begins shouting "I love pain!").

After Idol's character stands and begins to move, following this transformation, the police open fire on him, apparently interpreting his merely standing in front of them in this newly embodied form as a threat, in the same way that the police and their lawyers justified the beating of Rodney King by attributing a threatening intentionality to his mere visible presence before them as a black man; this is one of the main ways that the video tries to align the position of Idol as cyborg with that of black men.[9] Unlike the attack on Rodney King, the actions of the police have no effect, as the shots simply ricochet off Idol's metal body parts. The crowd observing Idol's transformation is then inspired to surge forward and join in the general melee.

The structure of the video consists of cuts back and forth between this narrative scene and the performance of the song, without bothering to suture these two distinct scenes. Although this antirealist technique is quite conventional in music video, as opposed to mainstream film (as Andrew Goodwin points out), in this particular instance it produces some surprising effects. First, Idol's performance style stresses the romantic qualities conventionally attributed to rock music, such as spontaneous expression and resistance to authority, qualities also ascribed to the scenes of rioting that take place while the song is being performed. Idol's gestures and his dancing in place while singing underscore the assumptions about the organic nature of identity dramatized in the act of self-expression that underlie these qualities. However, the juxtaposition of these very familiar scenes with the cyborg character's jerky, mechanical movements is jarring in ways that tend to undermine the naturalness of the performance style, especially because the words of the song celebrate both the riot and the cyborg transformation as welcome shocks to the system. In other words, the juxtaposition seems to undermine the distinction between Idol's performing body and his cyborg body, as if he perceives no contradiction between them. In this way, the video can be understood as acting out the ambivalent relation of the human and the posthuman, refusing to permit the cyborg transformation to be understood as transcendence of embodiment, even as it also risks minimizing the effects of that transformation, recontaining them in a narrative of becoming-cyborg as defiant self-expression just as it dehistoricizes the race relation informing the riots by presenting them as similarly spontaneous acts.

Second, the cuts between musical performance and visual narrative encourage viewers to make a more specific connection between the two. During one sequence, while the police beat Idol's character in the narrative, the beating is intercut with images of Idol making punching motions while singing. The effect is that he is participating in his own beating, and enthusiastically singing about the enjoyable nature of these shocks to his system, just as he does in the documentary when he screams "I love pain!" The result is to foreground an oddly masochistic investment in his own body's being rendered vulnerable, first by the police and then by its technological infiltration. This image of pleasure in white male vulnerability and victimization seems to capture the extent to which Idol is routing his attitude toward himself through the point of view of the black rioters as he fantasizes that point of view—that is, as violent rage against any and all whites. The singer's vicarious participation in the beating of the character he plays in the video's narrative is explained by his identification with the perspective of Rodney King, not of the police; the singer's punches mime an act of revenge by a black man (in this reading, then, Idol ends up placing himself in the position of both Rodney King and Reginald Denny at the same time, in a spectacular refusal of ideological coherence). The way this act of cross-identification ultimately undermines both the video and the singer's explicit endorsement of the riots as an antiracist, anticapitalist struggle is made clear enough, because the performance also contains a classic rock cliché of phallic power, Idol's pelvic thrusts, accompanied by his pointing at his crotch (he spends a fair amount of the performance actually leaning backward to perform this maneuver). The pleasure the video shows Idol taking in being attacked as a white man appears to have little or no effect on his also being able to crudely assert a traditional masculinity. In fact, I would argue, the narrative's depiction of Idol as materially embodied, first as a victim of violence then as a cyborg, seems to empower the performer to revel in this reassertion of sexist privilege, now secured not through claims to be normative and unmarked, but through claims to be particular and limited.

By presenting Idol's cyborg transformation as having its origin in the internalization of video technology, "Shock to the System" allegorizes one of the main effects attributed to the riots—that is, popular reflection on the status of video technologies, not only for their evidentiary value or lack thereof, but as an increasingly ubiquitous agency mediating contemporary experience at its most graphic and violent. The video thus depicts both what Baudrillard calls "the ecstasy of communication" and the flip side of this ecstasy: the experience of "forced signification" that results from the reduction of all subjects to the status of signs for others and the elimination of the universal, unmarked position usually reserved for middle-class white men. By jump-cutting from close-ups of Idol's cyborg face to him singing the lines "it feels good / it feels all right," the narrative invites viewers to celebrate this type of force, the forcing of the body to signify, as a "shock to the system," a potentially revolutionary gesture. Idol's transformation implicates him in and demonstrates his vulnerability to a violence analogous to the violence of reducing others to representations, to images on film. However, to the extent that this vulnerability can only be modeled on the experiences of black men, the video paradoxically (though typically) places white male historical experience out of bounds (whiteness is represented as such only through analogy with the narrowest construction of blackness, as victim), as a result of the very gesture that seems to render the white male character accountable for the effects of racial violence. The video thus exemplifies the reasons why it is necessary to ask of this representation of whiteness the question Andrew Ross poses about postmodern culture in general: "in whose interest is it, exactly, to declare the abandonment of universals?" ("Introduction," xiv).

The relation between the video's representation of the riots and its figuring of Idol as cyborg can be explained in several different ways. The body rhetorics about Rodney King produced during the trial by the policemen's defense team might have suggested this figuration. During the interminably prolonged, freeze-frame analysis of the videotape of the beating, police experts repeatedly referred to King's legs as "cocked" and his arms as being in a "trigger position"; after dozens of blows, they insisted on describing him as still having "access to his hands, access to his legs" and "visual sight of where the officers" were standing (Patricia Williams, 52–53). In fact, they describe him as a terminator, who won't stop, who just keeps coming, and whose body itself is a weapon, as Idol's seems to be by the end of the video. In terms of the varieties of gendered cyborgs I delineated at the beginning of this chapter, Idol's cyborg character moves from a hysterical representation of a vulnerable white male body deprived of the ability to retain the integrity of its ego boundaries or its physical form and toward a fortified, armored corporeality that aggressively reasserts those boundaries and recontains the crisis in white masculinity that his transformation dramatized. The relation established by the video between the riots and the cyborg narrative can also be understood in terms of the project of Idol's *Cyberpunk* album, to recoup some of the credibility he once possessed as the lead singer for Generation X, one of the original, late-1970s British punk bands. Idol is often regarded as one of the first punk sellouts, one of the first performers to market punk as a style detached from its musical subculture, primarily through the videos that appeared on MTV in the early 1980s. Idol's turn to *cyber*punk was an attempt to represent himself as still punk but in a new way, with the continuity suggested by the visual similarity of the performing Idol's spiked hair and the metal spikes protruding from the cyborg Idol's head. In that sense, his use of the riot imagery also attempts to put a bit more punk into cyberpunk, by including images of anarchistic violence and urban insurrection as the setting for his assumption of a cyberpunk persona. The representation of Idol's character as object of violence by the police and implicit object of revenge by the rioters (to the extent that he represents himself as both King and Denny) can also be understood as reproducing the adversarial relation between punk performer and audience, especially in the early British shows, where taunting the audience to spit at the band, for instance, was part of creating an alternative to consumer culture, offering another take on the masochistic elements of the video. In this reading, the video tends to transform the historical event of the L.A. riots into a stylistic signifier of a past moment of punk nostalgically recalled as a form of pure insurgence or anarchy, and not as a sustained alternative culture. This citation of punk recapitulates the very problem Idol was trying to overcome in the first place, the problem of revolution into style and his personal history of implication in that process. In their *Cyberpunk Fakebook,* a satirical take on cyberpunk trendiness, the editors of *Mondo 2000* magazine (St. Jude, R. U. Sirius, and Bart Nagel) include a section on "phonies, poseurs, and pretenders" that has a blank space with the words "photo of Billy Idol goes here" (35).

Idol's cyborg transformation should also be read in relation to MTV's preferred technology of racial representation—that is, morphing. The distortion of Idol's features as he assimilates or is assimilated to the machine that has entered his body evokes this computer-aided graphic technique, which William Sonnega describes as a means of visually representing "the sensations of spatial 'inbetweenness' that mark the lives of so many actual people" in postmodern cultures (47). But in videos like Michael Jackson's "Black or White" (1991), morphing tends to be deployed as a smooth crossing of identity boundaries that offer no significant resistance. When "cultural borders become 'morphs,'" border crossings function "not as a contestation of the normative patterns that maintain cultural boundaries," but instead as an escape from or transcendence of those norms (Sonnega, 49, 55).[10] In contrast, the special effects in "Shock to the System" seem intended to emphasize the conflict, pain, and effort involved in such cultural crossings. "Shock to the System" ends up, however, anarchistically celebrating the breakdown of normative boundaries and color lines in a way that evades historical responsibility for them just as much as morphing does.

All three of the analyses I've just outlined are valid, but I want to explore yet another possibility. Idol's tranformation into a cyborg can also be read as a response to the historical trauma opened by the videotaping of the attack on Rodney King. The usefulness of this reading would lie in the extent to which it makes possible a rereading of cyborg imagery in popular culture. "Shock to the System" suggests that other cyborg narratives might also be read as attempts to represent and assimilate an American history of racial violence on the level of embodiment, attempts that usually constitute strategies for managing and therefore recontaining that history.

Caruth's reading of trauma emphasizes the problem of access to historical experience. The experience of trauma foregrounds the ways in which we do not "own" our own experiences, and the question then becomes one of responsibility: how can anyone own up to such an experience? In Caruth's words, "for history to be a history of trauma means that it is referential precisely to the extent to that it is not fully perceived as it occurs; or to put it somewhat differently, that a history can be grasped only in the very inaccessibility of its occurrence" ("Introduction I," in *Trauma*, 8). Avital Ronell's essay "TraumaTV" reads Rodney King's beating and the L.A. riots as posing precisely these questions about history as trauma. Invoking the videotape of King's beating as a displacement of the Persian Gulf War, like Idol, Ronell argues that the King video "thematized unthematizable force fields of intensity" and brutality, and it therefore raises what she describes as "television's only question," the "relation between TV and violence" (318).

The video for "Shock to the System" both replicates some of Ronell's interpretive moves and demonstrates the limits of her analysis.[11] Idol's video also thematizes the riots as a "break in consciousness" that disconnects experience and meaning, a "break in the possibilities traditionally allowed for experiencing experience" (Ronell, 324). The cyborg narrative in Idol's video is an attempt to visually figure this kind of traumatic experience in an embodied form, as a "break" in the Idol character's relation to his own bodily experience. This kind of visual representation of trauma attempts to "own" that experience without minimizing the difficulty of doing so by assimilating the trauma to a familiar experiential schema. The trauma appears as such precisely through the undecidability performed in the video between owning the experience and being owned by it, between assimilating technology into the body and being assimilated to the machine. As Haraway argues, cyborg imagery figures the difficulty of distinguishing "who makes and who is made," and the same difficulty inheres in the relation of subjectivity to histories of trauma (*Simians*, 177).

But to the extent that "Shock to the System"'s representation of history as trauma depends on Idol's assuming Rodney's King's experience, the cyborg narrative is also a postmodern blackface performance of the type analyzed by Phillip Brian Harper, the transformation of the specific historical experiences of marginalized groups into empty signs of a generalized postmodern condition (27).[12] Where Eric Lott's analysis of historical blackface practices emphasizes the appropriation of a black image in order to dissociate from it and thereby consolidate working-class ethnic identities as white, the kind of postmodern blackface we find in Idol's video involves associating whiteness with the very qualities blackface had allowed whites to attribute to blacks and to expel from themselves; here the emphasis is on informing whiteness with these "black" qualities rather than dramatizing the difference between black mask and white face, and it is this inversion that Harryette Mullen identifies as the production of a black media cyborg through the "grafting" of "black soul as supplement to a white body" (86–87).

The implication is that, for Idol, the trauma of being subjected to racist violence and police harassment is more easily acknowledged, if not assimilated, than the very different "trauma" of being identified with the historical agents of racist violence and therefore being vulnerable to becoming the object of black anger. As Caruth defines it, traumatic experiences cut across the categories of subject and object, inside and outside; they constitute an intolerable eruption of violence that can neither be "owned" nor subjectively known directly, but which also cannot be distanced and known objectively, as a mere theme or topic of discourse. If this definition of trauma applies to the beating Rodney King suffered, then can or should it apply to the police who beat him? Should that violence be permitted to remain traumatic for all viewers of the videotape, or are there some of us who should contextualize it historically and "own" it in that form, not as a kind of violence whose proximity is overwhelming to us but as an event to which we are linked in a more mediated way? What Idol's video elides in its representation of the place of whiteness in the riots is the differential relations blacks and whites might have to racist histories. The video's deployment of the framework of trauma to conceptualize the riots paradoxically functions to suppress the question of how white people today might *historically* be implicated in this kind of violence precisely by implicating them instead in a generalized trauma that levels distinctions between violent acts and presents the beating of Rodney King and the riots as similarly traumatic in effect. The model of trauma usefully produces this sense of implication and proximity, which can be lost in more historically determinist analyses, that effectively displace responsibility for events into the past. But, in representations of history as continuing trauma, it is easy for this sense of complex *implication* to reduce to a simple *identification* with history's victims, as Hal Foster suggests.

To its credit, the video attempts to narrate the L.A. riots as a trauma for white Americans who might prefer to forget about the persistence of racism and who might need reminding that racist violence can have historical consequences for white Americans, too. In that sense, the video's goal seems to be to show how shared vulnerabilities do not necessarily lead to mutual assured destruction but instead can provide the very basis for an ethical relation. Instead, however, the video only ends up fantasizing the pleasures of being victimized like a black man.

On the one hand, the video's cyborg imagery allows a positive representation of how U.S. racial histories are traumatic for white men, as experiences white men can neither evade nor fully own; on the other hand, by placing Idol in the position of Rodney King, the video defines only the experience of having been subjected to racism as having traumatic effects, while it continues to disavow historical responsibility for the commission of racist violence, even in the minimal form of a trauma that cannot be assimilated.[13] In "Shock to the System," it is the historicity of American white masculinity that remains unrepresentable and disowned. In American history, it is the limits of white male experience that have never been produced as limits, and it is that experience that was "not fully perceived" by white men "as it occur[red]" and that we must therefore now attempt to grasp "in the very inaccessibility of its occurrence," in the form of violence and victimization that seems not to have occurred to "us." At the same time, Idol's video usefully demonstrates how this assumption of responsibility can easily slide into an assertion of victimization that only reproduces the traditional white privilege of ignoring color lines. The video also suggests how similar problems emerge when cyborg imagery is used to represent the process by which white masculinity is experienced as a particularized racial category.

Idol's video, then, indicates the extent to which the deuniversalizing project of postmodernism remains unfinished, as well as the extent to which the figure of the cyborg might reproduce racial norms that long precede the postwar period. This reading complicates the understanding of cyborg narratives as posthumanist critiques, but it also opens the possibility of rereading other cyborg narratives in relation to U.S. racial histories (rather than in relation to the history of U.S. feminism, as Haraway tends to do, where the interventions of women of color are placed under the heading of "fractured identities").[14] The place to begin this rereading would be the film *Robocop* (1987), which precedes

Idol's video in articulating extreme bodily trauma and the redefinition of white, male subjectivity that this trauma elicits with the transformation of the white male body into a technologically mediated form, a cyborg; *Robocop* also contextualizes these challenges to white masculinity in terms of the beleaguered position of the white male within a multicultural postmodern city marked by race and class divisions.

"That's Life in the Big City": White Men as Vulnerable/White Men as Victims in *Robocop*

Paul Verhoeven's 1987 film *Robocop* and its two sequels are commonly noted, along with the *Terminator* films, for having widely popularized narratives of cyborg transformation, and as one of the most symptomatic examples of the meanings attributed to such narratives. For example, Mark Poster argues that, no matter how conventional the first *Robocop* film might be in its adaptation of cyborg themes to the typical conventions of Hollywood action or "cops-and-robbers" movies, the ultimate effect of *Robocop* nevertheless exceeds the familiar limits imposed on it by its narrative models, because "the political impact of the film is to expose the bizarre repositioning of *the body* in the mode of information" (Poster, *Second*, 140; my emphasis). Poster concludes his chapter on *Robocop* by asserting that "a posthumanist discourse is called for to map the new domains of the body in its new configurations with technology," seemingly without registering the contradiction between the rhetoric of the "posthuman" and the way that the rhetoric of "the body" reintroduces the universalizing tendencies of humanism.[15] To what extent is it possible and necessary to understand "the body" in this film as a particular white male one?

Claudia Springer offers a more specifically gendered reading of *Robocop*, as the narrative of a masculinized body's transformation into a cyborg form, where it continues to signify as masculine, albeit in a displaced and technologically mediated manner. She argues that, in action films about male cyborgs like *The Terminator* and *Robocop*, "fusion with the technological" is presented as no more fundamental a change than "stepping into a suit of armor" (*Electronic Eros*, 108). In this reading, Robocop's mechanical body only provides a new technological means of reinforcing the fixed ego boundaries traditionally associated with masculinity, as figured by the "fortified bodies" of armored cyborgs (109).[16]

In contrast to both these critical traditions, I read *Robocop* for the ways in which the cyborg character's body is not just gendered but also racialized, as a specifically *white* male body.[17] When Springer argues that Robocop's transformation into a cyborg amounts to no more than a man donning a suit of armor, she also suggests that the film critiques our assumptions about the essentially human, but only in order to reinscribe assumptions about the essential nature of gender and masculinity, in what Bukatman describes as an example of "the *defensive* drive toward a techno-humanoid fusion" (304). But by focusing exclusively on gender rather than gender and race, Springer's reading overlooks the ways in which the narrative logic of a film like *Robocop*, centrally organized around a white man's violent and traumatic transformation into a cyborg, requires the film to produce the white male body as such and therefore to at least complicate that body as an unmarked norm by which all forms of humanity are to be measured. For instance, from this perspective, putting on technology like a suit of armor is not to be dismissed as merely a superficial change, to the extent that such bodies can be read as an intervention in the semiotics of skin and skin color (I am here suggesting an extension of the argument I made in chapter 3 about the racial significance of Sorayama's gynoids or female robot bodies). The fact that *Robocop*'s gender dynamics have struck the film's critics as more spectacularly in evidence than its racial representations is partly explained by the structure of the film itself, in which race tends to be relegated to a subtext, but also by the tendency for technoculture studies to privilege gender over race. I will begin my reading by defining the ways in which *Robocop* conforms to cyberpunk conventions and to the familiar technocultural pattern of marginalizing racial concerns, and then turn to the ways in which *Robocop* departs from this pattern and offers some resources for thinking about the continuing importance of race in the social setting it imagines.

The specific way in which this denaturalization of the white male body appears in *Robocop* is in terms of a thematics of vulnerability, the exposure of the body of the white male police officer who becomes Robocop to physical and psychic trauma, which the film represents in graphic detail. At the time of the film's release, this necessity resulted in popular commentary on the risk taken by Peter Weller, the actor playing Robocop, with his star image, because Weller was agreeing to play a role that required him to spend most of the film inside a costume that either veiled his face or reduced that face to a grotesque component within a larger machine, when it is finally revealed. Moreover, his character has to submit to literal dismemberment, in the opening scene in which Officer Murphy is killed, allowing him to be turned into a cyborg. The narrative of cyborg transformation in *Robocop*, then, requires the film to open with the implicit failure of what Berlant calls the "prophylaxis" of citizenship, by which the nation "promises to protect [the citizen's] privileges and his local body" in return for the citizen's identification with the "abstract" body of the generically "American" (113). That protection has always more or less failed when it came to minoritized subjects, regarded as overembodied and incapable of transcending their own "narrow" self-interest, and films like *Robocop* make that failure explicit at the same time that they generalize it to apply to white men as well.

The narrative of cyborg transformation in *Robocop* literalizes Berlant's account of the construction of citizenship, as Murphy (the white male police officer) "acquires a new body," as the citizen does through "participation in the political public sphere" (ibid.). But Murphy gets his new cyborg body only after his "local body" has been declared legally dead, and his vulnerability has been graphically demonstrated, first on a physical level, then on a legal level. As J. P. Telotte points out, recent science-fiction films (during the last decade or so) often seem to use the image of the mechanized person to represent precisely the same repression of individual particularity that Berlant associates with the production of the public body of the American citizen (Telotte, 150–53). Visually, the robotic or cyborg body is usually figured as an abstract, simplified version of the human, while on the psychological level the fact that robots and cyborgs are programmed can be read as allegorizing the self-discipline historically required for participation in the public sphere (and the association of robots with purely logical thinking allegorizes the norms of rational discourse and argumentation associated with the public sphere, beginning in the eighteenth century). As Telotte also suggests, however, the thematization of publicness as roboticization also involves a critique of the historical construction of publicness and an implicit desire to reassert bodily particularity in the public sphere (153).[18] *Robocop* can, then, be read as a film that both recapitulates the traditional abstraction of white masculinity, its construction as generic, and also reveals that generic category to be falsely universal or artificial, in part by stressing the materiality of artifice.

It is precisely at this point that *Robocop*'s narrative of cyborg transformation also runs the risk of reinstating the privilege of white masculinity, but not by reproducing the traditional form that privilege took, the claim to possess an unmarked or generically human identity as well as a specifically male body. Murphy's transformation into Robocop also differs from Berlant's account of citizenship because his new body serves as a continual reminder of his original white male body's failure to remain safely abstract. Murphy's cyborg body remains "local" and particular, and therefore vulnerable, if not in quite the same way that his original body was. I disagree with readings of the film such as Springer's or Jeffords's (see note 16) because I do not believe that the representation of Robocop's "fortified" cyborg embodiment is more ambivalent than they suggest; I also do not believe that the film treats Murphy's vulnerability as a moment in the narrative that is then forgotten and overwhelmed by the spectacle of his impressively armed and armored body. In fact, the cyborg's mechanical implants, and the access to and control over his body and mind that they enable, never allow the audience to forget that he remains vulnerable after he has been shot; despite his resurrection as a cyborg, his legal death represents a permanent change in the status of his body, whose literal piercing by machinery is constantly on display, as is the reprogramming of his mind.

This representation of vulnerability to physical violence and social control is the *only* way in which the film is able to represent white masculinity as embodied particularity. At the same time, however, the film therefore runs the continual danger of *vulnerability* sliding over into *victimization*.[19] The representation of a white male police officer's body as vulnerable, rather than afforded the "prophylaxis" of the nation-state, tends irresistibly to veer into a representation of white men as victims of state violence, and from there it is a short (though somewhat illogical) step to representing white men as victimized by nonwhite others, in a way that is very similar to the Idol video's substitution of Idol for Rodney King. *Robocop* attempts to defend against this slide from vulnerability to victimization by presenting a corporation, dominated by white men, as primarily responsible for the violence that turns Murphy, the police officer, into Robocop. However, the film ultimately tends to blur this distinction (not least because the corporation, or one of its executives, turns out to be both funding the Detroit police force and funding organized crime).

It is hardly surprising that *Robocop* has received little attention for its representation of race and race relations. The two most striking plot features of the film are its critique of the privatization of the state apparatus, leading to corporate control and rampant consumerism, and the narrative of Officer Murphy's transformation into Robocop, followed by his struggle to regain some degree of humanity, in the face of corporate executives and scientists who repeatedly refer to him as just "product."[20] The thematics of both Murphy's body and Robocop as corporate property links these two plot strands.

On the level of cinematic technique, the most striking feature of *Robocop* is its use of pastiche, especially its incorporation of brief "newsbreaks" and commercials, reinforcing its representation of near-future America as not only increasingly run by corporations but also as thoroughly saturated by mass media, as demonstrated by the repeated scenes of various characters watching a deliberately idiotic sitcom whose catchphrase is "I'd buy that for a dollar!" The suggestion is that experience in this future world is increasingly mediated and commodified, in much the same way as the Robocop cyborg's visual apparatus. The other most striking and often-remarked technique in this film appears in scenes shot from Robocop's point of view, which emphasize that his visual field is being mediated through a video camera capable of recording and playing back whatever Robocop sees (at one point, one of the corporate executives exclaims, "his memory's admissible as evidence!"). By the same token, when the film shifts to Robocop's point of view, we are able to see the textual displays that his onboard computer projects in his field of vision, such as a targeting grid or textual reminders of the "prime directives" that have been programmed into him and that limit his potentially destructive behavior: (1) Serve the public trust; (2) Uphold the law; (3) Protect the innocent. Not only have Robocop's eyes become cameras, but that change is part of the implanted technology that allows him to be controlled and programmed like a computer. There is, then, a close similarity between Robocop's mediated visual experience and the way the film cuts between the fictional action of the narrative, footage from (fictional) television broadcasts, and scenes of characters watching television. This similarity suggests that both our experience as viewers of the film and the experience of the other characters in the film closely approximates Robocop's technologically mediated and "unnatural" mode of experience as a cyborg.[21]

These themes are fairly conventional in cyberpunk fiction, but they seem to have little direct relevance to questions of race. Robocop's representation of Omni Consumer Products (OCP) evokes the representation of the *zaibatsus* in Gibson's *Neuromancer* and cyberpunk's more general emphasis on the replacement of the nation-state and its forms of governance by multi- and transnational corporations (a topic I will investigate in more detail in the next chapter). *Robocop* is especially interesting for its focus on the way in which such corporations infiltrate and install their transnational values in local sites, in this case Detroit.[22] This thematics is articulated most clearly in one of the boardroom scenes, when the main corporate villain (Dick Jones) describes how OCP has "gambled in markets traditionally regarded as nonprofit: hospitals, prisons, space exploration," and now law enforcement.

After a disastrous attempt to create a purely mechanical automated policeman, which ends up accidentally killing a junior executive during a test run, OCP's corporate agenda, its desire for a more efficient and cost-effective substitute for the police ("a cop who doesn't need to eat or sleep"), leads to the creation of Robocop. It turns out that OCP has a backup plan. The company has been transferring prime candidates for becoming cyborgs to high-risk areas of the city, where they are likely to be killed, so that their bodies can be used by OCP.

Immediately after this boardroom scene, we witness Officer Murphy's brutal slaying at the hands of a criminal gang, which includes the leader blowing Murphy's right arm off with a shotgun blast and a protracted firing-squad scene where the rest of the gang pumps bullet after bullet into Murphy's body, followed by the leader finishing him off with a head shot. This scene is clearly designed to rub the audience's noses in the physical trauma that Murphy undergoes, a trauma that is then repeated by OCP, when they turn Murphy into Robocop. This conceptualization of the process of being "cyborged" as a repetition of violent physical trauma is made explicit when Robocop regains consciousness during the process. Through his camera eyes, we see the doctor supervising the procedure tell the OCP executive in charge of the project that they've been able to save the left arm from Murphy's body. The executive becomes enraged, and reminds the doctor that "we agreed on a full body prosthesis. Now lose the arm." One of the other executives present comments that "He signed the release forms when he joined the force, and he's legally dead. We can do pretty much what we want to him." Note the way that this scene links the legal status of the corpse as property with the effects of the contractual obligations Murphy entered into with OCP while still alive, as equal justifications for the disassembly and reassembly of Murphy's body. The parallel to the earlier scene, where the criminal leader blows off Murphy's other arm, is clear.

The rest of the film emphasizes the slow process by which Robocop begins to overcome his "hardwired" programming constraints, following the narrative model established in Gibson's *Neuromancer*, as I argued in the first chapter of this book. As Springer has pointed out, the main way in which Robocop is proven to be more than just a mechanism or a "product" is through the reemergence of repressed memory, a process that again invokes the concept of trauma, this time on a psychic level. During the scene in which the executives decide to remove Murphy's one salvageable limb, they also discuss how the doctors and technicians plan to "blank [Robocop's] memory" but retain the reflexes Murphy developed during his career as an exemplary police officer. As the head of the project puts it, Robocop is supposed to be "the best of both worlds: the fastest reflexes modern technology has to offer, onboard computer-assisted memory, and a lifetime of on-the-street law enforcement programming."

However, the film insists that it is not so easy to reduce experience and consciousness to the status of mere "programming," at least not completely. As Robocop sits off-line in Murphy's former police precinct, he begins to experience something like a dream, in which he relives Murphy's violent death. Robocop tries to exorcize these images by going out on an unscheduled patrol (by throwing himself into his work), but he only encounters Murphy's female partner, who attempts to address him by name, as Murphy. After brushing her off, Robocop then runs into one of Murphy's murderers, in the middle of robbing a gas station. Moreover, this murderer (mis)recognizes Robocop as Murphy on the basis of Robocop's manner of speaking, when he unconsciously repeats the same words Murphy used in trying to arrest this same gang member before he was captured and killed. After hearing this man say "You're dead. We killed you," Robocop is inspired to access the police database, where he encounters a record of Murphy's murder and for the first time learns his own previous name and address. He then visits his former home, where his memories of his wife and child play back before his eyes, in the format of video recordings (somewhat inexplicably, in that these scenes were never processed through the cyborg's video apparatus, though perhaps the suggestion is supposed to be that whatever memories the cyborg retains from his organic state are reformatted as video images, however that might be accomplished).

The rest of the plot then involves Robocop tracking down Murphy's murderers, who turn out to be backed by a senior OCP executive, Dick Jones. When

Robocop tries to confront Jones, Jones reveals that he has arranged for Robocop to be programmed with a fourth prime directive, which is classified even from Robocop himself: any attempt to arrest a senior officer of OCP results in a shutdown. Jones then turns the defective police robot, who earlier killed a junior OCP executive, on Robocop. During the fight that ensues, Robocop's cyborg body is damaged, most dramatically in the area of the facial visor. At least twice, the camera moves to a close-up on Robocop's "face," and specifically on the organic right eye revealed by the damage to the visor. The appearance of Robocop's "eye" within the mechanical body is clearly intended to suggest the reemergence of an at least partially autonomous "I" within the cyborg body and in contrast to its programmed limitations.

This iconography is reinforced, though ambiguously, when Robocop removes the visor completely during the process of repairing himself. In another graphic if not downright gruesome scene, Robocop uses a power tool to remove two titanium bolts, at least three inches in length, from each side of his head, approximately where his ears should be. When the visor is removed, we see that the back half of Robocop's head is mechanical, while the front half appears to be organic, though there are a number of tubes and other mechanical parts connecting the two halves. The effect is to return a human face to the cyborg, but at the same time Robocop's organic face appears unnatural, and not just because of its lack of hair. The face looks very much like a mask of organic skin and features stretched over a mechanical armature (something like the Terminator cyborg). As the director, Verhoeven, once stated in an interview, the narrative of the film is intended to depict Robocop as "becoming Murphy again, but in a new way," a way that accepts "what he has become," a condition of both "having less and having more" (quoted in Cronenworth, 35).

The film ends with another OCP boardroom scene, in which Robocop finally manages to get around Dick Jones's directive 4 programming constraint, though this triumph of will over programming, man over machine, is at least as ambiguous and partial as Robocop's "recovery" of Murphy's human face. In the final scene, Robocop uses his ability to record images to play back Dick Jones's confession of his criminal dealings to the assembled OCP executives. Jones panics and puts a gun to the head of the Old Man, demanding transportation out of Detroit. The Old Man fires Jones, so that Robocop's built-in inability to apply the law to the executives of OCP no longer applies, and he kills Jones. The film tries to emphasize the interpretation that takes this moment as a triumph for Robocop's residual humanity, by having the film end with Robocop reclaiming the name "Murphy" and identifying himself as such in response to the Old Man's questions. But it is obvious, though unremarked in the film, that Robocop's programming remains intact, and he is no more able to arrest an OCP executive than he ever was, though, of course, the film has suggested all along that this limitation is one that also applies to the human police force, which is owned and operated by OCP just as much as Robocop is.

"You're Gonna Be a Bad Motherfucker": Robocop's Racial Subtexts

So far, then, the film seems to explore a number of challenges to the definition of the "human," most interestingly by associating cyborg hybrids of people and machines with the effects of commodification, corporate control, and mass media more generally. But at no point do considerations of race seem to make a difference within this narrative. The effects of commodification and technology that the film depicts appear to affect all social subjects, regardless of race. The primary conflicts and relationships are between white characters, including Murphy/Robocop and his partner (the main woman character), Robocop and his corporate nemeses, and Robocop and the leader of the criminal gang who murdered him. On the other hand, the film is careful to portion out supporting roles to racially marked characters, with there being one black man among the OCP executives involved in creating Robocop, one black sergeant among the Detroit police, and one black and one Asian member of the criminal gang, with the leader and the majority of the gang being white men (as are most of the other criminal characters in the film, especially a drug lab run by a character whose Italian ethnicity is emphasized). The cast is at least superficially integrated at all levels, if only with token black characters, as if to defend against a reading of the film in terms of racial conflict or color lines.

However, themes of race relations are invoked in the first scene of the film, a news broadcast, and reinforced by the opening scenes of Murphy's transfer to an inner-city police precinct in Old Detroit. My argument is that these themes are subsequently displaced, but not erased, by the cyborg plot that privileges Murphy's trauma, beginning with the shooting scene in which Murphy dies. In fact, the opening scenes might be read instead as establishing a racial frame for the rest of the narrative. *Robocop* opens with a vista of the Detroit skyline, with the point of view sweeping in over the lake, a shot designed to emphasize the film's urban setting. It then cuts to a television broadcast called *Newsbreak*, which recurs throughout the film. The top story in this first broadcast focuses on the threat of nuclear confrontation in South Africa, where Pretoria is described as a "besieged city-state" ruled by a "white military government" (the film was made prior to Nelson Mandela's release). The news story is accompanied by images of a funeral with an exclusively black crowd carrying a coffin, followed by scenes of street riots, again consisting of black Africans. In response to this state of siege by unruly African persons, Pretoria has obtained a French-made nuclear bomb, as the "city's last line of defense."

The parallels between Pretoria and Detroit will, retrospectively, become clear as the film progresses. Instead of social unrest and resistance to white settler colonialism, Detroit (or at least Old Detroit) is presented as besieged by crime, a parallel that implicitly racializes Detroit's crime problem. In addition, OCP needs Robocop to ensure law and order, in order to permit OCP to replace Old Detroit with a planned community called Delta City, which seems likely to become something very similar to a white-majority city-state within Detroit, ruled by OCP. Robocop, as "the future of law enforcement," plays a role analogous to the French nuclear bomb, Pretoria's "last line of defense" in the news story, as suggested by the rhetoric later used by OCP to advertise and promote Robocop.

It is also important to note the way in which the shots of the African funeral point toward a different history than we find in the rest of *Robocop*. At least in the Western news media, this kind of event became an icon for the African National Congress's struggle against apartheid. However briefly and marginally, then, *Robocop* begins with an image that evokes the politically motivated murder and martyrdom of African persons by a white supremacist state. The whole ideological thrust of the film's narrative, however, is to rescript this history, and to replace the (presumably) black body in that coffin, a symbol of resistance to the state, with the traumatized body of a white male police officer, an agent of the state, in a way that compares to Idol's substitution of himself for Rodney King, in the "Shock to the System" video.[23]

The newscast then continues with another story, which I read as satirizing traditional concepts of whiteness. The other big story of the day concerns the U.S. president's first press conference from the "Star Wars orbiting peace platform" (a missile-defense satellite that is later reported to have misfired and destroyed thousands of acres of forest near Santa Barbara, in the process killing two former U.S. presidents, in a foreshadowing of Murphy's fate). Unfortunately, this orbital press conference got off to a "shaky start" because of a power failure that resulted in a "brief but harmless period of weightlessness for the visiting president and his staff." The president, a white man, is shown, apparently nauseated and in the throes of space sickness, bumping his head against a wall.

This story strikes me as an allegory of the traditional construction of white masculinity and the generic American citizen, at the same time that it emphasizes the failure that renders this power as a slapstick spectacle. In a film that so consistently foregrounds the specificity of the white male body, it seems to me no coincidence that the film opens with a story in which the white male symbolic representative of America is depicted as literally elevated above and abstracted from the material world, while at the same time the power that this position grants him is shown to be unstable and liable to failure, a failure that results in an especially embarrassing reemergence of white male bodily limitations and vulnerabilities. The film's opening scene, then, juxtaposes stories

⟶ *black unrest + besieged*
white privilege   REPLAYING THE L.A. RIOTS

about black unrest and besieged white privilege, while the rest of the film focuses more exclusively on besieged white privilege, and I take this opening scene as a glimpse into a set of connections that implicitly inform the remainder of the narrative. As I suggested, these newsbreak scenes get critical attention for dramatizing the expanded role of media technologies in shaping experience and subjectivity in this futuristic setting, but the specific content and historical referentiality of these scenes are universally ignored.

The scene that immediately follows this news broadcast introduces Murphy, in a way that also alludes to urban race relations in Detroit. Murphy walks into the police headquarters for the Old Detroit precinct, announces his name to the black sergeant working the desk, and briefly explains that he is transferring in from Metro South. The sergeant's comment on this information is "Nice precinct. You work for a living down here, Murphy. Get your armor and suit up." This brief exchange establishes a differential mapping of Detroit in the near future, a mapping that can hardly help but evoke today's distinctions between middle-class suburbs or gentrified districts and the rhetoric of the "inner city," economically underdeveloped and stereotypically associated with racial ghettos and gang activities. The presence of a presumably homeless, older black woman begging in the police station indirectly reinforces this set of assumptions and provides an image of an omnipresent black poverty infiltrating and interfering with the efficient operation of city services and state institutions (the sergeant's response of "Not now," as the woman tugs on his arm, can serve as an image of the film's generally successful deferral of racial considerations; race in this film can be overlooked or dismissed precisely because it is omnipresent).

Given Murphy's subsequent transformation into an armored cyborg body, the casual reference to body armor as standard equipment for police in this precinct is especially significant, because it suggests that Murphy's cyborgization might also be read as a defense against the local population of the inner city—that is, a defense against a perceived threat from a racialized underclass. This suggestion in turn is reinforced by the other police who welcome Murphy to Old Detroit by asking, "What brings you to this little paradise?" and, after finding out where Murphy had previously been stationed, adding, "Welcome to hell." Left unspoken are the reasons why this precinct might be an especially tough assignment, an ambiguity made possible by the conventions of a mildly dystopian, near-future urban setting, which (in conjunction with the mixed-race nature of the criminal gangs Robocop faces) allow viewers to imagine that crime generally has become more of a problem in this entire future Detroit, even though the film specifically cites this inner-city precinct as more and more violently crime-ridden and "hellish." This ambiguity is typical of the film's thinly veiled disavowals of racist characterizations of the inner city. The film provides another example of this disavowal in a later scene, where we learn that

OCP has "restructured the police department," to place "prime candidates" for the Robocop program "according to risk factor." These "risk factors" are never explicitly defined in terms of racial unrest and violence, but that implication is always there, diffused and generalized throughout the narrative, becoming clearer only if and when we retroactively connect that later statement to the scene in which Murphy arrives at an especially high-risk part of the city.

Rather than present specifically racialized or minoritized agents of violence, the film instead focuses obsessively on white male victims, in a way that points toward an absent set of racial conflicts. In this sense, the film can be read as dramatizing a historical trauma of the kind theorized by Silverman, as any "event . . . which brings a large group of male subjects into such an intimate relation with lack that they are at least for the moment unable to sustain an imaginary relation with the phallus." In *Robocop*, I want to suggest, that historical event is the emergence of the modern city as cosmopolitan site or contact zone, theorized in 1908 by Georg Simmel as the compulsory encounter with the figure of "the stranger." It is not coincidental, I believe, that Simmel's classic sociological work on the city corresponds so closely to Silverman's example of World War I as a moment of historical trauma for white masculinity. From this perspective, the racial mapping of urban space that informs *Robocop*'s opening scene is especially significant. Murphy's cyborg transformation figures the crisis of belief in dominant fictions of the male body that Silverman associates with such forms of collective trauma.

The thematics of white male vulnerability appears in the scene in which Murphy is introduced to his partner at this new precinct, Ann Lewis. He first sees Lewis when she subdues a handcuffed white male prisoner attempting to escape, and is described by the sergeant as "fucking around with your suspect," a formulation that emphasizes the sexual role reversal. Similarly, the whole Robocop project is only given a corporate go-ahead by OCP as a result of the accidental killing of a white OCP executive by a malfunctioning police robot prototype. In this scene, the executive is asked to play the role of a criminal and point a gun at the robot; when the machine's controllers are unable to override its programmed response to such provocation, even after the terrified executive throws the gun down, the robot executes him in a hail of bullets, in an exact parallel to the manner in which Murphy is killed (the self-conscious restaging of police violence, with a white man placed in the position of victim, should also remind us of the Billy Idol video and his displacement of Rodney King— that is, it is strongly suggested that what is being enacted here is a kind of cross-racial performance, which I am arguing is more central to the logic of the film than critics have recognized). The executive's death is dismissed with the comment "That's life in the big city."[24] Structural racial conflict tends to be suppressed as a risk factor for white men, in favor of women's power, technology, and random crime, despite the fact race relations might seem to have at least as much to do with the specificity of life in most big cities as these other factors.

The danger race poses is most explicitly represented in the scenes leading up to Murphy's shooting. The one black member of the gang that murders Murphy plays a key role in neutralizing Murphy's partner, his protection or backup. The scene begins with Murphy and Lewis being told that further backup from other police is unavailable, as part of OCP's plan to put Robocop candidates in high-risk situations. The two officers separate, and Lewis encounters the black man urinating. She tells him to put his hands up and turn around, and after doing so he uses his head to gesture downward, asking, "Mind if I . . . zip this up?" The camera focuses for a moment on Lewis's face, then we see her eyes look downward at the man's penis. In that moment of distraction, he disarms her and knocks her over a railing, where she lies unconscious, while Murphy is captured and executed by the rest of the gang. The effect of this scene depends on a racist fantasy about the size of the black penis, a mark of black men's overembodied natures—that is, the scene insinuates that, for Lewis to be distracted at this crucial juncture, this has to be not just any penis, but a particularly spectacular one.[25] The black character later suggests that he has raped Lewis, in order to taunt Murphy. Through the mediation of this scene's citation of a history of interracial sexual anxieties, Murphy's exposure to physical violence is indirectly attributed to the proximity of black and white bodies. In contrast to Silverman's argument, the loss of phallic power for white men is not necessarily accompanied by loss of belief in the power of the black penis; quite the opposite, it appears.

Murphy's vulnerability is extended and its implications elaborated when his dead body is appropriated as the corporate property of OCP, and his experience is commodified as "a lifetime of on-the-street law enforcement programming," which the creators of the Robocop cyborg intend to combine with "the fastest reflexes modern technology has to offer" and "onboard computer-assisted memory," in order to obtain "the best of both worlds." Legal scholar Cheryl Harris has argued that, in terms of the history of race relations in the U.S. context, "the racial line between white and black was extremely critical; it became a line of protection and demarcation from the potential threat of commodification," because "whites could not be enslaved or held as slaves" (279). This argument recalls Berlant's description of American citizenship as a "prophylaxis" or form of protection for white men. This rhetoric of protection is crucial to *Robocop*, and I argue that this rhetoric of protection is one of the main ways that the film encodes "whiteness" as a racial category. However, the narrative of cyborg transformation and the rendering of the white police officer as corporate property also indicate the ways in which this "racial line" can be blurred in technocultural contexts.

When Robocop tracks down Boddicker, leader of the gang who killed him, Boddicker desperately asserts that "I'm protected! I've got protection! There's another guy. He's OCP. It's Dick Jones! OCP runs the cops! You're a cop!" Similarly, when Robocop acts on this confession and confronts Dick Jones in the OCP headquarters, Jones reveals that he also has protection, or, as he puts it, "an insurance policy": the fourth prime directive hardwired directly into Robocop's computer-mediated consciousness, prohibiting him from taking action against OCP executives. It is in these scenes that the film invokes the traditional historical and legal construction of "whiteness." However, the film invokes this history only to reject or redefine it. Although Jones does secure Boddicker's release and uses directive 4 to thwart Robocop's first attempt to arrest Jones himself, Robocop eventually manages to kill both men, as their forms of protection lapse, just as Murphy's did.

At the very moment when Jones invokes his protection against being arrested by Robocop, he does so by emphasizing that Robocop *lacks* any such protection. In contrast to Boddicker, who escapes death by reminding Robocop that he is a cop, Jones asks, "What did you think? That you were an ordinary police officer? You're our product, and we can't have our product turning against us." In other words, Jones invokes what Harris refers to as "the threat of commodification," which historically the distinction between whiteness and blackness was supposed to ward off. That threat of commodification can then be read as invoking racial categories, even as it threatens to obliterate them, by reducing to the level of "product" the white male body on the basis of which Robocop was built. It is, of course, by declaring Murphy legally dead that OCP is able to do an end run around the legal protections provided by whiteness as a form of property. In this sense, Robocop's cyborg transformation allegorizes the potential for this protection to be withdrawn.

The implication is that cyborg embodiment renders Murphy available to racially coded processes of commodification, and this implication becomes most explicit during a scene, discussed earlier, in which we observe what is happening to the Robocop cyborg through his own intermittently conscious viewpoint, as OCP's technicians struggle to put him back into operation. This segment begins by establishing a parallel between the shooting and the technologizing of Murphy's body. Boddicker's first move is to blow Murphy's right arm off with a shotgun blast; later, Robocop overhears an OCP executive's response to being told that the doctors have been able to save Murphy's left arm. The executive impatiently reminds the doctor that "we agreed on a full body prosthesis. Now lose the arm," while another OCP representative (the black executive) comments: "He signed the release forms when he joined the force, and he's legally dead. We can do pretty much what we want to him." In the next scene, one of the scientists demonstrates a mechanical arm and explains that "the entire outer skin will be like this. It's titanium laminated with kevlar," suggesting how the technology makes reproduces and displaces a racial fascination with the "outer skin."[26]

Most important, the OCP executive heading the Robocop project then leans down into the camera—that is, into Robocop's "face"—and tells the cyborg, "You're gonna be a bad motherfucker." We don't need to remember the theme song to *Shaft* to realize that being a cyborg is here figured as the assumption of a black street persona (however clichéd). I would argue, however, that this figuration is not so much a form of racial cross-identification or blackface as it is a figuring of white masculinity as a victimized racial minority, justifying the violent reassertion of white privilege—becoming a bad motherfucker here means not becoming or masquerading as black, but instead remaking whiteness on the model of blackness.

One implication of this reading of *Robocop* is that its cyborg narrative needs to be placed in the context of urban vigilante films, such as *Death Wish* (1974), and their white male revenge fantasies, which similarly exploit the perceived threat of inner-city crime.[27] This comparison, however, can also highlight the ways in which cyborg narratives put new pressures on the racial revenge plot. Although a film like the original *Death Wish* deploys an initial experience of trauma as justification for further graphic violence, in such films it is not usually the body of the white male protagonist himself that is first endangered, but his family. Moreover, in *Robocop,* the white male subject is not just threatened but is actually put to death, a fate that it is rather more difficult to recover from and that therefore makes it more difficult to fully recuperate white male agency and privilege, which remains unstable in *Robocop.*[28] As a cyborg, the legal protections enjoyed by white men are permanently revoked, in contrast to *Death Wish*, where Charles Bronson's character Paul Kersey finds himself "protected" against his own will, by the state institutions that find it politically expedient to allow him to escape rather than to enforce the law in the face of public opinion favoring vigilantism. But in *Robocop* that very revoking of whiteness as property, or what George Lipsitz calls "the possessive investment in whiteness," also allows whiteness to be reasserted in a new way.

Although Springer emphasizes how Robocop's cyborg body represents a supplement to his lost masculinity, by technologically reinforcing and "fortifying" his bodily integrity and individual autonomy, it seems to me equally true that Robocop's continuing vulnerability is built into his body.[29] Most obviously, Robocop's right thigh opens like a wound, or the reminder of a wound, to provide access to his gun, which is stored inside his mechanical leg. This aspect of the Robocop costume effectively constitutes a reenactment of the bodily trauma that resulted in Murphy's death and the creation of Robocop, just as much as Robocop's "dreams" and repressed memories constitute the return of the death trauma that has been "blanked," an experience he can no longer access directly, but only read about in the police record of Murphy's death. But at the same time that the opening of Robocop's leg serves as a reminder of his bodily vulnerability, the transformation of a wound into a gun holster seems to allegorize the slide from vulnerability to victimization to revenge, which structures both *Robocop* and the urban vigilante film genre.

The functioning of Robocop's cyborg body, then, depends on its ability to literally open and close, in a way that an organic body could only if it were injured, and that ability is functional for the cyborg. This ability both facilitates Robocop's control over his new body (emphasized in the scenes where he repairs himself, most notably when he removes his visor by unscrewing a bolt that apparently pierces his skull from ear to ear) and allows others to manipulate and control that body. Robocop's armored integrity comes only at the price of his submitting to the possibility of such control. The film clearly sets up a series of parallels between the way in which the cyborg body is subject to dis- and reassembly by others, and the way in which Robocop's consciousness is subject to the control and "programming" of others. In this sense, too, Robocop's cyborg embodiment constitutes not a transcendence of bodily frailty and vulnerability, but an incessant repetition and intensification of that vulnerability, on the psychic rather than the physical level.

The sequel to *Robocop* supports this reading, because that film associates Robocop's vulnerability to being programmed and controlled with political correctness, as an attack on the privilege of white men. In *Robocop 2*, a female OCP executive decides that Robocop's prime directives should be extended to produce a more community-friendly cyborg, which the film presents as resulting in an absurdly long list of dos and don'ts designed to avoid offending any possible demographic group. The result is that Robocop experiences so many conflicting imperatives that he is effectively paralyzed and unable to act to prevent crime. In other words, the only way that the second film can acknowledge the existence of racialized constituencies in Old Detroit is in terms of the paralyzing effect that such an acknowledgment has on Robocop. Acknowledging the existence of a multicultural inner city is depicted as a kind of violence against white men, just like the psychic violence Robocop experiences when he is programmed against his will.

In the context of Billy Idol's "Shock to the System," it becomes much easier to read the racial subtext of *Robocop*. The lesson of both the music video and the film is that cyborg imagery provides an important and significant means of visually representing white masculinity as a distinct racial category, as a legible bodily signifier rather than a transparent norm.[30] Cyborg imagery helps to produce this ideological effect by emphasizing the vulnerability of white male bodies and their implication in systems of social control and power. New

human–machine interfaces then might have a role to play in the critical project of denaturalizing and producing "whiteness" as a racial category. At the
same time, my readings of these visual narratives also indicates the need for
critical skepticism toward their depictions of white masculinity, because in these
texts it is difficult, if not impossible, to extricate the progressive depiction of white
masculinity as vulnerable from the defensive depiction of white masculinity as
victimized. This coding of cyborg imagery as a reassertion of a white masculinity victimized by its "others" nevertheless means that whiteness remains open
to challenge and intervention in ways that cannot be fully foreclosed on.

How do we distinguish btwn progressive depiction of white masculinity as embodied vulnerable + the defensive depiction of white masculinity as victimized?

7

FRANCHISE NATIONALISMS

GLOBALIZATION, CONSUMER CULTURE, AND NEW ETHNICITIES

In a seemingly centerless world, centerlessness is not adequate
resistance. . . .   —Ben Agger, Fast Capitalism *(10)*

The franchise and the virus work on the same principle: what
thrives in one place will thrive in another. You just have to find
a sufficiently virulent business plan, condense it into a three-
ring binder—its DNA—xerox it, and embed it in the fertile lining
of a well-traveled highway, preferably one with a left-turn lane.
. . . McDonald's is Home, condensed into a three-ring binder
and xeroxed. "No surprises" is the motto of the franchise ghetto,
its *Good Housekeeping* seal. . . .
    The people of America, who live in the world's most surpris-
ing and terrible country, take comfort in that motto.
               —Neal Stephenson, Snow Crash *(178)*

It seems to me that, in the various practices and discourses of
black cultural production, we are beginning to see constructions
of . . . a new conception of ethnicity: a new cultural politics which
engages rather than suppresses difference and which depends,
in part, on the cultural construction of new ethnic identities.
               —Stuart Hall, "New Ethnicities" *(446)*

Globalization and/as Localization: The "Paradox" of Transnationalism

In the mid-1990s, Masao Miyoshi began to offer a historical account of the
transnationalization of late capitalism.[1] He emphasizes the shift from multinational corporations, still "headquartered in a nation" though "operating in a
number of countries," to a more fully decentralized, post-Fordist form of economic organization that is "no longer . . . tied to its nation of origin" but is

instead "adrift and mobile, ready to settle anywhere and exploit any state including its own, as long as the affiliation serves its own interest" ("Borderless," 736). Like David Harvey's work on the economic logic of postmodernity, Miyoshi's definition of transnationalism offers a critique of the very qualities that postmodern and postindustrial theorists often celebrate as progressive, such as decentralization and mobility. For Miyoshi, as for post-cyberpunk writer Neal Stephenson, it is precisely this globalizing principle, that "what thrives in one place will thrive in another" (*Snow Crash*, 178), that defines what is most "virulent" about late capitalism.

My focus in this chapter will be on the way that both cyberpunk narratives and transnational or post-Fordist forms of political economy demonstrate the coimplication of processes of globalization and localization. Although these processes might seem mutually exclusive on the surface, they are in fact structurally linked in these emergent information economies and network societies. In effect, this imbrication of the global and the local is an inversion of Wiegman's "paradox of particularity," discussed in the preceding chapter in the context of whiteness studies, because there the problem was how a previously universalized identity category can maintain its privilege when it is marked as particular. In contrast, globalization seems to privilege economic and cultural "flows" across regional boundaries, what Arjun Appadurai calls "scapes" or what Haraway describes as a shift from "essential properties" to a logic of "design, boundary constraints, rates of flows, systems logics" (*Simians*, 162). How can such a logic of boundary crossing, within which the local is recontextualized as always contingent and transcendable, also benefit from the reassertion of local differences? How can power simultaneously operate effectively both at the highest levels of abstraction and universality and at the most basic levels of concrete particularity? In part, this contradiction can be explained by noting that transnational or post-Fordist political economies are defined by contrast not to the local but to the national—that is, to an older, more limited ideal of universality, consensus, and cultural homogeneity. In cyberpunk narratives, for example, the nation-state is typically replaced by *zaibatsus* or transnational corporations (TNCs), and the result is not just globalization but the internal fragmentation and balkanization of the nation-state. The result is to qualify the typical postmodern focus on the local, or what Partha Chatterjee calls "bad nationalisms," nationalisms mobilized within and against state power, such as postcolonial or black nationalisms, as inherently resistant to globalizing economic institutions as well as national state apparatuses. Those globalizing power structures function in part by imposing an increased imperative to be local, where the commodification of local difference fuels capitalist development. At the same time, that process should be understood dialectically. If globalization also means that "the qualities of place stand thereby to be emphasized in the midst of the increasing abstractions of space,"as Harvey argues, then it may be possible to turn global capital's dependence on new or newly visible local "qualities" or points of difference against this new logic of capitalist organization (295).

Neal Stephenson's *Snow Crash* (1992) offers a rearticulation of the original cyberpunk framework that foregrounds this set of issues, especially through its representation of gated communities as "franchise nations," organized around an informational logic of reproducibility that allows them to mediate between the local and the global, to thrive in one place as well as another (178). In this way, Stephenson's novel also returns us to the topic of the relation between commodification and cultural identity in postmodern technocultures, a central theme of my reading of *Neuromancer* in chapter 2. By renarrating that crucial cyberpunk thematics within a global frame, however, Stephenson's novel connects this problem more directly to questions of race and ethnicity than is typical of most cyberpunk fiction, because these franchise nations are explicitly represented as new forms of ethnicity and community.[2] One of the key interpretive questions about this novel is how to evaluate the shift in ethnic identity that is embodied in the new structure of franchise nationalism. Is it merely an extension of the commodity system whose effects are primarily homogenizing and Americanizing, as the novel's own example of the McDonald's franchise suggests?[3] Or does this shift also define new possibilities for resistance, and if so, where are those possibilities to be located, if neither the global nor the local, abstract spaces nor particular places, define standpoints clearly oppositional to late capitalism?

Cyberpunk fiction is especially relevant to the tension between "space" and "place" that Harvey defines. The changing relation between the global and the local characteristic of transnational social relations is usually represented in cyberpunk texts as a relationship between the relatively abstract experience of cyberspace computer simulations and the materiality of urban locations. These narratives try to bring together, in one plot, what Manuel Castells calls "the space of flows" and "the space of places" (*Informational City*, 348). Stephenson's *Snow Crash* is especially useful for its relatively explicit representation of these relationships, between increasingly balkanized and fragmented urban spaces and the freedom of motion or "frictionless" boundary crossings that seem possible in global cyberspaces and infoscapes. Claire Sponsler argues that cyberpunk narratives are as much about learning to enjoy inhabiting an "urban landscape of decay," which, "wrecked though it is, offers . . . a playground of creative possibilities" ("Beyond the Ruins," 261), as they are about learning to inhabit the more radically denaturalized, if not actually disembodied, landscape of cyberspace.[4] Sponsler also suggests the connection between transnationalism and posthumanist diversity and multiculturalism, when she cites Brian McHale's argument about how the transnational "collapse of regimes and national boundaries" can be read as a figure for "the collapse of *ontological* boundaries" (ibid., 262–63; McHale, 45). What Sponsler's argument does not address is the ideological and often specifically racist subtext that informs the language of urban "ruin," "decay," or "blight," language more often used to describe racialized "inner-city" ghettos than cities in general, as we saw in the case of *Robocop*, in the preceding chapter. From this latter perspective, cyberpunk's celebration of urban decay appears more ambivalent, because its reevaluation of a blighted urban landscape as a creative site tends to accept and reify processes of ghettoization at the same time that it tries to contest such racial mappings of social space by emphasizing the value of a cosmopolitan practice of living together, in proximity to difference.

The franchise nations theme in fact connects and mediates between the two main scenes of action in *Snow Crash*, cyberspace or the "Metaverse" and the late-capitalist urban setting. The redefinition of communities as reproducible franchises exemplifies how the experience of virtual spaces and informational flows also feeds back into an understanding of collective identities, in a way that marks the difference between electronically mediated forms of "imagined community" and the print-based ones Benedict Anderson famously argues are characteristic of modernity and the democratic nation-state.[5] As Nicholas Negroponte puts it, "neighborhoods, as we have known them, are places. In the digital world neighborhoods cease to be places and become groups that evolve from shared interests," as exemplified by Internet listservs, chat rooms, and newsgroups. The result, in Negroponte's view, is that "each of us will have many kinds of 'being local'" (286). Negroponte's comments here help explain what it means for ontological boundaries to collapse, and (despite Negroponte's upbeat tone) those implications are not clearly progressive politically, both because of the ominous overtones of Negroponte's casual dismissal of "places," and because of a basic ambiguity in the "nature" of these self-evolved interest groups: How do the boundaries of "interest" map onto existing social differences? Will these interest groups be multicultural, multiracial, multisexual, as Sponsler claims, or will they be self-segregating? As the history of U.S. attempts at integration shows, creating new possibilities for proximity and connection (whether physical or virtual) is hardly a guarantee that any real contact and exchange will occur between different groups.

Snow Crash provides a useful site for considering these questions, because Stephenson's novel implicitly articulates the kind of technocultural shift in the experience of places and neighborhoods that Negroponte describes with the shift from race to ethnicity that Stuart Hall defines, in the "New Ethnicities" essay in which he calls for "the end of a certain critical innocence in black cultural politics" (449). This end of innocence is predicated on the understanding that "the black subject and black experience are not stabilized by Nature or by some other essential guarantee," but are instead "constructed historically, culturally, politically—and the concept which refers to this is 'ethnicity'" (446). For Negroponte, a similar end of innocence is involved in the shift from communities that are naturalized through a shared relation to place or territory (a key characteristic of traditional nationalism) toward interest groups that are explicitly understood as consensual constructions and therefore as relatively contingent products of human activity. The newness of Hall's concept of ethnicity resides in the way in which it "engages rather than suppresses *difference*" and therefore remains open-ended and ontologically ungrounded, committed to the cultural construction of new ethnicities" and not just to the preservation of the past (ibid.). It is only through this investment in the productive nature of ethnicity that Hall's "positive conception of the ethnicity of the margins, of the periphery," ethnicity as a critical category, can be distinguished from "the dominant notion which connects [ethnicity] to nation and 'race'" and therefore to concepts of fixity and conservative traditions (447). Hall's goal is to combine the sense that "we are all . . . *ethnically* located" with a refusal to accept that location as a place, to the extent that dominant, nationalist notions of both ethnicity and place have been defined by sharp, if not absolute, distinctions between internal and external spaces, those who belong and those who do not—that is, as means of "marginalizing, dispossessing, displacing, and forgetting other ethnicities" (ibid.).

Mark Poster suggests how technoculture studies might converge on Hall's theory of new ethnicities, when he argues that virtually mediated forms of ethnic identity might provide "an alternative to the binaries of particularism and universalism, parochialism and cosmopolitanism" (*What's the Matter*, 150); at the same time, Poster suggests that the notion of virtual ethnicity might also help to resist the definition of cyberspace as pure mind and instead define it as a kind of "territory," a new kind of location rather than a pure space of dislocation (152). Castells similarly argues that the only way local governments can maintain any autonomy within the flows of global capital and "avoid the deconstruction of their locales by the placeless logic of flows-based organizations" is by reconstructing "an alternative space of flows on the basis of the space of places" (*Informational*, 352–53).[6] It is precisely this possibility of reimagining the place of ethnicity along the lines of an informational model that underlies the "excitement" created in *Snow Crash* by "its creation of new configurations of ethnicity." At the same time, however, Nakamura also emphasizes the danger involved in the way these new configurations tend "to avoid overt references to race" (*Cybertypes*, 71).

The obvious danger in Stephenson's elaboration of these shifts, especially as they are fueled by the mediating logic of information, is that ethnicity will be valued over race purely for its qualities of greater flexibility and plasticity, and not for how it continues to value place and location even as it renders such "groundings" more provisional and open to change. This danger is explicit in posthuman narratives that stress technological transcendence and denaturalization. For instance, in George Zebrowski's novel *Macrolife* (1979), leaving the Earth to live in completely unnatural space habitats results in a posthuman condition referred to as "Humanity II," and these new technologically mediated conditions of existence, which foreground the constructed nature of human communities, are imagined to call "into doubt the age-long affirmations of ethnic and regional humanity" or "culture-bound man," in favor of "a highly fluid and critical personal and social identity" (193–94). Culture and ethnicity here take on qualities of fixity and stasis that nature and biology have lost, as the latter are imagined to be replaced by technology and techniques of manipulation and controlled change, as Sedgwick suggests (*Epistemology*, 43). Castells similarly questions whether ethnicity can maintain the dual nature Hall ascribes to it under the conditions of the "network society," because, in Castells's view, ethnicity "is based on primary bonds that lose significance, when cut from their historical context," and therefore cannot serve "as a basis for reconstruction of meaning in a world of flows and networks, of recombination of images, and reassignment of meaning" (*Power*, 59). The result, he argues, is that ethnicity tends either to be overgeneralized and dislocated to the point of meaninglessness, or overterritorialized and exclusive to the point of possessing meaning only for a narrowly and prescriptively defined group of insiders and remaining incomprehensible and incommunicable to all others (ibid.). *Snow Crash* constitutes a significant exploration of this implicit debate between Hall and Castells, over how to evaluate the transformations ethnicity undergoes in technocultural contexts.

A less obvious danger resulting from the sets of changes Stephenson's novel thematizes in the form of the franchise nations, however, is the possibility they suggest for conservative rather than progressive articulations of location and dislocation, particularity and openness. Stephenson's novel is explicit about how the phenomenon of the gated community facilitates a process of social resegregation, allowing the creation of communities that are "for whites only." The redefinition of these separatist, racially pure communities as franchises allows them to claim the particularity implied by such a slogan, without abandoning whiteness's traditional claims to universality and to a normative status. The reproducibility implied in the notion of franchising a particularized community, of selling it to others by emphasizing unique features that will be the same everywhere that a franchise can be located, allows these separatist spaces to also claim a kind of generality, both for their particular form of community and, perhaps more importantly, for a logic of segregation and enforced particularity itself.

It is relatively commonplace to hear cyberpunk fiction described as "an expression of transnational corporate realities," which attempts "to think the impossible totality" of the "new decentered global network" of late capitalism, as Fredric Jameson does in his *Postmodernism* book (38). Stephenson's *Snow Crash*, in fact, begins with an explicit lecture on one interpretation of transnationalism and its possible effects on the U.S. economy: "once things have evened out, they're making cars in Bolivia and microwave ovens in Tadzhikistan and selling them here . . . once the Invisible Hand has taken all those historical inequities and smeared them out into a broad global layer of what a Pakistani brickmaker would consider to be prosperity," then "there's only four things we [Americans] do better than anyone else": music, movies, writing code for software programs, and delivering pizza in less than thirty minutes (2–3).[7] The reference to writing code is especially significant, because computer technologies play a central role in globalization by making possible the efficient "transfer of capital" across national borders (Miyoshi, "Borderless," 740). As one commentator puts it, in an age of automatic teller machines, "cyberspace is where your money is."[8] This reading begins to undo the mystification of these economic processes, reified and alienated as supposed autonomous "market forces," through the figure of the "Invisible Hand." This passage is also symptomatic for its suggestion that transnationalism is a cure for colonialism, here coyly referred to as "historical inequities" (Miyoshi argues instead that transnationalism is a neocolonial intensification of these inequities). Moreover, in a move resembling the ones analyzed in the preceding chapter for representing white masculinity, the United States is represented as having been particularized precisely because of the seemingly progressive process of "evening out" differences in economic development. The result of this market-driven process is presented as global homogenization, with the result that Americans (like the narrator, apparently) are forced to seize on the few remaining fields of specialization that make the United States unique, to emphasize them, and therefore to encode and package them as forms of local color. The result is to present Americans as having been victimized, reduced to the level of pizza deliverers, because that list of four specialties amusingly levels the distinctions between popular forms of creativity (music and movies), software coding (as opposed to manufacturing), and pizza delivery (to the extent that pizza delivery involves negotiating space in creative ways, this leveling process works in the novel to elevate that service industry as well as to deflate Hollywood and Silicon Valley). The question that is evaded in this thumbnail sketch of transnational political economy is how power and class inequities continue to structure global capitalism, and the resegregating function of the franchise nations is one of the ways the novel succeeds in confronting this issue.

The consequences of the shift from print to electronic media and from nationalism to transnationalism are still unclear. But if the emergence of print culture in Europe resulted in the creation of national vernacular languages, it seems clear that the emergence of transnational institutions based on electronic media will require a different attitude toward language and linguistic diversity, one that privileges "the ability to converse and communicate" across national boundaries (Miyoshi, "Borderless," 747). This shift from national linguistic norms to a norm of translatability returns us to what Hayles calls the metaphor of inscription, in which the value of treating persons or objects as inscriptions is that they can be "be frictionlessly transferred into another medium" (Hayles, "Posthuman Body," 248). Like the extreme posthuman or transhuman discourses discussed in my Introduction, transnational corporations apply this norm of translatability not only to languages, but to cultures and persons, or what Appadurai calls "ethnoscapes" as well as "infoscapes." This analysis of transnational attitudes toward languages explains, I believe, the thematics of language acquisition in Stephenson's *Snow Crash* and the conflict between linguistic diversity and linguistic homogenization in it (discussed in the Conclusion to this book). This connection between posthuman metaphors of human minds and bodies as textual inscriptions, available to be copied and downloaded, and transnational concepts of language also explains William Gibson's association of multinational corporations and posthumanism: "Case had always taken it for granted that the real bosses, the kingpins in a given industry, would be both more and less than *people*. . . . He'd always imagined it as a gradual and willing accommodation of the machine, the system, the parent organism" (*Neuromancer*, 203).

In an anticipation of the development of cable and satellite alternatives to the broadcast networks' monopoly, feminist cyberpunk writer Pat Cadigan describes a process she calls "narrowcasting" or media niche marketing (*Synners*, 51). Owing in part to what Monroe Price calls the higher degree of "addressability" that characterizes electronic media (79), the electronic public sphere and the modes of social connection that it promotes tend to produce diversity and division as much as consensus, or rather the signs of diversity as cultural commodities in themselves. In contrast to the traditional public sphere, produced through the technology of print and associated with both liberal humanism and the democratic nation-state, the electronic public sphere tends to generate specialized subgroups rather than a generalized public. There is a strong tendency for these subgroups to function as demographic categories, more directly integrated into the privatized consumer relations that traditionally constitute civil society than the bourgeois national public sphere ever was, because the ideal function of the bourgeois public sphere was to mediate between state institutions and private citizens in civil society.[9]

As Miyoshi points out, transnationalization means not only a shift to globalism, but also that "'traditional' arts and forms are fragmented and decontextualized so as to be staged, museumized, collected, or merchandised," while "even local resistance and nativist resentment are open to the seduction of consumerism, as can be seen in the history of graffiti art and rap music" ("Sites," 69).[10] Such techniques represent not only a reappropriation and recontainment of the logic of multiculturalism and new social subjects, but also a renewed and increasingly desperate attempt to manage the ever-present capitalist crisis of accumulation—that is, the problem of making sure there are always enough new consumers for the unending supply of products the system spews forth. In this situation, it becomes necessary to look more closely at this transnational process of commodifying the local as a possible site of resistance to the very logic of transnationalism itself, as I believe Harvey does, in contrast to the tendency implicit in Miyoshi's argument to dismiss this process as a "seduction."

This analysis suggests the importance of cyberpunk's narrative self-consciousness about the replacement of national identities with subcultural affiliations. Gibson famously claims that, in his paradigmatic cyberpunk novels, "there is no indication . . . that the USA exists anymore"; the word *America* does not appear, because he "wanted the reader to question the political existence of the United States" (Maddox, "Eye to Eye," 26). In *Neuromancer*, it is not only the United States but also the Pentagon and the CIA that are explicitly described as having been "balkanized," not only the cultural form of the nation but also institutions of state power (83). At the same time, Gibson suggests that "we're moving toward a world where all the consumers under a certain age will probably tend to identify more with their consumer status or with the products they consume than they would with a sort of antiquated notion of nationality."[11] As Dick Hebdige has shown in his famous work on "style" in rock subcultures, these subcultural affiliations represent a process of resignifying consumer objects, creating "identities" that cut across national boundaries to the extent that the corporations producing these commodities also extend across those boundaries. Gibson, in other words, is describing the transnationalization of style and strategies of consumption that do not necessarily reproduce precisely the agendas of the transnational corporations, in contrast to Miyoshi's perhaps over-pessimistic assessment of the TNCs' abilities to co-opt all forms of localized resistance. *Snow Crash* at least initially seems to lean toward Miyoshi's assessment of this interaction between culture and commodity, given that the main form such subcultural formations take is the proliferation of "franchise ghettos" or "burbclaves," which are far from hotbeds of anarchy.

For Harvey, the "paradox" of transnational globalization is that as "the spatial barriers" of national boundaries become less important, "the greater the sensitivity of capital to the variations of place within space, and the greater the incentive for places to be differentiated in ways attractive to capital" (295–96). In this model, globalization has the contradictory effect of encouraging the production of local "difference." There has been a great deal of commentary on the apparent conflict between transnational globalization, facilitated by new communications and computer technologies, and what is often referred to as "tribalization" or the turn toward exclusive local communities (Castells uses the term to dismiss attempts to resist globalization by disengaging from the virtual "space of flows" [*Informational City,* 350]). In a popular account of this process, Benjamin Barber refers to this conflict as "Jihad vs. McWorld." The point is that the global and the local, processes of cultural homogenization ("McWorld") and cultural heterogeneity ("Jihad"), can no longer easily be mapped onto a distinction between domination and resistance. As Arjun Appadurai puts it, the relationship between these two processes, as "the central feature of global culture today," might best be understood as "the politics of the mutual effort of sameness and difference to cannibalize one another," through the simultaneous marketing and exportation of local cultures and the local repatriation of global commodity culture, for instance (*Modernity,* 43). Under these conditions, as Harvey puts it, "geopolitics and economic nationalism, localism and the politics of place, are all fighting it out with a new internationalism in the most contradictory of ways" (358). One of the key contradictions or paradoxes, then, is whether this "fight" contests or actually promotes the interests of the "new internationalism," whether it is part of a "mutual effort."

The consequences of this coimplication of globalization and localization for resistance movements are perhaps best illustrated by comparing the work on transnationalism and post-Fordism with accounts of postcolonial national resistance and its critique of Western nationalism, such as Partha Chatterjee's *The Nation and Its Fragments.* The weakening of national boundaries in transnational economies diminishes what Chatterjee has described as the state's claim to be "the only legitimate form of community" within a nation (236). Chatterjee argues that nationalist discourse in postcolonial contexts involves the detaching of "nation," associated primarily with indigenous spiritual traditions, from "state," associated with material institutions imposed by the West (6). In Western histories of national formation, "the state became the nation's singular representative embodiment" (236). But if the modern state "cannot recognize within its jurisdiction any form of community" except the nation, community functions as an internal limit to the "disciplinary power" of the state, and this limit always threatens to return in the form of "bad nationalism," which disrupts the homogeneity of the nation-state by "claiming an alternative nationhood with rights to an alternative state" (237–38). For Chatterjee, postcolonial nationalisms therefore displace the supposed opposition between the state and civil society onto an opposition between capital and community and thereby unleash those forms of "bad nationalism" (236, 237–38).

This process of fragmentation appears progressive, however, only in relation to nationalist ideologies that the transnational corporations are attempting to render obsolete. From the perspective of the TNCs, the emergence of these alternative claims to nationhood and the internal differentiation of national space that results are the very motor of transnational development, to the extent that these nationalisms can be assimilated to the process of becoming "differentiated in ways attractive to capital." As indispensible as Chatterjee's argument may be as a corrective to an exclusively Western perspective on nationalism, work like Miyoshi's and Harvey's implies that new transnational strategies for managing internal heterogeneity might be replacing the more traditional identification of nation and state. Specifically, transnationalism thrives on and cannot exist without the emergence of new forms of "community" from within what was once the jurisdiction of the nation-state, beginning with new forms of corporate affiliation that supersede national identifications. But, as Miyoshi points out, the transnationalist strategy is to allow the emergence of new "communities" only within the limits of the commodity form. Cultural commodification of the "local" replaces the universalizing of community into nation and the identification of nation with state power.

This shift in management strategies raises the question of where to locate resistance. Grewal and Kaplan argue that the category of the transnational is indispensable for understanding how both postmodernism and feminism "participate in a critique of modernity" (22). But what happens to this politics of resistance when modernity and its political form, the nation-state, seem reduced to straw men, when transnationalism is no longer an ally against nationalism, but instead provides the new norm of capitalist organization? At that point, Ben Agger's assertion that "in a seemingly centerless world, centerlessness is not adequate resistance" comes into play.[12]

Teresa Caldeira has suggested that this fragmentation of the national public sphere into attractively differentiated local spaces represents, on the material level of social space, the postmodern theoretical critique of liberal humanist claims to universality, because those claims take the form of "modern citizenship based on affiliation to a nation-state"; the fragmentation of social space that Harvey links to transnational globalization therefore suggests to Caldeira the possibility of rethinking "the criterion for participation in political life" on the basis of "local residence rather than national citizenship." In this argument, the disappearance of generally accessible public space both reveals and makes it possible to redress the exclusions that have always marked the limits of participation in the public sphere for women and racial minorities (326). Caldeira also here defines the logical connections between transnational and posthuman themes in cyberpunk fiction.

However, the postmodern critique of universality on the level of social space has a majoritarian form as well as a minoritarian one, as Mike Davis's chapter on "Fortress L.A." in *City of Quartz* should remind us. Most relevant to my argument here is Davis's analysis of the trend in L.A. toward privatized, gated communities, in a turn away from previous urban ideals of public accessibility toward the division of urban space into segregated enclaves (227). Davis describes this privatization as "a master narrative in the emerging built environment of the 1990s" (223), and Stephenson's *Snow Crash* extrapolates this master narrative into the form of "franchise ghettos," which precisely market "community" as commodity. The possibilities for new forms of local governance and citizenship that Caldeira locates in the fragmentation of social space therefore always run the danger of appropriation by this majoritarian logic of ghettoization and enforced self-ghettoization.

Franchise Nationalisms

In Stephenson's *Snow Crash*, globalization results in the proliferation of "franchise ghettos" or "burbclaves" within First World national boundaries, and the novel therefore dramatizes the difficulties in simultaneously resisting the TNCs' dual imperatives of globalization and localization. In *Snow Crash*, with the notable exceptions of "street people," "immigrants," "young bohos," and the "technomedia" elites, most people in the former United States now live in "Franchise-Organized Quasi-National Entities" (14). Mr. Lee's Greater Hong Kong, described as "the granddaddy of all FOQNEs" (42), advertises itself as a place where "all ethnic races and anthropologies" can "merge under a banner of the Three Principles" of "information, information, information!" "totally fair marketeering!" and "strict ecology!" followed by the disclaimer that "Mr. Lee's Greater Hong Kong is a private, wholly extraterritorial, sovereign, quasi-national entity not recognized by any other nationalities and in no way affiliated with the former Crown Colony of Hong Kong, which is part of the People's Republic of China. The People's Republic of China admits or accepts no responsibility for Mr. Lee, the Government of Greater Hong Kong, or any of the citizens thereof" (92).

In contrast to Mr. Lee's ethnic tolerance for all "anthropologies," these "franchise nations" are generally organized around principles of ethnic homogeneity or identification with regional qualities, however displaced, and this tension is exemplified by the fact that these communities are referred to as both franchise nations and franchise ghettos, as if those terms were interchangeable. Examples include the Anglophile franchise "The Mews at Windsor Heights," "The Farms of Cloverdelle," "Caymans Plus," "The Alps," and, more pointedly, "apartheid burbclaves" such as "Metazania," "New South Africa," "Dixie Traditionals," "White Columns," and "Pickett's Plantation"; there are also a smaller number of "Rainbow Heights" franchises for members of the black middle class (41–42). A franchise ghetto even exists for users of RVs, consisting of a two-thousand-mile stretch of the Alaskan Highway called "Alcan," which continually expands "as quickly as people can drive up to the edge of the wilderness and park their bagos in the next available slot" (273). The Alcan franchise allegorizes the extent to which these "local" communities in fact represent mobile commodities, which can be located anywhere, as the novel indicates when it describes how these franchise communities are laid out with exactly the same street plans and architectural layouts wherever they happen to be located, even if doing so requires chopping down mountain ranges and diverting the course of rivers, with no attention given to local differences (178, 12).

What these franchises sell, then, are prepackaged versions of subcultural or "bad" nationalisms. Although Halberstam and Livingston approvingly cite the way "posthuman bodies thrive in subcultures without culture," *Snow Crash* suggests that this response might be premature. In Stephenson's novel, it is true that "there are only subcultures," but the most visible results of the disappearance of any norm of national culture are the franchises and burbclaves (Halberstam and Livingston, 4). Stephenson's speculative representation of changing spatial relations under transnational regimes, in fact, only extends an existing trend identified by sociologist Mark Abrahamson. Abrahamson analyzes the current tendency toward consolidation of two historically distinct forms of urban community: on the one hand, the suburbs; and, on the other hand, ethnic or immigrant enclaves within the metropolis. Stephenson's coinage of the term "burbclaves" emphasizes this convergence of two formerly separate types of urban space (138–39). The consolidation of suburb and metropolitan enclave embodies the dual imperatives of transnationalism, its operation both on a global or standardized level, given the association of the suburbs with cultural homogenization, and on local or differentiated levels, given the association of ethnic enclaves with the assertion of ethnic difference and tradition. Stephenson's burbclaves confirm that these seemingly mutually exclusive processes can actually work together and reinforce one another.

Complete with their own private security forces and customs procedures for nonresidents, Stephenson's burbclaves are only slight exaggerations of practices already in effect in many of the estimated thirty-thousand gated communities currently existing in the United States. Stephen Graham and Simon Marvin point out more than one-third of all new communities built in Southern California are planned on what Davis calls the "fortress L.A." model, with walls, gates, security forces, and surveillance devices; already, Dallas, Texas, is home to twenty-five such gated communities (Graham and Marvin, 223; Davis, 221).[13]

What most strikingly distinguishes Stephenson's fictional burbclaves is the way they organize their claims to quasi-national sovereignty around their deliberate self-commodification as stereotypes of local color or ethnic identity, perhaps clearest in the "Narcolumbia" or "Nova Sicilia" franchises; "Nova Sicilia" specializes in pizza delivery and advertises for new residents with the slogan "you've got a friend in The Family" (8). Abrahamson notes how franchises like McDonald's have often been resisted within urban enclaves interested in retaining their own local specificity, but that increasingly such enclaves are themselves becoming the basis for new franchises, in a "McDonaldization of enclaves" (144). Developments like these seem to confirm Miyoshi's suspicions that the rise of "neoracism and neoethnicism in conjunction with the decline of the nation-state" might be only the flip side of multiculturalism as a transnational "import strategy" ("Borderless," 744, 748).

The cultural logic that produces the burbclaves and franchises also takes another form in *Snow Crash:* the proliferation of new ethnic categories, or, more accurately, the coding of all forms of social difference as ethnic difference. This proliferation is a recurrent motif in *Snow Crash,* and the emergence of these new modes of "ethnicity" is often related to changes in social space. We learn, for instance, that the protagonist of the novel spent his childhood in a succession of army towns, which were all "basically the same," no matter what country they were located in, "with the same franchise ghettos, the same strip joints, and even the same people" (58). The narrator goes on to describe this character's childhood friends: "their skins were different colors but they all belonged to the same ethnic group: Military" (ibid.). Racial difference becomes ethnicity here by being explicitly detached from any biological basis, such as skin color; instead, ethnicity is grounded, literally, in a shared relationship to a type of place that seems new partly because it is not located in a single place or defined by a bounded territory, but instead is geographically scattered across national boundaries; at the same time, the military base also seems to embody a new kind of spatial unity defined not by physical proximity but precisely as a function of its ability to support an ethnic identity (in this case, a multiracial one, like Mr. Lee's Greater Hong Kong)—that is, "Military" becomes a "place" as a result of a sense of ethnic unity, rather than ethnic unity being derived from a shared sense of place. Stephenson's humor here has a serious purpose: it offers a critical perspective on the weaker identity claims that the extension of the ethnic model produces, as compared to race (it is harder to take a "Military" ethnicity as seriously as we do, for instance, Jewish or Irish ethnicities). At the same time, this passage also dramatizes how the constructedness of ethnicity lends itself to expropriation by groups with all kinds of political agendas and rationales for asserting themselves as interest groups with a claim to social recognition (one reason it is hard to take a new military ethnicity as seriously as Jewish or Irish identities is that the military lacks the history of violently enforced difference, exile, and occupation that characterize these other ethnicities). The novel also stresses the way in which the emergence of "Military" as a new ethnic category disrupts and delegitimates older *cultural* markers of racial difference as well as *biological* markers. When they become part of the "Military" as ethnic group, "black kids didn't talk like black kids. Asian kids didn't bust their asses to excel in school. White kids, by and large, didn't have any problem getting along with the black and Asian kids" (ibid.). The novel therefore presents the emergence of new ethnic categories as progressive, in their challenge to older racial stereotypes, as these new categories supposedly make obsolete both strategies of retaining difference (dialects and slang) and assimilating (doing well in school).

This progressive interpretation of the emergence of new ethnic categories is problematized in the novel by the way it pushes the process of ethnic formation to extremes, as we have already seen in the case of the military. The novel also refers to "the longtime status of skateboarders as an oppressed ethnic group" (77; one of the main characters, the protagonist's sidekick, is a skateboarder). This is an especially interesting example because skateboarders are not defined by a specific location or place, even a scattered one such as the military bases; instead, skateboarders as an ethnic category are defined by their mobility, like the recreational vehicles making up the Alcan franchise, a mobility that allows the skaters to move across the boundaries fragmenting the urban space of Stephenson's cities (like pizza deliverers). The only "ground" for the skateboarders' ethnicity is their boards, not any piece of land. The reference to the skateboarders as an "oppressed ethnic group" seems intended as a ironic and depoliticized reference to the plight of refugees, forcibly evicted from the site of their cultural heritage. The equation of skateboarders with such refugee groups (thematized in the novel by a mass migration of "boat people" called "the Raft") empties the term "refugee" of any historical specificity; a similar implication might inhabit the discussion of the military as an ethnic group, where a job or profession as a soldier requires continual relocation, a demand that hardly seems to merit being equated with expulsion from one's homeland. From this perspective, the representation of ethnicity in *Snow Crash* threatens to collapse into the postmodern tendency Phillip Brian Harper defines, in which a "general public" denies the "specificity" of the experiences of historically marginalized racial and ethnic groups citing those experiences in order "to 'express' its own sense of dislocation" (Harper, 193).

On the other hand, though, Stephenson's novel also seems to suggest that, although it is certainly problematic to identify skaters or the military with diasporic cultures and forced exile, these groups do in fact embody significant processes of social differentiation (including late-capitalist class fractioning, especially in the case of the military, though skateboarders might also be identified with a downwardly mobile segment of the middle classes, faced with the prospect of either costly professionalization through college education or dead-end jobs in the service industries). The novel suggests that these processes can usefully be highlighted and made visible by, and perhaps only by, applying the model of new ethnicities to them. The problem, then, is whether it is possible to maintain differences among these differentiated groups, rather than collapsing them all into a dehistoricized model of "oppressed" racial minorities, and if so, how. An even better example of the lengths to which the thematics of new ethnic formations is taken as a model for all social differences in *Snow Crash* comes when the narrator describes a pair of truck drivers for a rock band as "an oppressed minority of two," when they go on strike by refusing to step outside the cab of their truck (120–21). The point, however, is that these kinds of seemingly absurd designations of minority status are merely logical extensions of the processes of spatial and ethnic transformation exemplified by the burbclaves and franchise communities, which are likely to strike readers as less extreme because they are relatively closer to existing modes of occupying urban space.[14]

This proliferation of ethnic categories results in a landscape saturated with signs of difference. In that sense, Stephenson's representation of ethnicity implicitly parallels the proliferation of different bodily forms possible within cyberspace. As the narrator of *Snow Crash* puts it, "your avatar" or virtual body image "can look any way you want it to, up to the limitations of your equipment. . . . You can look like a gorilla or a dragon or a giant talking penis" (36). I discussed a similar emphasis on possibilities of bodily metamorphosis in cyberspace in my reading of Greg Egan's novel *Diaspora* in chapter 1. *Snow Crash* and *Diaspora* diverge, however, because in *Snow Crash* this spectacular diversity of cyberspatial body images seems to differ only in degree, not in kind, from the diversity of ethnic affiliations and cultural identities in the "real world."

In fact, the thematics of out-of-control ethnic diversity in *Snow Crash* can in part be traced to the same root cause as the explosion of different body images in cyberspace: the unmooring of both ethnicity and body image from biological fixity, so that it is not inherited physical characteristics that determine ethnic affiliation but where one chooses to live or the products one consumes and uses, such as skateboards. This redefinition of ethnicity and the analogy the novel sets up between ethnic affiliation and virtual personae in cyberspace have effects that are as problematic as they are progressive. Harper's definition of postmodernism in terms of a generalized and often ahistorical "sense of dislocation" is specifically invoked in *Snow Crash* as a way of explaining the main character's racial hybridity. The narrator paraphrases the protagonist's attitude toward class, which he defines as "knowing where you stand in a web of social relations" (61). This phrase brings into conjunction two very different concepts of space and spatial relations, the space of places defined by clear boundaries that allow us to know where we stand and the very different topology implied by the figure of the "web" or what Haraway calls "a network ideological image, suggesting the profusion of spaces and identities and the permeability of boundaries in the personal body and in the body politic," typical of information societies (*Simians*, 170). The tension between these two concepts of space is central to the novel's representations of ethnicity, and those representations are of interest precisely to the extent that they retain this tension rather than either dissolving the specificity of a knowable standpoint into the contingency of being a mere node in a network, or reasserting the autonomy of those traditional standpoints.

The novel's main character, named Hiro Protagonist, is born of an African-American father and a Korean mother, and he is described as living in a state of "general disorientation" because he "didn't know whether he was black or Asian or just plain Army" (61). The novel tends to emphasize the benefits of this condition of "general disorientation," repeatedly dramatizing the inability of the other characters to classify Hiro and to "read" his ethnicity (187). In fact, when confronted with a virtual icon or avatar designed to morph into a form mirroring the physical features of the persons it encounters, Hiro is initially unable to "peg" his own "racial background" when he runs into another person possessing it (391), so that this virtual icon fails to have its intended effect: to reassure the people it interacts with by assuming a physical appearance similar to theirs. This scene suggests how the malleability of body images in cyberspace can serve to reinforce and mirror real-life racial expectations and stereotypes as well as to disrupt them. The reference to users of cyberspace being able to walk around looking like giant talking penises suggests the same thing about the relation of cyberspace body images to gender stereotypes. But Hiro's inability to know his own ethnicity also suggests that new ethnic categories like "Military" do not simply replace older racial and ethnic identities, but exist alongside them in a more complex relationship. This statement therefore contradicts and qualifies the seeming evacuation of historical categories of otherness, in the earlier reference to the military as an ethnicity superseding the meanings of white, black, and Asian embodiment. In this sense, ethnicity seems to function in this novel in much the same way as cyborg imagery, as discussed in chapter 2; both underline the disruption of racialized expectations and frameworks of bodily legibility. Another example is the character Raven, Hiro's main antagonist in the novel, an Aleutian Islander whose ambiguously "Asian" racial features are a frequent source of confusion for the other characters, just like Hiro's hybrid background (157).

The analogy between body images in cyberspace and new ethnic categories is best exemplified by the two examples of cyberspace body images that are granted ethnic status within the novel. In Stephenson's novel, to log on and participate in the Metaverse, the novel's term for cyberspace, a user's virtual point of view must be represented by an icon or avatar that makes the user visible to other users and therefore makes possible social interaction. But this same demand for visual representation also makes it impossible to avoid the importation of racial paradigms into cyberspace. In this system, differential access to computing power registers as different degrees of verisimilitude in one's avatar, the icon that embodies the user's perspective for other participants. Persons who cannot afford a custom-made avatar have to buy "off-the-shelf," standardized or generic images of themselves, the most popular being "Brandy and Clint" (37). The narrator describes the Metaverse as containing "enough Clints and Brandys to found a new ethnic group" (38).

Another widespread type of cyberspatial body image compared to an ethnic grouping is the "black-and-white people—persons who are accessing the Metaverse through cheap public terminals, and who are rendered in jerky, grainy black and white" (41). Like the Clints and Brandys, this type of body image belongs to people of a particular economic class who lack access to the necessary hardware and processing power or the programming background needed to create a more impressive, customized image of themselves in cyberspace. These forms of social difference are encoded as ethnic or racial difference in cyberspace. The reference to these lower-class users as "black-and-white people" clearly suggests that this new bodily signifier of difference both reproduces and cuts across traditional racial categories. This disruption of older frameworks for "reading" bodies and attributing racial meanings to them is reinforced when Hiro complains about how he is unable to "read [the] expression" on the face of one of the black-and-white people in cyberspace (68). When another character is forced to access the Metaverse through a public terminal, she notices how everyone is "giving her dirty looks" because "she's a trashy black-and-white person" (220). In this example, the colorless, low-resolution graphic as a new visual marker of bodily difference provokes prejudice in cyberspace in the same way that markers of racial difference do in the real world, and the novel's representation of racial hybridity or illegibility as a critical commentary on racial expectations tends to blur into a stereotype of racial others as inscrutable and massified or nonindividuated, as all looking alike.

Narrated by Hiro, a hacker and one of the original designers of the Metaverse, as focal character, the novel tends to present the black-and-white people and the Brandys and Clints as deviant cases of cyberspatial embodiment, a failure to realize the potential of the medium. However, it is also possible to read them as continuous with more creative uses of the bodily plasticity possible in cyberspace, to the extent that both sets of possibilities derive from the transformation of bodies into images. The result is to enable embodiment to be recrafted and redesigned, but also to facilitate the denaturalized mechanical reproduction of body images as commodities to be bought and sold. From this perspective, indeed, the privilege given to crafted and customized images might seem anachronistic, a harking back to precapitalist modes of production. The same tension inhabits the novel's representations of the burbclaves and franchise communities, which similarly possess both positive and negative consequences, precisely to the extent that they transform ethnic differences into matters of signification.

The negative effect is to standardize or make generic these forms of difference, an effect that is reinforced on a different level of the narrative by the names of two of the characters, which invoke generic categories: Hiro Protagonist, our "hero," and his friend and sidekick, Y.T., whose name is clearly intended as a pun on the word *whitey*. In both cases, the characters' conformity to generic categories is emphasized, though Hiro's name refers to a category of narrative agents and Y.T.'s name refers to a racial category. These punning names have the effect of reminding readers, every time we encounter the name in the novel, that these supposedly unique and individual characters are in fact also generic types. The burbclaves treat ethnic difference in precisely the same way, as both a unique identity and a generic type, often verging on a stereotype.

Snow Crash offers two main lines of flight or alternatives to the negative effects of social fragmentation and the commodification or standardizing of difference exemplified by the burbclaves. The first is to look to the future, to cyberspace computer networks and virtual communities. The second looks back to the once-cosmopolitan nature of city life. Neither of these alternatives ultimately seems effective, to the extent that they both evade the extension of commodity culture to the level of local community.

Snow Crash's Metaverse represents an attempt to reconstitute an idealized public sphere absent from the balkanized material reality of the United States, a new social space where "information, information, information" replaces "location, location, location" as the three main things to remember about real estate. Although Howard Rheingold celebrates the possibilities of online community as a "new electronic frontier" available for "homesteading," from a more political perspective some recent work on global computer networks suggests that what Gibson calls the "nonspace of the [computer] matrix" (63) might also provide a fertile ground for the nongovernment organizations that Miyoshi identifies as one major site of potential resistance to transnational corporations ("Sites," 72).[15] Howard Frederick both echoes and complicates Negroponte's claims about what it means to be local in cyberspace, when Frederick argues that both cyberspace and the NGOs might provide a basis for understanding how "today we are all members of many global 'nonplace' communities" (285). *Wired* magazine made similar claims in a story focused on computer networks in the Balkans themselves, as a technological antidote to the historical conflicts that gave us a model for the "balkanized" nation-state (Gessen).

Such celebrations of virtual community fall prey, however, to the trap of

resisting balkanization by valorizing the global access available through information technologies. Virtual reality and cyberspace can just as easily be understood as the proper site of the transnational elites themselves, a version of what
Arthur Kroker and Michael Weinstein call "the virtual class," whose "one gift,"
Miyoshi argues, "is, needs to be, an ability to converse and communicate with
each other" across ethnic and national boundaries ("Borderless," 747). Similarly, Stephen Graham and Simon Marvin's ethnographic study of the effects of
new technologies concludes that the social groups who seem to be taking full
advantage of electronic communication networks are those who already possess the privilege of physical mobility; for these groups, electronic media allow
them to travel freely while still maintaining the kinds of contacts that were previously possible only by staying at home or in one's neighborhood (192). In
this sense, Gibson's outlaw hackers and console cowboys might actually embody
the ideal of the transnational elites, precisely because in Gibson's novels it is
only the hackers who can move freely from one computer system to the next,
while legitimate users are confined within the metaphorical barriers of the intrusion countermeasures and firewalls that are intended to provide security for
corporate databases.[16]

In *Snow Crash*, one of the main features of the virtual space of the Metaverse is a public site called simply "The Street," which can be accessed by anyone
using public computer facilities. But rather than reconstituting an increasingly
inaccessible public sphere, Stephenson's virtual community in fact only results
in the extension of the logic of the franchise to the most basic level of individual personalities and bodies, as exemplified by the Clints and Brandys and
the black-and-white people.[17] The description of the features and body type of
the Clints in fact seems to invoke Clint Eastwood's film persona, as if that persona could be detached from cinematic narratives and sold as a commodity in
itself. For this class within the virtual community, to participate in cyberspace
is merely to become part of a franchise, to "do a Clint."[18] One way to read this
aspect of *Snow Crash* is as a gloss on the figure of Gibson's AI in *Neuromancer*,
who has limited Swiss citizenship, because it owns only its own thoughts, while
a multinational corporation owns its hardware and software (see chapter 2 in
this book). The way in which cyberspace technologies can function to reproduce the same, just as the franchises reproduce themselves across the face of
America, is emphasized in the narrator's description of what it's like to interact with one of the black-and-white people in cyberspace: it's "like talking to a
person who has his face stuck in a xerox machine, repeatedly pounding the
copy button, while you stand by the output tray pulling the sheets out one at
a time and looking at them" (38–39).

The application of the urban metaphor of the street to a virtual community marks the extent to which cyberspace is fantasized as a repository for social

interactions that are no longer possible in a balkanized postnational space. But the thematics of the Clints and Brandys and the black-and-white people shows that this utopian realm of free exchange is already contaminated by commodity relations. The idea that electronic spaces will assume the dominance once held in everyday life by urban ones is common enough, and is shared to varying degrees even by architects and city planners, such as Christine Boyer or William Mitchell. Graham and Marvin persuasively argue that this notion misrepresents the actual complex interactions that are developing between urban sites and electronic networks. But the power of this misreading dominates *Snow Crash's* representation of the consequences of replacing older forms of urban and public culture by privatized communities (assuming that those forms are not simply nostalgic idealizations in the first place); cyberspace comes to seem like a possible alternative public sphere, rather than the two functioning as "parallel constructions" (Graham and Marvin, 377).

Besides cyberspace, then, the other main alternative to the franchise ghetto is the city, or rather the ideal of the modernist city as a space of public access. Immediately after the description of how Americans have embraced the franchise ghetto, because they live in the most surprising and terrible country in the world, the narrator of *Snow Crash* tells us that by doing so they flee "the true America, the America of atomic bombs, scalpings, hip-hop, chaos theory, cement overshoes, snakehandlers, spree killers, space walks, buffalo jumps, drive-bys, cruise missiles, Sherman's March, gridlock, motorcycle gangs, and bungee jumping" (178–79). This truth of America lies in its status as an idealized contact zone of cultural hybridity and a supposedly even playing field of mutual vulnerability to violence, as indicated by the references to "scalpings" and "drive-bys."

In contrast to the suburban refugees from this America are the characters "who take the risk of living in the city because they like stimulation and they know they can handle it" (179). The effectiveness of the city as a model of resistance to the franchise ghettos is, however, limited by the fact that, where the distinction between the local and the cosmopolitan once corresponded to the distinction between the provincial and the larger national culture, today being cosmopolitan "involves an intellectual and aesthetic stance of openness towards divergent experiences from *different* national cultures," precisely the stance cultivated by the transnational corporations (Lash and Urry, *Economies,* 308). The tendency in transnationalism is to transform both sides of the oppositions global/local or provincial/cosmopolitan into forms that profit the corporations. The novel's figuration of the cosmopolitan space of the city as an alternative to the commodified and fortified enclaves of the suburbs depends on nostalgia for a social form that the novel itself depicts as anachronistic.[19]

Both of *Snow Crash's* alternatives to the franchise ghettos seem to fail because, in their very attempts to define a space outside the logic of transnationalism and its commodification of local cultures, they lend themselves to reappropriation by that logic. This problem is more briefly allegorized in Stephenson's contribution to a special issue of *Wired* magazine called *Wired Scenarios: The Future of the Future*. Stephenson imagines transforming the Internet and the World Wide Web into what he calls a "global neighborhood watch." By digitizing the output from cameras hooked up to motion sensors and tying those images into the Web, it would be possible for the appearance of an intruder on Stephenson's property to trigger an alarm and alert a computer user in another global time zone, where it would be daylight. Computer users around the world would therefore watch over one another's property while the owner slept in peace and security. Stephenson then acknowledges how this utopian scenario of technological boundary crossing and neighborhood formation will necessarily be interrupted by the realities of the global division of labor. He points out that "the US is so large, computerized, and crime-ridden that Global Neighborhood Watch will probably be a seller's market in the long run. Companies will establish giant air-conditioned warehouses in Malaysia where workers sit in front of screens keeping an eye on" American property (146). In contrast to the American television programs exported to places like Malaysia, these workers will see not "crime, crime, crime," but mostly "stray dogs, blowing branches, paper carriers, and—every so often—crime. That's an improvement, but it's so boring that they'll have to be paid to watch it" (ibid.). Typically, Stephenson suggests that new transnational media will break down national and ethnic stereotypes, revealing the United States to be more boring but less violent than TV programs suggest, even as they perpetuate and exploit economic inequities. He then takes this commercialization of the global neighborhood a step further, by suggesting that "if we could develop image-processing and pattern-recognition software good enough to filter out dogs and tree branches, then it would be crime, crime, crime again, and maybe they'd watch it for free. We cut out the Hollywood middleman. The solution to our crime problem becomes their entertainment" (ibid.). This scenario encapsulates the transnational cycle of cultural commodification, in a typical postmodern move to a logic of simulation, where "our crime problem becomes their entertainment." But Stephenson's speculations here also indicate how the reconstitution of local resistance and agency on a global level through the mediation of computer technology, finding global solutions to local problems and vice versa, merely results in the transformation of both the categories of the "global" and the "local" into resources to be exploited by transnational capitalism.

If such parables define the problems we face in a transnational economy, the implication is that it will be necessary to rethink the notions of resistance and opposition, in the absence of critical distance or utopian sitings. Haraway accurately sums up both the project of transnationalism and one basis for the production of cyborg imagery and cyberpunk narratives when she defines the common tendency of both "communications sciences" and modern biologies as the translation of "the world into a problem of coding, a search for a common language in which all resistance to instrumental control disappears and all heterogeneity can be submitted to disassembly, reassembly, investment, and exchange" (*Simians*, 164). As is characteristic of the posthuman formations discussed throughout this book, neither information nor material bodies (biology) escape such transformations. But the transnational context also suggests how these transformations can be understood as breaking down the distinction between information and materiality, mind and body, text and context, in ways that can have either conservative or progressive effects. As Harvey and Miyoshi suggest, within transnationalism, "heterogeneity" or local particularities do not exactly disappear; instead, they circulate within global commodity relations, in a system that prizes heterogeneity precisely to the extent that it "submits" to such integration and assimilation. But it is a mistake to assume that such assimilation can ever be total and that these necessary elements of local culture do not also continue to represent potential points of resistance that can be managed more or less successfully, but never eliminated. The transnational context, then, qualifies Haraway's argument about the informatics of domination, as Miyoshi (undoubtedly one of the most pessimistic and skeptical commentators on these changes) suggests when he argues that the challenge of resistance in a transnational economy is "how to balance the transnationalization of economy and politics with the survival of local culture and history—without mummifying them with tourism and in museums" ("Borderless," 747).

It is important to note that, in the context of transnational capitalism, "survival" has to mean something other than defensive assertions of autonomy or "innocence," to use Hall's phrase, because that kind of assertion is precisely the basis for the transnational commodification of local cultures, as Castells points out when he links "the globalization of power flows and the tribalization of local communities" (*Informational*, 350). Price similarly argues that the qualities of "addressability" and "interactivity" that characterize electronic media encourage the development of closed communication circuits between writers and readers, speakers and audience, leading to the development of "intense and exclusive diasporic communities, assembled along ethnic, class, or interest lines," in a closing of the "speech terrain" (79–80). This tendency represents a contrast to the "normally impersonal" medium of print, in which readers incorporate "an awareness of the potentially limitless others who may also be reading" and therefore gain a sense of participation in a general public (Warner, *Letters*, xiii). As Castells elaborates, "faced with the variable geometry of the space of [informational] flows, grassroots mobilizations" tend to become "so culturally specific that their codes of self-recognizing identity become non-communicable" (*Informational City*, 350). It is this process that Castells refers to as "tribalization" and that Stephenson's *Snow Crash* represents through the thematics of franchise communities. In other words, this thematics of the balkanization of the nation-state represents one possible story about the interconnections between new communications and computer technologies and transformations in public space. These processes are progressive to the extent that they presuppose a critique of the false universality attributed to the bourgeois public sphere in the early national period, in which the supposedly universal realm of rational debate was actually constructed through the exclusion of women and racialized groups, but these same processes can also play into the hands of new capitalist strategies of niche marketing, narrowcasting, and the proliferation of new demographic categories as "new ethnicities."

However, it is equally important to note the implications of analyses that suggest that this process of commodification is not simply one of co-optation, but also offers possibilities for preserving differences, in the new, more self-conscious form that Hall has in mind when he defines "new ethnicities." For instance, Harvey argues that the very demand for local self-commodification also defines sites of resistance, or at least negotiation: "if capitalists become increasingly sensitive to the spatially differentiated qualities of which the world's geography is composed, then it is possible for the peoples and powers that command those spaces to alter them in such a way as to be more rather than less attractive to highly mobile capital" (295). Similarly, this process of self-commodification seems to offer an opportunity to reconstruct "place-based social meaning" by rearticulating "the meaning of places to this new functional space" of transnational flows, a rearticulation that Castells proposes as the necessary precondition for resisting those flows (*Informational City*, 350). Using the example of British "heritage cities," in *Consuming Places*, John Urry suggests that the alternative to "tribalization," the self-commodification of local communities, is not necessarily a simple capitulation to the TNCs, but can instead result in self-reflection on and contestation of what is "authentic" about local histories and who can claim the right to speak in the name of the community (27). Where Miyoshi sees the recent history of rap music as an example of the vulnerability of "local resistance and nativist resistance" to the seductions of consumerism, the kind of contestation and debate that Urry describes seems much more apt as an account of the debates generated by the marketing of rap music.

In Stephenson's novel, while the apartheid burbclaves practice strict ethnic cleansing, franchises like Nova Sicilia or Mr. Lee's Greater Hong Kong actively recruit members who are not Italian or Asian (92). In the case of these franchises, the very act of self-commodification undermines the essentializing logic behind seeking "stable places of being," which Harvey sees as typical of post-Fordist cultures (339). The novel thereby supports Harvey's suggestion that the franchises' attempts at the "mechanical reproduction of value systems, beliefs, cultural preferences, and the like is impossible, not in spite of but precisely because of the speculative grounding" and drive to expansion "of capitalism's inner logic" (345). The very logic of the reproducibility of the franchise communities, which seems to produce only homogeneity, can in fact lead to the kind of ethnic engagement with internal differences that Hall calls for, in effect resisting the process of resegregation exemplified by the white supremacist burbclaves.

The emergence of this possibility for resistance highlights one of the key subtexts in Stephenson's novel, the analogy between the franchises and computer software. This analogy emerges most directly in the narrator's claim that the essence of a franchise is the "three-ring binder" that contains the franchise's business plan. In other words, the franchise is defined as information, and more specifically as a set of formal rules, for which the metaphor is the DNA code (178). It is this definition of what is essential to the franchise that makes it portable and underlies the comparison between the franchises and viruses, each able to thrive as well in one place as another. The contradictory, and potentially resistant, nature of this definition emerges when we realize that franchises are therefore not just reproducible forms of information, but also potentially forms of shareware, to use the contemporary term for software that is *not* treated as intellectual property, but which is freely distributed and copyable. Mr. Lee's Greater Hong Kong, with its openness to all "anthropologies," is a franchise that treats ethnicity as a form of shareware, by resisting the analogy between ethnic identity and private property that informs the white supremacist burbclaves. In this sense, Mr. Lee's Greater Hong Kong seems to realize the abstract potential for cooperation that Hardt and Negri locate in informational economies (293–94). Mr. Lee's Greater Hong Kong is a franchise community in which the hacker slogan "information wants to be free" (intended to capture the ways in which information resists objectification as property) is rewritten in terms of ethnicity and possessive investments in it.[20]

This rethinking of ethnicity is still marked by contradiction and ambivalence, because it tends to elide the distinction between the traditional "possessive investment in whiteness" (Lipsitz) as a model for new commodified forms of ethnicity and resistant forms of identity politics that, as Chatterjee argues, mobilize alternative investments or "bad nationalisms." To the extent that a redefinition like Mr. Lee's Greater Hong Kong opens onto the new cultural politics of difference that Hall calls for, it seems progressive, but Stephenson's novel also demonstrates how easily such a redefinition slips into what Coco Fusco calls a "backlash against identity politics" that might find an unexpected ally in the posthuman critique of "the integrity of the human organism as the basis of identity" (xvi). Stephenson's franchise nations, as embodying an information logic or software analogy at the level of group identity, demonstrate that the same critique is being applied to models of ethnic integrity and the organic relation between groups and their cultural heritages.

CONCLUSION: THE ANTINOMIES OF POSTHUMAN THOUGHT

Classical philosophy did, it is true, take all the antinomies of its life-basis to the furthest extreme it was capable of in thought; it conferred on them the highest possible intellectual expression. But even for this philosophy they remain unsolved and insoluble. Thus classical philosophy finds itself historically in the paradoxical position that it was concerned to find a philosophy that would mean the end of bourgeois society, and to resurrect in thought a humanity destroyed in that society and by it. In the upshot, however, it did not manage to do more than provide a complete intellectual copy and the *a priori* deduction of bourgeois society. It is only the manner of this deduction, namely the dialectical method that points beyond bourgeois society. And even in classical philosophy this is only expressed in the form of an unsolved and insoluble antinomy.

—*Georg Lukács, "The Antinomies of Bourgeois Thought," in* History and Class Consciousness *(148)*

GEORG LUKÁCS'S CRITIQUE of classical philosophy (by which he means philosophical modernity, beginning with Kant) identifies the ways in which this movement of critical thought remained bound up within the limitations of classic liberalism, specifically what Lukács calls the "reified structure of consciousness" or the romantic problem of alienation, the a priori separation of individual mind from social world (110–11). In other words, classical philosophy only intensifies the antinomies or dualisms of the bourgeois way of life that it tries to resolve, to the extent that this philosophy remains a form of thought. For Lukács, the failure of classical philosophy is its failure to abolish itself by realizing its ideas in practice and creating an alternate society that could materialize the "humanity destroyed by [bourgeois class] society" and resurrected only in thought by the philosophical exercise of critical reason.

On one level, the forms of posthuman thought I have analyzed throughout this book hold out the promise of resolving these antinomies in ways classical philosophy could not, to the extent that the technological mediation of embodiment and subjectivity undoes the ideology of possessive individualism, the material basis for the alienation of self and world, mind and body. New theories of extended minds, which incorporate external, technological elements as part of the cognitive process, and embodied cognition, emerging out of evolutionary psychology as it blurs the distinction between biological and cultural modes of development, promise to put "brain, body, and world together again," to cite the subtitle of one of Andy Clark's books. But this scientific realization of the project of classical philosophy also calls into question the category of "authentic humanity" that Lukács argues would have been produced if classical philosophy could have put its ideas into practice (Lukács, 136). From this perspective, posthumanism suggests a new, more powerful statement of what Lukács calls "the necessity of going beyond this historical stage in mankind's development," the stage theorized by classical philosophy (121), but the most recent versions of this "evolution" seem to call into question Lukács's humanist vision of "the true essence of man liberated from the false, mechanising forms of society: man as a perfected whole who has inwardly overcome, or is in the process of overcoming, the dichotomies of theory and practice, reason and content; man whose tendency to create his own forms does not imply an abstract rationalism which ignores concrete content; man for whom freedom and necessity are identical" (136–37).

Or do they? As we have seen, some forms of posthuman thought and some visions of scientific progress, at least, intensify these same antinomies, in the very act of attempting to abolish them, in ways that pose a much more extreme challenge to the dialectical method's ability to resolve and mediate these dualisms, even in thought, than industrial society and wage labor ever could. Posthuman fantasies of technological transcendence and freedom from the limits of embodiment (exemplified in chapter 1 by Hans Moravec and the Extropian movement, as well as fictions of immigrating into cyberspace) define an impulse to deny the very existence of a world of material practice that might seem very familiar to Lukács, who offers a biting critique of the subjectivist and solipsist tendencies of Kantian epistemology. What Lukács could not have anticipated is what Edward Wilson calls the imminent decommissioning of "human nature" itself (303), which in some posthuman formulations threatens to destroy humanity more thoroughly and resurrect it as pure mind more abstractly than Lukács could possibly have imagined.

Moreover, posthuman technocultures suggest that the movement beyond dualistic and dichotomous habits of thought (Lukács's antinomies) is not necessarily progressive, as Mary Ann Doane suggests when she asks how "the collapse of oppositions represented by the cyborg" can be "liberating or potentially productive" when "the collapse of these oppositions" becomes "the norm," in information economies where social relations are organized around flexible networks and permeable boundaries ("Cyborgs," 213).[1] The other touchstone I have cited in developing this critique throughout this book has been Phillip Brian Harper's argument about the dehistoricizing effects of a postmodern "categorical collapse" that appropriates experiences of social marginality as signifiers of this general dislocation and disorientation. N. Katherine Hayles defines technocultures in general as informed by a basic interpenetration of information and materiality, which she calls the "condition of virtuality" (*How We Became Posthuman,* 13–14), but she also argues that only one possible outcome of this process of breaking down dualisms has tended to dominate the new cultures of technological embodiment—that is, that materiality can be assimilated or collapsed into to a model of information (18). This definition also suggests the possibility of posthuman alternatives to some of the more extreme claims of posthuman transcendence, alternatives that would define more complex interactions between information and materiality, minds and bodies. Throughout this book I have attempted to define this ambivalence within posthumanism, but part of the problem is that technocultures are inherently more ambivalent, in terms of how both domination and resistance function, than the forms of bourgeois thought and society that Lukács takes as his object. Posthumanism, then, functions like popular cultures as Stuart Hall defines them, as sites of "strategic contestation" that are "bound to be contradictory, and this is not because we haven't fought the cultural battle well enough" ("What Is This 'Black,'" 471). I want to consider now the ways in which dualistic habits of thought are both reproduced and displaced within posthumanism in analogical forms. Specifically, I will argue that Stephenson's *Snow Crash* demonstrates how Hayles's condition of virtuality may only invert the categories of nature and culture; as material bodies become more malleable, new forms of cultural rigidity are produced. This failure to break down the dualism of materiality and information is the central antinomy of posthuman thought.

"The Franchise and the Virus Work on the Same Principle": The Analogical Structures of Posthuman Narrative

To conclude this book with a final reflection on the sources of this posthuman ambivalence, I would now like to return briefly to a reading of *Snow Crash,* which focuses more directly on the issues foregrounded by the plot, in contrast to my focus in the preceding chapter on the novel's more lateral elements of setting, place, and ethnicity as they are redefined by processes of globalization, facilitated by new information technologies and the economic structures they support. As critics like Hayles and David Porush have pointed out, Stephenson's novel can be read as a kind of metacommentary on one of the central tendencies of posthuman narratives: the analogical linkage they make between computer software and human minds and bodies, both of which tend to be represented through metaphors of textuality or inscription, to use Hayles's term, and both of which tend to be understood, more or less reductively, as problems of coding, to use Haraway's phrase. *Snow Crash* foregrounds the role of a specific conception of language in providing the basis for this analogical structure. The novel therefore offers a unique opportunity to consider the validity of posthumanist analogies between bodies, minds, and information. I want to stress, however, that *Snow Crash* has particular value within the speculative tradition of posthuman narratives because it also extends this analogical structure further than almost any other such narrative. The analogical structure Stephenson's novel sets up includes metaphorical equivalences not only between computer software, human beings, and language, but also between all of those things and place or social space and ethnicity.

Hayles's reading of *Snow Crash* begins with the insight that the world of the novel "is driven by a single overpowering metaphor: humans are computers" (*How We Became Posthuman*, 272).[2] The novel's title refers to a computer virus that is designed to affect the brains of human beings who have learned computer programming languages, and therefore, as the novel imagines, have developed neural structures that can be accessed and externally manipulated or rewired by anyone who understands the techniques required. The narrative concerns the way in which a group of characters, especially Hiro and Y.T., learn of the existence of these techniques of mind control; reeducate themselves (along with readers of the novel) in the fields needed to account for the existence of these techniques, especially theories of language and sociobiological accounts of the origins of human consciousness; and ultimately join in resistance to the mind-control conspiracy launched by the technique's developers. In other words, the plot of the novel revolves around the redefinition of embodiment and subjectivity implicit in the metaphor of hardwiring; in fact, the novel sets out to bridge the use of this concept in neuroscientific study of brain structures, especially to define the role of learned practices and behavior in creating biological features in the brain, with its use in computer science, to define a particular level within a computational system where software and hardware become difficult to distinguish absolutely.

The novel's central narrative strategy is therefore to literalize and collapse the metaphorical chain that equates human minds and bodies (or brain structures) with texts and in turn equates such texts with computer software programs. As Hayles puts it, "the novel's central premise" is that "a computer virus can also infect humans, acting at once as an infection, a hallucination [recalling Gibson's definition of cyberspace as a "consensual hallucination"], and a religion" (ibid.). David Porush calls attention to the same narrative strategy when he describes how the idea that human brains could be "hacked" or infected by a computer virus "breaks the barrier between worlds" and "effects a transcendence of the categories *natural* and *artificial*, between the biological world and the simulated reality of cyberspace" (563).[3] Porush points out that this breakdown of conceptual barriers can be understood as literalizing the process of metaphor itself, in its function of linking distinct categories, rather than any specific metaphor. Porush's reading of *Snow Crash* is based on his argument that "the brain . . . is a metaphor machine, operating continuously to carry meaning between realms that are in the largest sense thoroughly incommensurable"—that is, between the objective world and the subjective (Porush, 550). Porush therefore reads *Snow Crash* as the ultimate example of a general postmodern tendency to exteriorize "the codes of metaphoresis represented in the hard-wiring of the brain itself" (ibid.). We might also note that this privileging of the process of metaphorization as Porush idiosyncratically defines it becomes more problematic when read as a version of the abstraction of information from material context that Hayles critiques, because metaphors involve a process of transfer or substitution. Porush's argument needs to be qualified, however, by the way in which *Snow Crash* also constitutes a metacommentary on the typical cyberpunk use of "hardwiring" to thematize posthuman analogies between humans and machines.

The Snow Crash computer virus to which computer programmers are especially vulnerable is most easily distributed through cyberspace. But there is another, more general aspect to this mind-control conspiracy, whose techniques of affecting human minds directly, at the level of deep brain structures, are generalizable because of an analogy between the effects of computer programming languages on the brain and the effects of language in general. Hiro learns about the more general effects of the Snow Crash virus during an extended didactic sequence set in cyberspace, consisting of a dialogue between Hiro and a digital agent or expert system specializing in information retrieval, called the Librarian. The Librarian outlines for Hiro the linguistic debates between the relativists, like Sapir and Whorf, who believe that different languages determine modes of thought and perception, and the universalists, like Chomsky, who believe that there are general deep structures unifying all languages, linguistic structures that might correspond to brain structures. The novel proposes a synthesis of these two positions, by developing a computer analogy. In this synthesis of relativist and universalist positions, Stephenson's novel imagines that language acquisition creates and alters deep neurological structures, which are therefore not simply inherited or built into our brains but actively produced after birth. As a result, it is true that "the newborn human brain has no structure—as the relativists would have it," but it is also true that "as the child learns a language, the developing brain structures itself accordingly . . . as the universalists would have it" (277). In other words, language hardwires itself into the brain during the process of learning one's first language. The novel explicitly compares this process to the programming of a computer chip, specifically to PROMs, or programmable read-only memory chips, which can be programmed with information only once. As soon as the information is recorded in the chip, "it transmutes into hardware," so that "you can read it out" but "you can't write" anymore (ibid.). Similarly, the novel suggests that during language acquisition, "language gets 'blown into' the hardware and becomes a permanent part of the brain's deep structure" (ibid.). In the terms of the computer metaphor, language begins as software, as information recorded and stored in our memories, and becomes hardware, a permanent part of our brain structure. This crossover from hardware to software, from culture and ideology to biology, is precisely what is meant by the term "hardwiring" in cyberpunk fiction more generally, and in this sense Stephenson's novel can be read as an extended reflection on the implications of that key metaphor, like the analogy Gibson's *Neuromancer* sets up between Case and Molly and the artificial intelligence they work for and try to free from its hardwired programming constraints (see chapter 2).

These deep structures are both linguistic and neurological, both software and hardware, and it is on the basis of this linguistic speculation that the novel can imagine the possibility of "hacking" a human brain in the same way that it is possible to hack into a computer. Hiro raises this possibility when he compares the deep structures wired into the brain during language acquisition to "machine code," a programming language that functions at a more fundamental level than any other and that takes its name from the fact that it is designed to be "read" primarily by machines; programmers work in another language, which is then translated or compiled into the more basic commands of machine code, which is not usually directly legible or accessible to most programmers, much less users (*Snow Crash*, 278).[4]

This analogy between the neurolinguistic deep structures of the brain and machine code is significantly different than the analogy between those brain structures and PROMs. Specifically, it is possible, though extraordinarily difficult, for a programmer to work in machine code. Even when access to the machine-code level is mediated through other programming languages (assembly languages, specifically), it is still possible to rewrite such code, whereas the information that has transmuted into hardware in a PROM chip is untouchable. The shift from the PROM analogy to the machine-code analogy may seem like a minor change, but it is absolutely necessary to justify the novel's vision of neurolinguistic mind-control, which would be impossible if the brain's deep structures were analogous to PROMs. Hiro later elaborates on this neurolinguistic theory to convince another character to help him resist the mind-control conspiracy. Hiro explains that there is an underlying "tongue based in the deep structures of the brain, that everyone shares," and "these structures consist of basic neural circuits that have to exist in order to allow our brains to acquire higher languages" (395). The "output side" of this fundmental ur-language is glossalalia, or speaking in tongues, "where the deep linguistic structures hook into our tongues and speak, bypassing all the higher, acquired languages" (ibid.). But Hiro insists that there must also be "an input side" to this ur-language, which means that "someone who knows the right words" can "go past all your defenses and sink right into your brainstem" (ibid.). This neurolinguistic hacking is analogous to programming in machine language, which involves "controlling the computer at its brainstem, the root of its existence" (278). Note here how the metaphor reverses itself, so while the novel sometimes compares human brains to computers, it also sometimes compares computers to human brains. But what this reversibility makes possible, the novel suggests, is the direct programming and manipulation of human minds, moving the human–computer analogy toward a fairly traditional conception of the reduction of humans to automatons "with no choice but to run the programs fed into [them]," as Hayles notes (273).

The novel pays little or no attention to the possibility that, if cultural "software" can transform itself into biological "hardware," then the reverse might also be true: what we regard as biologically fixed qualities defining our "natures" might be better understood as learned cultural patterns and codes. *Snow Crash's* lack of attention to this possibility is especially surprising, given its usual willingness to invert its own metaphorical equations. As I have argued, what gives the trope of hardwiring the critical potential it possesses is precisely the possibility of reversing the metaphorical equation of culture and biology and defining the analogical crossing from culture to biology as working both ways.

Given this shift from conceptualizing neurolinguistic structures as permanent, by analogy with PROMs, to constructing them as "vulnerable" to hacking and external manipulation, by analogy with machine code (124), there is another possible interpretation of the novel's central analogy, one that is less defensive about the implications of that analogy. In this second reading, which moves against the grain of *Snow Crash*, the novel's theory of how language and culture transform and institutionalize themselves as biology is *not* as essentialist as it seems it should be, because the biological encoding of linguistic structure is *not* absolutely fixed and unchanging. The novel displays considerable anxiety, if not outright panic, over the interpretation of these deep structures as a threat to human autonomy. By extension, the novel displays that same anxiety about the analogy between humans and computers that underlies this linguistic theory. But the very representation of such neurolinguistic structures or "programs" as a threat also implies that these deep structures can be rewritten. And if they can be rewritten, then they could be rewritten not to manipulate people, but instead in order to critique and call into question cultural assumptions and social norms as they are embedded in different languages, in a technocultural restatement of one of the basic insights of contemporary ideology critique.

As Hayles points out, *Snow Crash* seems to resist this reading of how the novel's own speculative premises make it "possible to imagine someone 'hacking the brainstem' for liberatory purposes" (276).[5] Greg Egan's story "Chaff," discussed in chapter 1, offers a narrative of precisely the "liberatory" effects of technologies that make it possible to alter the "wiring" of the brain's structures. The contrast between these two narratives and their attitudes toward the metaphor of hardwiring and the analogical linkage of humans and computers points to important differences in the interpretation of this analogical structure.

The Snow Crash virus, and the neurolinguistic theory on which it is based, have their origins in the desire of a media tycoon, L. Bob Rife, to exercise proprietary control over the information contained in the brains of his employees. Rife argues that when a computer programmer works for him, "information is going into [the programmer's] brain. And it's staying there." As a result, Rife's corporation invents the Snow Crash virus as a refinement of "our management techniques so that we can control that information no matter where it is—on our hard disks or even inside the programmers' heads" (116). In this corporate rhetoric of information as intellectual property, the analogy between human brains and computer disks clearly serves the purposes of extending the commodity structure and relations of ownership, and not just to the body or the labor value of the employee but to the employee's inner subjective world, which cannot be clearly distinguished from what the employee learns on the job. As Rife puts it, a programmer inevitably absorbs information that "travels with him when he goes home at night" and "gets all tangled up into his *dreams*" (ibid.). The language of this passage exactly parallels the language of Hiro's description of how information or software becomes transformed into hardware after being entered into a onetime read-only memory chip. In other words, what Rife is resisting is the idea that information ceases to be manipulable or revisable once it has been entered into the brains of his human employees. Rife prefers to be able to treat his employees' brains as if they were structured like machine code rather than a PROM, and Rife's attitude certainly seems to justify the novel's panic about the implications of this analogy between brain structures and computer programming languages. In effect, Stephenson imagines a scenario in which human beings are threatened with being reduced to the status of an artificial intelligence, like the one in Gibson's *Neuromancer,* where a corporation owns its brain and what it knows, but the AI's "thoughts have Swiss citizenship" (132).

It is also significant that Rife owns a religious franchise called Reverend Wayne's Pearly Gates, where customers have to present their credit cards to be allowed into the chapel. Rife uses these franchises as a front to distribute Snow

Crash as a drug, to infect people who aren't computer programmers. This bio-technologically delivered infection produces one dominant symptom. In addition to being rendered suggestible, those infected lose their "higher language functions" and begin to babble chains of nonsense syllables. As Hiro puts it, glossalalia is the output side of the universal neurolinguistic deep structures. This element of *Snow Crash*'s plot emphasizes the association of ethnicity, in the form of religion, with the hardwired deep structures of language, given that religion is one of the forms that the Snow Crash virus takes. The association of such forms of cultural hardwiring with processes of cultural homogenization and massification is dramatized in the novel when Rife uses Snow Crash to take over a mass migration of refugees, permanent "boat people," who are compared to a horde of army ants (*Snow Crash*, 273). At this point, the novel's depiction of the negative effects of this theory of linguistic hardwiring begins to generate its own conservative reaction, in the form of a reassertion of the humanist values of individuality, which results in the conflation of racist stereotypes with the imagined effects of posthuman technologies and their threat of mind control. As Hayles notes, in the face of the possibilities for social control and abuse created by both new technologies and theories of language that analogize humans and computers, *Snow Crash* suggests "it is better to have a white middle-American consciousness than no consciousness at all" (277). By polarizing the options in this way, the novel falls prey to what I have called the antinomies of posthuman thought. But this pessimistic conclusion is generated by a suspect interpretation of the posthuman analogy between people and software, not necessarily by that analogy itself.

In *Snow Crash*, the diversity of the "higher language functions," as opposed to the universality of neurolinguistic deep structure, functions as a defense against direct manipulation of minds. The novel sets up two alternatives, pure homogeneity or pure heterogeneity, direct understanding without the need for conscious thought or the misunderstanding and miscommunication that results from not knowing one another's languages and never being able to truly learn. The novel effectively rewrites the biblical story of the destruction of the Tower of Babel in terms of an elaborate Sumerian mythology.[6] Stephenson suggests that these neurolinguistic deep structures correspond to an original universal language, which was shattered into today's divergent tongues by an ancient neurological hacker (taken from Sumerian mythology). This ancient hacker caused Babel to happen by introducing a virus that would have the opposite effect of Rife's Snow Crash—that is, this ancient virus rewired or rewrote the deep structures of the brain to render them inaccessible to anyone else; it edited brains in such a way as to make them uneditable from then on. The result is the loss of any common, shared language, intelligible to all persons. As Hayles astutely puts it, Stephenson's myth revision writes the posthuman back into ancient history, in order to argue that we are all always potential posthumans because we possess these basic brain structures that are analogous to computer programs and that always threaten to shift from unchanging hardware back to manipulable and rewritable software (278–79).

This countervirus is the main way Stephenson's novel ever admits that neurolinguistic hacking can have "liberatory purposes." But the only such purpose the novel is willing to imagine is the foreclosure of any similar acts for any other purposes, and the novel tends therefore to conflate manipulation and mind control with critical interventions, which thereby are reduced to oppressive forms of "political correctness." The Snow Crash virus, and the whole plot of the novel, result from Rife's discovery that people have become vulnerable again to manipulation of these neurolinguistic structures, precisely because of the shift from spoken and written languages to a predominantly visual mode of communication exemplified by virtual reality. The novel ends with Hiro and his allies overcoming Rife's conspiracy by reintroducing the original countervirus into the population. In effect, Snow Crash ends with its heroes discovering how to stabilize the ambiguous status of these neurolinguistic deep structures, so that they revert to a stable foundational "hardware" rather than functioning as a programming language, however mediated our access to that language is through layers of other "codes." In effect, the novel collapses the ambiguities created by the trope of hardwiring, in order to suggest that there are no distinctions to be made between layers of programming languages, and that they are all vulnerable to instrumental control precisely because they function as texts that can be rewritten at will, offering no resistance.[7] As Hayles puts it, Snow Crash's revisionist mythology implies that these neurolinguistic deep structures are necessary because "they allow the human to emerge out of the posthumans we have always already been" (279). The novel therefore reasserts the human over the posthuman, to present human autonomy and self-control as a process of subordinating and repressing our logically prior susceptibility to manipulation and "programming." But paradoxically, the heroic narrative of Snow Crash reasserts the human over the posthuman only by technologically producing brain structures as hardware, as machines resistant to change, rather than as software or texts that can easily metamorphose.

Stephenson's novel therefore resists the implications of the metaphor of human minds as inscriptions rather than as embodied and material only at the cost of giving up on changing or decentering the norms of "white middle-class American consciousness" (277). This recontainment of the possibilities for critique and change that might be implicit in posthuman technological metaphors and analogies seems to me to be the result of Stephenson's relentless literalizing of these analogies. I argued in earlier chapters that the trope of hardwiring combines the qualities of malleability and resistant materiality, by implying that cultural patterns and norms can be modeled on texts and so are open to revision or reprogramming; at the same time, this trope often suggests that such patterns and norms are embedded in people at a deep enough level to resist their transformation into manipulable signifiers and thus their commodification and control. The distinction here would be between software that functions as part of an operating system and software that runs as an application on an operating system. The operating system's software works at a more fundamental level than the applications and is therefore relatively harder to access or alter, but it is not inherently impossible to do so; it just takes considerable skill and effort, and is likely to have more far-reaching consequences on the rest of the system. In this sense, hardwired structures are both built in and built, both "essential" and "constructed." In contrast, in *Snow Crash*, hardwiring tends to be associated more definitely with resistant materiality, though the whole plot of the novel dramatizes the fact that this simpler definition of hardwiring has to be achieved through a long and difficult struggle. The implication that hardwired or built-in structures, like language, are built and can be rebuilt is associated with purely negative effects. Hardwiring as inscription is associated only with human *pro*grammability rather than *re*programmability or *self*-programmability.

There's a relatively minor scene in *Snow Crash* that perfectly exemplifies this reductive interpretation of the trope of hardwiring. In this scene, Hiro is trying to turn off a piece of equipment with a powerful built-in computer system. He reflects that "computers this powerful are supposed to shut themselves down, after you've asked them to. Turning one off with the hard switch is like lulling someone to sleep by severing their spinal column" (386). This passage reverses the normal way in which the hardwiring metaphor is used, comparing the computer to a human body rather than reading the human body as a computer. The point of the comparison is that using the "hard switch," or affecting either a computer or a person through their hardwired structures, is analogous to physical violence and violation, in contrast to the self-regulation of the system through its own software. Given the way *Snow Crash* systematically operates through reversible metaphors of humans as computers and computers as humans, this passage invites the conclusion that human "hardwiring" cannot be altered without killing or mutilating the person, that "hacking" the brainstem is literally to "hack" the spinal cord in half. The entire plot of the novel seems bent on reinforcing this same conclusion. The corollary is that fundamental human change is not possible without similar violence, so that in this reading *Snow Crash* does indeed end up reasserting a humanist ideology, at the same time that it presents the stability of that ideology as always in danger of dissolving into malleable software architectures.

The novel is ultimately unable or unwilling to sustain the ambiguity that establishes hardwired structures as *both* biological *and* cultural, as mutual

contexts for each other, despite the possibilities for social and political intervention that are implicit in the novel's own references to such structures as "the
operating system of society" (257). It is at this point that the novel seems to
draw back from the implications of its own analogical structure. When the novel
plays on the word *hack* as a metaphor for such interventions that collapses into
counterproductive violence at the first attempt to literalize it, the novel tries to
convert its key analogy between the human mind and computer systems into
a metaphor, characterized by sharp distinctions between the figurative and the
literal rather than the reversibility of terms typical of analogy. The novel ends
by emphasizing the possibility of culture becoming biology, human products
becoming hardwired into our brain structures, our anatomy, but not the reverse.
Stephenson's version of the human–computer analogy, which compares neurolinguistic structures to the "collection of rules that tell [a computer] how to
function" (ibid.), seems to make it equally plausible to read cultural norms and
"rules" through the metaphor of hardwiring, and not just neural structures. But
Snow Crash tries to foreclose on that possibility, even as its use of these basic
posthuman analogies cannot help but raise it as a possibility. The result is to
emphasize the reification of those norms and rules, like Dennett's example of
how language acquisition exemplifies a form of "post-natal self-design" (or what
Stephenson's novel calls hardwiring, by analogy with the PROM chips) that
amounts to no more than the process by which an individual brain "turns itself
into a Swahili or Japanese or English brain" (*Consciousness Explained*, 200; see
chapter 1 for a discussion of Dennett). Like Stephenson's conservative reassertion of the Babel myth, Dennett here implies that cultural differences are built
into the structures of our minds in ways that we can never truly change.

    Snow Crash therefore dramatizes both the value and the limitations of post-
human analogies, by pushing them to the point of literalization. *Snow Crash*'s
claim that "humans are computers" collapses an analogical structure into a relation of identity, which in turn generates a defensive rejection of any overlapping
of the categories of the "human" and the "computer" (Hayles, *How We Became
Posthuman*, 272). Other posthuman narratives invoke this same analogical
structure to present more complex explorations of the relationship between
these categories. In *The Cassini Division*, for example, one of Ken MacLeod's
characters points out that it is likely to be impossible to "hack human minds,
even minds in computers," downloaded and encoded as software, because even
in that form there won't be any built-in "access path" or "memory addresses"
in the downloaded human mind, as there are in computer operating systems
(*Cassini Division*, 147).

    At the same time, *Snow Crash* serves, in my view, as a warning against the
inherent tendency of this analogical structure to move toward a relation of
identity. It is difficult to maintain a more complex relationship of simultaneous

similarity and difference between the terms of this analogy, though that is exactly what is being attempted in the passage from MacLeod's *Cassini Division* quoted in the preceding paragraph. It is difficult to treat biology and culture as metaphors for each other without privileging one of them as the literal term, the "truth" of the other. Throughout this book I have tried to define the benefits as well as the dangers of maintaining this difficult balance in our thinking about the cultural effects of the technological mediation of embodiment.

"No Piece of Software Is Ever Bug Free": Hardwiring the Linguistics of Contact

So far, in this discussion of what *Snow Crash* has to teach us about the analogical structure of posthuman narrative, I have focused on the novel's representation of and commentary on the analogy between humans and computers, including the trope of hardwiring. I want to turn now to the way in which *Snow Crash* foregrounds the role of language in this chain of posthuman metaphors. In the preceding chapter, I discussed how transnational culture privileges the concept of linguistic translatability and how this concept of language functions as a metaphor for spatial mobility across cultural and ethnic borders. But we can now see how concepts of language appropriate to a transnationalized world appear in *Snow Crash* in relation to the trope of hardwiring.

In Stephenson's novel, hardwired deep structures in the brain are associated with a particular fantasy about language, which Mary Louise Pratt refers to as the "linguistics of community" (49). With specific reference to Chomsky's theory of linguistic deep structure, Pratt critiques the way "our modern linguistics of language, code, and competence" takes for granted "a unified and homogeneous social world in which language exists as a shared patrimony"; she goes on to point out that this is precisely the assumption behind Benedict Anderson's analysis of print culture, which makes it possible for him to define nationalism as a process of imagining community through the technology of print (50). The problem with such a "linguistics of community" is that it cannot conceptualize how speakers of the same language "constitute each other relationally and in difference, how they enact differences in language" (60). Pratt refers to this alternative as a "linguistics of contact," where language practices function as sites of contact across cultural boundaries rather than as a site for the reproduction of a homogeneous cultural heritage (ibid.).

In *Snow Crash,* the deep linguistic structure hardwired into our brains during language acquisition constitutes just such a "linguistics of community," in the form of a supposedly universal ur-language, which renders differences between people meaningless. The novel foregrounds the dangers represented by such a "dream of a common language," and Stephenson therefore seems to offer a critique of what Haraway describes as the founding logic of transnational or post-Fordist information economies: as "*the translation of the world into a problem of coding*, a search for a common language in which all resistance to instrumental control disappears and all heterogeneity can be submitted to disassembly, reassembly, investment, and exchange," the "common move" of both communications science and modern biology (*Simians*, 164). Haraway's wording here is especially important: translating the world into a problem of coding turns out to mean making the world translatable or mobile, on the assumption that meaning can be abstracted more or less completely from the material medium that communicates it.[8]

However, this reading returns us to the problem of the franchise communities discussed in the preceding chapter. In terms of the thematics of language, the alternative to the universal deep structure, the ur-language, is a linguistics that privileges diversity, misunderstanding, noise, and obstacles to free communication, a linguistics that recognizes that the playing field is never level and that the free exchange of ideas is always subject to the interferences of unequal power relations—Pratt's "linguistics of contact." But the thematics of the franchise nations shows that, in the transnational technocultural context *Snow Crash* imagines, that very diversity can be translated into a reproducible and generalizable form not unlike that of the ur-language the novel's main characters struggle to suppress. The franchise nations represent closed communities and exclusive cultural identities that become commodities that can be bought and sold precisely because of their exclusivity. Through this process of commodification, the assertion of local difference is paradoxically harnessed to the production of Pratt's "homogeneous social world," and signs of local difference are indifferently distributed across the entire globe, just as the Snow Crash virus obliterates cultural differences by infecting people with the realization of the dream of a linguistics of community. To the extent that the novel shows how forms of cultural and linguistic separatism can actually play into the transnational commodity system, *Snow Crash* demonstrates that it is possible to market and sell noncommunicability, a prospect Castells doesn't seem to have anticipated when he criticizes "grassroots" attempts to resist globalization by making themselves "so culturally specific that their codes of self-recognizing identity become non-communicable" to outsiders (*Informational City*, 350). Harvey, however, anticipates precisely this problem when he defines the paradoxical nature of transnationalism (295–96).

As a result, the situation of linguistic diversity *Snow Crash* attempts to privilege starts to seem no less subject to manipulation, control, and commodification than the linguistic universality it rejects and demonizes. In other words, linguistic, cultural, and ethnic differences seem to suffer the same fate as the franchise communities: the assertion of difference itself promotes a kind of

indifference. This slippage between difference and indifference is exactly captured in the novel's pun on "Babel" and "babble." The glossolalia that afflicts
those persons infected with the Snow Crash virus is clearly intended to represent the empty sounds that result from pushing the qualities of universal translatability to such an extreme that words lack not only cultural specificity but
any meaning whatsoever. The contrast is the extreme fragmentation of languages represented by the Babel story, in which no one can understand anyone
else because everyone has their own specific language.

At one point in the novel, however, these two extremes become conflated.
In a discussion of language practices among the refugee "boat people," one of
the characters describes how "babbling" has become a fad among these people.
He explains the popularity of these nonsense syllables in terms of the effects of
cultural difference, rather than cultural homogeneity: "They all speak different
languages, you know, all those different ethnic groups. It's like the fucking Tower
of Babel. I think when they make that sound—when they babble at each other—
they're just imitating what all the other groups sound like" (363). At this point,
"babble" refers not to a language that functions at a universally accessible, "deep,"
or hardwired level. Instead, it refers to exactly the opposite, to the acknowledgment of difference and the imperfection of mutual intelligibility. Babble here
means *noise*, not perfect translatability. This acknowledgment of imperfection
is precisely what Haraway means when she talks about "powerful infidel hetero-
glossia" (*Simians*, 181). The textual metaphor of inscription and the analogy
between computer software and human beings may promote a posthuman ideal
of our minds and bodies as existing in a form that "can be frictionlessly transferred into another medium," as Hayles argues ("Posthuman Body," 248). But,
as one of Stephenson's cyborg characters puts it, "no piece of software is ever
bug free" (*Snow Crash*, 363). This assertion, however, is rather atypical. The
tendency of the novel is to treat "babble" not as a marker of the limitations of
communications systems and therefore as pointing toward a different metaphor
for human embodiment and cultural difference; instead, *Snow Crash* tends to
interpret "babble" as promising a utopian ideal of universal linguistic community, which the novel then reveals to be a nightmare of linguistic control. And
linguistic control means control of the world and the people in it, because they
are all understood on a textual model of software, as so many inscriptions. It
should be possible, however, to redefine this textualization of the world on the
model of Pratt's linguistics of context, rather than the linguistics of community.
Stephenson's novel dramatizes what might happen *only* if assumptions about
language as a homogenizing force are correct. Pratt's theory of the linguistics
of contact is intended to suggest that those assumptions are not necessarily or
completely accurate.

The analogical structure of posthuman narratives depends on the application of textual metaphors to both computer software and the minds and bodies of human beings. This reading of *Snow Crash* exemplifies one of the general points of this book: it is crucial not to overgeneralize about the consequences of post-human technological transformations. The metaphorical equation of persons and computers in such narratives often seems to reproduce a logic of commodification and control. But that metaphorical equation is mediated by a further analogy, which equates both persons and computers with language or textuality. To fully understand the cultural consequences of this analogical structure it is necessary to consider exactly what concept of language underlies the metaphor of persons as computer software. Posthuman narratives ambivalently but inextricably connect empowering uses of new technologies, new possibilities for self-control and self-definition, and new possibilities for cultural diversity outside the universalizing framework of the normative human form, with increased possibilities for external control and manipulation of those same uses and possibilities. It is precisely this internal debate over the meaning of these new possibilities for understanding and changing ourselves that makes posthuman narratives a model for the dialectical relation critics need to develop toward new technologies and technocultures: a combination of unbounded pleasure in the horizons they open up and unceasing skepticism toward what we might find when we get there.

NOTES

Introduction

1. The main example of these earlier traditions discussed in the next chapter is James Blish's 1957 collection of stories, *The Seedling Stars,* especially "Watershed," though I will also argue that versions of the posthuman can be traced back at least to H. G. Wells. Gardner Dozois's *Supermen* anthology offers other examples.

2. Chris Hables Gray makes a similar point about cyborg embodiment in general (*Cyborg Citizen,* 11, 187–90).

3. See Charles Stross's play with posthumanism's revolutionary rhetoric in his 2003 novel *Singularity Sky,* which includes an Extropian and Cyborgs' Soviet (130). In a recent interview, Stross in fact argues that "socialism makes a fairly good fit with extropianism," if only because both movements "believe in the perfectibility of human nature" (or at least its historical mutability). He sees the fact that they have "had to swallow, subliminally and unconsciously, some things that are considered axiomatic for socialism" as a bit of a joke on the "hardcore libertarians and conservatives" who dominate the Extropian movement ("Exploring Distortions," 86).

4. A conference on this topic took place at Yale University at the end of June 2003. The quotation from James Hughes, secretary of the World Transhumanist Association, that serves as an epigraph to this Introduction is taken from Erik Baard's article on this conference, posted on the *Village Voice* Web site on July 29, 2003; see http://www.villagevoice.com/issues/0331/baard.php. The article notes that the transhumanist association constitutes "a community of people who feel the inevitability of revolution in their bones." For more information, see the association's Web site at www.transhumanism.org.

5. Baard's article notes that transhumanism is a broader umbrella within which the Extropian movement might be included (see chapter 1, note 19). In the next chapter, I will discuss the Extropian definition of this term. Mark Dery's book *Escape Velocity* also discusses this movement. Wilson's "genetically conservative" argument about the dangers of biotechnology, which extends and accelerates the processes of natural evolutionary change, will be discussed in greater detail at the beginning of the next chapter.

6. *Mississippi Review* 47/48 (summer 1988); this issue includes a "Cyberpunk Forum/Symposium," in which a number of participants suggest that the movement is merely a promotional gimmick masquerading as a revolution in the science-fiction genre (22, 26, and 41). This tendency to lament the co-optation of cyberpunk was epitomized by the

1995 publication of *The Real Cyberpunk Fakebook*, by the editors of *Mondo 2000* magazine (Jude, Sirius, and Nagel). Sterling's introduction parodically indulges in the same game of one-upmanship by suggesting that the only "actual cyberpunks" are science-fiction writers (9). A more interesting version of this response is found in attempts to define alternative takes on cyberpunk, such as K. W. Jeter's term "steampunk" (for Victorian or alternate history cyberpunk) or Paul Di Filippo's "ribofunk," an SF subgenre organized around biotech rather than infotech.

7. *New York Times*, January 7, 1991; see also Sterling's response to Shiner and an argument for cyberpunk's continued relevance beyond its immediate moment, in Sterling's "Cyberpunk in the Nineties" (39–41).

8. Compare Pat Cadigan's description of herself as "the accidental tourist of cyberpunk" ("Interview," 89) among an otherwise all-male group including (besides Gibson, Sterling, and Cadigan herself) Rudy Rucker and John Shirley as core members, with other writers more or less closely affiliated (sometimes only temporarily or in some of their fiction), such as Greg Bear, Tom Maddox, Paul Di Filippo, Lewis Shiner, Michael Swanwick, and Richard Kadrey.

9. Loyd Blankenship, *GURPS Cyberpunk: High-Tech Low-Life Roleplaying* (118). Published in 1990, this roleplaying game was realistic enough (or the boundary between cyberpunk fiction and technological reality was still confused enough) that the company producing it had its offices raided by the U.S. Secret Service, which thought they were confiscating a guide to cutting-edge computer crime (Sterling, "Report," 47–51; and Sterling, "War," 4–5). Andrew Ross discusses this game's codification of cyberpunk assumptions in *Strange Weather* (159–61).

10. Jean Baudrillard describes this same postmodern experience of cultural commodification as a condition of "forced signification," a "cold" pornography of "information and communication, . . . of circuits and networks, of functions and objects in their legibility, availability, [and] regulation" (Baudrillard, *Ecstasy*, 22).

11. In Gibson's *Neuromancer*, cyberspace is defined as a "consensual hallucination" and a "graphic representation of data abstracted from the banks of every computer in the human system" (5, 51). Originally written as an internal document for the Autodesk company, one of the earlier designers of virtual reality, John Walker's essay "Through the Looking Glass" exemplifies how the literary metaphor of cyberspace was taken up by computer researchers and programmers. Specifically, Walker used cyberspace to argue for replacing conversation as the dominant metaphor for human–computer interfaces (as when the computer "asks" us "save document: y/n?") with the metaphor of entering another space, the virtual space on the other side of the computer screen (443). For more on the history of these kinds of responses to the cyberspace metaphor, see Benedikt; Laurel; and Stone.

12. MacLeod in fact identifies himself as such a third-generation writer when he asserts that his "emulation text was Neal Stephenson's *Snow Crash*" ("Singularity Skies," 42), one of the most well known responses to Gibson's cyberpunk fiction. Other examples of this emergent third generation of post-cyberpunk writing might include works by Cory Doctorow, John C. Wright, Dan Simmons, Tony Daniel, Robert Reed, Wil McCarthy, Alastair Reynolds, and Justina Robson, as well as some of Ted Chiang's stories.

Many of these texts demonstrate a tendency to make Sterling's posthumanism more central to third-generation cyberpunk.

13. Grossberg's main example of such a nonnecessary articulation is rock music, which brought together several formerly distinct musical styles, including rhythm and blues and country and western, with an "apocalyptic rhetoric, youth, bohemianism, and juvenile delinquency" (70).

14. Ross suggests a similar cultural analysis of "the struggle over values and meaning . . . in the debate about technology," with reference to hacking, not cyberpunk (*Strange Weather*, 98–99). See also Dani Cavallaro's book on the generalization of "cyberpunk" into "cyberculture," and the permeable boundary between popular fiction and actually existing uses of new information technologies in the contributions to Bell and Kennedy's *Cybercultures Reader*.

15. In an interview with Tom Maddox, William Gibson points out that the words *America* and *U.S.* are completely absent from *Neuromancer*, because he wanted his readers "to question the political existence of the United States" ("Eye to Eye," 26); see chapter 7 in this volume.

16. McHale's *Constructing Postmodernism* offers the fullest consideration of this connection, first suggested by Jameson's comments on "high-tech paranoia" as an attempt to imagine the "impossible totality" of new global systems (Jameson, *Postmodernism*, 38; McHale, 178–80).

17. One of the few early commentators to note the "symbolic depth" of Sterling's trope, as opposed to Gibson's more spectacular cyberspace metaphor, was Tom Maddox, a fiction writer included in the *Mirrorshades* anthology (McCaffrey, *Storming*, 327; originally published in the 1988 special cyberpunk issue of the *Mississippi Review*). More recently, British author Ken MacLeod argues that "the idea of the post-human sets the agenda of 90s SF" (*Poems and Polemics*, 25). Key critical texts on posthumanism include Bukatman (272–78); Hayles's *How We Became Posthuman*, whose definition of posthumanism in terms of the technological mediation of subjectivity and as a challenge to the political philosophy of liberal humanism (4–5) has been a major influence on my thinking on this topic; Halberstam and Livingston's *Posthuman Bodies* collection, which is especially useful for situating posthumanism in relation to queer theory; Dery's more ethnographic survey (*Escape Velocity*); Mark Poster's definition of posthumanism in terms of Baudrillard's critique of the humanist subject's "dramatic interiority" (*Second Media Age*, 140); Allucquère Roseanne Stone's discussion of how virtual systems and computer-mediated communication "call into question the structure of meaning production by which we recognize each other as human" (*War*, 173); and Graham's book on popular culture. Wolmark's book on contemporary feminist SF does not explicitly use the term "posthuman," but her analyses of figures of otherness in this fiction is directly relevant to the topic, as are the poststructuralist essays in Cadava's collection *Who Comes after the Subject?*.

18. Another example of this shift to the posthuman would be Haraway's redefinition of cyborg imagery as just one of a group of "excessive and dislocated figures that can never ground what used to be called 'a fully human community'" ("Actors," 25). Another contemporary codification of posthumanism as subsuming cyberpunk, like Dozois's,

appears in the decision by one of the first companies to produce a cyberpunk role-playing game, Steve Jackson Games, to introduce a new line of games titled *Transhuman Space,* beginning from the premise that the transformation of humanity "from a single, evolved species to a multitude of artificial races" will be part of the exploration and colonization of outer space (Pulver, 7). Cyberpunk is retained in the form of "core technologies" (62–69).

19. Of special interest is Sterling's essay "Precessing the Simulacra for Fun and Profit," on his own reading in postmodern theory, after having his writing categorized in this way. Bukatman identifies a tradition of postmodern science fiction, broader than but including cyberpunk. For other examples, see Hollinger; Pfeil; Hayles, (*Chaos Bound,* 275–78); Jameson (*Postmodernism,* 39, 419 n. 1); McHale, *Constructing Postmodernism* (especially 223–67); McCaffery's collection *Storming the Reality Studio,* which combines postmodern theory and selections of cyberpunk fiction; the special issue of *Critique* (33 [spring 1992]) edited by McHale; and part 3 of the Slusser and Shippey collection, "The Question of Newness: Cyberpunk and Postmodernism," especially the essays by Huntington, Olsen, and Landon. Featherstone and Burrows interestingly argue that cyberpunk revives "utopian impulses" within a generally more pessimistic postmodern framework (*Cyberspace,* 1). Tabbi and Johnston both situate cyberpunk fiction within a tradition of postmodern metafiction.

20. I discuss Moravec's fantasy of copying or "downloading" human consciousness into machine form at greater length in the next chapter, along with Hayles's critical response to it. In the reading of *Neuromancer* that I offer in chapter 2, I will argue that this neat distinction is in fact a reductive and oversimplified reading of cyberpunk fiction. To quote Bukatman, if there is increasing acceptance that "the body must become a cyborg to retain its presence in the world," there is little agreement about whether this reconceptualization of embodied existence "represents a continuation, a sacrifice, a transcendence, or a surrender of 'the subject'" (245). For critiques of cyberpunk and posthumanism for associating new technologies with disembodiment, see Morse; Nixon; Stockton; Kendrick; Land; "Deleting the Body," chapter 1 of Springer's book; chapter 5 of Balsamo's book; and Dery, *Escape Velocity,* chapter 6, on "obsolete bodies and posthuman beings." Work that attempts to offer an alternative to this trope of disembodiment, or to read in such narratives a more complex history, would include Tomas; Hayles's *How We Became Posthuman,* which places this trope more firmly in the history of cybernetics and systems theory; the rest of Springer's book, which argues that "speculation about the bodily obsolescence" is combined with "a desire to preserve bodily pleasures" (161); Balsamo's reading of Pat Cadigan's feminist cyberpunk novel *Synners* in Balsamo's chapter 6 (140–46); most of the essays in Featherstone and Burrows's *Cyberspace/Cyberbodies/ Cyberpunk* collection, especially Lupton, Clark, and Sobchack; and some work on text-based virtual communities, such as Cherny; Lang; and Argyle and Shields.

21. The context for this reference to Butler's novel is the main character's waking up to realize she has been abducted by an alien race and noting that there is a new scar on her abdomen; the narrator's next words are "she didn't even own herself" (5). The possibility that her body has been modified by her captors, and the question of how to respond to that possibility, is central to the plot of this novel, because its premise is that

the aliens reproduce by trading genetic material with other species, in what they call a "trade," so that this race alters its physical embodiment and those of its partner species in every new generation, in a version of posthuman self-modification.

22. I will return to the (mis)reading of the "post-biological world" as synonymous with a "post-body age" in chapter 3. I discuss the relevance of narratives of virtual reality to representations of embodiment in chapters 3 and 4. For more complex emplotments of the relation between the human and the posthuman, see Bukatman (278) and Nancy (5).

23. Both Bukatman (278) and Dery (*Escape Velocity*, 297) discuss this undoing of the initial opposition between the Shaper and Mechanist factions.

24. In later chapters, I will discuss the ways in which Stone's definition of citizenship too quickly blurs important distinctions between forms of gender performativity, as theorized by Judith Butler, and forms of racial performativity, as exemplified by Kobena Mercer for Stone. For Gray, cyborg citizenship is both defined discursively and always embodied (*Cyborg Citizen*, 25, 29–30). Gray's model of cyborg citizenship is problematized by Hayles's reading of the Turing test for intelligence, which uses a discursive standard, as dramatizing both the denaturalization of social categories and the reduction of embodiment to a purely formal construct (*How We Became Posthuman*, xi–xiv).

25. See Butler, *Gender Trouble* (135), for another critique of the soul as figure of interiority; Butler stresses the way in which this concept of the soul also implies that the body is merely an inert signifying surface across which external social meanings are deterministically inscribed.

26. Similarly, Eric Lott's analysis of the history of blackface minstrelsy in the United States suggests that "what seems 'blackest'" about such performers is precisely their "commodification" (62).

27. Cameron Bailey suggests a similar reading of the persistence of race in cyberspace (29), citing Benedikt's argument that cyberspace can be defined as "the world of objective, real, and public structures which are the not-necessarily-intentional products of the minds of living creatures" but "with the ballast of materiality cast away" (3, 4). The collapse of depth models that Jameson sees as central to postmodern culture is what Harper has in mind when he refers to a "categorical collapse" (*Postmodernism*, 15). Lisa Nakamura applies this critique to issues of racial representation in technoculture contexts, pointing out how racial stereotypes continue to circulate as such in communicational situations where those stereotypes cannot be naturalized (*Cybertypes*, 31–40; see chapter 5). Paul Gilroy's *Against Race* offers a more optimistic assessment of the effects of technocultural denaturalizations of the color line.

28. The best popular example of a narrative that explicitly represents the effects of technological mediation on the figure of the "soul" would be David Brin's *Kiln People*. This novel imagines a technology of "soulistics" that permits people to make temporary copies of themselves, for the purposes of completing particular tasks, in effect inverting and reembodying the contemporary concept of digital agents that can be sent out over the Internet to gather and filter information.

29. See also Robert Walser's argument that white critics of black jazz performances were more comfortable explaining this music as an expression of a distinct black interiority than they were with the musicians' own explanations of how their music was

informed by the social context of U.S. race relations. Both interiorizing black soul as the essence of racial difference and externalizing and rendering it accessible to others can have dehistoricizing effects.

30. Poster sums up these debates in a chapter on "virtual ethnicity" (*What's the Matter*, 150–52).

31. I take this to be one of the main points of Nelson and Tu's collection, with its focus on "race and everyday life" (2), as well as in the special issue of *Social Text* on "Afrofuturism," edited by Nelson.

32. See also Nelson's discussion of a similar temporality in Reed's novel *Mumbo Jumbo* ("Introduction," 6–8). Hortense Spillers's analysis of the "cultural vestibularity" created by slavery's dehumanizing practices suggests a similar "short-circuiting" or rewriting of the development of subjectivity (67).

33. The phrase "intentional stance" provides the title of one of Dennett's books; see his *Consciousness Explained* for a succinct summary of why adopting this stance is necessary, whatever its "dangers" (76–77). This stance is the basis for Gray's proposal of a "Turing test for citizenship," with citizenship based on the ability to participate in a discourse community (*Cyborg Citizen*, 25–26, 31), though note also Gray's critique of the political implications of more extreme versions of the intentional stance, such as Bruno Latour's (ibid., 30–31); Gray observes: "That everything can be called a system does not mean that all systems can think, or act, or practice politics in any real way" (30).

1. The Legacies of Cyberpunk Fiction

1. To suggest how these ideas have begun to find their way into popular culture, see the citation of Wilson on the dangers of decommissioning natural selection on the back cover of *Unnatural Selection*, a 2002 comic book about a genetic engineering experiment (Starkings, Casey, and Ladronn). Another example would be Michael Crichton's thriller novel *Prey* (2002), which begins with a short essay on the topic of "artificial evolution" and its potential dangers. See also Terranova's essay.

2. Dennett derives this definition of virtual machines directly from early work on cybernetics by Alan Turing and John von Neumann (210–17). Dennett is defining what he calls the Baldwin effect, the evolutionary selection for brain structures that permit later, "postnatal" forms of learning and training, as an element of relatively early human evolution.

3. For instance, MCI's 1997 advertisement "Anthem," for its Internet service, proclaims that on the Internet "there is no race. There is no gender. There is no age. There are no infirmities. There are only minds" (quoted in Nakamura, *Cybertypes*, 89; see her excellent analysis of this ad [89–90] and a number of others). Similarly, Barlow's "A Declaration of the Independence of Cyberspace" proclaims cyberspace to be "the new home of Mind" in order to reject state regulation of Internet communications (28).

4. For Hayles's definition of the posthuman in terms of the mediation of subjectivity, see *How We Became Posthuman* (4). Michelle Kendrick offers a similar argument (146).

5. Hayles makes a similar point in her analysis of the Turing test for the successful achievement of artificial intelligence in computers, a test based on a human audience's

inability to distinguish a computer-generated text from a human-authored one (see chapter 3). Hayles finds in the Turing test both a denaturalization of the human that can reveal internal diversity and a decontextualization of identity and a reduction of it to the ability to formally manipulate "informational patterns" (xi).

6. See Steven Pinker's *Blank Slate* for a defense of evolutionary psychology like the one I suggest here.

7. Vinge argues, for instance, that the technological ability to design more intelligent minds constitutes "a regime as radically different from our human past as we humans are from the lower animals," who depend purely on natural selection for adaptability. Both Vinge and Joy are far less optimistic than Moravec about the ability of human beings to redesign ourselves in ways that will make us competitive with advanced machines. By "singularity," Vinge refers to the possibility of technological development reaching "an exponential runaway beyond any hope of control," arguing that "from the human point of view this change will be a throwing away of all the previous rules, perhaps in the blink of an eye." For an elaboration of Vinge's ideas see Damien Broderick's *The Spike*. Stross cites Vinge in the introduction to *Toast and Other Ruste'd Futures* (2002), a collection of stories; see especially the title story and "Antibodies."

8. Bey cites the title of Sterling's 1988 novel *Islands in the Net* (98). Bey in fact argues that the temporary autonomous zone can combine an "Ultra-Green . . . luddite" camp and cyberpunk, "futuro-libertarians" like the Extropians, and "Reality Hackers" (the title of one of the magazines that became *Mondo 2000* and that attempted to articulate the surviving hippy counterculture with the new technoculture); these latter groups are seen by Bey as all believing in "the Net as a step forward in evolution" (110–11). This combination is perhaps best represented by the Lo Tek subculture in Gibson's story "Johnny Mnemonic" (see chapter 2). For another fictional representation of the temporary autonomous zone, see Gómez-Peña's "barrios of resistance," in the title performance piece in his book *The New World Border* (38), and my discussion of this piece ("Cyber-Aztecs," 57–58). The Ludlow collection on "pirate utopias" and "crypto anarchy" represents an important set of critical responses to models of resistance like Bey's. For other examples of the politics of ontology, see also Haraway, *Simians* (150) and Tomas ("Feedback," 37).

9. Clark's other metaphors include the "scaffolded" (45–46) and the "leaky" mind (53). In *Mindware*, Clark uses the example of the artist's sketchbook, arguing that it functions not just as an example of "external memory," but instead shows that "the iterated process of externalizing and reperceiving is integral to the process of artistic cognition itself" (149). Clark thereby emphasizes the technological mediation of subjectivity, Derrida's "archive fever." For a historical precursor to Clark's theory, see Gregory Bateson's chapter "The Cybernetics of 'Self'" (originally published as an article in 1971) in *Steps to an Ecology of Mind* (317), especially his famous example of a blind man with a stick as a system of extended mind or self (318).

10. This critique of assumptions about space is central to the postmodern geography movement; see Smith and Katz (75).

11. See Markley ("Boundaries," 72) and Sobchack's ("Beating the Meat," 209–10) use of Ihde's theory of doubled desire. Hayles emphasizes how cybernetics challenges liberal subjectivity by situating that "autonomous subject" within feedback loops "between the

subject and the environment," thereby putting the subject's boundaries in question (*How We Became Posthuman*, 2).

12. This rethinking of the space of subjectivity as social rather than privatized is also typical of postmodern literary theory; see Catherine Belsey for a critique of expressive subjectivity (3) and Tony Davies for a fuller definition of the humanist tradition, especially its romantic version (10–13). Stone draws on Foucault and others to make a similar critique (97). See Butler (*Gender Trouble*, 134) and Jameson (*Postmodernism*, 11–12, 15) for the two touchstone critiques of expressive interiority in postmodern theory.

13. See also John Johnston's reading of *Synners* (262–63).

14. The title piece in Gómez-Peña's *The New World Border* imagines a similar reversal, as whites and English-only monocultures become minoritized in a near-future social setting where transnational hybridity has become a new norm.

15. For work on embodied cognition, see especially Lakoff and Johnson; Varela, Thompson, and Rosch; and Damasio.

16. Clynes and Kline's essay is reprinted in Gray's *Cyborg Handbook*. See also chapter 12 of D. S. Halacy Jr.'s more popular 1965 book, *Cyborg—Evolution of the Superman*.

17. See Ross's analysis of the discourse of self-transformation in New Age spirituality, especially his discussion of biofeedback technologies for gaining conscious control over one's body (*Strange Weather*, 30–37). This New Age formation is certainly one of the main strands of Extropian philosophy as well. One popular source for these ideas about breaking down the distinction between mind and body in order to gain greater control over both is John Lilly's 1972 book on "metaprogramming" and the "human biocomputer," which seems to have influenced such cyberpunk texts as Michael Swanwick's *Vacuum Flowers* (1987) and Ted Chiang's story "Understanding"(1991).

18. This glossary contains, for instance, entries for the verbs "deanimalize" (as a process of becoming a cyborg), "deflesh," and the noun "demortalization" (More, "Futique Neologisms," 33). The contradiction I note here is a version of the same problem Hayles locates in the Turing test (*How We Became Posthuman*, xi, xiv).

19. This focus on transhumanism rather than posthumanism can be traced back to the work of biologist and evolutionary theorist Julian Huxley. See also Dery's concluding discussion of the Extropy group (*Escape Velocity*, 301–6). Within science fiction, Brian Stableford has written a series of six novels outlining a future history organized around life extension technologies or what he calls "emortality." Perhaps most relevant to this discussion of the Extropy movement is his *The Fountains of Youth* (2000), whose narrator is a cultural historian writing the definitive book about death as an obsolete phenomenon.

20. For a different fictional take on the same question, see Greg Egan's story "Learning to Be Me."

21. Miller is here undoubtedly influenced by Marvin Minsky's argument in *The Society of Mind* that the sense of possessing a coherent ego is an illusion that mystifies the functioning of a set of relatively autonomous subprograms that actually constitute the human mind.

22. For one characteristic formulation of this argument, see Butler,"Imitation" (18).

23. The main fictional model for this notion of emergent systems and self-organization is Sterling's references in *Schismatrix* to Ilya Prigogine's work, though this same set of

issues is central to contemporary systems theory. Of special interest in Kelly's book are his two chapters on "artificial evolution" (15) and "postdarwinism" (19).

24. For another version of this critique, see especially Harvey's claim that "what is most interesting about the current situation is the way in which capitalism is becoming ever more tightly organized *through* dispersal, geographical mobility, and flexible responses in labour markets, labour processes, and consumer markets, all accompanied by hefty doses of institutional, product, and technological innovation" (*Condition*, 159). Also relevant here is Jameson's discussion of the "more intimate symbiosis between the market and the media" characteristic of information economies (*Postmodernism*, 275). Nick Dyer-Witheford offers a critique of the analogy between free markets and information systems, with specific reference to Moravec (36–37). The "Informatics of Domination" section of Haraway's "Cyborg Manifesto" (in *Simians*) remains an important critique of the disembodying logics of information economies, one too often overlooked in readings of the essay.

25. See Hayles's discussion of the ideology of possessive individualism, which emphasizes the challenge posed to it by posthuman discourses, not the (more or less displaced) reproduction of it within certain of those discourses (*How We Became Posthuman*, 3), though Hayles does note that "the erasure of embodiment is a feature common to *both* the liberal humanist subject and the cybernetic posthuman," because possessive individualism implied that we have bodies, not that we are bodies (4).

26. In the early 1980s, prior to the publication of *Neuromancer*, Sterling promoted cyberpunk (or "The Movement") as a radical break with the rest of the field of contemporary science fiction, in a series of reviews, manifestos, and attacks. This material appeared in his self-published fanzine *Cheap Truth*, under the pseudonym of Vincent Omniaveritas, and is now available in a Web archive at www.io.com/~ftp/usr/shiva/ SMOF-BBS/cheap.truth. In particular, Sterling was invested in defining cyberpunk in contrast to a group of self-identified humanist science-fiction writers generally associated with the Sycamore Hill writing workshops; this group included such figures as James Patrick Kelly, John Kessel, Kim Stanley Robinson, and Connie Willis. One result of this polemic was Veronica Hollinger's characterization of cyberpunk as "antihumanist" rather than posthumanist, but Sterling deliberately included writers like Kelly in *Mirrorshades* (who went on to write at least one [post]cyberpunk novel, *Wildlife*), and writers such as Michael Swanwick became associated with both groups. The result has been to break down the more or less artificial distinctions between cyberpunk and science fiction generally. The best account of this history is Swanwick's essay "A User's Guide to the Postmoderns," but see also Kelly's column "On the Net: Cyberpunk," as well as the 1988 special issue of the *Mississippi Review* on "The Cyberpunk Controversy." For other accounts of these controversies and interventions in the definition of cyberpunk, especially in relation to earlier SF, see Rucker's *Seek;* Cadigan's anthology *The Ultimate Cyberpunk;* Pfeil; Suvin; Fitting; Slusser and Shippey's essay collection.

27. See Ross's discussion of Toffler (*Strange Weather*, 179–80). We might also note that Toffler was one of the authors of "A Magna Carta for the Knowledge Age, Release 2.0," prepared by Newt Gingrich's Peace and Freedom Foundation, available on the World Wide Web; see Hayles (*How We Became Posthuman*, 18).

28. Another example of this conflation of cyberpunk with less critical forms of libertarian politics might be David Brande's essay on the ways the cyberspace metaphor fits into a model of capitalist expansion. See also the essays by Rosenthal and Whalen.

29. Schroeder also offers a unique take on posthumanism's evolutionary rhetoric (*Permanence*, 175, 177). The theme of the naturalizing of technology, its becoming a taken-for-granted element of the environment, is a critical and potentially dystopian revision of the central premise of Schroeder's previous novel, *Ventus*, which imagined a planet in which the natural environment is completely mediated and informed by a global artificial intelligence.

30. What is imagined here is a technological literalization of the romantic project of overcoming alienation and the subject/object split, while the techniques of the Rights Economy demonstrate that such a project can also have repressive political effects. This theme of technology as way out of romantic epistemological dilemmas is more explicit in Schroeder's previous novel *Ventus*, where the isomorphism between a global AI and the natural environment of a planet extends the concept of ubiquitous computing and presents the weaving together of technology and nature to create a "smart world" as breaking down romantic dualisms.

31. This representation of an information economy, then, challenges Extropian optimism in what they call call "agoric open systems," or "computer operating systems in which system resources such as memory and processing cycles are traded by programs and processes on an internal open market" (Krieger, 25), as the basis for an analogy between such open systems and an ideal free market. Schroeder's novel shows how this analogy can also work the other way, as informational models produce an even more totalized and tightly regulated capitalist system.

32. The main contemporary form of resistance to such models is the open source computing movement; see Torvalds and Diamond as well as Sam Williams. The open source movement seeks to make the source code of computer operating systems accessible to users, so that it becomes possible to rewrite those programs rather than simply accepting the options and limitations built into them. Julian Stallybrass usefully connects this movement to Hardt and Negri's argument about the potentially cooperative nature of "immaterial labor" (144). For a nonfiction account of new "technologies of cooperation" like those Sterling imagines, see Rheingold's *Smart Mobs* (2002). The main problem in Sterling's story is his mapping of the distinction between cooperative and commercial uses of computer networks with racial and cultural stereotypes of both Japan and the United States.

33. See Rodney Brooks's critique of the plausibility of Moravec's scenario (204–6), for a sense of the debates within the fields of artificial intelligence and cognitive science over these speculations.

34. Hayles makes a similar distinction between a "nightmare" of "a culture inhabited by posthumans who regard their bodies as fashion accessories"and the "dream"of "a version of the posthuman that embraces the possibilities of information technologies without being seduced by fantasies of unlimited power and disembodied immortality" (*How We Became Posthuman*, 5). One of the best fictional explorations of this "nightmare" is Nancy Kress's story "Always True to Thee, in my Fashion" (in her collection *Beaker's Dozen*).

35. Other examples of the use of this concept of hardwiring in cyberpunk and post-cyberpunk fiction might include Walter Jon Williams's *Hardwired;* Barnes; Laidlaw; Rosenblum's *Chimera* (14); Carter (44, 53); Rucker's *Software* (114); the title story in Egan's *Axiomatic* (100); Robert Charles Wilson's *Memory Wire* (151); James (46, 159). Although they do not use the term "hardwiring" explicitly, Gray and Mentor similarly offer a reading of cyborg body prostheses as "models for political structures that subject and partially construct us" (229).

36. In both cases, the existence of a biological basis for homosexual practices and behaviors can offer a validation for gay people and counter the conservative impulse to present homosexuality as a choice or an addiction that can be cured by the right kind of therapy, while at the same time the acceptance of biological explanations for homosexuality still carries with it the dangers of essentialism, especially the stigmatizing or ghettoizing of homosexuals as so fundamentally different from straight people that there is no possibility of exchange or community.

37. For another version of this same process, see Chiang's story "Understand" (reprinted in Dozois's posthuman anthology).

38. This conflict between posthumanist technologies and a traditional concept of the humanities, especially literature, is also central to Egan's story "The Planck Dive," which has the same setting as *Diaspora* (discussed later in this chapter).

39. See Steven Pinker, *The Language Instinct,* for an elaboration of this aspect of Chomsky's thinking.

40. The novel that spells out this understanding of the trope of hardwiring most explicitly is Neal Stephenson's *Snow Crash;* see chapter 7 of this book. This argument about how representations of hardwiring can trouble the hardware/software divide might be compared to Friedrich Kittler's claim that "there is no software" (in the essay of that title in Kittler, *Literature*), or, more specifically, to David Gelernter's argument that software is not simply "a highly specialized kind of document" (40), or is so only prior to actually being run on a computer. Until a software program is running, "the machine [we're] looking at has no body" (Gelernter, 89), but actually turning a "working infomachine" on necessarily results in "the embodiment of [that] disembodied machine" (39, 40). Like Hayles's rereading of the history of cybernetics, in chapter 3 of *How We Became Posthuman,* Gelernter here challenges the association of information technologies with processes of disembodiment.

41. Compare to Latour's technoscientific hybridity, which precedes the institution of the nature/culture distinction (10–12); or to Brockman's idea of a "third culture." See, however, Slavoj Žižek's critique of the tendency for such formulations to move too quickly from "biological-evolutionist concepts to the study of the history of human civilization" ("Cultural Studies," 22).

42. See Egan's *Permutation City* (1994) for another fictional treatment of virtual community.

43. Emily Apter notes the thematic of racelessness in cyberpunk (220), and she cites an example from Gibson's 1993 novel *Virtual Light,* in which that representation is applied to a homeless man—that is, without reference to any technological agency (Gibson, *Virtual,* 215).

44. Because Warner, drawing on Habermas, also emphasizes the role of print culture in producing a norm of impersonality or abstraction in the modern public sphere (Warner, *Letters*, xiii), it is noteworthy that the norm or "constant" for body images in Konishi polis is compared to writing, but in a form that *precedes* print technology, specifically, "the letter A in a hundred mad monks' illuminated manuscripts" (Eagan, *Diaspora*, 15).

45. We will see a similar metaphor of faking it applied to artificial intelligence in Ken MacLeod's novel *The Cassini Division* (in the next section of this chapter), but the use of the word *puppet* to refer to the body in this passage alludes to Gibson's *Neuromancer* and its trope of the "meat puppet," a trope analyzed in detail in chapter 2 of this book. This same passage also suggests the critical possibilities inherent in Gibson's definition of cyberspace as a "consensual hallucination," another form of faking it, in *Neuromancer*. Swanwick glosses this definition in his novel *Stations of the Tide*, by asserting that cyberspace is not a "place" but rather "an agreed-upon set of conventions within which people may meet and interact" (125).

46. More specifically, Yatima's notion of the polis citizens as defined by an immutable but nevertheless formalizable and translatable essence, one that can be copied from one storage medium to another, conflates the distinction between real and nominal essences proposed by John Locke; on this distinction, see Fuss (*Essentially Speaking*, 4). For Yatima, mathematical principles are "real" in the sense of being "irreducible and unchanging," but "nominal" in the sense of being formalized and encoded in a purely symbolic form. See also Hayles's discussion of how "incorporating practices are not necessarily more 'natural' than inscribing practices," so that "embodiment" is also "not more essentialist than the body" (*How We Became Posthuman*, 201). Hayles goes on to suggest, as I do here, that "it is difficult to see what essentialism would mean" in this technocultural context, where "a coherent, continuous, essential self" is not "necessary or sufficient to explain embodied experience" (ibid.).

47. Žižek offers the following formula for the operation of cynical reason: "they know very well what they are doing, but still, they are doing it" (*Sublime*, 29).

48. The title of the novel might derive from two possible sources: Dennett's comment on Dawkins's concept of the meme or a self-replicating idea (he says he's "not initially attracted by the idea of my brain as a sort of dung heap in which the larvae of other people's ideas renew themselves, before sending out copies of themselves in *an informational Diaspora*" [*Consciousness Explained*, 202; my emphasis]); and an article in *Extropy* 15, which tries to define a diasporic model of the "cybernexus," a "synthesis of virtual communities on computer networks" (Reilly Jones, 43–44).

49. See MacLeod's account of his own political history (in *Poems and Polemics*, 10–11), as a Trotskyist and later a "quite sincere member of the Communist Party," who then became attracted to libertarian ideas "about sex and drugs and rock and roll," as well as free speech, even though his "enthusiasm for the free market" remains "a great deal more conditional than theirs." Underscoring his ambivalent attitude toward the libertarian tradition of "anarchocapitalism" (which he tries to redefine as "socialist anarchism"), MacLeod calls his first novel, *The Star Fraction*, "a libertarian novel about communists," and a later novel (*The Stone Canal*) "a communist novel about libertarians" (11).

50. MacLeod has his posthumanists directly appropriate Moravec's ideas about creating

"smart-matter"—that is, converting the physical world into computing resources, in an ultimate version of Hayles's condition of virtuality, where information interpenetrates the material world (MacLeod, *Cassini Division*, 75; Moravec, *Robot*, 164–67).

51. The designation of the posthumanist faction as the Outwarders seems to constitute another allusion to Sterling's *Schismatrix* (285), but it also associates the posthumans with the expansionist libertarian philosophy espoused by writers like Zebrowski. The Earth Tendency, on the other hand, is associated with an extreme left anarcho-communist ideology, referred to as the "true knowledge."

52. Cyberpunk representations of the body as "meat" originate with Gibson's *Neuromancer* and will be discussed at length in chapter 2. We have already seen how Cadigan's *Synners* picks up on this motif. I might here point out that similar references can be traced back at least to L. Frank Baum's 1914 children's novel *Tik-Tok of Oz*, whose title character is introduced as "the Clockwork Man—who works better than some meat people" (79).

53. Turing also argues that the only other way to know for certain that human beings are sentient and self-aware and machines are not is to argue theologically and to posit the existence not only of a soul but of a soul that only human beings can possess (443).

54. This struggle over the legal rights of intelligent machines is one of the central plot elements of MacLeod's novel *The Stone Canal*, published just prior to *The Cassini Division*.

55. In chapter 1 of *Figures of Black*, Gates focuses specifically on how African-American literature historically functioned as a kind of test of whether persons of African descent possessed the qualities necessary to be classified as "human."

56. Note the return of the problematic of possessive individualism or self-ownership, which for MacLeod's AI characters, as for Gibson's, is only possible after a prior condition of having been owned. The existence of such characters implicitly suggests a breakdown of the traditional protections associated with whiteness in the U.S. context, because as Cheryl Harris points out, "the racial line between white and black . . . became a line of protection and demarcation from the potential threat of commodification" (279). MacLeod's and Gibson's artificial intelligences dramatize the breakdown of this "line of protection," with a challenge to the power of the color line remaining as an implicit subtext. I am indebted to Eva Cherniavsky for pointing out the significance of this passage from Harris; for a fuller discussion of it, see her forthcoming book *The Body Politics of Capital*.

2. Meat Puppets or Robopaths

1. I am indebted to Anne Balsamo for bringing this moment in *Circuitry Man* to my attention.

2. The source of the term "robopath" is Louis Yablonsky's book on the dehumanizing effects of technology, long before cyberpunk or the Internet. *Antibodies* literalizes this process of becoming a robot, through the thematics of prosthetic body parts, and the novel should therefore be placed in a countercultural literary tradition of body-modification fiction established by Bernard Wolfe's *Limbo* (1952; see Hayles, *How We Became Posthuman*, chapter 5), and Katherine Dunn's *Geek Love* (1989). See also Dery, *Escape Velocity*, (274–85), on cultures of actual body modification as forms of popular posthumanism; and Balsamo's feminist readings of women bodybuilders (chapter 2) and cosmetic surgery

(chapter 3), which she reads in relation to "the anti-aesthetics of cyberpunk" and its critique of "romantic conceptions of the 'natural' body" (79).

3. See Adrienne Rich for the classic feminist statement of the distinction between "the body" and "my body" (*Blood,* 215). Hayles resituates this distinction within technocultural contexts, by drawing a distinction between "the body," as a normative construct denaturalized by postmodern culture, and "embodiment," as the material "enactment" or performance of a specific cultural positionality "generated from the noise of difference" (*How We Became Posthuman,* 193, 196). Hayles associates the concept of "the body" with the models of "inscription" and the concept of "embodiment" with the models of "incorporation" (193).

4. For the cyberpunks, then, as for Baudrillard, science fiction "is no longer an elsewhere, it is an everywhere" ("Simulacra," 312).

5. Cherniavsky makes a similar point in her reading of how *Neuromancer* reproduces sentimental and maternal traditions, in a denaturalized form ("[En]Gendering Cyberspace").

6. Judith Butler similarly argues that "the inquiry into the kinds of erasure and exclusion by which the construction of the subject operates" and the category of the human is produced "is no longer constructivism, but neither is it essentialism" (*Bodies That Matter,* 8). Hardwiring figures what Butler calls a "return to the notion of matter . . . as *a process of materialization*" (9).

7. This reductive reading tends to take a negative form, but it can also appear in work that celebrates this same presumed devaluation of organic embodiment, such as Tomas's work on Gibson. For feminist critiques of cyberpunk as offering a relatively familiar devaluation of embodied particularity, see Ross (*Strange Weather,* chapter 4); Nixon; and Stockton. Sponsler ("Cyberpunk") and Collins (*Architectures,* chapter 1) offer more general critiques of the conflict between familiar plot structures and technological innovation in Gibson's fiction. In chapter 4, I will address the extent to which these limitations are inherent in cyberpunk fiction and the extent to which they reflect the specific shortcomings of some of these male authors, including Gibson. I still believe it is important, however, to acknowledge the way that the conventions of cyberpunk fiction require authors who are not particularly feminist in their political convictions (and sometimes quite the opposite) to engage with gender and sexuality as explicit cultural constructs.

8. This institutional moment is perhaps best demonstrated by the inclusion of a section on cyberpunk and technoculture in the Norton anthology of *Postmodern American Fiction* (Geyh, Leebron, and Levy).

9. For a general account of these changes, see Kroker and Kroker's *Body Invaders* and Donald Lowe. On the relevance of such theories to postmodern science fiction more specifically, see the section "Terminal Flesh" in Bukatman (chapter 4) and Ross's discussion of "cyberpunk and difference" (*Strange Weather,* 156–60).

10. Bukatman (278) makes a similar point about the posthuman as a dangerous supplement to the human, in Sterling's *Schismatrix.*

11. For feminist responses to Haraway's very influential essay, see especially Kirkup et al.; Balsamo (32–35); and the commentaries collected in Weed (205–17). Plant's and Braidotti's cyberfeminisms should also be read as responses to Haraway, at least in part. More general responses to Haraway's work can be found in Penley and Ross's *Technoculture* and

Gray's collection *The Cyborg Handbook*. Les Levidow and Kevin Robins offer a different critique by choosing to emphasize the negative side of cyborg technology as Haraway defines it, especially its roots in military research.

12. Christina Crosby and Joan W. Scott both question whether Haraway's cyborg myth evacuates the specificity of women's experiences (in Weed, *Coming to Terms*, 207–8, 216–17). Kroker and Kroker push this tendency to the extreme, with the sweeping assertion that "women's bodies have always been postmodern" (24).

13. I am indebted here to Stone's reading of Gloria Anzaldúa and her figure of the mestiza or "boundary-subject," in "Will the Real Body Please Stand Up?" (112). For a similar reading of the relevance of Haraway's cyborg myth for women of color and post-colonial theory, see Sandoval ("New Sciences") and Gabifondo. In contrast, Gonzalez ("Envisioning," 275–78; "Appended," 48), Hammonds (315–17), and Fusco (xvi), like Mullen, are more skeptical of the ways in which new technologies only reproduce old conventions for managing racial miscegenation and hybridity. See also Weheliye's discussion of how Hayles's concept of the posthuman, especially as (self-)critique of white masculinity, has to be revised to apply African-American musical recording practices (23–25). Nakamura's attention to the ways in which racist stereotypes continue to circulate in technocultural contexts, even as their denaturalized form makes possible new modes of critical intervention, is exemplary; see especially chapter 2 of *Cybertypes*, which incorporates her well-known essay on racial passing on the Internet.

14. I am quoting from issue 2 of the continuing series (12–13; ellipses in original). The full passage can be found in Du Bois (215).

15. See Priscilla Wald's discussion of the complexity of Du Bois's formulation of double consciousness, which is intended to legitimate African-American participation in processes of national self-formation and self-consciousness, but also to disrupt and critique the "comfortable and continouous correspondence between perception and experience" on which both mainstream concepts of national consciousness and the exclusion of African-Americans from it were based (187–88).

16. See Baker's argument for the need to "explode" the duality of self and other in critical discussions of race ("Caliban's Triple Play," 389).

17. The term "postbiological" is Moravec's (*Mind Children*, 1). Case's initial attitude toward cyberspace seems to fit the interpretive tradition Elaine Scarry defines, in which disembodiment is interpreted as the possibility for self-extension without limits (207).

18. See Hayles on the significance of this redefinition of point of view (*How We Became Posthuman*, 39). Stone offers an important general theory of virtual systems as the end product of a progressive detachment of self from body in modern culture (*War*, 39–42).

19. See Simone de Beauvoir for the source of this terminology of immanence and transcendence (xxxiii–xxxiv). Glenn Grant offers one of the first readings of the desire for technological transcendence in *Neuromancer*.

20. The thematics of the "meat puppet" was first introduced in the title story of the collection *Burning Chrome*, where it is described as a way of negotiating the conflict "between needing someone and wanting to be alone at the same time, which has probably always been the name of that particular game, even before we had the neuroelectronics to allow them [the johns] to have it both ways" (Gibson, *Burning Chrome*, 199).

21. This lack of attention is probably explained in part by the fact that the represen-tation of Zion, a separatist Rastafarian space satellite (*Neuromancer*, 103), is a more obvi-ous representation of a kind of high-tech racial formation, though less interesting than Hideo precisely to the extent that it associates racial difference with resistance to moder-nity and as a retreat from technology, as implied when one of the inhabitants of Zion dismisses cyberspace as "Babylon" (106). This primitivizing representation of racial dif-ference also problematizes Gibson's later use of voodoo as a means of conceptualizing cyberspace, with artificial intelligence programs as loas, in the two sequels to *Neuro-mancer, Count Zero* and *Mona Lisa Overdrive*. I would distinguish these primitivist rep-resentations from the figure of Hideo, because primitivism depends on a naturalization of difference, which is precisely what is missing from Hideo's character. See Heim for a primitivizing reading of the representation of the Zionites in Gibson's novel (80) and Bailey's critique of this danger, as it applies both to the Zionites and to Gibson's use of voodoo metaphors (44–45).

22. This character, however, does strongly resemble the narrator of Gibson's story "Burning Chrome" (in *Burning Chrome*).

23. Later in this chapter I make a similar point about the character Molly, whose cyborg prostheses are presented as transforming the body from container for subjectiv-ity into the signifying surface of a style. This rethinking of embodiment in relation to subcultural practices of stylistic self-(re)definition, paradigmatically punk rock, offers an answer to the question George McKay poses: "much critical attention has been paid to the *cyber* of cyberpunk—but what about the *punk*?" (49). One of the best popular explo-rations of already-existing subcultural practices of body modification as a context for cyborg prostheses and enhancements is the three-issue limited-series comic book *Mek*, written by Warren Ellis and published in 2003 by DC Comics.

24. The same problem recurs in the movie that was made of this story, in which Ice-T is cast as the leader of the Lo Teks.

25. For a similar analysis of the relation of sexuality and technology, see Springer (*Electronic Eros*, 50–51). Gibson has described his interest in "garbage," including art that incorporates found objects or uses techniques of pastiche and image scavenging, as hav-ing "something to do with fetishism, the sexuality of junk" (Tatsumi, "Eye to Eye," 12).

26. See also Pfeil's comments on how cyberpunk perpetuates a "masculinist frame" even in a situation where castration anxiety seems obsolete (88–89).

27. I take this to be one possible implication of arguments like bell hooks's or Cornel West's, that completely detaching the experience of marginal groups from the changes characteristic of postmodernity can be as problematic as assimilating them too quickly to a general characterization of those changes. Valerie Smith makes a similar critique, of what she sees as a tendency among white critics, including feminists, to treat the expe-rience of African-American women as a "historicizing presence" in contrast to the effects of postmodernism (45–46).

28. Manuel Castells theorizes this impossibility in terms of the disjunction between the "space of places" and the global space of informational "flows," with the latter space being literally uninhabitable (*Informational City*, 348–49), or, as Jameson puts it, "unthinkable."

29. See also Koestenbaum (182–83).

30. In addition to the works discussed in later chapters, these multicultural writers and artists would include Gómez-Peña (see my essay on his work), as well as Native American postmodernist Gerald Vizenor.

31. See Winner's statement of this problem (187–91), and Pfeil's argument that cyberpunk's rejection of the traditional science-fictional polarity of the utopian and the dystopian represents a rejection of either instrumental control by or instrumental mastery of technology (84–85).

32. The trope of hardwiring is continued in the sequel to *Neuromancer, Count Zero* (1986). One of the characters, a corporate mercenary, escapes to his childhood home in a plane described as being "smart, smart as any dog, with hard-wired instincts of concealment" (125). On the next page, the narrator observes some squirrels who are similarly "hard-wired" to ignore static objects, even a hunter waiting for a good shot. Observing this behavior, repeated by the squirrels exactly as he remembers from his childhood, the mercenary thinks, "You're like me. . . . I always come back" (126). This character's story involves altering these hardwired behavior patterns, specifically his attraction to a life of violence and action; the character ends up settling down with a wife by the end of the novel. This example both extends Gibson's use of the hardwiring trope to the construction of masculinity and implies an internal critique of adventure narrative conventions, even as it reiterates a traditional heterosexual narrative teleology.

33. On this point, I tend to disagree with Hayles, who reads the phrase "data made flesh" as implying that information takes ontological priority over embodiment, that the data came first (*How We Became Posthuman*, 5). It seems to me equally plausible to read this phrase as implying that information only becomes valuable, perhaps even accessible, when it is embodied.

34. For examples of such feminist readers, see Gordon; Hollinger; Cadora; and Wolmark's chapter 5, "Cyberpunk, Cyborgs, and Feminist Science Fiction" (especially 138).

3. The Sex Appeal of the Inorganic

1. For other perspectives on this topic, see McLuhan's vision of simultaneously enlarging "the domain of sex by mechanical technique" and possessing "machines in a sexually gratifying way" (94). Dery offers a critique of this passage from McLuhan, whose vision he argues has not been realized ("Sex Machine," 42–43). Like Dery, Bukatman argues that cyberpunk fiction offers only a delibidinizing of the body to produce a "sexualized machine" (328).

2. This is the key question, about the effects of the literalizing of Deleuze and Guattari's concept of the machinic assemblage (rather than the subject), that organizes Johnston's book on information narratives.

3. On the Freudian origins of the split between desire and identification in the production of compulsory heterosexuality, see Fuss (*Identification Papers*, 11). I analyze the way in which virtual reality computer interfaces challenge this distinction in my essay "'Postproduction'" (481–85).

4. Springer analyzes these same two pages from this comic book in the original essay version of "The Pleasure of the Interface," but she ends up emphasizing only the narrative of disembodiment (308–9, 322). When the essay is reprinted as a chapter in her book

Electronic Eros, only the first of the two pages is included, the page that interprets entry into cyberspace as a process of becoming a disembodied mind (63).

5. Rheingold's teledildonics scenario will be discussed in more detail in the next chapter, especially in terms of its direct influence on how feminist science-fiction writers have responded to cyberpunk. For an example of how these ideas have been embraced by the sex industry as well as futurist commentators like Rheingold, see Robinson and Tamosaitis's *The Joy of Cybersex,* which includes both a survey of actually existing erotic applications of computer technology and an overview of science-fictional speculations about cybersex.

6. See Grosz for the value of such a critique of mind/body dualisms of feminism (5–13). Both Andy Clark *(Being There)* and Stone argue for non-Cartesian understandings of the effects of new technologies, while Penny (231–32, 242–44), O'Brien (56), and Žižek *(Indivisible Remainder,* 193–94) argue the opposite case. Tomas associates the Cartesian tendencies within cyberspace with the replication of Euclidean geometry in these new computer simulations and offers some alternative non-Euclidean geometries that might structure cyberspace in a different way ("Old Rituals," 33–45). See also Žižek's critique of virtual personae as merely reproducing classic Lacanian forms of "symbolic identification" in ways that leave dualistic categories basically intact *(Plague,* 139).

7. See Hayles *(How We Became Posthuman,* 193). One of the main arguments of Hayles's book is that technocultural rhetorics of disembodiment are grounded in early forms of information theory that are at best only partially relevant to contemporary developments (17–20).

8. Stephanie Smith and William Sonnega both offer critiques of more naive versions of this belief in the liberatory effects of shape-changing or computer "morphing" technologies. In contrast, Haraway is arguing for a project of *"materialized refiguration"* that would harness the "generative forces of embodiment" released by the lesson that "what counts as human is not, and should not be, self-evident," a lesson implicit in both the new technoculture and "feminist, antiracist, multicultural science studies" ("Game," 64). Compare this statement by the curator of the Post Human art exhibit that toured Europe from September 1992 to May 1993: "our current post-modern era can be characterized as a transitional period of the disintegration of the self. Perhaps the coming 'post-human' period will be characterized by the reconstruction of self" (Deitch, 33).

9. In a similar critique, Deleuze and Guattari famously suggest replacing "that organization of the organs called the organism" with the figure of the "body without organs" *(A Thousand Plateaus,* 158).

10. These particular photos of Sherman's were included in the Post Human exhibit; for examples see Deitch (132–33).

11. Here I am in substantial agreement with Judith Butler's critique of Žižek and the concept of the Real as that which resists symbolization absolutely; Butler argues that this formulation mystifies the way in which what is outside symbolic structures is an effect of historical and cultural processes of abjection and constitutive exclusion (see chapter 7 in *Bodies That Matter*).

12. As an example of the capacity of new technologies to render "consciousness . . . as commodity experience," consider the claim that, in an information-saturated age, "the

thing we will pay a premium for is point of view"—that is, the franchising of personalities as customized information filters (Lohr, 3; see also Negroponte, 144). Lohr fantasizes that "famous people will license their tastes and attitudes to be simulated" by expert systems, so that we would pay to "watch the news reports and television shows or read the books that interest, say, John Kenneth Galbraith—or David Letterman, Madonna, or Rush Limbaugh" (3).

13. See Jean-François Lyotard's "Can Thought Go on without a Body?" a philosophical dialogue in which one of the interlocutors argues: "it's appropriate to take the body as model in the manufacture and programming of artificial intelligence if it's intended that artificial intelligence not be limited to the ability to reason logically" (16).

14. In print science fiction, see Dorsey's story "(Learning About) Machine Sex" (in *Machine Sex*) for a similar critique of the gender ideologies informing the design principle of interactivity.

15. For a restatement of this argument, see Haraway, "The Promises of Monsters" (301).

16. For a negative assessment of Sorayama's paintings, see Springer, *Electronic Eros* (148–49). Springer argues that the familiarity of the sexual representation recontains any uncanny quality the images might evoke, of "inanimate objects [that] have taken on human life" (149). I argue exactly the opposite, that the formal conventionality of the images is rendered uncanny by their robotic content, in a way that makes it difficult for male viewers to ignore the unreality of these idealized feminine images, as our culture has taught me to do with more "natural" representations.

17. In this sense, Sorayama's work seems to anticipate and contest the emergent phenomenon of computer-generated female characters, such as the virtual film star in the movie-within-the-movie in the film *S1m0ne*. In Japan, such virtual icons are called *idoru*, and Gibson's 1996 novel of that title centers on an American rock star's plan to marry one of these virtual characters; Gibson's next novel, *All Tomorrow's Parties* (1999), ends by imagining a technology that allows this virtual character to become embodied in real life.

18. See De Fren (63). She notes that as of the summer of 2002 there were three U.S. companies working to materialize these fantasies commercially by producing robot sex dolls, including one called "Realdoll" and another called the "Cyborgasmatrix," the latter based on a "full-body lifecast" of porn star Pandora Peaks (64).

19. See Butler on the possibility that "perhaps gender itself might be understood on the model of the fetish" (*Bodies,* 283 n. 15; Butler attributes this suggestion to Mandy Merck). On the implications of such a redefinition, see Mercer's argument about the possibility of mutuality and reversibility of subject–object relations between spectator and fetish object in homoerotic representations (195).

20. Calder seems to take the term "gynoid" from a British feminist science-fiction writer Gwyneth Jones. Sorayama acknowledges both Calder and Jones in a prefatory note to his most recent collection, *The Gynoids.*

21. Tatsumi discusses Calder's work in precisely this way, in his essay "A Manifesto for Gynoids."

22. M. Christian's story "State," published in one of Cecilia Tan's polymorphous SF porn anthologies, focuses on a similar representation in a more directly eroticized fashion. The main character is a female prostitute who specializes in imitating a sex robot.

23. Mercer is specifically critical of such analogies for obscuring the specificity of the photos' homoeroticism, in his own earlier critique of Mapplethorpe for fetishizing racial difference. For an example of an argument that reproduces this analogy, see Modleski's comment that the film *Blonde Venus* "requires us to apply the insights of *both* a Homi Bhabha and a Laura Mulvey," but in a strictly additive fashion, as if those insights functioned in the same way (127).

24. Fuchs offers a different reading of cyborg imagery through the framework of Butler's theory of performativity, focusing on male cyborgs (114–15).

25. Mosquito is in fact a character in *Dead Girls,* and one of the sources or vectors of the doll plague. The next two novels take this generalization of gender fantasies to the most extreme possible lengths, as the whole universe is rewritten as a decadent sex and death game. To my mind, this hyperbolic development of the initial premise of the short stories loses a good deal of its critical potential. See Fran Mason for a reading of *Dead Girls* as a critique of Haraway's claims for the cyborg's feminist potential (124).

26. See also Halberstam (441–45). Curtain argues that "Turing technology" can trigger "deep homosexual panic," as the Internet does by calling into question the "strict alignment between on-line and off-line gender presentations" (145). For more general discussions of Turing and the Turing test, see Collins (chapter 13), and Biddick, who discusses Turing's personal history and his sexuality in relation to contemporary work on computer-simulated artificial life, and its challenge to definitions of the "human" (174–75).

27. Koestenbaum is here articulating the main tenets of what Dollimore defines as one of the two main traditions in gay culture, the tradition of Oscar Wilde as opposed to the tradition of André Gide, with the latter privileging realistic representation and a politics based on equal rights, not the stylization of difference. As I suggested earlier, Calder's allusions to the decadent movement suggest an application of this Wildean tradition to technologically mediated forms of embodiment.

4. Trapped by the Body

1. Stone is critical of how the term "cyberspace" has become an overly general and abstract rubric, diverting attention from the specificity of the different forms taken by the "network of electronic communication prosthetics" (*War*, 35). This critique is elaborated in Markley's essay collection (*Virtual Reality*, 2). Such comments again emphasize the ways in which real life seems to have caught up with cyberpunk fiction.

2. A partial list of other significant attempts to produce feminist responses to or versions of cyberpunk, besides the ones discussed in this chapter, would include Gwyneth Jones's trilogy (*White Queen, North Wind, Phoenix Café*) and novels or story collections by Rosenblum; Misha; Lisa Mason; Ore; and Robson.

3. For work on sexual or gender performativity and virtual embodiment, see Case; Fraiberg: Woodland; and Senft and Horn's special issue of *Women and Performance* on "Sexuality and Cyberspace: Performing the Digital Body," especially Senft's introduction and the essays by O'Brien and Ehrlich.

4. For reasons that I will discuss at the end of this essay, much less work has been done on the topic of race and performativity. Nakamura's essay on racial passing, subsequently incorporated into chapter 2 of her book, was a groundbreaking application of

Butler's theory of performativity to questions of racial passing and masquerade or minstrelsy in cyberspace. See also Dery's comments about "Afrofuturism," in his introduction to the interviews with Samuel R. Delany, Greg Tate, and Tricia Rose (Dery, "Black to the Future," 736–43); the special issue of *Social Text* on this topic, edited by Nelson; Gómez-Peña's "Virtual Barrio" essay; Hayles's intriguing suggestion that cyberspace and narratives about it demonstrate the themes of "marked bodies" and "invisibility" associated with African-American literary texts such as Ralph Ellison's *Invisible Man* ("Seductions," 183); Shohat and Stam's speculations on the possibility of using virtual reality as part of a "multicultural or transnational pedagogy" (165–66); and the section of Case's book that focuses on Chicana lesbian writer Cherríe Moraga and her concept of "queer Aztlán" (Case, 161–64).

5. Jon McKenzie similarly notes that virtual reality combines two paradigms of performance, human and technological (the latter defined in terms of efficiency and input/output ratios), into a new configuration that both "heightens the oppositions that structure it—presence/absence, originality/derivativeness, organic/inorganic, authenticity/inauthenticity, immediacy/mediation—while also exposing a certain cohabitation" between them (101).

6. See also Jameson's argument that postmodernism in general is defined by critiques of how "the very concept of expression presupposes . . . a whole metaphysics of the inside and outside" and therefore a "conception of the subject as a monadlike container" (*Postmodernism*, 11, 15).

7. McHugh is perhaps better known for her novels, and of those *China Mountain Zhang* (1992) is most comparable to the stories I will discuss here, because that novel appropriates the cyberpunk thematics of "jacking in" to computer networks or prosthetic enhancements through direct neural interfaces (within the overall context of a futuristic setting in which China has replaced the United States as the dominant world superpower); see Gray, Mentor, and Figueroa-Sarriera's reference to this novel in their introduction to *The Cyborg Handbook* (11).

8. Carole-Anne Tyler's critique of Butler's account of drag performance raises similar questions (53–58). Tyler points out that drag performances often depend on stereotypes about racialized or lower-class women in order to mark the difference between a "subversive" or denaturalizing drag performance and a naturalizing performance of gender; that is, drag performances often mark their excess or their ironic distance from white, middle-class norms of femininity by reproducing stereotypes about women who do not conform to those white, middle-class norms.

9. See Sedgwick on this problem ("Queer Performativity"), and Butler's response (*Bodies That Matter*, 226–33 and 282–83 n. 11).

10. This withholding of the characters' "real" names seems particularly suggestive in relation to Ellison's similar strategy in *Invisible Man*. This reading of the convention of "unmasking" in narrative about virtual reality technologies should be compared to Žižek's discussion of the formation of virtual body images as a process of "symbolic identification," defined as "assuming a mask which is more real and binding than the true face beneath it" (*Plague*, 139). This definition seems to me to ignore the ways in which the narratives I'm examining call into question the distinction between mask and face, rather

than simply inverting the hierarchy between them, to privilege the mask as more real than the face.

11. Jay David Bolter similarly theorizes immersive virtual reality computer interfaces as a medium that works primarily through the manipulation of point of view ("Ekphrasis," 267–69). In a short piece in *Wired* magazine, he claims that "computer graphics is showing itself to be a technology for generating points of view" and that this medium is not "just about morphing objects" but, more important, "about morphing the view and the viewer" ("You Are What You See," 113). Bolter also defines the medium of virtual reality as nonexpressive: "you don't 'express' yourself in defining your computer graphic identity. Instead, you occupy various points of view, each of which constitutes a new identity" (114).

12. See Fuchs's suggestion that cyborg body images that combine organic and mechanical elements might be read in a similar way. Fuchs quotes Butler's argument that "if every performance repeats itself to institute the effect of identity, then every repetition requires an interval between the acts, as it were, in which risk and excess threaten to disrupt the identity being constituted" (Butler, "Imitation," 28); Fuchs goes on to define these "intervals" as the "breaks in cyborg identity encoded by their 'divided' selves" (114).

13. Sonnega raises a similar issue, in the context of a critique of the computer graphic technique of morphing as a favored mode of racial representation on MTV. Sonnega points to the difficulty performance techniques, with their emphasis on the visual, have in accounting "for the sensations of spatial 'inbetweenness' that mark the lives of so many actual people" in postmodern culture (46–47). He goes on to critique morphing for construing "intercultural performance not as a contestation of the normative patterns that maintain cultural boundaries, but as an escape from them" (55). Morphing, then, functions as a painless form of border crossing or identity tourism, much like the modes of cross-identification that initially excite Cobalt in McHugh's story.

14. Similarly, O'Brien distinguishes between sexual performances coded as fiction that only reconfirm the knowledge of "our 'physical reality,'" such as "a white 40-something male middle-manager who goes online" as a woman and has text-based cybersex with a black man, and performances that more successfully resist such categorization, her example being a "self-identified lesbian" who has anal sex with a gay man using a dildo (62–63). O'Brien also notes that current netiquette involves the assumption that any Internet user identified as a woman who is also "cruising for sex" and "hypergendered" is actually "a guy trying to 'trick' other men into having sex" (60). This assumption clearly functions as a strategy for reinstating a clear hierarchy between "real life" and virtual personae, in particular by ruling out possibilities for female female impersonation. I am trying to define the ways that these narratives of virtual reality imagine what O'Brien ends by calling for, more "cross-over between those in queer and straight spaces" online (66).

15. *Trouble and Her Friends* arguably engages more directly with cyberpunk conventions than any of Scott's other novels, but she has produced a considerable body of work taking up cyberpunk tropes. *Dreamships, Dreaming Metal,* and *The Shapes of Their Hearts* are all concerned with the rights of AIs; *Burning Bright* focuses on virtual reality gaming; *Night Sky Mine* combines cyberspace with artificial life technologies (software programs designed to evolve through competition); and *The Jazz* focuses on the immediate future of the Internet as a technology of disinformation, manipulated by corporate interests.

16. O'Brien's essay begins with an analysis of an ad for online services in the *Advocate*, which uses the slogan "There are no closets in Cyberspace" and which claims that online chat rooms are "meeting places so free and open and wild and fun they make Castro Street look Victorian" (55). Scott's novel and its more complex mapping of connections between cyberspace and the closet can be read as an intervention in this kind of popular discourse.

17. As early as 1988, cyberpunk writers themselves began to question this figure of the romanticized outlaw hacker. Examples would include Sterling's *Islands in the Net*, which deliberately tries to invert the typical cyberpunk scenario by presenting a positive model of the transnational corporation and taking an employee of such a corporation as its main character. Gibson's *Virtual Light* can also be read as an attempt to resist the transformation of the hacker as cyberpunk protagonist into a formulaic narrative figure.

18. Mixon has published two other novels since *Glass Houses*, both of which center on telepresence technologies and can therefore be read as elaborating on the concerns of this earlier work; I discuss the first of the two novels, *Proxies*, in my essay "Postproduction."

19. Laurel's *Computers as Theatre* also clearly participates in this attempt to foreground questions of human performance modes within VR technologies.

20. Mary Catherine Harper also offers a reading of Ruby's "hybridized subjectivity" (413–15). Both Harper and Cadora draw primarily on Haraway's "Cyborg Manifesto" as a theoretical model for reading *Glass Houses*, with the result that they overlook the performative aspect of the novel's representation of telepresence technologies—that is, they both read Ruby as a feminist cyborg, rather than as a user of virtual reality, as theorized by Stone.

21. See Hayles's argument that cybernetic technocultures redefine Lacan's mirror stage, replacing the dialectic of presence and absence with a dialectic between randomness and pattern ("Seductions," 186); as well as Haraway's redefinition of Lacan ("Promises," 301). See also my reading of Egan's *Diaspora* in chapter 1.

22. Butler raises the question of "what will constitute a subversive or de-instituting repetition," given that all identities are constituted through acts of repetition, imitation, and impersonation ("Imitation," 25, 27). Tyler's essay elaborates on the difficulties in drawing this distinction. Turkle addresses the question of how virtual experiences might feed back into "real-life" experiences by suggesting that cyberspace can function as a "transitional space" like that of a psychoanalyst's office (*Life*, 262–63). As I have argued, Stone seems to offer a more useful model of this relationship between the physical and the virtual, through her description of both the physical and the virtual as composed of discursive and performative elements.

23. The implications of this disjunction between gender or sexual and racial performativity will be explored in the next chapter. Michael Rogin criticizes Lott for implicitly assimilating blackface to forms of cross-dressing such as drag or butch-femme, which tend to be coded as liberatory within postmodern theory (30).

5. The Souls of Cyberfolk

In the first heading, I am quoting a famous phrase from the two-part episode of *Star Trek: The Next Generation* titled "The Best of Both Worlds," in which the crew of the *Enterprise* encounters a race of cyborgs known as the Borg, whose culture is organized around "assimilating" other species.

1. See also Warner's account of this process ("Mass Public," 397); Wiegman discusses these same issues, in the context of theorizing the relationship between race and gender (*American Anatomies*, 50).

2. Yvonne Yarbro-Bejarano has critiqued the tendency to analyze racial performativity by analogy with gender in Butler's work (129). To a greater or lesser extent, most feminist technoculture studies work to date also demonstrates this tendency to at best only occasionally invoke questions of race rather than to attempt to incorporate them more substantially into the analysis of gender and sexuality; examples might include Turkle, Springer, and Balsamo, whose books otherwise constitute major contributions to the field, like Stone's. This tendency has only begun to be corrected, with the publication of Kolko, Nakamura, and Rodman's collection *Race in Cyberspace;* Nakamura's *Cybertypes;* Nelson and Tu's *Technicolor;* Nelson's *Social Text* special issue on Afrofuturism; and Lee and Wong's *AsianAmerica.Net* collection, an emerging body of work that is making it possible to begin articulating feminist and critical race approaches to technoculture.

3. See Stuart Hall's "New Ethnicities" for the argument that ethnicity foregrounds the constructedness of subaltern experience (446–47); Poster's chapter on "Virtual Ethnicity" in *What's the Matter with the Internet?* makes a similar argument, as does Bailey (29–31).

4. This process is particularly apparent in Haraway's "The Promises of Monsters" and "Ecce Homo," as well as *Modest Witness.* "Ecce Homo" turns away from cyborg figurations entirely, in order to focus on Sojourner Truth. Wiegman's *American Anatomies* offers the best critique of this analogical mode of thinking about race.

5. Baudrillard theorizes a similar integrated circuit, in a form that more explicitly re-universalizes a postmodern critique of the falsely universal form of the humanist subject. Baudrillard argues that the infiltration of popular media into the fabric of everyday life breaks down traditional modernist distinctions between individuals and society, so that alienation from the society of the spectacle as represented by the figures of the "mirror and the scene" is replaced by the "screen and network" (*Ecstasy,* 12). The result is what Baudrillard famously describes as "a pornography of information and communication" and a condition of "forced signification," in which everyone functions as signs for others (22).

6. This seems to me to be one implication of Doane's critique, which asks what happens when "the collapse of oppositions represented by the cyborg" becomes normative ("Cyborgs," 213).

7. This argument is elaborated in Sandoval's *Methodology.*

8. I am following Sinker in suggesting that it may be possible to find examples of African-American technoculture studies in unexpected places. Sinker's essay on black science fiction argues that the relatively small number of black science-fiction writers does not mean that science fiction holds no interest for black cultural workers, but instead that black science fiction is more likely to be found in media other than print fiction, such as the music and videos of Sun Ra, George Clinton, or Public Enemy. See Weheliye's essay on black posthumanism and the music industry.

9. Nakamura's work is the best exploration of this connection. Her suggestion that all forms of virtual role-playing might be understood as forms of "passing" (*Cybertypes*, 36) exemplifies the double nature of the relationship between histories of racial performance and new technologies of "technosociality." If everyone must "pass" on the Internet, then histories of racial performance offer a framework for understanding the racial implications of new technologies and their modes of sociality; at the same time, those technologies and new modes of sociality threaten to generalize and efface the specificity of these racial histories of performing "blackness," for example.

10. See Jeffrey Brown (15–26) for a reading of these early attempts.

11. After McDuffie and Cowan's departures, Wright produced two final story arcs, in which *Deathlok* finally turned even further in the direction of a standard Marvel superhero comic. The focus turned to investigating the history of character Deathlok and his previous incarnations by introducing an enormously complicated plot involving alternate time lines. This plot seems designed to appeal mainly to readers who knew the prior history of the comic book character rather than to readers interested in racial issues. As a result, the comic lost its audience and was canceled after issue 34, ending an almost three-year run. McDuffie and Cowan went on to become partners in Milestone, a multicultural line of comics, published by Marvel's rival DC Comics and devoted to producing racialized versions of classic superhero tropes. Milestone began publishing in 1993 and continued through the 1990s, until it folded for financial reasons (though an animated version of one of the characters, Static, later appeared on television). See Brown's book on Milestone for an excellent account of this subsequent history. Brown mentions Deathlok only very briefly (26–27, 31, 85), but these brief passages are useful for indicating the importance of this collaboration on the Deathlok book for their later work.

12. This aspect of *Deathlok*'s plot seems to be echoed in the film *Solo*, in which Mario van Peebles plays a black version of the Terminator, a human-appearing robot soldier designed by the U.S. Army who is used to intervene in a Central American uprising.

13. Similar issues are raised in relation to the android Data on *Star Trek: The Next Generation*, especially in the episode titled "The Measure of a Man," in which Data has to go to court to prove that he has the rights of a person rather than a machine. See also Gray's reading of this episode (*Cyborg Citizen*, 21–22), as an example of the problem of citizenship in technocultural contexts. The jokes in *Deathlok* are repeated in the film *Robocop 3*; at one point when Robocop is under attack, he tells his assailant that the assailant is under arrest for attacking a police officer. When the attacker then cuts off Robocop's arm with a sword, Robocop adds that the attacker is also under arrest for destroying police property.

14. See Baker's definition of African-American modernism in terms of two possible responses to the stereotypes that Baker refers to as the minstrel mask (*Modernism*). The first of these positions was "the mastery of form," by which Baker means learning to accept and manipulate these stereotypes, and the second was "the deformation of mastery," the act of revising the minstrel mask by creating alternative black performances grounded, for example, in black vernacular or musical practices, as a counterimage to contest the stereotypes of the minstrel mask.

15. Stone makes a similar point about the difference between mask and prosthesis (*War*, 2–4), noting that "there are some out at the margins who have always lived comfortably with the idea of floating identities" where even the "'root persona'" is assumed to be a mask, "and inward from the margins there are a few who are beginning, just a bit, to question" (2–3).

16. The question of why Deathlok does not give up searching for his organic body is explicitly raised in a story written by McDuffie for the first *Deathlok* annual comic. This story is a dream sequence in which Deathlok's son takes him to class for show-and-tell, and one of the children asks why he continues to search for his organic body. Deathlok's reply is that "that body isn't just a piece of meat. It's my *humanity*" (27). Another child, meanwhile, accuses Deathlok of being "a liberal and out of touch with the American mainstream" (26). See "Show and Tell," *Deathlok Annual* 1 (August 1992): 24–29.

17. This same ambivalence appears in the thematics of the family in *Deathlok*. Roddy Reid quotes the 1993 report of the national commission on America's Urban Families, which defines the family as "the most economical system for keeping human beings human," in an argument that links the posthuman with the postfamilial (177, 194). Although Deathlok acknowledges that his family can no longer keep him human and that as long as he remains a cyborg he can never play the same roles in his family, Deathlok is nevertheless as unable to simply abandon his relationship to his wife and son as he is to forget his relationship to his organic, his "human" body. McDuffie begins many of his issues of the monthly *Deathlok* comic with Deathlok writing letters to his wife that he never expects to be able to send, and one of McDuffie's later story arcs involves Deathlok's attempted reunion with his family, a classic convention in African-American slave narratives and post-Emancipation fiction, such as Frances E. W. Harper's *Iola Leroy*. In this respect, it is also interesting to consider the way that Deathlok's relation to his son is initially mediated through cyberspace and video games.

18. Other popular representations of black cyborgs would include *Virtuosity* (1995), starring Denzel Washington, and Mario van Peebles's character in *Solo*, a cyborg soldier who chooses to appear black because he wants to "be like Mike" after watching one of Michael Jordan's Nike commercials. The main televisual example would be the Fox network program *M.A.N.T.I.S.* (1994–95), whose main character (played by Carl Lumbly) was a paralyzed black scientist who invents a full-body prosthesis that he uses to fight crime. Of particular interest is Jimmie Robinson's comic *Cyberzone*, whose main character is a black lesbian and which was published independently by Jet-Black Graphics in Oakland. A more mainstream example is the black character Cyborg in *Tales of the New Teen Titans* (an animated version of this comic began airing on the Cartoon network in July 2003). As Springer points out, this character is also depicted as being "aware of racial divisions in society" (*Electronic Eros*, 135), though in contrast to both *Deathlok* and *Cyberzone*, the *Teen Titans* comic is not produced by an African-American creative team.

19. This shift in emphasis away from racial issues in later issues of *Deathlok* is perhaps best summed up by the opening scenes of Wright's issue 26, which begins with Deathlok and his son playing a video game Deathlok has designed, a fighting game (like Mortal Kombat) called Borgs N the Hood. The contrast to Deathlok's intervention in his son's video game in issue 1 of the limited series is illuminating. This scene allegorizes

the way in which racial themes gradually become overwhelmed by action plots, after McDuffie and Cowan's departures from *Deathlok*.

20. See also chapter 4 n. 21.

21. See Lyotard (2) for this distinction.

22. It is this folding of the virtual and the discursive back into the physical that makes it theoretically possible for cyberspace and VR to function as what Turkle calls "transitional spaces," spaces of therapeutic experimentation that should ideally lead to greater self-awareness outside the therapist's office (*Life*, 262–63; see also chapter 4 n. 22).

23. See also Hayles's critique of claims that VR might replace physical embodiment in *How We Became Posthuman* (e.g., 283–84).

24. The implication here is that the technosocial modes of articulating physical and virtual spaces that Stone tends to define as "new" have a long history in racial contexts. This critique of Stone is similar in many ways to Phillip Brian Harper's critique of Jameson's account of the postmodern "decentering" of subjectivity (Harper, 11; Jameson, *Postmodernism*, 63). The problem here is one of the complex relation of African-American histories and traditions to periodizing definitions of the postmodern or technosocial.

25. Compare this statement to Naomi Schor's analysis of how power is constructed through simultaneous processes of "saming" and "othering" ("Essentialism," 45–46). Both Warner ("Mass Public," 397) and Wiegman (*American Anatomies*, 50) identify the tension between universalization and particularity as central to recent changes in the structure and function of the public sphere. I would also note that the AI's condition of "philosophical agony" seems to echo Amiri Baraka's poem "An Agony. As Now," which begins with the lines "I am inside someone / who hates me. I look / out from his eyes." The thematics of being either (or both) too different and too much the same also appears in Langston Hughes's poem "Theme for English B."

26. See Phillip Brian Harper's reading of Rinehart as a figure for the specificity of black experiences of self-division, multiplicity, and "decenteredness" (142–43).

27. Wald argues that Du Bois's *Souls of Black Folk* defines double consciousness in formal, literary terms as the necessity of "always telling one's story through the narratives of others" (12)—that is, as formally revisionary in its techniques. This same necessity for cultural revision is thematized in *Deathlok* through the notion of hardwiring.

28. See Wald (176–77) and, for more detail on Du Bois's sources, Dickson's essay on double consciousness.

29. Wilcox's essay on the android character Data on *Star Trek: The Next Generation* offers an interesting reading of the ways in which Data might be understood as attempting not only to "pass" for human (which is Data's explicit project in the series) but more specifically to pass for "white" (72–79).

30. In the context of a possible reading of the Deathlok cyborg as a blackface performance (by a black man), the internal dialogues between Deathlok and the onboard computer seem significant as well. In those dialogues, the computer's precision, emotionlessness, and incomprehension of jokes and sarcasm seem to drive Deathlok toward a more vernacular mode of speech in reaction, such as the use of the word *ain't*. These speech patterns seem surprising considering Michael Collins's background, but they might be read as a tendency toward black dialect.

6. Replaying the L.A. Riots

1. For versions of this argument, see Frankenberg's introduction to her collection *Displacing Whiteness* (5); Wray and Newitz's *White Trash* collection (3–5); and Dyer (1–2). Roediger goes further in arguing for the "abolition" or the "withering away of whiteness" (12). See Nealon for a critique of this latter position (140, 163). Although he does not specifically refer to the white male body, Telotte's account of how "the body itself seems no longer quite hidden from history or from our own gaze," in films about cyborgs, suggests the connection of cyborg imagery to the concerns of whiteness studies (167).

2. Springer specifically cites Klaus Theweleit's analyses of fascist anxieties (see note 16 in this chapter); see also Bukatman's contrast of this representation to cyberpunk's (304–8). Ross makes a similar contrast, arguing that cyberpunk represents the disappearance of the "guarantee of invulnerability" with which cyborg embodiment is associated in such films as *The Terminator* (*Strange Weather,* 152–53). See Pfeil for an analysis of how this very vulnerability can reinscribe certain forms of masculine privilege.

3. On this discourse of victimization (the "angry white male"), see Nealon's chapter 7.

4. A longer version of this argument appears in Foster's book *The Return of the Real,* chapter 5.

5. Other examples of this convention would include a series of novels by Ings, all of which include characters who are left traumatized by the removal of cyborg implants, and most recently Stross's story "Tourists" (2002), where the main character, Manfred Macx (a near-future information entrepreneur), suffers the theft of what is variously described as his exobrain or metacortex (the "whole slew of high-level [digital] agents that collectively form a large chunk of the society of mind that is their owner's personality" [18]). This thematics highlights the potential vulnerability of what Andy Clark calls "the expanded mind" or "wideware" (see chapter 1 of this book).

6. This reference to "duality" is from the video of "Shock to the System" marketed by Chrysalis Records in 1993, which also contains a "Shockumentary" about the making of the video, including some commentary by Idol.

7. Avital Ronell makes the same connection, not to the riots themselves, but to the video of Rodney King's beating, where the use of massive force against a black body by the police evokes for her the similar use of massive force in a "police action" against "helpless brown bodies in Iraq" (315). She also notes that L.A. Chief of Police Darryl Gates drew the same analogy when he accused the media of turning Rodney King's beating "into something bigger than the Gulf War" (318; Gates was quoted to this effect on the broadcast news, June 27, 1992).

8. I take this to be the point of Springer's argument that SF film shifted, around 1995 (the year in which *Strange Days, Johnny Mnemonic,* and *Virtuosity* were all released, along with such Internet thriller movies as *Hackers* and *The Net*), from representing the technological mediation of bodies in films such as the Terminator and Robocop series to representing the manipulation of minds in cyberspace ("Psycho-Cybernetics," 204; Sterling's comments on both body and mind invasion, in the Introduction to the *Mirrorshades* anthology, indicate how cyberpunk fiction had already anticipated this shift). Springer's own earlier reading of *Robocop* emphasizes the psychological frameworks used

to represent the radical nature of his transformations, specifically the classic traumatic symptom of repressed memories.

9. See Butler's essay in Gooding-Williams's collection *Reading Rodney King/Reading Urban Uprising* for an analysis of the visual structure of racial paranoia exhibited by the police in their response to King, a structure replicated and reinforced during the trial when the defense lawyers successfully insisted that King's beaten body itself constituted evidence of a threat against the police beating him.

10. See Stephanie Smith for another critique of postmodern fantasies of metamorphosis.

11. Fred Moten offers a critique of the desire to produce new readings of Rodney King, with reference to both Ronell and the Gooding-Williams book, which he suggests replicate the logic of the police defense team and their approach to the videotape of King's beating. Hunt's *Screening the Los Angeles "Riots"* offers a useful corrective to such tendencies, by focusing on the different ways that black, white, and Latino "informants" constructed the meaning of these events.

12. The song's allusion to Kipling's "The Man Who Would Be King" is relevant here (or more likely the film version of it), because that story consists of a traditional narrative of "going native" by two British men who leave India to set themselves up as rulers in Kafiristan and whose claims to godlike powers are revealed as a hoax when one of the men is bitten by the "native" woman he wants to marry and he bleeds. The story therefore presents physical vulnerability as a deflation of white male pretensions, a narrative that Idol's video rewrites, to present vulnerability as a precondition for reasserting white privilege.

13. The wordplay between "King" and "king" in the song lyrics seems to dramatize this status of trauma as an event that cannot properly be experienced subjectively, in a version of the same critique of possessive individualism and claims to uniqueness that cyborg imagery applies to possession of one's own body.

14. Silverman's use of the notion of "historical trauma" to define the instability of male subjectivity provides the basis of such an alternate model of cyborg masculinity, though Silverman's argument tends to associate such trauma with World War II, and to distinguish between such, to her, properly "historical" traumas and two other distinct sources of instability for men, the symbolic "Law of Language" and "oppression experienced in relation to class, race, ethnicity, age, and other ideologically determined 'handicaps'" (47). The result of this distinction is to suggest that only members of minoritized racial groups can experience race as a form of historical trauma, with the result that the whiteness of masculinity remains a category that cannot be specified.

15. The same tension between a critique of the generically human and a definition of the value of that critique in generic terms occurs in Bukatman's comments on the film. He argues that "the hybrid superhero bodies of Robocop and the Terminator embrace technology at the same time as they armor *the human* against the technological threat" and that films like *Robocop* dramatize "an uneasy but consistent sense of human obsolescence, and at stake is the very definition of *the human*" (20; my emphasis); see also Holland (160).

16. Springer is here drawing on Klaus Theweleit's famous analysis (in *Male Fantasies*)

of the gender assumptions implicit in protofascist rhetoric in Germany, which projected anxieties about the "dissolution of self" onto women and communists, associating both groups with "fluid ego boundaries." This analysis is indebted to Susan Jeffords's work on the trope of the male "hard body" in Reagan-era film (24–28); Jeffords also argues that Robocop comes to epitomize this reconstructed ideal of masculinity, precisely to the extent that he succeeds in recovering his humanity (his memories, his emotions), in order to resist his reduction to a commodity, so that this reduction primarily serves as a justification or alibi for the film's reassertion of masculinity. In relation to this trope of the "hard body" more generally, it is interesting to note that Dyer devotes a whole chapter (chapter 4) to bodybuilding as a form of *white* and not just masculine embodiment.

17. Rushing and Frentz's book on "the cyborg hero in American film" does not refer specifically to *Robocop*, but their situating of cyborg figures in relation to Americanist myths, especially the figure of the hunter (5), suggests possibilities for reading cyborg narratives in terms of racial and colonial histories.

18. See also Seltzer on "wound culture" and the "pathological public sphere," as mutations in the contemporary public sphere, organized now around display and spectacularization of embodied particularity, not abstraction. His discussion of how this construction of publicness links "sociality" with "the excitations of the torn and opened body . . . as public spectacle" (254) is especially relevant to *Robocop*, as is his suggestion that "sociality" can be defined as an "opening toward others," and therefore as a positive form of "wounding" or trauma (258).

19. In their introduction to their *White Trash* collection, Wray and Newitz indicate the need "to criticize the idea that whiteness can only be assimilated into a multicultural society once it is associated with victimhood" and to "question why we believe that whites (or anyone) need to be victimized before they can adopt an anti-racist, multiculturalist perspective" (6).

20. For an example of criticism focusing on *Robocop*'s critique of the corporation and its extension of corporate power into areas formerly controlled by state institutions, see Schelde (209). Jeffords points out that the city services Omni Consumer Products (OCP) takes over in Detroit are the same ones that were being privatized under the Reagan administration (107–8). Sobchack's chapter on "Postfuturism," added to the second edition of *Screening Space*, applies Jameson's argument about postmodernism as an expansion of the commodity structure to previously untouched areas of human experience to a wide range of science-fiction film (Sobchack, *Screening Space*, 236), though *Robocop* appeared after this chapter was written. For examples of criticism focusing on the narrative of Robocop overcoming his built-in limitations, see Schelde (212), Telotte (156), and Poster (*Second Media Age*, 139–40), as well as Jeffords (see note 16 above).

21. For examples of criticism focusing on the technological mediation of Robocop's vision, see Bukatman (254–55); Poster (*Second Media Age*, 139–40); and Holland (161). Sobchack offers a reading of the technique of postmodern "pastiche" in science-fiction film (245), though again without direct reference to *Robocop*. Collins devotes a whole chapter (chapter 3) to the problem of the "'recycled' nature" of recent Hollywood film (*Screening Space*, 125).

22. See Beller for a reading of *Robocop II* in terms of transnational capitalism. OCP

creates Robocop as part of an urban-renewal scheme to wipe out crime in Old Detroit, not to benefit the residents of the inner city, but instead in order to make it possible to tear down Old Detroit and replace it with Delta City, a planned community. This thematics of corporate urban renewal and its impact on lower-class and minoritized urban populations becomes more explicit in the sequels to *Robocop,* especially *Robocop 3,* which focuses on OCP's attempts to use Robocop to evict the inhabitants of Old Detroit.

23. Poster offers the only commentary I have found on this opening newscast, though he reads the news stories in more general terms, as "figuring *the body* in danger," without any reference to the specific content of the stories—that is, racial unrest and white anxieties about it (*Second Media Age,* 138).

24. In fact, the rhetoric of "life in the big city" as a self-evident explanation for random and inexplicable acts of violence evokes nothing if not the popular association of urban unrest and street violence with minoritized racial populations, especially African-Americans, an association prominently displayed in the news coverage of the L.A. "riots," which typically "labeled 'blacks' as the event insiders," despite the participation of other groups in the unrest following the acquittal, as Hunt points out (168).

25. Schelde offers a brief commentary on this scene, associating it with other forms of phallic imagery in the film, rather than focusing on the specific historical stereotype about black anatomy (210).

26. Dyer's chapter 3 on the centrality of lighting techniques in the development of both photography and film, as a way of constructing an image of whiteness (122), offers another suggestive account of the role technology might play in the project of spectacularizing whiteness. As I pointed out in chapter 3, Dyer's distinction between the diffuse haze or "glow" associated with white body images and the more hard-edged "shine" associated with people of color seems especially relevant to any attempt to decode the racial meanings of cyborg imagery (ibid.); like Calder's gynoids, Robocop's skin has a silvery color whose nearest racial analogue would seem to be Caucasian skin, but the shiny metal surface invokes the lighting conventions applied to nonwhite bodies in Hollywood film.

27. Urban vigilante films seem to depend on the concept of trauma theorized by Caruth, in which the initial acts of violence are especially shocking because they are presented as random and senseless eruptions that cannot be assimilated to the characters' ongoing life stories. But the traumatic nature of the initial attack is used not just to justify subsequent acts of violence, to make them narratable in terms the audience as well as the character *can* understand and assimilate, but also to present the initial attack as coming out of nowhere, as an event without any history that we can grasp or should try to grasp. Robocop follows some of the conventions of these films quite closely, almost to the point of seeming like a deliberate parody of them; for instance, the level of violence that Robocop commits against the gang who killed Murphy escalates to absurd levels, as it does in vigilante films, where forms of violence that are often more graphic and should be more traumatic than the original attacks are coded as acceptable.

28. The thematics of Murphy's death as the precondition for his becoming a cyborg suggests both a recapitulation and a redefinition of the traditional association of whiteness and death that Dyer discusses (208), in which death signifies whiteness's capacity

for transcendence, its ability to become a generic category rather than a particular and embodied one.

29. For a related reading of Robocop as vulnerable rather than just fortified, see Telotte's discussion of how Robocop can be read as combining masculine and feminine qualities, as suggested by the scene in which his partner Lewis has to physically adjust Robocop's posture to help him aim his gun in order to repair his targeting system, a scene that seems designed to emphasize Robocop's dependence rather than his armored autonomy (Telotte, 156).

30. By focusing on the figure of the cyborg as a *visual* strategy for producing whiteness in film and video contexts, I am taking Dyer's argument about the importance of learning "to see whiteness" in a different direction (9).

7. Franchise Nationalisms

1. A few of the other key originating texts on the cultural implications of contemporary processes of transnationalization would include Appadurai *(Modernity at Large);* the Wilson and Dissanayake collection, especially the essays by Dirlik and Featherstone on the relation between global and local; and Ong. The essays in Grewal and Kaplan make a feminist intervention into this discourse.

2. Nakamura describes *Snow Crash* as a novel that "keeps a foot in two worlds: one in the world of first-generation cyberpunk, and one in [the] more contemporary 'real world' of the 1990s, where ethnicity and race are in the process of being actively reconfigured" (*Cybertypes,* 70).

3. See Buell for a critique of globalization as deterritorialized Americanization, with specific reference to cyberpunk as an example (565–69).

4. Sponsler goes on to argue that "an acceptance of the decay of the physical world—especially the urban environment—seen not as a frightening specter but simply as home, the place where we live . . . coupled with a fascination with simulated, interior space—the world of cyberspace or virtual reality—may be one of the enduring themes of cyberpunk" ("Beyond the Ruins," 261–62). This definition of cyberpunk suggests its resistance to the traditional utopian/dystopian polarity in SF, as I argued in the Introduction to this book.

5. Anderson famously connects the democratic public sphere to what he calls print capitalism, as embodied in the power of cultural forms such as the newspaper and the novel to create a sense of common participation in the life of the nation (42–46). The role of print culture in creating standardized national vernacular languages is also crucial to Anderson's argument, and defines the model of language that *Snow Crash* presents as breaking down, as we will see. See Buell on the shift from print to electronic media as a crisis in the definition of national community (564–65). From this perspective, it seems especially significant that the promoters of virtual community and free speech on the Internet often appropriate the rhetoric of early national culture and its founding documents, as in the case of Barlow's "A Declaration of the Independence of Cyberspace" (see the Introduction to this book) and the "Magna Carta for the Knowledge Age," collaboratively authored and later posted on the World Wide Web by Newt Gingrich's Peace and Freedom Foundation (Dyson et al.).

6. See also Dirlik's argument that a critical localism can only consist of being simultaneously local and translocal, in order to resist the logic of multinational corporations, which assert their dominance precisely by both "thinking globally and acting locally" (34, 41–42).

7. The influence of *Snow Crash*'s fictional representation of transnationalism is suggested by the inclusion of an excerpt from the novel in the postmodern geography essay collection *The Spaces of Postmodernity* (Dear and Flusty).

8. John Perry Barlow, quoted in Rheingold, *Virtual Community*, 75. See also Rheingold's discussion of the "convergence" between monetary "transaction systems" and computerized "representation systems" (*Virtual Reality*, 367). This convergence (or disjunction) is the central concern of Castells's work, especially the three-volume series on "The Information Age," published after *The Informational City*.

9. See Turow for an account of the history of this shift to narrowcasting within the advertising industry, and for a critique of its effects on the national public sphere.

10. See also Miyoshi's argument that transnational capital is progressive to the extent that it destroys the fiction of the nation-state as an internally homogeneous "imagined community" and reveals the emptiness of "such official 'traditional' culture" ("Sites," 70), but exploitative because it also "means the destruction of local and regional culture" (ibid., 69). This argument defines where Miyoshi departs from Harvey, who sees transnationalism as transforming local and regional cultures in more ambivalent ways.

11. I am quoting an interview with Gibson from Marianne Trench's film *Cyberpunk*.

12. Recall here Doane's critique of Haraway for ignoring how the cyborg, as a figure for the "collapse" of dualistic structures, might function as an oppressive norm within a society in which "oppression is no longer organized through dualisms" ("Cyborgs at Large," 213). Harvey's work on post-Fordism raises a similar question about postmodernism in general.

13. See also Dillon's essay "Fortress America," and especially Blakely and Snyder's *Fortress America*, for more empirical data on gated communities. Evan McKenzie's book offers a more ambivalent assessment of homeowner associations as "privatopias," with a focus on them as models for local styles of governance.

14. Nakamura points out that this thematics of new ethnicities continues in Stephenson's next novel, *The Diamond Age* (1995), where it is applied to a political grouping of twelve-year-old girls referred to as the Mouse Army (Nakamura, *Cybertypes*, 71; Stephenson, *Diamond*, 446).

15. See also Grewal and Kaplan's discussion of feminist NGOs, as models for coalition building in transnational feminist practices, in their introduction to *Scattered Hegemonies* (23–29).

16. Gibson's self-consciousness about this point is suggested in *Neuromancer* when the narrator comments that transnational corporations tolerate black market trafficking in high-tech commodities because they realize that "burgeoning technologies require outlaw zones," and that the black market is not there "for its inhabitants," but instead "as a deliberately unsupervised playground for technology itself" (11).

17. The trope of franchising one's personality is recurrent in cyberpunk fiction. Two of the best examples can be found in Pat Cadigan's novels *Mindplayers* and *Fools*.

18. This thematics in cyberpunk fiction and contemporary technoculture should also be read in relation to theories of performativity, and especially histories of racial performance. Doing "a Clint" in *Snow Crash* might well evoke Ralph Ellison's representation of "doing a Rinehart," in *Invisible Man* (507), which is how that novel encodes what Baker calls "mastery of form" or the manipulation of the "minstrel mask" produced by white stereotypes imposed on African-Americans *(Modernism)*. The suggestion is that virtual technologies result in a generalizing of these histories of racial performance, which now apply to white subjects as well.

19. The same recourse to the city as a model of cosmopolitan resistance to the balkanizing logic of gated communities and enclaves appeared in an episode of Michael Moore's *TV Nation*, in a segment on Rosemont, a northwestern suburb of Chicago, which enjoys public funding and the use of armed Chicago police as guards on the entrances to the community. *TV Nation's* African-American correspondent, filmmaker Rusty Cundieff, set up a gate on the road leading out of Rosemont into Chicago, to suggest how these burbclaves attempt to have things both ways—to retain free access to the benefits of cosmopolitan life and to retain the privilege of withdrawing at will from engagement with the contact zone of the big city. The problem that emerges here is the tendency to reify the city's cosmopolitan nature, effacing urban histories of ghettoization as well as the emergence of gated communities within metropolitan areas.

20. See chapter 1, note 32, on the open source movement in computing, as a related attempt to redefine information and software outside the model of private intellectual property, but instead as a collaborative production.

Conclusion

1. Schroeder's novels *Ventus* and *Permanence* are two of the best examples of how new technocultures might overcome the antinomies of bourgeois thought or romantic epistemological dilemmas, but not necessarily in a liberatory form; see my reading of *Permanence* in chapter 1 and note 30 to that chapter, on *Ventus*.

2. Hayles's reading of *Snow Crash* was initially published in a slightly different form, in the essay "The Posthuman Body." Although I will generally quote the book version, certain relevant passages appear only in the essay version, and will be cited as such. Page references that do not include a title are to *How We Became Posthuman*, and references to the essay version will be indicated by "Posthuman Body."

3. There are two important sources for Stephenson's use of this premise. The more familiar source is Dawkins's influential theory of the meme or self-replicating idea, in his book *The Selfish Gene* (see my discussion of how Daniel Dennett's uses this concept in his theory of the evolution of consciousness, in chapter 1 below). The other source is a postmodern literary influence, specifically the "Jes Grew" plague or "psychic epidemic" (5) in African-American postmodernist Ishmael Reed's novel *Mumbo Jumbo* (Pynchon's influence on Stephenson in particular and cyberpunk in general is much more widely acknowledged; see McHale), suggesting the influence of postmodern concepts of race on the central trope of Stephenson's novel, the snow crash virus. See Nelson's reading of "Jes Grew" as an example of afrofuturism ("Introduction" 6–8). Reed's novel has influenced Chicano science fiction writer Ernest Hogan's attempt to produce an ethnic intervention

in cyberpunk conventions; Hogan's *High Aztech* represents religions as communicable faith viruses, imagining artificial virus technologies that allow people to "fully understand each other's religions and belief systems" or to "access each other's programs" (233). This novel begins with an epigraph from Reed.

4. Hayles offers an excellent discussion of machine code and of the qualities that make it an interesting metaphor for the neurolinguistic structures *Snow Crash* imagines, given that this programming language is performative—that is, the making of statements makes something happen in the program (*How We Became Posthuman*, 274–75).

5. This argument is actually Hayles's interpretation of Porush. In his essay on *Snow Crash*, Porush calls attention to the female hacker character, Juanita, who allows herself to become infected with the Snow Crash virus in order to learn the techniques of neurolinguistic hacking. In contrast to Hiro, she is specifically described as being interested in the power she could gain from such knowledge to control her own neural structures, to hack her own brain. Porush argues that for Juanita this ability to hack neurolinguistic structures is attractive because of its irrationality and its connotations of mystical transcendence (568–69), and he suggests that Juanita's and Hiro's different reactions to this ability are gendered along the lines of a split between masculinized rationality and feminized irrationality. Hayles's reading differs from Porush's in its suggestion that Juanita might have more of a social motive to want to change the more metaphorically hardwired structures of gender and racial expectations.

6. Porush describes this revisionist mythology as a syncretic mixture of Chomsky's linguistic theories and the sociobiological theories of Edward Jayne, who argues that modern concepts of self-consciousness and self-reflection, as well as religious concepts of self-transcendence, can be traced back to changes in the structure of the brain, primarily the neural connections between the right and left hemispheres (Porush, 564). As Porush points out, Stephenson acknowledges Jayne as an influence in his foreword to *Snow Crash*.

7. To get a sense of Stephenson's grasp of these distinctions, see his *In the Beginning . . . Was the Command Line*, a critique of what he sees as the dumbing down of operating systems, as we move toward the convention of graphic user interfaces (Windows as opposed to DOS), interfaces that effectively naturalize the operating system's software for people who wish only to be "end users" and therefore allow fewer possibilities to manipulate the operating system more directly.

8. For a variety of other, more recent attempts to theorize linguistics on a relational or differential model rather than a homogenizing or communitarian one, see Lingis; Arteaga; and Budick and Iser. My use of the term "translatability" is indebted to this latter collection, which defines it both as involving a desire to know "the other" and as marking the limits of that knowledge. Of particular interest is Chang's attempt to apply poststructuralist theories of writing to communication technologies in general, precisely in order to resist the privileging of communication over "noise." Hayles's critique of how early information theory abstracted information from its material medium should be read in relation to the kind of communicational situation that Pratt critiques, in which messages or signals are received within the overall context of "a unified and homogeneous social world" (Pratt, 50).

WORKS CITED

Abrahamson, Mark. *Urban Enclaves: Identity and Place in America.* New York: St. Martin's Press, 1996.

Agger, Ben. *Fast Capitalism: A Critical Theory of Significance.* Urbana and Chicago: University of Illinois Press, 1989.

Anderson, Benedict. *Imagined Communities: Reflections on the Origin and Spread of Nationalism.* Revised edition. New York: Verso, 1991.

Anzaldúa, Gloria. *Borderlands/La Frontera: The New Mestiza.* San Francisco: Spinsters/ Aunt Lute, 1987.

Appadurai, Arjun. "Disjuncture and Difference in the Global Cultural Economy." *Public Culture* 2.2 (spring 1990): 1–24.

———. *Modernity at Large: Cultural Dimensions of Globalization.* Minneapolis: University of Minnesota Press, 1996.

Apter, Emily. *Continental Drift: From National Characters to Virtual Subjects.* Chicago: University of Chicago Press, 1999.

Argyle, Katie, and Rob Shields. "Is There a Body in the Net?" In *Cultures of Internet: Virtual Spaces, Real Histories, Living Bodies,* ed. Rob Shields. London: Sage Publications, 1996. 58–69.

Armstrong, Nancy. *Desire and Domestic Fiction: A Political History of the Novel.* New York: Oxford University Press, 1987.

Arteaga, Alfred, ed. *An Other Tongue: Nation and Ethnicity in the Linguistic Borderlands.* Durham, NC: Duke University Press, 1994.

Baard, Erik. "Inside the Movement for Posthuman Rights: Cyborg Liberation Front." http://www.villagevoice.com/issues/0331/baard.php. Posted July 29, 2003.

Bailey, Cameron. "Virtual Skin: Articulating Race in Cyberspace." In *Immersed in Technology: Art and Virtual Environments,* ed. Mary Anne Moser. Cambridge: MIT Press, 1996. 29–49.

Baker, Houston A., Jr. "Caliban's Triple Play." In *"Race," Writing, and Difference,* ed. Henry Louis Gates Jr. Chicago: University of Chicago Press, 1986. 381–95.

———. *Modernism and the Harlem Renaissance.* Chicago: University of Chicago Press, 1987.

Balsamo, Anne. *Technologies of the Gendered Body: Reading Cyborg Women.* Durham, NC: Duke University Press, 1996.

Barber, Benjamin R. *Jihad vs. McWorld: How Globalism and Tribalism Are Reshaping the World*. New York: Ballantine Books, 1995.

Barlow, John Perry. "Being in Nothingness: Virtual Reality and the Pioneers of Cyberspace." *Mondo 2000* 2 (summer 1990): 34–43.

———. "A Declaration of the Independence of Cyberspace." In ed. Peter Ludlow. *Crypto-Anarchy, Cyberstates, and Pirate Utopias*, Cambridge: MIT Press, 2001. 27–30.

Barnes, John. *Orbital Resonance*. New York: Tor, 1991.

Bateson, Gregory. *Steps to an Ecology of Mind*. New York: Ballantine, 1972.

Baudrillard, Jean. *The Ecstasy of Communication*. Trans. Bernard and Caroline Schutze. New York: Semiotext(e), 1987.

———. "Simulacra and Science Fiction." Trans. Arthur B. Evans. *Science-Fiction Studies* 18 (November 1991): 309–20.

———. *The Transparency of Evil*. Trans. James Benedict. New York: Verso, 1992.

———. "The Year 2000 Has Already Happened." Trans. Nai-fei Ding and Kuan-heng Chen. In *Body Invaders: Panic Sex in America*, ed. Arthur Kroker and Marilouise Kroker. New York: St. Martin's Press, 1987. 35–44.

Baum, L. Frank. *Tik-Tok of Oz*. Chicago: Reilly and Lee, 1914.

Bell, David, and Barbara M. Kennedy. *The Cybercultures Reader*. New York: Routledge, 2000.

Beller, Jonathan L. "Desiring the Involuntary: Machinic Assemblage and Transnationalism in Deleuze and *Robocop 2*." In *Global/Local: Cultural Production and the Transnational Imaginary*, ed. Rob Wilson and Wimal Dissanayake. Durham, NC: Duke University Press, 1996. 193–218.

Belsey, Catherine. *Critical Practice*. New York: Routledge, 1980.

Benedikt, Michael, "Introduction." In *Cyberspace: First Steps*. Cambridge: MIT Press, 1991. 1–29.

———, ed. *Cyberspace: First Steps*. Cambridge: MIT Press, 1991.

Benford, Gregory. "A Hunger for the Infinite." In *Far Horizons*, ed. Robert Silverberg. New York: Eos, 2000. 415–54.

Benjamin, Walter. *Charles Baudelaire: A Lyric Poet in the Era of High Capitalism*. Trans. Harry Zohn. New York: Verso, 1983.

Benston, Kimberly W. "Performing Blackness: Re/Placing Afro-American Poetry." In *Afro-American Literary Study in the 1990s*, ed. Houston A. Baker Jr. and Patricia Redmond. Chicago: University of Chicago Press, 1989. 164–93.

Berlant, Lauren. "National Brands/National Body: *Imitation of Life*." In *Comparative American Identities: Race, Sex, and Nationality in the Modern Text*, ed. Hortense J. Spillers. New York: Routledge, 1991. 110–40.

Bey, Hakim. *T.A.Z.: The Temporary Autonomous Zone, Ontological Anarchy, Poetic Terrorism*. New York: Autonomedia, 1991.

Bhabha, Homi. *The Location of Culture*. New York: Routledge, 1994.

Biddick, Kathleen. "Stranded Histories: Feminist Allegories of Artificial Life." *Research in Philosophy and Technology* 13 (1993): 165–82.

Blakely, Edward J., and Mary Gail Snyder. *Fortress America: Gated Communities in the United States*. Cambridge: Brookings Institution, 1997.

Blankenship, Loyd. *GURPS Cyberpunk: High-Tech Low-Life Roleplaying*. Austin, TX: Steve Jackson Games, 1990.

Blish, James. *The Seedling Stars*. New York: Gnome Press, 1957.

Bolter, Jay David. "Ekphrasis, Virtual Reality, and the Future of Writing." In *The Future of the Book*, ed. Geoffrey Nunberg. Berkeley: University of California Press, 1996. 253–72.

———. "You Are What You See." *Wired* 5.1 (January 1997): 113–14.

Bourdieu, Pierre. *Outline of a Theory of Practice*. Trans. Richard Nice. New York: Cambridge University Press, 1977.

Boyer, M. Christine. *Cyber Cities: Visual Perception in the Age of Electronic Communication*. Princeton, NJ: Princeton Architectural Press, 1996.

Boyne, Roy. "Crash Theory: The Ubiquity of the Fetish at the End of Time." *Angelaki* 4.2 (September 1999): 41–52.

Braidotti, Rosi. "Toward a New Nomadism: Feminist Deleuzian Tracks; or Metaphysics and Metabolism." In *Gilles Deleuze and the Theater of Philosophy*, ed. Constantin V. Boundas and Dorothea Olkowski. New York: Routledge, 1994. 159–86.

Brande, David. "The Business of Cyberpunk: Symbolic Economy and Ideology in William Gibson." In *Virtual Realities and Their Discontents*, ed. Robert Markley. Baltimore: Johns Hopkins University Press, 1996. 79–106.

Brin, David. *Kiln People*. New York: Tor, 2001.

Brockman, John, ed. *The Third Culture*. New York: Touchstone of Simon & Schuster, 1996.

Broderick, Damien. *The Spike: How Our Lives Are Being Transformed by Rapidly Advancing Technologies*. New York: Tor, 2001.

———. *Transcension*. New York: Tor, 2002.

Brooks, Rodney. *Flesh and Machines: How Robots Will Change Us*. New York: Pantheon, 2002.

Brown, Jeffrey A. *Black Superheroes, Milestone Comics, and Their Fans*. Jackson: University Press of Mississippi, 2001.

Brunner, John. *The Shockwave Rider*. New York: Harper & Row, 1975.

Budick, Sanford, and Wolfgang Iser, eds. *The Translatability of Cultures: Figurations of the Space Between*. Stanford, CA: Stanford University Press, 1996.

Buell, Frederick. "Nationalist Postnationalism: Globalist Discourse in Contemporary American Culture." *American Quarterly* 50.3 (September 1998): 548–91.

Bukatman, Scott. *Terminal Identity: The Virtual Subject in Postmodern Science Fiction*. Durham, NC: Duke University Press, 1993.

Burroughs, William. *Naked Lunch*. New York: Grove Press, 1959.

Butler, Judith. *Bodies That Matter: On the Discursive Limits of "Sex."* New York: Routledge, 1993.

———. "Endangered/Endangering: Schematic Racism and White Paranoia." In *Reading Rodney King/Reading Urban Uprising*, ed. Robert Gooding-Williams. New York: Routledge, 1993. 15–22.

———. *Gender Trouble: Feminism and the Subversion of Identity*. New York: Routledge, 1990.

———. "Imitation and Gender Insubordination." In *Inside/Out: Lesbian Theories, Gay Theories*, ed. Diana Fuss. New York: Routledge, 1991. 13–31.

Butler, Octavia. *Dawn*. New York: Popular Library, 1987.

Cadava, Eduardo, Peter Connor, and Jean-Luc Nancy, eds. *Who Comes after the Subject?* New York: Routledge, 1991.

Cadigan, Pat. *Fools*. New York: Bantam Spectra, 1992.

———. "Interview." With Andy Watson. *Journal Wired* (spring 1990): 83–118.

———. *Mindplayers*. New York: Bantam Spectra, 1987.

———. "Pretty Boy Crossover." In Pat Cadigan, *Patterns*. Kansas City, MO: Ursus Imprints, 1989. 127–39.

———. *Synners*. New York: Bantam, 1991.

———, ed. *The Ultimate Cyberpunk*. New York: ibooks, 2002.

Cadora, Karen. "Feminist Cyberpunk." *Science-Fiction Studies* 22.3 (November 1995): 357–72.

Caldeira, Teresa P. R. "Fortified Enclaves: The New Urban Segregation." *Public Culture* 8.2 (winter 1996): 303–28.

Calder, Richard. "The Allure." *Interzone* 40 (October 1990): 36–41.

———. *Dead Boys*. New York: St. Martin's Press, 1994.

———. *Dead Girls*. London: HarperCollins, 1992.

———. *Dead Things*. New York: St. Martin's Press, 1996.

———. "The Lilim." *Interzone* 34 (March–April 1990): 5–12.

———. "Mosquito." *Interzone* 32 (November–December 1989): 5–11.

———. "Toxine." In *Interzone: The 4th Anthology*. ed. John Clute, David Pringle, and Simon Ounsley. London: Simon & Schuster, 1989.

Carter, Raphael. *The Fortunate Fall*. New York: Tor, 1996.

Caruth, Cathy. *Trauma: Explorations in Memory*. Baltimore: Johns Hopkins University Press, 1994.

Case, Sue-Ellen. *The Domain-Matrix: Performing Lesbian at the End of Print Culture*. Bloomington: Indiana University Press, 1996.

Castells, Manuel. *End of Millennium*. Cambridge: Blackwell Publishers, 1998.

———. *The Informational City: Information Technology, Economic Restructuring, and the Urban-Regional Process*. Cambridge: Blackwell Publishers, 1989.

———. *The Power of Identity*. Cambridge: Blackwell Publishers, 1997.

———. *Rise of the Network Society*. Cambridge: Blackwell Publishers, 1996.

Cavallaro, Dani. *Cyberpunk and Cyberculture*. New Brunswick, NJ: Athlone Press, 2000.

Chang, Briankle G. *Deconstructing Communication: Representation, Subject, and Economies of Exchange*. Minneapolis: University of Minnesota Press, 1996.

Chatterjee, Partha. *The Nation and Its Fragments: Colonial and Postcolonial Histories*. Princeton, NJ: Princeton University Press, 1993.

Cherniavsky, Eva. "(En)Gendering Cyberspace in *Neuromancer*: Postmodern Subjectivity and Virtual Motherhood." *Genders* 18 (winter 1993): 32–46.

Cherny, Lynn. "'Objectifying' the Body in the Discourse of an Object-Oriented MUD." In *CyberSpaces: Pedagogy and Performance on the Electronic Frontier*, ed. Charles J. Stivale. Special issue of *Works and Days* 13.1/2 (1995). 151–72.

Chiang, Ted. *Stories of Your Life.* New York: Tor, 2002.

Christian, M. "State." In *Selling Venus,* ed. Cecilia Tan. Boston: Circlet Press, 1995. 19–30.

Clark, Andy. *Being There: Putting Brain, Body, and World Together Again.* Cambridge: MIT Press, 1997.

———. *Mindware: An Introduction to the Philosophy of Cognitive Science.* New York: Oxford University Press, 2001.

Clark, Nigel. "Rear-View Mirrorshades: The Recursive Generation of the Cyberbody." In *Cyberspace/Cyberbodies/Cyberpunk: Cultures of Technological Embodiment,* ed. Mike Featherstone and Roger Burrows. London: Sage Publications, 1995. 113–33.

Clifford, James. "On Collecting Art and Culture." In *The Cultural Studies Reader,* 2d ed. ed. Simon During. New York: Routledge, 1999. 57–76.

Clynes, Manfred E., and Nathan S. Kline. "Cyborgs and Space." In *The Cyborg Handbook,* ed. Chris Hables Gray. New York: Routledge, 1995.

Collins, Jim. *Architectures of Excess: Cultural Life in the Information Age.* New York: Routledge, 1995.

Crichton, Michael. *Prey.* New York: HarperCollins, 2002.

Cronenworth, Brian. "Man of Iron." *American Film* 13.1 (1987): 33–35.

Curtain, Tyler. "The 'Sinister Fruitiness' of Machines: *Neuromancer,* Internet Sexuality, and the Turing Test." In *Novel Gazing: Queer Readings in Fiction,* ed. Eve Kosofsky Sedgwick. Durham, NC: Duke University Press, 1997. 128–48.

Cyberpunk. Directed by Marianne Trench. Intercon Production, 1990.

Damasio, Antonio R. *Descartes' Error: Emotion, Reason, and the Human Brain.* New York: G. P. Putnam's Sons, 1994.

Daniel, Tony. *Metaplanetary.* New York: Eos, 2001.

Daniels, Wayne. "Reasons to Be Dual: Comprising the Person in Two Stories by Greg Egan." *New York Review of Science Fiction* 12.4 (December 1999): 1, 6–7.

Davies, Tony. *Humanism.* New York: Routledge, 1997.

Davis, Mike. *City of Quartz: Excavating the Future in Los Angeles.* New York: Verso, 1990.

Dawkins, Richard. *The Selfish Gene.* New York: Oxford University Press, 1976.

Dear, Michael J., and Steven Flusty, eds. *The Spaces of Postmodernity: Readings in Human Geography.* Malden, MA: Blackwell, 2002.

de Beauvoir, Simone. *The Second Sex.* Trans. H. M. Parshley. New York: Vintage, 1974.

De Fren, Allison. "Future Sex: The Evolution of Erotic Robots." *Res* 5.3 (May–June 2002): 62–64.

Deitch, Jeffrey. *Post Human.* New York: Distributed Art Publisher, 1992.

Delany, Samuel R. "Some *Real* Mothers." Interview with Takayuki Tatsumi. *Science Fiction Eye* 1 (March 1988): 5–11.

Deleuze, Gilles. *Masochism: An Interpretation of Coldness and Cruelty.* Trans. Jean McNeil. New York: George Braziller, 1971.

Deleuze, Gilles, and Félix Guattari. *A Thousand Plateaus: Capitalism and Schizophrenia.* Trans. Brian Massumi. Minneapolis: University of Minnesota Press, 1987.

Dennett, Daniel. *Consciousness Explained.* Boston: Little, Brown and Company, 1991.

———. *Darwin's Dangerous Idea: Evolution and the Meanings of Life.* New York: Touchstone of Simon & Schuster, 1995.

————. *The Intentional Stance.* Cambridge: MIT Press, 1987.

Derrida, Jacques. *Archive Fever.* Trans. Eric Prenowitz. Chicago: University of Chicago Press, 1996.

Dery, Mark. "Black to the Future: Interviews with Samuel R. Delany, Greg Tate, and Tricia Rose." *South Atlantic Quarterly* 92.3 (fall 1993): 735–78.

————. *Escape Velocity: Cyberculture at the End of the Century.* New York: Grove Press, 1996.

————. "Sex Machine, Machine Sex: Mechano-Eroticism and Robo-Copulation." *Mondo 2000* 5 (spring 1991): 42–43.

Dickson, Bruce D., Jr. "W. E. B. Du Bois and the Idea of Double Consciousness." *American Literature* 64 (June 1992): 299–309.

Di Filippo, Paul. *Ribofunk.* New York: Four Walls Eight Windows, 1996.

Dillon, David. "Fortress America." *Planning* (June 1994): 8–12.

Dirlik, Arif. "The Global in the Local." In *Global/Local: Cultural Production and the Transnational Imaginary,* ed. Rob Wilson and Wimal Dissanayake. Durham, NC: Duke University Press, 1996. 21–45.

Doane, Mary Ann. "Cyborgs, Origins, and Subjectivity." In *Coming to Terms: Feminism Theory and Politics,* ed. Elizabeth Weed. New York: Routledge, 1989. 209–14.

————. "Technophilia: Technology, Representation, and the Feminine." In *Body/Politics: Women and the Discourse of Science,* ed. Mary Jacobus, Evelyn Fox Keller, and Sally Shuttleworth. New York: Routledge, 1990. 163–76.

Doctorow, Cory. *Down and Out in the Magic Kingdom.* New York: Tor, 2003.

Dollimore, Jonathan. *Sexual Dissidence: Augustine to Wilde, Freud to Foucault.* New York: Oxford University Press, 1991.

Dorsey, Candas Jane. *Machine Sex and Other Stories.* Victoria, British Columbia: Porcepic Books, 1988.

Dozois, Gardner, ed. *Supermen: Tales of the Posthuman Future.* New York: St. Martin's Press, 2002.

Dreyfus, Hubert L. *What Computers Still Can't Do: A Critique of Artificial Reason.* Cambridge: MIT Press, 1992.

Du Bois, W. E. B. *The Souls of Black Folk.* In *Three Negro Classics,* ed. John Hope Franklin. New York: Avon, 1965. Originally published 1903.

Dunbar, Paul Laurence. *The Complete Poems of Paul Laurence Dunbar.* New York: Dodd, Mead, 1913.

Dunn, Katherine. *Geek Love.* New York: Knopf, 1989.

Dyer, Richard. *White.* New York: Routledge, 1997.

Dyer-Witheford, Nick. *Cyber-Marx: Cycles and Circuits of Struggle in High-Technology Capitalism.* Urbana: University of Illinois Press, 1999.

Dyson, Esther, George Keyworth, George Gilder, and Alvin Toffler. "Cyberspace and the American Dream: A Magna Carta for the Knowledge Age." *New Perspectives Quarterly* 11 (fall 1994): 26–37.

Egan, Greg. "Chaff." In *Our Lady of Chernobyl.* Paramatta, Australia: MirrorDanse Books, 1995.

————. *Diaspora.* London: Millennium, 1997.

————. "Learning to Be Me." In *Axiomatic.* London: Millennium, 1995. 157–71.

————. *Permutation City.* New York: HarperPrism, 1994.

————. "The Planck Dive." *Asimov's Science Fiction* 22.6 [266] (February 1998): 118–45.

Ehrlich, Michael. "Turing, My Love." In *Sexuality and Cyberspace: Performing the Digital Body,* ed. Theresa Senft and Stacy Horn. Special issue of *Women and Performance* 9. 1 (1996). 187–203.

Ellis, Warren, Steve Rolston, and Al Gordon. *Mek.* New York: Homage Comics of DC Comics, January–March 2003.

Ellison, Ralph. *Invisible Man.* New York: Vintage, 1989. Originally published 1950.

Featherstone, Mike. "Localism, Globalism, and Cultural Identity." In *Global/Local: Cultural Production and the Transnational Imaginary,* ed. Rob Wilson and Wimal Dissanayake. Durham, NC: Duke University Press, 1996. 46–77.

Featherstone, Mike, and Roger Burrows, eds. *Cyberspace/Cyberbodies/Cyberpunk: Cultures of Technological Embodiment.* London: Sage Publications, 1995.

Ferlinghetti, Lawrence. *A Coney Island of the Mind.* New York: New Directions, 1958.

Fiske, John. *Understanding Popular Culture.* Boston: Unwin Hyman, 1989.

Fitting, Peter. "The Lessons of Cyberpunk." In *Technoculture,* ed. Constance Penley and Andrew Ross. Minneapolis: University of Minnesota Press, 1991. 295–315.

Foster, Hal. "Obscene, Abject, Traumatic." *October* 78 (fall 1996): 107–24.

————. *The Return of the Real: The Avant-Garde at the End of the Century.* Cambridge: MIT Press, 1996.

Foster, Thomas. "Cyber-Aztecs and Cholo-Punks: Guillermo Gómez-Peña's Five Worlds Theory." *PMLA* 117.1 (January 2002): 43–67.

————. "'The Postproduction of the Human Heart': Desire, Identification, and Virtual Embodiment in Feminist Narratives of Cyberspace." In *Reload: Rethinking Women + Cyberculture,* ed. Mary Flanagan and Austin Booth. Cambridge: MIT Press, 2002. 469–504.

Fraiberg, Allison. "Electronic Fans, Interpretive Flames: Performing Queer Sexualities in Cyberspace." In *CyberSpaces: Pedagogy and Performance on the Electronic Frontier,* ed. Charles J. Stivale. Special issue of *Works and Days* 13.1/2 (1995). 195–207.

Frankenberg, Ruth, ed. *Displacing Whiteness: Essays in Social and Cultural Criticism.* Durham, NC: Duke University Press, 1997.

Frederick, Howard. "Computer Networks and the Emergence of Global Civil Society." In *Global Networks: Computers and International Communication,* ed. Linda M. Harasim. Cambridge: MIT Press, 1993. 283–95.

Freud, Sigmund. "The 'Uncanny.'" Trans. Alix Strachey. In Sigmund Freud, *Collected Papers,* vol. 4. New York: Basic Books, 1959. 368–407.

Fuchs, Cynthia J. "'Death Is Irrelevant': Cyborgs, Reproduction, and the Future of Male Hysteria." *Genders* 18 (winter 1993): 113–33.

Fukuyama, Francis. *Our Posthuman Future: Consequences of the Biotechnology Revolution.* New York: Farrar, Straus and Giroux, 2002.

Fusco, Coco. *The Bodies That Were Not Ours and Other Writings.* New York: Routledge, 2001.

Fuss, Diana. *Essentially Speaking: Feminism, Nature, and Difference.* New York: Routledge, 1989.

————. *Identification Papers.* New York: Routledge, 1995.

Gabifondo, Joseba. "Postcolonial Cyborgs: Subjectivity in the Age of Cybernetic Reproduction." In *The Cyborg Handbook,* ed. Chris Hables Gray. New York: Routledge, 1995. 423–32.

Garber, Marjorie. "Fetish Envy." *October* 54 (fall 1990): 45–56.

Gates, Henry Louis, Jr. *Figures in Black: Words, Signs, and the "Racial" Self.* New York: Oxford University Press, 1987.

————. *The Signifying Monkey: A Theory of African-American Literature.* New York: Oxford University Press, 1988.

Gelernter, David. *Mirror Worlds: Or, the Day Software Puts the Universe in a Shoebox . . . How It Will Happen and What It Will Mean.* New York: Oxford University Press, 1991.

Gessen, Masha. "Balkans Online." *Wired* 3.11 (November 1995): 158–62, 220–22.

Geyh, Paula, Fred G. Leebron, and Andrew Levy, eds. *Postmodern American Fiction.* New York: Norton, 1998.

Gibson, William. *All Tomorrow's Parties.* New York: Putnam, 1999.

————. *Burning Chrome.* New York: Ace Books, 1987.

————. *Count Zero.* New York: Ace Books, 1986.

————. *Idoru.* New York: Putnam, 1996.

————. *Mona Lisa Overdrive.* New York: Bantam, 1988.

————. *Neuromancer.* New York: Ace Books, 1984.

————. *Virtual Light.* New York: Bantam, 1993.

Gilroy, Paul. *Against Race: Imagining Political Culture beyond the Color Line.* Cambridge: Belknap Press of Harvard University Press, 2000.

Gómez-Peña, Guillermo. *The New World Border.* San Francisco: City Lights, 1996.

————. "The Virtual Barrio @ the Other Frontier (or the Chicano Interneta)." In *Clicking In: Hot Links to Digital Culture,* ed. Lynn Hershman Leeson. Seattle: Bay Press, 1996. 173–79.

Gonzalez, Jennifer. "The Appended Subject: Race and Identity as Digital Assemblage." In *Race in Cyberspace,* ed. Beth E. Kolko, Lisa Nakamura, and Gilbert B. Rodman. New York: Routledge, 2000. 27–50.

————. "Envisioning Cyborg Bodies: Notes from Current Research." In *The Cyborg Handbook,* ed. Chris Hables Gray. New York: Routledge, 1995. 267–79.

Gooding-Williams, Robert, ed. *Reading Rodney King/Reading Urban Uprising.* New York: Routledge, 1993.

Goodwin, Andrew. *Dancing in the Distraction Factory: Music Television and Popular Culture.* Minneapolis: University of Minnesota Press, 1992.

Goonan, Kathleen Ann. *Mississippi Blues.* New York: Tor, 1999.

Gordon, Joan. "Yin and Yang Duke It Out." *Science Fiction Eye* 2 (February 1990): 37–39.

Graham, Elaine L. *Representations of the Post/Human: Monsters, Aliens and Others in Popular Culture.* New Brunswick, NJ: Rutgers University Press, 2002.

Graham, Stephen, and Simon Marvin. *Telecommunications and the City: Electronic Spaces, Urban Places.* New York: Routledge, 1996.

Grant, Glenn. "Transcendence through Detournement in William Gibson's *Neuromancer.*" *Science-Fiction Studies* 17 (1990): 41–49.

Gray, Chris Hables. *Cyborg Citizen: Politics in the Posthuman Age.* New York: Routledge, 2001.

⸺, ed. *The Cyborg Handbook.* New York: Routledge, 1995.

Gray, Chris Hables, and Steven Mentor. "The Cyborg Body Politic and the New World Order." In *Prosthetic Territories: Politics and Hypertechnologies,* ed. Gabriel Brahm Jr. and Mark Driscoll. Boulder, CO: Westview Press, 1995.

Gray, Chris Hables, Steven Mentor, and Heidi J. Figueroa-Sarriera. "Cyborgology: Constructing the Knowledge of Cybernetic Organisms." In *The Cyborg Handbook,* ed. Chris Hables Gray. New York: Routledge, 1995. 1–14.

Grewal, Inderpal, and Caren Kaplan, eds. *Scattered Hegemonies: Postmodernity and Transnational Feminist Practices.* Minneapolis: University of Minnesota Press, 1994.

Griggers, Cathy. "Lesbian Bodies in the Age of (Post)Mechanical Reproduction." In *The Lesbian Postmodern,* ed. Laura Doan. New York: Columbia University Press, 1994. 118–33.

Grossberg, Lawrence. *We Gotta Get Out of This Place: Popular Conservatism and Postmodern Culture.* New York: Routledge, 1992.

Grosz, Elizabeth. *Volatile Bodies: Toward a Corporeal Feminism.* Bloomington: Indiana University Press, 1994.

Habermas, Jürgen. *The Structural Transformation of the Public Sphere.* Trans. Thomas Burger. Cambridge: MIT Press, 1989.

Halacy, D. S., Jr. *Cyborg—Evolution of the Superman.* New York: Harper & Row, 1965.

Halberstam, Judith. "Automating Gender: Postmodern Feminism in the Age of the Intelligent Machine." *Feminist Studies* 17 (fall 1991): 439–60.

Halberstam, Judith, and Ira Livingston. "Introduction: Posthuman Bodies." In *Posthuman Bodies,* ed. Judith Halberstam and Ira Livingston. Bloomington: Indiana University Press, 1995. 1–19.

Hall, Stuart. "New Ethnicities." In *Stuart Hall: Critical Dialogues in Cultural Studies,* ed. David Morley and Kuan-Hsing Chen. New York: Routledge, 1996. 441–49.

⸺. "The Problem of Ideology: Marxism without Guarantees." In *Stuart Hall: Critical Dialogues in Cultural Studies,* ed. David Morley and Kuan-Hsing Chen. New York: Routledge, 1996. 25–46.

⸺. "What Is This 'Black' in Black Popular Culture?" In *Stuart Hall: Critical Dialogues in Cultural Studies,* ed. David Morley and Kuan-Hsing Chen. New York: Routledge, 1996. 465–75.

Hammonds, Evelyn M. "New Technologies of Race." In *The Gendered Cyborg: A Reader,* ed. Gill Kirkup, Linda Janes, Kathryn Woodward, and Fiona Hovenden. New York: Routledge, 2000.

Haraway, Donna. "The Actors Are Cyborg, Nature Is Coyote, and the Geography Is Elsewhere: Postscript to 'Cyborgs at Large.'" In *Technoculture,* ed. Constance Penley and Andrew Ross. Minneapolis: University of Minnesota Press, 1991. 21–26.

⸺. "Cyborgs at Large: Interview with Donna Haraway." With Constance Penley and Andrew Ross. In *Technoculture,* ed. Constance Penley and Andrew Ross. Minneapolis: University of Minnesota Press, 1991. 1–20.

⸺. "Ecce Homo, Ain't (Ar'n't) I a Woman, and Inappropriate/d Others: The Human in a Post-Humanist Landscape." In *Feminists Theorize the Political,* ed. Judith Butler and Joan W. Scott. New York: Routledge, 1992. 86–100.

———. "A Game of Cat's Cradle: Science Studies, Feminist Theory, Cultural Studies." *Configurations* 2.1 (winter 1994): 59–71.

———. *Modest Witness@Second Millennium.Female Man© Meets Oncomouse™: Feminism and Technoscience.* New York: Routledge, 1997.

———. "The Promises of Monsters: A Regenerative Politics for Inappropriate/d Others." In *Cultural Studies,* ed. Lawrence Grossberg, Cary Nelson, and Paula Treichler. New York: Routledge, 1992. 295–337.

———. *Simians, Cyborgs, and Women: The Reinvention of Nature.* New York: Routledge, 1991.

———. "When Man™ Is on the Menu." In *Incorporations,* ed. Jonathan Crary and Sanford Kwinter. New York: Zone Books, 1992. 38–43.

Hardt, Michael, and Antonio Negri. *Empire.* Cambridge: Harvard University Press, 2000.

Harper, Frances E. W. *Iola Leroy, or Shadows Uplifted.* Boston: Beacon Press, 1999.

Harper, Mary Catherine. "Incurably Alien Other: A Case for Feminist Cyborg Writers." *Science Fiction Studies* 22.3 (November 1995): 399–420.

Harper, Phillip Brian. *Framing the Margins: The Social Logic of Postmodern Culture.* New York: Oxford University Press, 1994.

Harris, Cheryl I. "Whiteness as Property." In *Critical Race Theory: The Key Writings That Formed the Movement,* ed. Kimberle Crenshaw, Neil Gotanda, Gray Peller, and Kendall Thomas. New York: New Press, 1995. 276–91.

Harvey, David. *The Condition of Postmodernity: An Enquiry into the Origins of Cultural Change.* Cambridge, MA: Blackwell, 1990.

Hayles, N. Katherine. *Chaos Bound: Orderly Disorder in Contemporary Literature and Science.* Ithaca, NY: Cornell University Press, 1990.

———. *How We Became Posthuman: Virtual Bodies in Cybernetics, Literature, and Informatics.* Chicago: University of Chicago Press, 1999.

———. "The Posthuman Body: Inscription and Incorporation in *Galatea 2.2* and *Snow Crash.*" *Configurations* 5.2 (spring 1997): 241–66.

———. "The Seductions of Cyberspace." In *Rethinking Technology,* ed. Verena Andermatt Conley. Minneapolis: University of Minnesota Press, 1993. 173–90.

Hebdige, Dick. *Subculture: The Meaning of Style.* New York: Routledge, 1979.

Heim, Michael. "The Erotic Ontology of Cyberspace." In *Cyberspace: First Steps,* ed. Michael Benedikt. Cambridge: MIT Press, 1991. 59–80.

Hodges, Andrew. *Alan Turing, the Enigma.* New York: Simon & Schuster, 1983.

Hogan, Ernest. *High Aztech.* New York: Tor, 1992.

Holland, Samantha. "Descartes Goes to Hollywood: Mind, Body, and Gender in Contemporary Cyborg Cinema." In *Cyberspace/ Cyberbodies/Cyberpunk: Cultures of Technological Embodiment,* ed. Mike Featherstone and Roger Burrows. London: Sage Publications, 1995. 57–174.

Hollinger, Veronica. "Cybernetic Deconstructions: Cyberpunk and Postmodernism." In *Storming the Reality Studio: A Casebook of Cyberpunk and Postmodern Fiction,* ed.

Larry McCaffrey. Durham, NC: Duke University Press, 1991. 203–18. Originally published in *Mosaic* 23 (spring 1990): 29–44.

hooks, bell. "Postmodern Blackness." In *Yearning: Race, Gender, and Cultural Politics*. Boston: South End Press, 1990. 23–31.

Hunt, Darnell M. *Screening the Los Angeles "Riots": Race, Seeing, and Resistance*. New York: Cambridge University Press, 1997.

Huxley, Julian. *New Wine for New Bottles: Essays*. London: Chatlo and Windus, 1957.

Huyssen, Andreas. *After the Great Divide: Modernism, Mass Culture, Postmodernism*. Bloomington: Indiana University Press, 1986.

Ihde, Don. *Technology and the Lifeworld: From Garden to Earth*. Bloomington: Indiana University Press, 1990.

Ings, Simon. *Headlong*. London: HarperCollins, 1999.

———. *Hot Head*. London: Grafton of HarperCollins, 1992.

———. *Hotwire*. London: HarperCollins, 1995.

James, Peter. *Host*. New York: Villard, 1995. Originally published 1993.

Jameson, Fredric. *Marxism and Form: Twentieth-Century Dialectical Theories of Literature*. Princeton, NJ: Princeton University Press, 1971.

———. *Postmodernism, or, The Cultural Logic of Late Capitalism*. Durham, NC: Duke University Press, 1991.

———. "Reification and Utopia in Mass Culture." *Social Text* 1 (winter 1979): 130–48.

Jayne, Edward. *The Origins of Consciousness in the Breakdown of the Bicameral Mind*. New York: Houghton Mifflin, 1976.

Jeffords, Susan. *Hard Bodies: Hollywood Masculinity in the Reagan Era*. New Brunswick, NJ: Rutgers University Press, 1994.

Johnston, John. *Information Multiplicity: American Fiction in the Age of Media Saturation*. Baltimore: Johns Hopkins University Press, 1998.

Jones, Gwyneth. *Divine Endurance*. New York: Tor, 1984.

———. *North Wind*. New York: Tor, 1994.

———. *Phoenix Café*. London: Victor Gollancz, 1997.

———. *White Queen*. New York: Tor, 1991.

Jones, Reilly. "Consciousness: Spontaneous Order and Selectional Systems, Part II." *Extropy* 15 (2d–3d quarter 1995): 38–44.

Joy, Bill. "Why the Future Doesn't Need Us." *Wired* 8.4 (April 2000): 238–62.

Jude, St., R. U. Sirius, and Bart Nagel. *Cyberpunk Handbook: The Real Cyberpunk Fakebook*. New York: Random House, 1995.

Kelly, James Patrick. "On the Net: Cyberpunk." *Asimov's Science Fiction* 25.1 (January 2001): 9–13.

Kelly, Kevin. *Out of Control: The New Biology of Machines, Social Systems, and the Economic World*. Reading, MA: Addison-Wesley, 1994.

Kendrick, Michelle. "Cyberspace and the Technological Real." In *Virtual Reality and Its Discontents*, ed. Robert Markley. Baltimore: Johns Hopkins University Press, 1996. 143–60.

Kendrick, Neil. "Cybermusic." *U.: The National College Magazine* (August/September 1993): 36.

Kirkup, Gill, Linda Janes, Kathryn Woodward, and Fiona Hovenden, eds. *The Gendered Cyborg: A Reader.* New York: Routledge, 2000.

Kittler, Friedrich. *Literature, Media, Information Systems.* Trans. John Johnston. New York: Routledge, 1997.

Koestenbaum, Wayne. "Wilde's Hard Labor and the Birth of Gay Reading." In *Engendering Men: The Question of Male Feminist Criticism,* ed. Joseph A. Boone and Michael Cadden. New York: Routledge, 1990. 176–89.

Kolko, Beth, Lisa Nakamura, and Gilbert B. Rodman, eds. *Race in Cyberspace.* New York: Routledge, 2000.

Kress, Nancy. *Beaker's Dozen.* New York: Tor, 1998.

Krieger, David. "A Conversation with Mark S. Miller." *Extropy* 10 (winter/spring 1993): 25–29.

Kroker, Arthur, and Marilouise Kroker. "Theses on the Disappearing Body In the Hyper-Modern Condition." In *Body Invaders: Panic Sex in America,* ed. Arthur Kroker and Marilouise Kroker. New York: St. Martin's Press, 1987. 10–34.

Kroker, Arthur, and Michael A. Weinstein. *Data Trash: The Theory of the Virtual Class.* New York: St. Martin's Press, 1994.

Lacan, Jacques. *Écrits: A Selection.* Trans. Alan Sheridan. New York: Norton, 1977.

Laidlaw, Marc. *Kalifornia.* New York: St. Martin's Press, 1993.

Lakoff, George, and Mark Johnson. *Philosophy in the Flesh: The Embodied Mind and Its Challenge to Western Thought.* New York: Basic Books, 1999.

Lamos, Colleen. "The Postmodern Lesbian Position: On Our Backs." In *The Lesbian Postmodern,* ed. Laura Doan. New York: Columbia University Press, 1994. 85–103.

Land, Nick. "Meat (or How to Kill Oedipus in Cyberspace)." In *Cyberspace/Cyberbodies/Cyberpunk: Cultures of Technological Embodiment,* ed Mike Featherstone and Roger Burrows. London: Sage Publications, 1995. 191–204.

Lang, Candace. "Body Language: The Resurrection of the Corpus in Text-Based VR." In *Cyber Spaces: Pedagogy and Performance on the Electronic Frontier,* ed Charles J. Stivale. Special issue of *Works and Days* 13.1/2 (1995). 245–58.

Lash, Scott, and John Urry. *Economies of Sign and Space.* London: Sage Publications, 1994.

———. *The End of Organized Capitalism.* Madison: University of Wisconsin Press, 1987.

Latour, Bruno. *We Who Have Never Been Modern.* Trans. Catherine Porter. Cambridge: Harvard University Press, 1993.

Laurel, Brenda. *Computers as Theatre.* 2d ed. Reading, MA: Addison-Wesley, 1993.

Lee, Rachel, and Sau-ling Cynthia Wong, eds. *AsianAmerica.Net: Ethnicity, Nationalism, and Cyberspace.* New York: Routledge, 2003.

Levidow, Les, and Kevin Robins. *Cyborg Worlds: The Military Information Society.* London: Free Association Books, 1991.

Lilly, John C. *Programming and Metaprogramming in the Human Biocomputer.* New York: Julian Press, 1972.

Lingis, Alphonso. *The Community of Those Who Have Nothing in Common.* Bloomington: Indiana University Press, 1994.

Lipsitz, George. *The Possessive Investment in Whiteness: How White People Profit from Identity Politics.* Philadelphia: Temple University Press, 1998.

Locke, John. *An Essay concerning Human Understanding*. Vol. 1. New York: Dover, 1959.

Lohr, Steve. "Who Will Control the Digital Flow?" *New York Times*, October 17, 1993, section 4, pages 1, 3.

Lott, Eric. *Love and Theft: Blackface Minstrelsy and the American Working Class*. New York: Oxford University Press, 1993.

Lowe, Donald M. *The Body in Late-Capitalist USA*. Durham, NC: Duke University Press, 1995.

Ludlow, Peter, ed. *Crypto-Anarchy, Cyberstates, and Pirate Utopias*. Cambridge: MIT Press, 2001.

Lukács, Georg. *History and Class Consciousness: Studies in Marxist Dialectics*. Trans. Rodney Livingstone. Cambridge: MIT Press, 1971.

Lupton, Deborah. "The Embodied Computer/User." In *Cyberspace/Cyberbodies/Cyberpunk: Cultures of Technological Embodiment*, ed. Mike Featherstone and Roger Burrows. London: Sage Publication, 1995. 97–112.

Lyotard, Jean-François. *The Inhuman: Reflections on Time*. Trans. Geoffrey Bennington and Rachel Bowlby. Stanford, CA: Stanford University Press, 1991.

MacLeod, Ken. *The Cassini Division*. London: Orbit, 1998.

———. *Poems and Polemics*. Minneapolis: Rune Press, 2001.

———. "Singularity Skies." *Locus: The Magazine of the Science Fiction and Fantasy Field* 511 (August 2003): 41–42.

———. *The Star Fraction*. London: Legend, 1995.

———. *The Stone Canal*. London: Legend, 1996.

Macpherson, C. B. *The Political Theory of Possessive Individualism: Hobbes to Locke*. New York: Oxford University Press, 1962.

Maddox, Tom. "Eye to Eye: Disclave 1986 Guest of Honor Interview with William Gibson." *Science Fiction Eye* 1.1 (winter 1987): 18–26.

———. "The Wars of the Coin's Two Halves: Bruce Sterling Mechanist/Shapter Narratives." In *Storming the Reality Studio: A Casebook of Cyberpunk and Postmodern Fiction*, ed. Larry McCaffery. Durham, NC: Duke University Press, 1991. 324–30.

Markley, Robert. "Boundaries: Mathematics, Alienation, and the Metaphysics of Virtual Reality." In *Virtual Reality and Its Discontents*, ed. Robert Markley. Baltimore: Johns Hopkins University Press, 1996. 55–77.

———. "Introduction: History, Theory, and Virtual Reality." In *Virtual Reality and Its Discontents*, ed. Robert Markley. Baltimore: Johns Hopkins University Press, 1996. 1–10.

———, ed. *Virtual Reality and Its Discontents*. Baltimore: Johns Hopkins University Press, 1996.

Marx, Karl, and Frederick Engels. *The German Ideology*. New York: International Publishers, 1985.

Mason, Fran. "Loving the Technological Undead: Cyborg Sex and Necrophilia in Richard Calder's *Dead* Trilogy." In *The Body's Perilous Pleasures: Dangerous Desires and Contemporary Culture*, ed. Michele Aaron. Edinburgh: Edinburgh University Press, 1999. 108–25.

Mason, Lisa. *Arachne*. New York: William Morrow, 1990.

————. *Cyberweb*. New York: William Morrow, 1995.

Mayer, Bernadette. *The Formal Field of Kissing*. New York: Catchword Papers, 1990.

McCaffrey, Larry. "An Interview with William Gibson." *Mississippi Review* 47/48 (summer 1988): 217–36.

————, ed. *Storming the Reality Studio: A Casebook of Cyberpunk and Postmodern Fiction*. Durham, NC: Duke University Press, 1991.

McCallum, E. L. *Object Lessons: How to Do Things with Fetishism*. Albany: State University of New York Press, 1999.

McCarthy, Wil. *Bloom*. New York: Del Rey of Ballantine, 1998.

————. *The Collapsium*. New York: Del Rey of Ballantine, 2000.

McClintock, Anne. *Imperial Leather: Race, Gender and Sexuality in the Colonial Contest*. New York: Routledge, 1995.

————. "Maid to Order: Commercial Fetishism and Gender Power." *Social Text* 11 (winter 1993): 87–116.

McDuffie, Dwayne, and Denys Cowan. "The Souls of Cyber-Folk." *Deathlok* 2–5 (August–November 1991). New York: Marvel Comics.

McDuffie, Dwayne, and Gregory Wright, Jackson Gaice, Scott Williams, Denys Cowan, Rick Magyar, Kyle Baker and Mike DeCarlo. *Deathlok* limited series 1–4 (July–October 1990). New York: Marvel Comics.

McHale, Brian. *Constructing Postmodernism*. New York: Routledge, 1992.

McHugh, Maureen F. *China Mountain Zhang*. New York: Tor, 1992.

————. "A Coney Island of the Mind." In *Isaac Asimov's Cyberdreams*, ed. Gardner Dozois and Sheila Williams. New York: Ace Books, 1994. 83–90. Originally published 1992.

————. "Virtual Love." In *Nebula Awards 30*, ed. Pamela Sargent. New York: Harcourt Brace & Company, 1996. 99–110. Originally published 1994.

McKay, George. "'I'm So Bored with the USA': The Punk in Cyberpunk." In *Punk Rock: So What? The Cultural Legacy of Punk*, ed. Roger Sabin. New York: Routledge, 1999. 49–67.

McKenzie, Evan. *Privatopia: Homeowner Associations and the Rise of Residential Private Government*. New Haven: Yale University Press, 1994.

McKenzie, Jon. "Virtual Reality: Performance, Immersion, and the Thaw." *TDR: The Drama Review* 38.4 (winter 1994): 83–106.

McLuhan, Marshall. *The Mechanical Bride: Folklore of Industrial Man*. New York: Vangaurd Press, 1951.

Mercer, Kobena. *Welcome to the Jungle: New Positions in Black Cultural Studies*. New York: Routledge, 1994.

Minsky, Marvin. *The Society of Mind*. New York: Touchstone of Simon & Schuster, 1988.

Misha. *Red Spider, White Web*. Scotforth, England: Morrigan Books, 1990.

Mitchell, William J. *City of Bits: Space, Place, and the Infobahn*. Cambridge: MIT Press, 1995.

Mixon, Laura J. *Burning the Ice*. New York: Tor, 2002.

————. *Glass Houses*. New York: Tor, 1992.

————. *Proxies*. New York: Tor, 1998.

Miyoshi, Masao. "A Borderless World? From Colonialism to Transnationalism and the Decline of the Nation-State." *Critical Inquiry* 19.4 (summer 1993): 725–51.

————. "Sites of Resistance in the Global Economy." *boundary 2* 22.1 (spring 1995): 61–84.

Modleski, Tania. *Feminism without Women: Culture and Criticism in a "Postfeminist" Age.* New York: Routledge, 1991.

Moore, Lisa. "Teledildonics: Virtual Lesbians in the Fiction of Jeanette Winterson." In *Sexy Bodies: The Strange Carnalities of Feminism*, ed. Elizabeth Grosz and Elspeth Probyn. New York: Routledge, 1995. 104–27.

Moravec, Hans. *Mind Children: The Future of Robot and Human Intelligence.* Cambridge: Harvard University Press, 1988.

————. "Pigs in Cyberspace." *Extropy* 10 (winter/spring 1993): 5–7.

————. *Robot: Mere Machine to Transcendent Mind.* New York: Oxford University Press, 1999.

More, Max, comp. "Futique Neologisms." *Extropy* 7 (spring 1991): 33–36.

————. "Order without Orderers." *Extropy* 7 (spring 1991): 21–32.

————. "Technological Self-Transformation: Expanding Personal Extropy." *Extropy* 10 (winter/spring 1993): 15–24.

————. "Transhumanism: Towards a Futurist Philosophy." *Extropy* 6 (summer 1990): 5–10.

Morley, David, and Kuan-Hsing Chen. *Stuart Hall: Critical Dialogues in Cultural Studies.* New York: Routledge, 1996.

Morse, Margaret. "What Do Cyborgs Eat? Oral Logic in an Information Age." in *Culture on the Brink: Ideologies of Technology*, ed. Gretchen Bender and Timothy Druckrey. Seattle: Bay Press, 1994. 157–89.

Moten, Fred. "Music against the Law of Reading the Future and *Rodney King.*" *Journal of the Midwest Modern Language Association* 27.1 (spring 1994): 51–64.

Mullen, Harryette. "Optic White: Blackness and the Production of Whiteness." *Diacritics* 24.2–3 (summer–fall 1994): 71–89.

Murray, Timothy. *Drama Trauma: Specters of Race and Sexuality in Performance, Video, and Art.* New York: Routledge, 1997.

Nakamura, Lisa. *Cybertypes: Race, Ethnicity, and Identity on the Internet.* New York: Routledge, 2002.

————. "Race In/For Cyberspace: Identity Tourism and Racial Passing on the Internet." In *CyberSpaces: Pedagogy and Performance on the Electronic Frontier*, ed. Charles J. Stivale. Special issue of *Works and Days* 13.1/2 (1995). 181–93.

Nancy, Jean-Luc. "Introduction." In *Who Comes after the Subject?* ed. Eduardo Cadava, Peter Connor, and Jean-Luc Nancy. New York: Routledge, 1991. 1–8.

Nealon, Jeffrey T. *Alterity Politics: Ethics and Performative Subjectivity.* Durham, NC: Duke University Press, 1998.

Negroponte, Nicholas. "Being Local." *Wired* 4.11 (November 1996): 286.

Nelson, Alondra. "Introduction: Future Texts." *Social Text* 20.2 (summer 2002): 1–15. Special issue on "Afrofuturism."

Nelson, Alondra, and Thuy Linh N. Tu, eds. *Technicolor: Race, Technology, and Everyday Life.* New York: New York University Press, 2001.

Nichols, Bill. "The Work of Culture in the Age of Cybernetic Systems." *Screen* 29 (winter 1986): 22–46.

Nixon, Nicola. "Cyberpunk: Preparing the Ground for Revolution or Keeping the Boys Satisfied?" *Science-Fiction Studies* 19 (1992): 219–35.

O'Brien, Jodi. "Changing the Subject." In *Sexuality and Cyberspace: Performing the Digital Body*, ed. Theresa Senft and Stacy Horn. Special issue of *Women and Performance* 9.1 (1996). 54–67.

Ong, Aihwa. *Flexible Citizenship: The Cultural Logics of Transnationality*. Durham, NC: Duke University Press,1999.

Ore, Rebecca. *Gaia's Toys*. New York: Tor, 1995.

Otter. "Against Man, the Challenger." *Dropout* (summer 1992): 22–24.

Penley, Constance, and Andrew Ross. "Cyborgs at Large: Interview with Donna Haraway." In *Technoculture*, ed. Constance Penley and Andrew Ross. Minneapolis: University of Minnesota Press, 1991.

Penny, Simon. "Virtual Reality as the Completion of the Enlightenment Project." In *Cultures on the Brink: Ideologies of Technology*. Seattle: Bay Press, 1994. 231–48.

Pfeil, Fred. "These Disintegrations I'm Looking Forward To: Science Fiction from New Wave to New Age." In *Another Tale to Tell: Politics and Narrative in Postmodern Culture*. New York: Verso, 1990. 83–94.

Pinker, Steven. *The Blank Slate: The Modern Denial of Human Nature*. New York: Viking, 2002.

———. *The Language Instinct: How the Mind Creates Language*. New York: HarperCollins, 1995.

Plant, Sadie. *Zeroes + Ones: Digital Women + the New Technoculture*. New York: Doubleday, 1997.

Porush, David. "Hacking the Brainstem: Postmodern Metaphysics and Stephenson's *Snow Crash*." *Configurations* 2.3 (fall 1994): 537–71.

Poster, Mark. *The Mode of Information: Poststructuralism and Social Context*. Chicago: University of Chicago Press, 1990.

———. *The Second Media Age*. Cambridge, MA: Polity Press, 1995.

———. *What's the Matter with the Internet?* Minneapolis: University of Minnesota Press, 2001.

Pratt, Mary Louise. "Linguistic Utopias." In *The Linguistics of Writing: Arguments between Language and Literature*. New York: Methuen, 1987. 48–66.

Price, Monroe E. "Free Expression and Digital Dreams: The Open and Closed Terrain of Speech." *Critical Inquiry* 22.1 (autumn 1995): 64–89.

Pulver, David L. *Transhuman Space*. Steve Jackson Games Incorporated, 2002.

Reed, Ishmael. *Flight to Canada*. New York: Atheneum, 1989. Originally published 1976.

———. *Mumbo Jumbo*. New York: Scribner's, 1996. Originally published 1972.

Reed, Robert. *Marrow*. New York: Tor, 2000.

Reid, Roddey. "'Death of the Family,' or, Keeping Human Beings Human." In *Posthuman Bodies*, ed. Judith Halberstam and Ira Livingston. Bloomington: Indiana University Press, 1995. 177–99.

Reynolds, Alastair. *Revelation Space*. London: Victor Gollancz, 2000.

Rheingold, Howard. *Smart Mobs: The Next Social Revolution*. New York: Perseus, 2002.

———. *The Virtual Community: Homesteading on the Electronic Frontier*. New York: HarperPerennial, 1993.

————. *Virtual Reality.* New York: Summit Books, 1991.

Rich, Adrienne. "Notes toward a Politics of Location." In *Blood, Bread, and Poetry: Selected Prose 1979-1985.* New York: Norton, 1986. 210–31.

Robinson, Phillip, and Nancy Tamosaitis. *The Joy of Cybersex: An Underground Guide to Electronic Media.* New York: Brady Publishing, 1993.

Robson, Justina. *Mappa Mundi.* London: Macmillan, 2001.

————. *Natural History.* London: Macmillan, 2003.

————. *Silver Screen.* London: Macmillan, 1999.

Roediger, David. *Towards the Abolition of Whiteness: Essays on Race, Politics, and Working Class History.* New York: Verso, 1994.

Rogin, Michael. *Blackface, White Noise: Jewish Immigrants in the Hollywood Melting Pot.* Berkeley: University of California Press, 1996.

Ronell, Avital. *Finitude's Score: Essays for the End of the Millennium.* Lincoln: University of Nebraska Press, 1994.

Rosenblum, Mary. *Chimera.* New York: Del Rey, 1993.

————. *Synthesis and Other Virtual Realities.* Sauk City, WI: Arkham House, 1996.

Rosenthal, Pam. "Jacked In: Fordism, Cyberpunk, Marxism." *Socialist Review* 21 (January–March 1991): 79–103.

Ross, Andrew. "Introduction." In *Universal Abandon? The Politics of Postmodernism,* ed. Andrew Ross. Minneapolis: University of Minnesota Press, 1988. vii–xviii.

————. *Strange Weather: Culture, Science, and Technology in the Age of Limits.* New York: Verso, 1991.

Rucker, Rudy. *Seek: Selected Nonfiction.* New York: Four Walls Eight Windows, 1999.

————. *Software.* New York: Avon Books, 1982.

Rushing, Janice Hocker, and Thomas S. Frentz. *Projecting the Shadow: The Cyborg Hero in American Film.* Chicago: University of Chicago Press, 1995.

Saenz, Mike, Ken Holewczynski, and Norm Dwyer. "The Cybersex 2 System." *Future Sex* 2 (1992): 28–31.

Sandoval, Chela. *Methodology of the Oppressed.* Minneapolis: University of Minnesota Press, 2000.

————. "New Sciences: Cyborg Feminism and the Methodology of the Oppressed." In *The Cyborg Handbook,* ed. Chris Hables Gray. New York: Routledge, 1995. 405–21.

Sawyer, Robert J. *The Terminal Experiment.* New York: HarperPrism, 1995.

Scarry, Elaine. *The Body in Pain: The Making and Unmaking of the World.* New York: Oxford University Press, 1985.

Schelde, Per. *Androids, Humanoids, and Other Science Fiction Monsters: Science and Soul in Science Fiction Films.* New York: New York University Press, 1993.

Schor, Naomi. "Female Fetishism: The Case of George Sand." In *The Female Body in Western Culture,* ed. Susan Rubin Suleiman. Cambridge: Harvard University Press, 1986. 363–72.

————. "This Essentialism Which Is Not One: Coming to Grips with Irigaray." *differences* 1.2 (summer 1989): 38–58.

Schroeder, Karl. *Permanence.* New York: Tor, 2002.

————. *Ventus.* New York: Tor, 2000.

Scott, Melissa. *Burning Bright.* New York: Tor, 1993.

————. *Dreaming Metal.* New York: Tor, 1997.

————. *Dreamships.* New York: Tor, 1992.

————. *The Jazz.* New York: Tor, 2000.

————. *Night Sky Mine.* New York: Tor, 1996.

————. *The Shapes of Their Hearts.* New York: Tor, 1998.

————. *Trouble and Her Friends.* New York: Tor, 1994.

Sedgwick, Eve Kosofsky. *Epistemology of the Closet.* Berkeley: University of California Press, 1990.

————. "Queer Performativity: Henry James's *The Art of the Novel.*" *GLQ* 1.1 (1993): 1–16.

Seltzer, Mark. *Serial Killers: Death and Life in America's Wound Culture.* New York: Routledge, 1998.

Senft, Theresa. "Introduction: Performing the Digital Body—A Ghost Story." In *Sexuality and Cyberspace: Performing the Digital Body,* ed. Theresa Senft and Stacy Horn. Special issue of *Women and Performance* 9.1 (1996). 9–33.

Senft, Theresa, and Stacy Horn, eds. *Sexuality and Cyberspace: Performing the Digital Body.* Special issue of *Women and Performance* 9.1 (1996).

Sheppard, Nathaniel, Jr. "Trashing the Information Superhighway: White Supremacy Goes Hi-Tech." *Emerge* 7.9 (July/August 1996): 34–40.

Shohat, Ella, and Robert Stam. "From the Imperial Family to the Transnational Imaginary: Media Spectatorship in the Age of Globalization." In *Global/Local: Cultural Production and the Transnational Imaginary,* ed. Rob Wilson and Wimal Dissanayake. Duke, NC: Durham University Press, 1996. 145–70.

Silverman, Kaja. *Male Subjectivity at the Margins.* New York: Routledge, 1992.

Simmel, Georg. *On Individuality and Social Forms: Selected Writings.* ed. Donald N. Levine. Chicago: University of Chicago Press, 1971.

Simmons, Dan. *Ilium.* New York: Eos of HarperCollins, 2003.

Sinker, Mark. "Loving the Alien: Black Science Fiction." *Wire* 96 (February 1992): 30–33.

Skal, David J. *Antibodies.* New York: Worldwide Library, 1989.

Slusser, George, and Tom Shippey, eds. *Fiction 2000: Cyberpunk and the Future of Narrative.* Athens: University of Georgia Press, 1992.

Smith, Neil, and Cindi Katz. "Grounding Metaphor: Towards a Spatialized Politics." In *Place and the Politics of Identity,* ed. Michael Keith and Steve Pile. New York: Routledge, 1993. 67–83.

Smith, Stephanie. "Morphing, Materialism, and the Marketing of *Xenogenesis.*" *Genders* 18 (winter 1993): 67–86.

Smith, Valerie. "Black Feminist Theory and the Representation of the 'Other.'" In *Changing Our Own Words: Essays on Criticism, Theory, and Writing by Black Women.* New Brunswick, NJ: Rutgers University Press, 1989. 38–57.

Sobchack, Vivian. "Beating the Meat/Surviving the Text, or How to Get Out of This Century Alive." In *Cyberspace/Cyberbodies/Cyberpunk: Cultures of Technological Embodiment,* ed. Mike Featherstone and Roger Burrows. London: Sage Publications, 1995. 205–14.

————. *Screening Space: The American Science Fiction Film.* 2d ed. New York: Ungar, 1987.

Sonnega, William. "Morphing Borders: The Remanence of MTV." *Drama Review* 39.1 (spring 1995): 45–61.

Sorayama, Hajime. *The Gynoids*. Tokyo: Treville, 1992.

———. *Hajime Sorayama*. Berlin: Benedikt Taschen Verlag, 1991.

———. *Sexy Robot*. Tokyo: Genko-sha Publishing, 1983.

Spillers, Hortense. "Mama's Baby, Papa's Maybe: An American Grammar Book." *Diacritics* 17.2 (summer 1987): 65–81.

Sponsler, Claire. "Beyond the Ruins: The Geopolitics of Urban Decay and Cybernetic Play." *Science-Fiction Studies* 20.2 (July 1993): 251–65.

———. "Cyberpunk and the Dilemmas of Postmodern Narrative: The Example of William Gibson." *Contemporary Literature* 33.4 (winter 1992): 625–44.

Springer, Claudia. *Electronic Eros: Bodies and Desire in the Postindustrial Age*. Austin: University of Texas Press, 1996.

———. "Psycho-Cybernetics in Films of the 1990s." In *Alien Zone II: The Space of Science Fiction Cinema*, ed. Annette Kuhn. New York: Verso, 1999. 203–18.

Stableford, Brian. *The Fountains of Youth*. New York: Tor, 2000.

Stallybrass, Julian. "Digital Commons." *New Left Review* 15; 2d series (May–June 2002): 141–46.

Starkings, Richard, Joe Casey, and Ladronn. *Unnatural Selection*. Los Angeles: Active Images, September 2002.

Stephenson, Neal. *The Diamond Age*. New York: Bantam, 1995.

———. "Global Neighborhood Watch." *Wired Scenarios: The Future of the Future* (special issue, September 1995): 100, 146.

———. *In the Beginning . . . Was the Command Line*. New York: Avon Books, 1999.

———. *Snow Crash*. New York: Bantam Spectra, 1992.

Sterling, Bruce. *Crystal Express*. New York: Ace Books, 1990.

———. "Cyberpunk in the Nineties." *Interzone* 48 (June 1991): 39–41.

———. *Islands in the Net*. New York: Ace Books, 1988.

———. "Letter from Bruce Sterling." *REM* 7 (April 1987): 4–7.

———. "Maneki Neko." In *A Good Old-Fashioned Future*. New York: Bantam, 1999.

———. "Processing the Simulacra for Fun and Profit." *Monad: Essays on Science Fiction* 1 (September 1990): 52–65.

———. "Report on the Cyberpunk Bust." *Interzone* 44 (February 1991): 47–51.

———. *Schismatrix*. New York: Ace Books, 1986.

———. "War on the Electronic Frontier." *American Book Review* 13 (April–May 1991): 4–5.

———, ed. *Mirrorshades*. New York: Ace Books, 1988.

Stivale, Charles J., ed. *CyberSpaces: Pedagogy and Performance on the Electronic Frontier*. Special issue of *Works and Days* 13.1/2 (1995).

Stockton, Sharon. "'The Self Regained': Cyberpunk's Retreat to the Imperium." *Contemporary Literature* 36.4 (winter 1995): 588–612.

Stone, Allucquère Rosanne. *The War of Desire and Technology at the Close of the Mechanical Age*. Cambridge: MIT Press, 1995.

———. "Will the Real Body Please Stand Up? Boundary Stories about Virtual Cultures." In *Cyberspace: First Steps*, ed. Michael Benedikt. Cambridge: MIT Press, 1991. 81–118.

Stross, Charles. "Charles Stross: Exploring Distortions." Interview. *Locus: The Magazine of the Science Fiction and Fantasy Field* 511 (August 2003): 84–86.

————. *Singularity Sky*. New York: Ace Books, 2003.

————. *Toast and Other Rusted Futures*. Holicong, PA: Cosmos Books, 2002.

————. "Tourists." *Asimov's Science Fiction* 26.2 (February 2002): 14–38.

Sullivan, Caitlin, and Kate Bornstein. *Nearly Roadkill: An Infobahn Erotic Adventure*. New York: High Risk Books/Serpent's Tail, 1996.

Suvin, Darko. "On Gibson and Cyberpunk SF." *Foundation* 46 (1989): 40–51.

Swanger, David. "Mrs. Brown's Prefrontal Cortex: The Promise of Hard Character SF." *New York Review of Science Fiction* 12.4 (December 1999): 7–10.

Swanwick, Michael. *Stations of the Tide*. New York: Avon Books, 1991.

————. "A User's Guide to the Postmoderns." In *Moon Dogs*. Framingham, MA: NESFA Press, 2000. 257–74. Originally published 1986.

————. *Vacuum Flowers*. New York: Arbor House, 1987.

Tabbi, Joseph. *Postmodern Sublime: Technology and American Writing from Mailer to Cyberpunk*. Ithaca, NY: Cornell University Press, 1995.

Tatsumi, Takayaki. "Eye to Eye: An Interview with William Gibson." *Science Fiction Eye* 1 (winter 1987): 6–17.

————. "A Manifesto for Gynoids: Reading Richard Calder." *Science Fiction Eye* 9 (November 1991): 82–85.

Telotte, J. P. *Replications: A Robotic History of the Science Fiction Film*. Urbana: University of Illinois Press, 1995.

Terranova, Tiziana. "Posthuman Unbounded: Artificial Evolution and High-Tech Subcultures." In *FutureNatural: Nature, Science, Culture*, ed. George Robertson, Melinda Mash, Lisa Tickner, Jon Bird, Barry Curtis, and Tim Putnam. New York: Routledge, 1996.

Theweleit, Klaus. *Male Fantasies*. 2 vols. Trans. Chris Turner. Minneapolis: University of Minnesota Press, 1987.

Toffler, Alvin. *The Third Wave*. New York: Bantam, 1981.

Tomas, David. "Feedback and Cybernetics: Reimaging the Body in the Age of the Cyborg." In *Cyberspace/Cyberbodies/Cyberpunk: Cultures of Technological Embodiment*, ed. Mike Featherstone and Roger Burrows. London: Sage Publications, 1995. 21–43.

————. "Old Rituals for New Space: *Rites de Passage* and William Gibson's Cultural Model of Cyberspace." In *Cyberspace: First Steps*, ed. Michael Benedikt. Cambridge: MIT Press, 1991. 31–47.

————. "The Technophilic Body: On Technicity in William Gibson's Cyborg Culture." *New Formations* 8 (1989): 113–29.

Tooby, John, and Leda Cosmides. "The Psychological Foundations of Culture." In *The Adapted Mind*, ed. Jerome Barkow, John Tooby, and Leda Cosmides. New York: Oxford University Press, 1992. 19–136.

Torvalds, Linus, and David Diamond. *Just for Fun: The Story of an Accidental Revolutionary*. New York: HarperBusiness of HarperCollins, 2001.

Turing, Alan. "Computing Machinery and Intelligence." *Mind* 59 (October 1950): 433–60.

Turkle, Sherry. *Life on the Screen: Identity in the Age of the Internet*. New York: Simon & Schuster, 1995.

————. *The Second Self: Computers and the Human Spirit*. New York: Simon & Schuster, 1984.

Turow, Joseph. *Breaking Up America: Advertisers and the New Media World.* Chicago: University of Chicago Press, 1997.

Tyler, Carole-Anne. "Boys Will Be Girls: The Politics of Gay Drag." In *Inside/Out: Lesbian Theories, Gay Theories,* ed. Diana Fuss. New York: Routledge, 1991. 32–70.

Urry, John. *Consuming Places.* New York: Routledge, 1995.

Varela, Francisco J., Evan Thompson, and Eleanor Rosch. *The Embodied Mind: Cognitive Science and Human Experience.* Cambridge: MIT Press, 1993.

Varley, John. *The Ophiuchi Hotline.* New York: Dial Press, 1977.

Vinge, Vernor. "The Coming Technological Singularity: How to Survive in the Post-Human Era." http://www.rohan.sdsu.edu/faculty/vinge/misc/singularity.html. Originally published in the *Whole Earth Review* (winter 1993).

Vizenor, Gerald. *The Heirs of Columbus.* Hanover, NH: Wesleyan University Press/ University Press of New England, 1991.

———. *Landfill Meditation: Crossblood Stories.* Hanover, NH: Wesleyan University Press/ University Press of New England, 1991.

Von Neumann, John. *The Computer and the Brain.* New Haven: Yale University Press, 1958.

Wald, Priscilla. *Constituting Americans: Cultural Anxiety and Narrative Form.* Durham, NC: Duke University Press, 1995.

Walker, John. "Through the Looking Glass." In *The Art of Human-Computer Interface Design,* ed. Brenda Laurel. Reading, MA: Addison-Wesley, 1990. 439–47.

Walser, Randal. "Spacemakers and the Art of the Cyberspace Playhouse." *Mondo 2000* 2 (summer 1990): 60–61.

Walser, Robert. "Deep Jazz: Notes on Interiority, Race, and Criticism." In *Inventing the Psychological: Toward a Cultural History of Emotional Life in America,* ed. Joel Pfister and Nancy Schnog. New Haven: Yale University Press, 1997. 271–96.

Warner, Michael. "Fear of a Queer Planet." *Social Text* 29 (1991): 3–17.

———. *The Letters of the Republic: Publication and the Public Sphere in Eighteenth-Century America.* Cambridge: Harvard University Press, 1990.

———. "The Mass Public and the Mass Subject." In *Habermas and the Public Sphere,* ed. Chris Calhoun. Cambridge: MIT Press, 1992. 377–401.

Weed, Elizabeth, ed. *Coming to Terms: Feminism, Theory, and Politics.* New York: Routledge, 1989.

Weheliye, Alexander G. "'Feenin': Posthuman Voices in Contemporary Black Popular Music." *Social Text* 20.2 (summer 2002): 21–47.

Wells, H. G. "The Limits of Individual Plasticity." In *H. G. Wells: Early Writings in Science and Science Fiction,* ed. Robert M. Philmus and David Y. Hughes. Berkeley: University of California Press, 1975. 36–39. Originally published in *Saturday Review* 79 (January 19, 1895): 89–90.

West, Cornel. "Black Culture and Postmodernism." In *Remaking History,* ed. Barbara Kruger and Phil Mariani. Seattle: Bay Press, 1989. 87–96.

Whalen, Terence. "The Future of a Commodity: Notes toward a Critique of Cyberpunk and the Information Age." *Science-Fiction Studies* 19 (March 1992): 75–88.

Wiedemann, Julius. *Digital Beauties: 2D & 3D Computer Generated Digital Models, Virtual Idols and Characters.* New York: Taschen, 2001.

Wiegman, Robyn. *American Anatomies: Theorizing Race and Gender*. Durham, NC: Duke University Press, 1995.

――――. "Whiteness Studies and the Paradox of Particularity." *boundary 2* 26.3 (fall 1999): 115–50.

Wiener, Norbert. *The Human Use of Human Beings: Cybernetics and Society*. New York: Da Capo, 1954.

Wilcox, Ronda. "Dating Data: Miscegenation in *Star Trek: The Next Generation*." In *Enterprise Zones: Critical Positions on Star Trek*, ed. Taylor Harrison, Sarah Projansky, Kent A. Ono, and Elyce Rae Helford. Boulder, CO: Westview Press, 1996. 69–92.

Wilde, Oscar. *The Artist as Critic: Critical Writings of Oscar Wilde*. ed. Richard Ellmann. Chicago: University of Chicago Press, 1969.

Williams, Patricia J. "The Rules of the Game." In *Reading Rodney King/Reading Urban Uprising*, ed. Robert Gooding-Williams. New York: Routledge, 1993. 51–55.

Williams, Sam. *Free as in Freedom: Richard Stallman's Crusade for Free Software*. Sebastopol, CA: O'Reilly, 2002.

Williams, Walter Jon. *Hardwired*. New York: Tor, 1986.

Wilson, Edward O. *Consilience: The Unity of Knowledge*. New York: Vintage, 1998.

Wilson, Rob, and Wimal Dissanayake, eds. *Global/Local: Cultural Production and the Transnational Imaginary*. Durham, NC: Duke University Press, 1996.

Wilson, Robert Charles. *Memory Wire*. New York: Bantam, 1987.

Winner, Langdon. *Autonomous Technology: Technics-out-of-Control as a Theme in Political Thought*. Cambridge: MIT Press, 1977.

Wolfe, Bernard. *Limbo*. New York: Random House, 1952.

Wolmark, Jenny. *Aliens and Others: Science Fiction, Feminism and Postmodernism*. Iowa City: University of Iowa Press, 1994.

Woodland, J. Randal. "Queer Spaces, Modem Boys, and Pagan Statues: Gay/Lesbian Identity and the Construction of Cyberspace." In *CyberSpaces: Pedagogy and Performance on the Electronic Frontier*, ed Charles J. Stivale. Special issue of *Works and Days* 13.1/2 (1995). 221–40.

Wray, Matt, and Annalee Newitz, eds. *White Trash: Race and Class in America*. New York: Routledge, 1997.

Wright, John C. *The Golden Age*. New York: Tor, 2002.

――――. *The Golden Transcendence*. New York: Tor, 2003.

――――. *The Phoenix Exultant*. New York: Tor, 2003.

Yablonsky, Louis. *Robopaths*. Indianapolis: Bobbs-Merrill, 1972.

Yarbro-Bejarano, Yvonne. "Expanding the Categories of Race and Sexuality in Lesbian and Gay Studies." In *Professions of Desire: Lesbian and Gay Studies in Literature*, ed. George E. Haggerty and Bonnie Zimmerman. New York: Modern Language Association, 1995.

Yoshimoto, Mitsuhiro. "Real Virtuality." In *Global/Local: Cultural Production and the Transnational Imaginary*, ed. Rob Wilson and Wimal Dissanayake. Durham, NC: Duke University Press, 1996. 107–18.

Zebrowski, George. *Macrolife*. New York: Harper & Row, 1979.

Žižek, Slavoj. "Cultural Studies versus the 'Third Culture.'" *South Atlantic Quarterly* 101.1 (winter 2002): 19–32.

———. *Enjoy Your Symptom! Jacques Lacan in Hollywood and Out.* New York: Routledge, 1992.

———. *The Indivisible Remainder: An Essay on Schelling and Related Matters.* New York: Verso, 1996.

———. *The Plague of Fantasies.* New York: Verso, 1997.

———. *The Sublime Object of Ideology.* New York: Verso, 1989.

INDEX

②

Steatopygia. These images belong to the past but also to the present as Jennings rethinks their embodiment via the interface btwn technology + flesh via the processes of banal cultural commodification that cre For scholars like Haraway, the cyborg the cy presents us w/ an opportunity to redefine technolo moving away from binarisms of bodies + machines as tools under our control. Rather technology, like a lover is seen as "pervasive, utterly intimate. Not outside us, but next to us" (Sterling in Foster, xii). Jennings' palimpsestic characters, like the Mammy with cybernetic tendrils protruding from her breast, trouble an overly optimistic view of the cyborg. Rather he shows that the process of enslavement + race attempted to convert body into machine, resulting in hybrid entities that more often than not, served conservative agendas more than progressive ones. Jennings' images shows that disembodiment is in fact not an escape from the traumatic embodiment of race. Rather the monstrosity of Jennings' cyborg draws our attention to the monstrosity of the slave body as it was forcibly removed from categories of the human + converted into prosthetic limbs, organs + orifices for the slave master. The beach body, Jennings' seems to suggest, has always been a cyborg.

Yet Jennings does not map a bleak world ~~where~~ where late capitalism has reduced us all to posthuman cyborgs that perpetuate very old racial stereotypes. Rather his images ~~insist on~~ are also counter movement as they refuse to displace considerations of social justice. The ~~by~~ injury, the commodification and an insistence on

Thomas Foster is associate professor of English and director of the cultural studies program at Indiana University, where he also has adjunct appointments in American studies and cognitive science. He is author of *Transformations of Domesticity in Modern Women's Writing: Homelessness at Home* and has published essays on cyberpunk and technoculture in *PMLA, Contemporary Literature, Modern Fiction Studies,* and *Genders,* and in the books *Reload: Rethinking Women + Technoculture, Cyberspace Textuality,* and *The Cyberculture Reader.*

recognizing the consequences of imperial actions where Africans were converted into factors, manufactured in the 1st factories — the slave fort. While increasingly new technologies appear to displace the old, Jennings shows the instead aggregation of representations of commodity — celebrity / disenfranchised bag lady / destitute African

Utterly Intimate: John Jennings Cyborg Pieces.

Sean Puffy Combs has been credited for the saying "Rosa sat so Martin could walk so Barack could run + our children could fly". In this construction we see the construction of a teleological model of racial progress, culminating in the end of the Civil Rights movement with a black president who will ensure a non-racist America for the future. Indeed, the president comes to stand in for this very future — a man whose presence, putatively, announces that slavery is dead. In the wake of Obama's election, John Jennings has created a brilliant series " " that counters such models of progress. Instead he reveals not the ~~factual~~ demise of regimes of race but their constant reinvention through new technologies of embodiment. These technologies of embodiment ~~reveal both~~ that Harryette Mullen states is technoculture's " forcible ~~exteriorization~~ of 'the souls of black folks,'" whereby they, as cyborgs, are rendered ~~fungible~~ to (white) consumers. That Jennings illustrates with such poignancy, construct an alternate geneology to the one previously mentioned by Sean Combs. Instead we see how the black body is haunted by the specters of slavery, colonialization + racialization — how these ghosts are always present, revealing themselves in the outlines of the images. Look mama, here is a Negro — Uncle Ben looking at us over his shoulder, Sarah Baartman, the Venus Hottentot, stubbornly performing her